Hawai'i

Kaua'i

O'ahu

Moloka'i

Lāna'i

Maui

Hawai'i

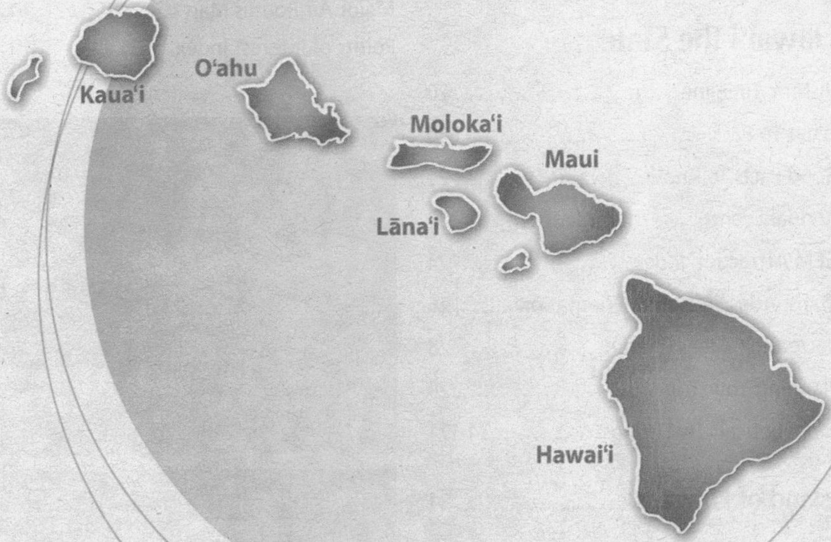

Published by AAA Publishing
1000 AAA Drive, Heathrow, FL 32746-5063
Copyright AAA 2015, All rights reserved

The publisher has made every effort to provide accurate, up-to-date information but accepts no responsibility for loss or injury sustained by any person using this book. TourBook® guides are published for the exclusive use of AAA members. Not for sale.

Advertising Rate and Circulation Information: (407) 444-8280

Printed in the USA by Quad/Graphics

This book is printed on paper certified by third-party standards for sustainably managed forestry and production.

 Printed on recyclable paper.
Please recycle whenever possible.

Stock #5035

CONTENTS

Featured Information

We Get You ...

Sigrid Olsson / Alamy

- **Where you want to go -**
  with TripTik® Travel Planner maps and directions

- **What you want to know -**
  with hotel, discount and gas price information

- **Help along the way -**
  with easy road service request

Our apps keep you mobile.
Download today.

AAA.com/mobile | CAA.ca/mobile

Going the Extra Mile

Every year AAA experts travel North America to check out places for members to see, stay, dine and play.

Professional Inspectors - conduct in-person hotel and restaurant evaluations, providing ratings, notes and tips to guide your decisions.

Seasoned Travel Writers - gather destination insight, providing itineraries and top picks including AAA GEM attractions.

A to Z City Listings

Cities and places are listed alphabetically within each state or province. Attractions, hotels and restaurants are listed once — under the city in which they are physically located.

Cities that are considered part of a larger destination city or area have an expanded city header. The header identifies the larger region and cross-references pages that contain shared trip planning resources:

- Destination map – outline map of the cities that comprise a destination city or area
- Attraction spotting map – regional street map marked with attraction locations
- Hotel/restaurant spotting map and index – regional street map numbered with hotel and restaurant locations identified in an accompanying index

Cities that are not considered part of a larger destination city or area but have a significant number of listings may have these resources within the individual city section:

- Attraction spotting map
- Hotel/restaurant spotting map and index

Location Abbreviations

Directions are from the center of town unless otherwise specified, using these highway abbreviations:

Bus. Rte.=business route
CR=county road
FM=farm to market
FR=forest road
Hwy.=Canadian highway
I=interstate highway
LR=legislative route
R.R.=rural route
SR/PR=state or provincial route
US=federal highway

Maps

Use the navigable road maps and accompanying legend in the Atlas Section for route planning. Check the destination maps for general location reference. In select cities only, refer to the mass transit overview maps to cross-reference station names and numbers. For attraction and hotel/restaurant spotting maps, see the legend below to identify symbols and color coding.

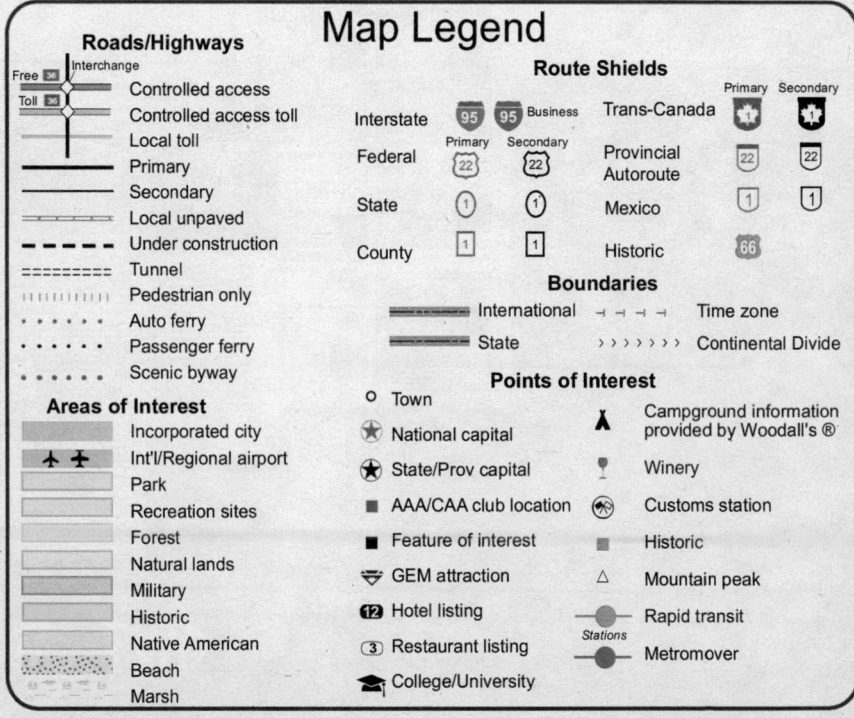

Map Legend

Roads/Highways

Free / Toll / Interchange
- Controlled access
- Controlled access toll
- Local toll
- Primary
- Secondary
- Local unpaved
- Under construction
- Tunnel
- Pedestrian only
- Auto ferry
- Passenger ferry
- Scenic byway

Areas of Interest

- Incorporated city
- Int'l/Regional airport
- Park
- Recreation sites
- Forest
- Natural lands
- Military
- Historic
- Native American
- Beach
- Marsh

Route Shields

	Primary	Secondary	
Interstate	95	95 Business	Trans-Canada
Federal	22 (Primary)	22 (Secondary)	Provincial Autoroute
State	1	1	Mexico
County	1	1	Historic 66

Boundaries

- International
- State
- Time zone
- Continental Divide

Points of Interest

- o Town
- National capital
- State/Prov capital
- AAA/CAA club location
- Feature of interest
- GEM attraction
- 12 Hotel listing
- 3 Restaurant listing
- College/University
- Campground information provided by Woodall's ®
- Winery
- Customs station
- Historic
- △ Mountain peak
- Rapid transit / Stations
- Metromover

About Listed Establishments

AAA/CAA Approved hotels and restaurants are listed on the basis of merit alone after careful evaluation and approval by full-time, professionally trained AAA/CAA inspectors. An establishment's decision to advertise in the TourBook guide has no bearing on its evaluation or rating; nor does inclusion of advertising imply AAA endorsement of products and services.

Information in this guide was believed accurate at the time of publication. However, since changes inevitably occur between annual editions, please contact your AAA travel professional, visit AAA.com or download the AAA mobile app to confirm prices and schedules.

Attraction Listings

> **[GEM] [SAVE] ATTRACTION NAME,** 3 mi. n. off SR 20A (Main Ave.), consists of 250 acres with Olmsted-designed gardens, a 205-foot marble and coquina bell tower and a Mediterranean-style mansion. One of the state's oldest attractions, the tower and gardens were dedicated to the American people in 1929 by President Calvin Coolidge on behalf of their founder, a Dutch immigrant.
>
> **Hours:** Gardens daily 8-6. Last admission 1 hour before closing. Visitor center daily 9-5. Estate tours are given at noon and 2. Carillon concerts are given at 1 and 3. Phone ahead to confirm schedule. **Cost:** $10; $3 (ages 5-12). Gardens and estate $16; $8 (ages 5-12). **Phone:** (555) 555-5555.
> [icons] Dupont Circle,13

[GEM] AAA/CAA travel experts may designate an attraction of exceptional interest and quality as a AAA GEM — a *Great Experience for Members®. See GEM Attraction Index (listed on CONTENTS page) for a complete list of locations.*

Consult the online travel guides at AAA.com or visit AAA Mobile for additional things to do if you have time.

Cost

Prices are quoted without sales tax in the local currency (U.S. or Canadian dollars). Children under the lowest age specified are admitted free when accompanied by an adult. Most establishments accept credit cards, but a small number require cash, so please call ahead to verify.

Adventure Travel

Activities such as air tours, hiking, skiing and white-water rafting are listed to provide member information and do not imply AAA/CAA endorsement. For your safety, be aware of inherent risks and adhere to all safety instructions.

Icons

[SAVE] AAA Discounts & Rewards® member discount

[icon] Electric vehicle charging station on premises. Domestic station information provided by the U.S. Department of Energy. Canadian station information provided by Plug'n Drive Ontario.

[GT] Guided Tours available

[icon] Camping facilities

[icon] Food on premises

[icon] Recreational activities

[icon] Pets on leash allowed

[icon] Picnicking allowed

In select cities only:

[icon] Mass transit station within 1 mile. Icon is followed by station name and AAA/CAA designated station number within listing.

Information-Only Attraction Listings

Bulleted listings, which include the following categories, are listed for informational purposes as a service to members:

- **Gambling establishments** (even if located in a AAA/CAA Approved hotel)
- **Participatory recreational activities** (those requiring physical exertion or special skills)
- **Wineries that offer tours and tastings**

Mobile Tags

 Scan QR codes throughout the TourBook guide to see online offers, menus, videos and more on your smartphone or tablet. If you need a QR scanner app, download one for free from your app store.

If you see a non-QR code in an ad, check the nearby text for details on which app you'll need to scan it.

Hotel and Restaurant Listings

1 Diamond Rating – AAA/CAA Approved hotels and restaurants are assigned a rating of one to five Diamonds. Red Diamonds distinguish establishments that participate in the AAA/CAA logo licensing program. For details, see p. 11 or AAA.com/Diamonds.

fyi indicates hotels and restaurants that are not AAA/CAA Approved and/or Diamond Rated but are listed to provide additional choices for members:

- **Hotels** may be unrated if they are too new to rate, under construction, under major renovation or have not yet been evaluated; or if they do not meet all AAA requirements. Hotels that do not meet all AAA requirements may be included if they offer member value or are the only option; details are noted in the listing.

- **Restaurants** may be unrated if they have not yet been evaluated by AAA.

2 Classification or Cuisine Type – Noted after the Diamond Rating.

- **Hotel Classifications** indicate the style of operation, overall concept and service level. Subclassifications may also be added. (See p. 12.)

- **Restaurant Cuisine Types** identify the food concept from more than 100 categories. If applicable, a classification may also be added. (See p. 13.)

3 Dollar Amounts – Quoted without sales tax in the local currency (U.S. or Canadian dollars), rounded up to the nearest dollar. Most establishments accept credit cards, but a small number require cash, so please call ahead to verify.

- **Hotel Rates** indicate the publicly available two-person rate or rate range for a standard room, applicable all year.

- **Restaurant Prices** represent the minimum and maximum entrée cost per person. Exceptions may include one-of-a-kind or special market priced items.

4 Spotting Symbol – Ovals containing numbers correspond with numbered location markings on hotel and restaurant spotting maps.

5 Parking – Unless otherwise noted, parking is free, on-site self parking.

6 Hotel Value Nationwide – Blue boxes highlight member benefits available at AAA/CAA Approved locations across a hotel chain. (See Just For Members section for details.)

7 Hotel Unit Limited Availability – Unit types, amenities and room features preceded by "some" are available on a limited basis, potentially as few as one.

8 Hotel Terms – Cancellation and minimum stay policies are listed. Unless otherwise noted, most properties offer a full deposit refund with cancellations received at least 48 hours before standard check-in. Properties that require advance payment may not refund the difference for early departures. "Resort fee" indicates a charge may apply above and beyond the quoted room rate.

9 Hotel Check-in/Check-out – Unless otherwise noted, check-in is after 3 p.m. and check-out is before 10 a.m.

10 Restaurant Dress Code – Unless otherwise noted, dress is casual or dressy casual.

11 Restaurant Menu – Where indicated, menus may be viewed in a secure online environment at AAA.com or, if a mobile tag is provided, via the restaurant's website.

12 Hotel Icons – May be preceded by CALL and/or SOME UNITS.

Member Information:

SAVE Member rates: discounted standard room rate or lowest public rate available at time of booking for dates of stay.

ECO Eco-certified by government or private organization.

⊞ Electric vehicle charging station on premises. Domestic station information provided by the U.S. Department of Energy. Canadian station information provided by Plug'n Drive Ontario.

☒ Smoke-free premises

In select cities only:

🚇 Mass transit station within 1 mile. Icon is followed by station name and AAA/CAA designated station number within listing.

Services:

🛬 Airport transportation

🐾 Pets allowed (Call property for restrictions.)

$🐾 Pets allowed (Call property for restrictions and fees.)

🍴 Restaurant on premises

🍴 Restaurant off premises

🍽 Room service for 2 or more meals

🍸 Full bar

HOTEL LISTING

RESTAURANT LISTING

🛏 Child care

BIZ Business area

♿M Accessible features (Call property for available services and amenities.)

Activities:

🎰 Full-service casino

🏊 Pool

💪 Health club on premises

In-Room Amenities:

HS High-speed Internet service

sHS High-speed Internet service (Call property for fees.)

📶 Wireless Internet service

s📶 Wireless Internet service (Call property for fees.)

📶 No wireless Internet service

🎬 Pay movies

🧊 Refrigerator

▤ Microwave

☕ Coffee maker

K No air conditioning

TV No TV

📞 No telephones

13 Restaurant Icons

SAVE AAA Discounts & Rewards® member discount

ECO Eco-certified by government or private organization.

🔌 Electric vehicle charging station on premises. Domestic station information provided by the U.S. Department of Energy. Canadian station information provided by Plug'n Drive Ontario.

K No air conditioning

♿M Accessible features (Call property for available services and amenities.)

◣ Designated smoking section

B Breakfast

L Lunch

D Dinner

24 Open 24 hours

LATE Open after 11 p.m.

🐾 Pet-friendly (Call property for restrictions.)

In select cities only:

🚇 Mass transit station within 1 mile. Icon is followed by station name and AAA/CAA designated station number within listing.

Just For Members

Understanding the Diamond Ratings

Hotel and restaurant evaluations are unscheduled to ensure our professionally trained inspectors encounter the same experience members do.

- When an establishment is Diamond Rated, it means members can expect a good fit with their needs. The inspector assigns a rating that indicates the type of experience to expect.
- While establishments at high levels must offer increasingly complex personalized services, establishments at every level are subject to the same basic requirements for cleanliness, comfort and hospitality. Learn more at AAA.com/Diamonds.

Hotels

Budget-oriented, offering basic comfort and hospitality.

Affordable, with modestly enhanced facilities, décor and amenities.

Distinguished, multifaceted with enhanced physical attributes, amenities and guest comforts.

Refined, stylish with upscale physical attributes, extensive amenities and high degree of hospitality, service and attention to detail.

Ultimate luxury, sophistication and comfort with extraordinary physical attributes, meticulous personalized service, extensive amenities and impeccable standards of excellence.

Restaurants

Simple, economical food, often self-service, in a functional environment.

Familiar food, often cooked to order, served in relaxed surroundings.

Popular cuisine, skillfully prepared and served, with expanded beverage options, in enhanced setting.

Imaginative, market-fresh food creatively prepared and skillfully served, often with wine steward, amid upscale ambience.

Cutting-edge cuisine of the finest ingredients, uniquely prepared by an acclaimed chef, served by expert service staff led by maître d' in extraordinary surroundings.

What's the difference?

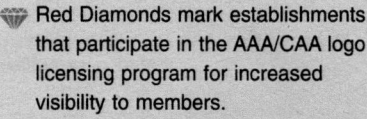 Red Diamonds mark establishments that participate in the AAA/CAA logo licensing program for increased visibility to members.

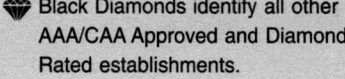 Black Diamonds identify all other AAA/CAA Approved and Diamond Rated establishments.

Hotel Classifications

Quality and comfort are usually consistent across each Diamond Rating level, but décor, facilities and service levels vary by classification.

Berry Manor Inn, Rockland, ME

Bed & Breakfast — Typically owner-operated with a high degree of personal touches. Guests are encouraged to interact during evening and breakfast hours. A continental or full, hot breakfast is included in the room rate.

Killarney Lodge, Algonquin Provincial Park, ON

Cabin — Often located in wooded, rural or waterfront locations. Freestanding units are typically rustic and of basic design. As a rule, essential cleaning supplies, kitchen utensils and complete bed and bath linens are supplied.

Hyatt Regency Clearwater Beach Resort & Spa, Clearwater Beach, FL

Condominium — Apartment-style accommodations of varying design or décor, units often contain one or more bedrooms, a living room, full kitchen and an eating area. As a rule, essential cleaning supplies, kitchen utensils and complete bed and bath linens are supplied.

Montpelier Plantation and Beach, St. Kitts and Nevis

Cottage — Often located in wooded, rural, or waterfront locations. Freestanding units are typically home-style in design and décor. As a rule, essential cleaning supplies, kitchen utensils and complete bed and bath linens are supplied.

Nottoway Plantation & Resort, White Castle, LA

Country Inn — Although similar in definition to a bed and breakfast, country inns are usually larger in scale with spacious public areas and offer a dining facility that serves breakfast and dinner.

The Shores Resort & Spa, Daytona Beach Shores, FL

Hotel — Typically a multistory property with interior room entrances and a variety of guest unit styles. The magnitude of the public areas is determined by the overall theme, location and service level, but may include a variety of facilities such as a restaurant, shops, a fitness center, a spa, a business center and meeting rooms.

All Star Vacation Homes, Kissimmee, FL

House — Freestanding units of varying home-style design. Typically larger scale, often containing two or more bedrooms, a living room, a full kitchen, a dining room and multiple bathrooms. As a rule, essential cleaning supplies, kitchen utensils and complete bed and bath linens are supplied.

Bryce View Lodge, Bryce Canyon City, UT

Motel — A one- or two-story roadside property with exterior room entrances and drive up parking. Public areas and facilities are often limited in size and/or availability.

Vista Verde Guest Ranch, Clark, CO

Ranch — Typically a working ranch featuring an obvious rustic, Western theme, equestrian-related activities and a variety of guest unit styles.

Hotel Subclassifications

These additional descriptives may be added to the classification for more information:

- **Boutique** — Often thematic, typically informal yet highly personalized; may have a luxurious or quirky style that is fashionable or unique.
- **Casino** — Extensive gambling facilities are available, such as blackjack, craps, keno and slot machines.
- **Classic** — Renowned and landmark properties, older than 50 years, well known for their unique style and ambience.
- **Contemporary** — Overall theme reflects characteristics of present mainstream trends.
- **Extended Stay** — Offers a predominance of long-term accommodations with a designated full-service kitchen area within each unit.
- **Historic** — More than 75 years old with one of the following documented historical features: Maintains the integrity of the historical nature, listed on the National Register of Historic Places, designated a National Historic Landmark or located in a National Register Historic District.
- **Resort** — Extensive recreational facilities and programs may include golf, tennis, skiing, fishing, water sports, spa

treatments or professionally guided activities.

- **Retro** — Overall theme reflects a contemporary design that reinterprets styles from a past era.
- **Vacation Rental** — Typically houses, condos, cottages or cabins; these properties are "home away from home" self-catering accommodations.
- **Vintage** — Overall theme reflects upon and maintains the authentic traits and experience of a past era.

Service Animals

Under the Americans with Disabilities Act (ADA), U.S. businesses that serve the public must allow people with disabilities to bring their service animals into all areas of the facility where customers are normally allowed to go.

Businesses may ask if an animal is a service animal and what tasks the animal has been trained to perform. Businesses may not ask about the person's disability, require special identification for the animal or request removal of the animal from the premises except in limited cases that require alternate assistance. Businesses may not charge extra fees for service animals, including standard pet fees, but may charge for damage caused by service animals if guests are normally charged for damage they cause.

Call the U.S. Department of Justice ADA Information Line: (800) 514-0301 or TTY (800) 514-0383, or visit ada.gov. Regulations may differ in Canada.

Restaurant Classifications

If applicable, in addition to the cuisine type noted under the Diamond Rating, restaurant listings may also include one or both classifications:

- **Classic** — Renowned and landmark operation in business for 25 plus years; unique style and ambience.
- **Historic** — Meets one of the following: Listed on National Register of Historic Places, designated a National Historic Landmark or located in a National Register Historic District.

AAA/CAA Approved Hotels

For members, AAA/CAA Approved means quality assured.

- Only properties that meet basic requirements for cleanliness, comfort and hospitality pass inspection.
- Approved hotels receive a Diamond Rating that tells members the type of experience to expect.

Guest Safety

Inspectors view a sampling of rooms during evaluations and, therefore, AAA/CAA cannot guarantee the presence of working locks and operational fire safety equipment in every guest unit.

Member Rates

AAA/CAA members can generally expect to pay no more than the maximum TourBook listed rate for a standard room. Member discounts apply to rates quoted within the rate range and are applicable at the time of booking. Listed rates are usually based on last standard room availability. Rates may fluctuate within the range and vary by season and room type. Obtain current AAA/CAA member rates and make reservations at AAA.com.

Exceptions

- Rates for properties operating as concessionaires for the U.S. National Park Service are not guaranteed due to governing regulations.
- Special advertised rates and short-term promotional rates below the rate range are not subject to additional member discounts.
- During special events, hotels may temporarily increase room rates; not recognize discounts or modify pricing policies. Special events may include Mardi Gras, the Kentucky Derby (including pre-Derby events), college football games, holidays, holiday periods and state fairs. Although some special events are listed in the TourBook guides and on AAA.com, it's always wise to check in advance with AAA travel professionals for specific dates.

If you are charged more than the maximum TourBook listed rate, question the additional charge. If an exception is not in effect and management refuses to adhere to the published rate, pay for the room and contact AAA/CAA. The amount paid above the stated maximum will be refunded if our investigation indicates an unjustified charge.

Reservations and Cancellations

When making your reservation, identify yourself as a AAA/CAA member and request written confirmation of your room type, rate, dates of stay, and cancellation and refund policies. At registration, show your membership card.

To cancel, contact the hotel, your AAA/CAA club office or AAA.com, depending on how you booked your reservation. Request a cancellation number or proof of cancellation.

If your room is not as specified and you have written confirmation of your reservation for a specific room type, you should be given the option of choosing a different room or receiving a refund. If management refuses to issue a refund, contact AAA/CAA.

Contacting AAA/CAA About Approved Properties

If your visit to a AAA/CAA Approved attraction, hotel or restaurant doesn't meet your expectations, please tell us about it — **during your visit or within 30 days**. Be sure to save your receipts and other documentation for reference.

Use the easy online form at AAA.com/TourBookComments to send us the details.

Alternatively, you can email your comments to: memberrelations@national.aaa.com or submit them via postal mail to: AAA Member Comments, 1000 AAA Dr., Box 61, Heathrow, FL 32746.

AAA/CAA Preferred Hotels

All AAA/CAA Approved hotels are committed to providing quality, value and member service. In addition, those designated as AAA/CAA Preferred Hotels also offer these extra values at Approved locations nationwide. Valid AAA/CAA membership required.

- **Best AAA/CAA member rates for your dates of stay**.
- **Seasonal promotions and special member offers.** Visit AAA.com to view current offers.
- **Member benefit.** See the blue boxes in hotel listings for the chains shown in the right-hand column below to find values offered at AAA/CAA Approved locations nationwide, subject to availability. Details valid at the time of publication and may change without notice.

- **Total satisfaction guarantee.** If you book your stay with AAA/CAA Travel and your stay fails to meet your expectations, you can apply for a full refund. Bring the complaint to the hotel's attention during the stay and request resolution; if the complaint is not resolved by the hotel, ask your AAA/CAA travel agent to request resolution through the AAA/CAA Assured Stay program.

	BEST WESTERN®, BEST WESTERN PLUS®, EXECUTIVE RESIDENCY, Vib, BEST WESTERN PREMIER® and BW Premier Collection SM
Hilton	Hilton Hotels & Resorts, Waldorf Astoria™ Hotels & Resorts, Conrad® Hotels & Resorts, Canopy by Hilton, Curio - A Collection by Hilton™, DoubleTree by Hilton™, Embassy Suites Hotels™, Hilton Garden Inn™, Hampton Inn™, Homewood Suites by Hilton™, Home2 Suites by Hilton™ and Hilton Grand Vacations™
	Park Hyatt®, Andaz®, Grand Hyatt®, Hyatt Centric®, Hyatt®, Hyatt Regency®, Hyatt Place®, HYATT house®, Hyatt Zilara® and Hyatt Ziva®
	JW Marriott®, Autograph Collection® Hotels, Renaissance® Hotels, Marriott Hotels®, Delta Hotels and Resorts®, Gaylord Hotels®, AC Hotels by Marriott®, Courtyard®, Residence Inn®, SpringHill Suites®, Fairfield Inn & Suites® and TownePlace Suites®
	Bellagio®, ARIA®, Vdara®, MGM Grand®, The Signature at MGM Grand®, Mandalay Bay®, Delano™ Las Vegas, The Mirage®, Monte Carlo™, New York-New York®, Luxor®, Excalibur® and Circus Circus® Las Vegas
	St. Regis®, The Luxury Collection®, W®, Westin®, Le Méridien®, Sheraton®, Four Points® by Sheraton, Aloft®, element® and Tribute Portfolio™

Member Discounts

Visit AAA.com/searchfordiscounts to find locations and available member discounts. Your AAA/CAA club may offer even greater discounts on theme park tickets. Amtrak and theme park discounts may be used for up to six tickets; restaurant savings may be used for up to six patrons. Other restrictions may apply. All offers subject to change. For complete restrictions, visit your AAA office or AAA.com/restrictions.

ATTRACTIONS

Six Flags

- Save on admission at the gate, participating AAA/CAA offices or AAA.com/SixFlags.

- Save 10% on merchandise of $15 or more at in-park stores.

Universal Orlando Resort and Universal Studios Hollywood

The Entertainment Capital of L.A.

- Save on tickets at select AAA/CAA offices or AAA.com/Universal. In-park savings available in FL.

- Save 10% on Blue Man Group tickets and at select food and merchandise venues at Universal CityWalk®.

DINING

Hard Rock Cafe

- Save 10% on food, nonalcoholic beverages and merchandise at all locations in the U.S. and Canada, plus select international locations. Visit AAA.com/HardRock for full listing.

Landry's Seafood House, The Crab House, Chart House, Oceanaire, Saltgrass Steak House, Muer Seafood Restaurants and Aquarium Restaurants

- Save 10% on food and nonalcoholic beverages at all of the above restaurants.

- Save 10% on merchandise at Aquarium, Downtown Aquarium and Rainforest Cafe restaurants.

SHOPPING

adidas Outlet

- Save 20% on the entire purchase. Visit AAA.com/adidasoutlet for list of locations.

Reebok & Rockport Outlet

- Save 20% on the entire purchase. Visit AAA.com/Reebok for list of locations.

Tanger Outlet Centers

- Receive a free coupon book with discounts up to 50% at select merchants.

TRANSPORTATION

Amtrak

- Save 10% on rail fare booked at least three days in advance of travel date at AAA.com/Amtrak.

El Monte RV

- Save up to 10% on nightly rates booked at least 24 hours in advance of pickup at AAA.com/ElMonteRV or (800) 337-2156.

Hertz

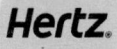

- Save on daily, weekend, weekly and monthly rentals at AAA.com/Hertz or (800) 654-3080.

RACK UP THE REWARDS

Make membership an even more rewarding experience.

The AAA Member Rewards Visa® credit card lets you earn reward points on all of your purchases. Apply for an account today and let the rewards start rolling in!

- ✓ Earn 1 point for every $1 in purchases with your AAA Member Rewards Visa® card!*

- ✓ Earn 2X points for gas, grocery and drug store purchases!

- ✓ Earn 3X points on qualifying AAA and travel purchases!

- ✓ Redeem for cash or get a AAA Voucher that gives you up to 40% more value!**

- ✓ Exclusive rewards to make you smile!

VISIT AAA.com/creditcard   **STOP BY** any AAA branch

Haleakalā National Park, Maui

Hawai'i the State

As you feast on *kalua* pig and *poi*, an ocean breeze tickles the orchid that garnishes your cocktail. On the stage before you, beautiful women adorned in ti-leaf skirts and fragrant *lei* sway seductively to the melody of a plucking *'ukulele*. Entranced and re-laxed, you bite into a juicy pineapple and enjoy the show.

But things here weren't always so easygoing. For ancient Hawaiians, the *hula* was a hallowed ritual. Performers danced for *hula* goddesses Laka and Hi'iaka, offering to the deities the sacred *lei* worn in the dance. Each move had to be performed impeccably—the slightest mistake could be punishable by death.

And still there are other gods to appease. Assuming natural forms, they reign in a state steeped in mythical allusion, serving as explanations for the wondrous geologic features that make up Hawai'i's island paradise.

Meet Pele, volcano goddess, who came to

Surf on O'ahu's North Shore

Hawai'i Island in search of a suitable home. She found Kīlauea, now considered part of Hawai'i Volcanoes National Park. Aila'au, the fire god who originally held court at Kīlauea, so feared Pele's powers that he fled.

Local lore says that Pele still resides in Halema'uma'u, a depression within Kīlauea Caldera. And she makes her presence known—with spitting fire and thick, rolling lava. Quite possibly the longest temper tantrum in history, Pele's wrath has caused steady eruptions of Kīlauea since 1983.

The demigod Māui stalked the sun from Haleakalā's crest; at 10,023 feet, the dormant, lunar-like "House of the Sun" is definitely a high point on the island of Maui. Goddess Hina complained that the sun slept late and sped across the sky to make up time, leaving little daylight for her chores. Her son Māui captured the sun with a coconut-fiber rope and only consented to its release with the agreement that it would travel more slowly.

The result is nearly 13 hours of daylight in summer to enjoy Maui's grasslands, green valleys and teal waters that lap black volcanic sand. And the sun's morning stretch across the summit of Haleakalā's sunken crater—a watercolor canvas in warm golds and oranges—is an unforgettable sight.

The Rainbow Connection

While visiting the islands you'll come across countless rainbows. The colorful arches, which grace lush gorges, plummeting waterfalls and the Honolulu skyline, are provided courtesy of the goddess Ānuenue.

Legend holds that in a valley on Kaua'i, a resident tossed a brightly colored cloth into the pool at Nāmolokama Falls. The colors spread into a magnificent rainbow, and the goddess emerged from an underwater prison, grateful to the villager for freeing her to roam the islands. To this day she continues her wanderings, bestowing a multihued blessing on the landscape.

In Hilo, Hawai'i, you may have the chance to meet Ānuenue firsthand. She frequents 'Akaka Falls and Waiānuenue (also known as Rainbow Falls), where evidence of her polychrome wand gleams amid the splash of tumbling water.

Recreation

From the ocean floor to volcanic peaks, Hawai'i is an inviting land of extremes. Warm azure water and pristine natural wonders are the calling cards of this compact tropical paradise.

Marine Life Conservation Districts off O'ahu, Hawai'i, Lāna'i and Maui are perfect playgrounds for underwater exploration and photography. Kealakekua Bay, the largest district at 315 acres, is nestled along the western coast of Hawai'i Island near Captain Cook Monument. Crystal-clear water, depths to 120 feet and diverse species make it a favorite stop on the scuba diving circuit.

O'ahu's public beaches welcome walk-ons and walk-ins, including snorkelers. Hānauma Bay, in Honolulu, has a sandy-bottomed reef that extends about 100 yards offshore. During low tide at Pūpūkea Beach Park, north of Hale'iwa, the kids can snorkel in tide pools at Shark's Cove. Don't let the cove's name scare you away—shark sightings are no more prevalent here than at any other inlet.

Surfers find swell action on O'ahu's North Shore, where the big ones roll in. Waikīkī Beach, on the other hand (and the other side of the island), beckons the novice rider with its gentler waves. Those who dare to meet the crests without a board can attempt bodysurfing at Po'ipū Beach on Kaua'i. World-class windsurfing off Ho'okipa, east of Kahului, is a Maui specialty.

An island's hiking trails often provide the only access to deep rain forests, volcanic craters or steep ocean-side cliffs. Always check weather conditions, including information about tides and waves, before camping or hiking.

The challenging 11-mile Kalalau Trail, on Kaua'i's Nāpali Coast, begins at Ke'e Beach near Hā'ena and follows the coastline along a footpath cut in the 1800s—rising over towering cliffs, dipping into five valleys and spilling onto deserted beaches.

For a sweeping panorama of O'ahu, make the three-quarter-mile trek to the top of Diamond Head, in southeast Honolulu. Contact the Division of State Parks for trail guides and hiking permits.

Bicycle paths thread across some 65 miles of O'ahu's Ko'olau and Wai'anae ranges. Take in the extended views from the ridges, being careful not to pedal off the path: Erosion caused by tire ruts is an environmental concern here and on all the islands.

Hawai'i Island offers bicyclists the ultimate pedaling and sightseeing combo—an 11-mile circle tour along the rim of Kīlauea Caldera in Hawai'i Volcanoes National Park; the visitor center is a good place to start.

Hawai'i has verdant golf courses bordering rugged coastlines, lush fairways in jewellike mountain settings and year-round golfing weather. For information about the state's golf courses, contact the Hawai'i Visitors and Convention Bureau.

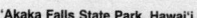

'Akaka Falls State Park, Hawai'i

Historic Timeline

1778	Capt. James Cook lands two ships on Kaua'i and christens his find the Sandwich Islands.
1782	Kamehameha I rises to power on Hawai'i; he rules a unified Hawai'i 1810-19.
1839	The Declaration of Rights and the Edict of Toleration are issued and lead to the kingdom's first written constitution.
1842	The United States recognizes Hawai'i as an independent nation.
1893	Queen Lili'uokalani is overthrown and a provisional government backed by the United States assumes power.
1941	The United States enters World War II following the Japanese attack on Pearl Harbor and other O'ahu sites.
1959	Hawai'i becomes the nation's 50th state.
1983	Kīlauea erupts, beginning a voluminous outpouring of lava that continues today.
1992	Hurricane Iniki creates havoc on Kaua'i.
1993	President Bill Clinton issues a resolve apologizing for the 1893 overthrow of the Hawaiian Kingdom.
2009	Honolulu-born senator Barack Obama is sworn in as the United States' first African-American president.

What To Pack

Temperature Averages Maximum/Minimum	JANUARY	FEBRUARY	MARCH	APRIL	MAY	JUNE	JULY	AUGUST	SEPTEMBER	OCTOBER	NOVEMBER	DECEMBER
Hilo	79/64	79/64	79/65	79/66	81/67	82/68	82/69	83/69	83/69	83/69	81/67	79/65
Honolulu	80/66	81/65	82/67	83/68	85/70	87/72	88/74	89/75	89/74	87/73	84/71	82/68
Kahului	80/63	81/63	81/65	83/66	84/67	86/69	87/71	88/71	88/70	87/69	84/68	82/65
Kalaupapa	78/63	78/63	79/64	80/65	82/67	83/69	85/70	86/71	86/71	85/70	82/68	79/65
Lāna'i City	72/60	73/59	73/60	74/61	75/62	76/64	77/65	78/66	79/66	77/65	76/64	74/61
Līhu'e	78/65	78/66	78/67	79/69	81/70	83/73	84/74	85/74	85/74	83/73	81/71	79/68

From the records of The Weather Channel Interactive, Inc.

Good Facts To Know

ABOUT THE STATE

POPULATION: 1,211,537.

AREA: 10,932 square miles; ranks 43rd.

CAPITAL: Honolulu.

HIGHEST POINT: 13,796 ft., Mauna Kea, Island of Hawai'i.

LOWEST POINT: Sea level, Pacific Ocean.

TIME ZONE(S): Hawai'i-Aleutian. The state observes standard time all year. When daylight saving time is observed on the mainland, an additional hour is added to the time difference between the two, making Hawai'i 3 hours behind the West Coast and 6 hours behind the East Coast.

REGULATIONS

TEEN DRIVING LAWS: No more than one passenger under age 18 is permitted; household members are exempt. Driving is not permitted 11 p.m.-5 a.m. The minimum age for an unrestricted driver's license is 17. For more information, phone (808) 587-2150.

SEAT BELT/CHILD RESTRAINT LAWS: Seat belts are required for individuals ages 18 and over. Children 8-18 are required to be in a seat belt; appropriate child restraints are required for children under age 8 who are less than 57 inches tall. AAA recommends the use of seat belts and appropriate child restraints for the driver and all passengers.

CELLPHONE RESTRICTIONS: Hawai'i state law prohibits the use of handheld cellphones while driving. Texting while driving also is prohibited. Maui has a complete ban on cellphone use for novice drivers.

HELMETS FOR MOTORCYCLISTS: Required for riders under age 18; windscreen or eye protection required for all.

RADAR DETECTORS: Permitted.

MOVE OVER LAW: Drivers are required to slow down and vacate the lane nearest stopped emergency vehicles using flashing signals; if possible, drivers must move two lanes over. The law also requires drivers to move over for tow truck drivers assisting motorists.

FIREARMS LAWS: Vary by state and/or county. Contact the Firearms Division of the Honolulu Police Department; phone (808) 529-3371.

HOLIDAYS

HOLIDAYS: Jan. 1 ■ Martin Luther King Jr. Day, Jan. (3rd Mon.) ■ Washington's Birthday/Presidents Day, Feb. (3rd Mon.) ■ Prince Jonah Kūhiō Kalaniana'ole Day, Mar. 26 ■ Good Friday ■ Easter ■ Memorial Day, May (last Mon.) ■ King Kamehameha I Day, June 11 ■ July 4 ■ Statehood Day, Aug. (3rd Fri.) ■ Labor Day, Sept. (1st Mon.) ■ Discoverer's Day, Oct. (2nd Mon.) ■ Veterans Day, Nov. 10 ■ Election Day, Nov. (1st Tues. following 1st Mon.) ■ Thanksgiving, Nov. (4th Thurs.) ■ Christmas, Dec. 25.

STATEWIDE EVENTS: Wesak Day, Apr. (1st Sun.) ■ Bodhi Day, Dec. (Sun. nearest Dec. 7) ■ Princess Bernice Pauahi Bishop's Birthday, Dec. 19.

MONEY

TAXES: Hawai'i has a general excise tax of 4 percent (4.712 percent in Honolulu and 4.5 percent in Oahu). There also is a 9.25 percent Transient Accommodations Tax on lodgings for stays of less than 180 consecutive days.

VISITOR INFORMATION

INFORMATION CENTERS: Information is available Mon.-Fri. 8-4:30, except holidays, at the Hawai'i Visitors and Convention Bureau, 2270 Kalākaua Ave., Suite 801, Honolulu, HI 96815. Phone (800) 464-2924.

PHONE RATES:
Calls made to any part of the same island are local calls (no toll); calls from one island to another are toll calls. Dial 911 for emergency phone calls on all the islands.

FISHING AND HUNTING REGULATIONS:
Division of Aquatic Resources, Fishing Licenses
Dept. of Land and Natural Resources
1151 Punchbowl St., Room 330
Honolulu, HI 96813
(808) 587-0100
(808) 587-0109 (Fishing Licenses)

Division of Conservation and Resource Enforcement, Hunter Education
Hawai'i Hunter Education Program
1130 N. Nimitz Hwy., A-212
Honolulu, HI 96817
(808) 587-0200

DIVING AND SNORKELING INFORMATION:
Hawai'i Visitors and Convention Bureau
2270 Kalākaua Ave., Suite 801
Honolulu, HI 96815
(808) 923-1811
(800) 464-2924

RECREATION INFORMATION:
Division of State Parks
Dept. of Land and Natural Resources
1151 Punchbowl St., Kalanimoku Building, Room 310
Honolulu, HI 96813
(808) 587-0300
(808) 587-0400

Hawai'i Annual Events

Please call ahead to confirm event details.

JANUARY

- Hyundai Tournament of Championship / Lahaina
  808-669-2440
- New Year's 'Ohana Festival
  Honolulu
  808-945-7633
- Ka Moloka'i Makahiki (Ancient Hawaiian Games)
  Kaunakakai
  808-553-3214

FEBRUARY

- Punahou School Carnival
  Honolulu
  808-944-5711
- Waimea Town Celebration
  Waimea
  808-645-9996
- World Whale Day / Kīhei
  808-249-8811, ext. 1

MARCH

- Kona Brewers Festival
  Kailua-Kona
  808-331-3033
- Honolulu Festival
  Honolulu
  808-833-3378
- Big Island International Marathon / Hilo
  808-969-7400

APRIL

- Banyan Tree Birthday Party
  Lahaina
  808-667-9194
- Merrie Monarch Festival
  Hilo
  808-935-9168
- Hawai'i International Film Festival Spring Showcase
  Honolulu
  808-792-1577

MAY

- Waikiki Spam Jam
  Honolulu
  808-255-5927
- Maui Onion Festival
  Lahaina
  808-243-2290
- World Fireknife Dance Competition and Samoa Festival / Lā'ie
  808-367-7060

JUNE

- Kapalua Wine and Food Festival / Lahaina
  808-669-0244
- King Kamehameha Celebration and Floral Parade / Honolulu
  808-586-0333
- Pan-Pacific Festival Matsuri / Honolulu
  808-926-8177

JULY

- Volcanoes Cultural Festival
  Volcano
  808-967-8333
- Concert in the Sky / Līhu'e
  808-245-7277
- Koloa Plantation Days
  Kōloa
  808-652-3217

AUGUST

- Volcano Rain Forest Runs
  Volcano
  808-967-8240
- Hookuikahi Establishment Day Hawaiian Cultural Festival / Kawaihae
  808-882-7218
- Hilo Orchid Society Show and Sale / Hilo
  860-380-7964

SEPTEMBER

- Aloha Festivals / Honolulu
  808-483-0730
- Kauai Mokihana Festival
  Kapa'a
  808-822-2166
- Hawaii Food and Wine Festival / Honolulu
  808-738-6245

OCTOBER

- Moloka'i Hoe Outrigger Canoe Championship
  Maunaloa
  808-330-4774
- Halloween in Lahaina
  Lahaina
  808-667-9174
- Coconut Festival / Kapa'a
  808-651-3273

NOVEMBER

- Kona Coffee Cultural Festival / Kailua-Kona
  808-326-7820
- Waikiki Holiday Parade
  Honolulu
  888-892-5877
- Christmas in the Country
  Volcano
  808-967-7565

DECEMBER

- Holiday Lighting of the Banyan Tree / Lahaina
  808-667-9194
- Waimea Lighted Christmas Parade / Waimea
  808-337-1005
- Pearl Harbor Day Commemoration / Honolulu
  808-422-3300

Pu'uhonua o Hōnaunau National Historical Park, Hawai'i

Akatsuka Orchid Gardens, Hawai'i

King Kamehameha Statue draped with *lei*, O'ahu

Hawaiian green sea turtle

Byodo-In Temple, O'ahu

Index: Great Experience for Members

AAA editor's picks of exceptional note

Polynesian Cultural
Center

Hawai'i Tropical
Botanical Garden

Hawai'i State Capitol

USS *Arizona*
Memorial

See Orientation map on p. 26 for corresponding grid coordinates, if applicable.

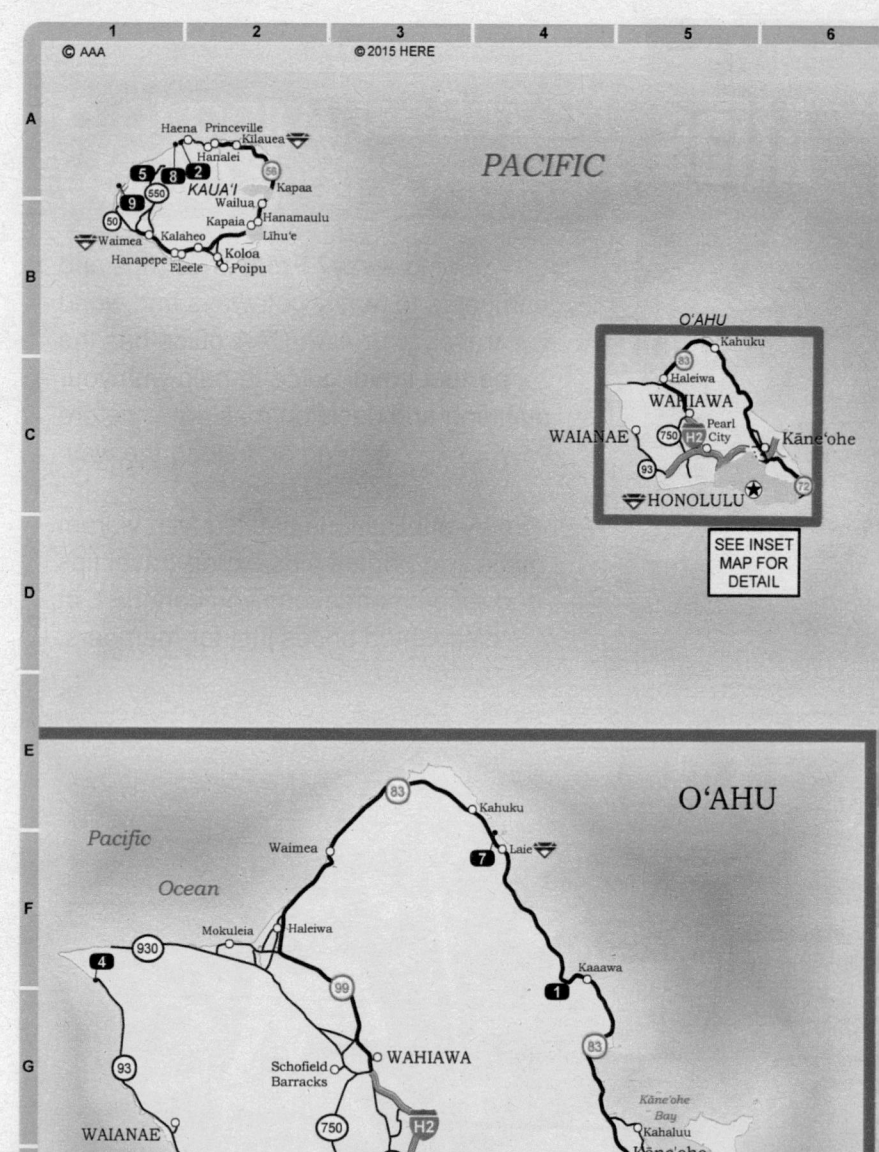

7 8 9 10 11 12

4090-16

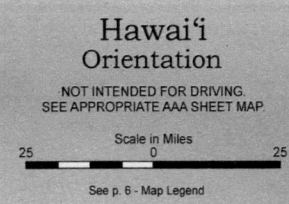

Hawai'i
Orientation

NOT INTENDED FOR DRIVING.
SEE APPROPRIATE AAA SHEET MAP.

Scale in Miles
25   0   25

See p. 6 - Map Legend

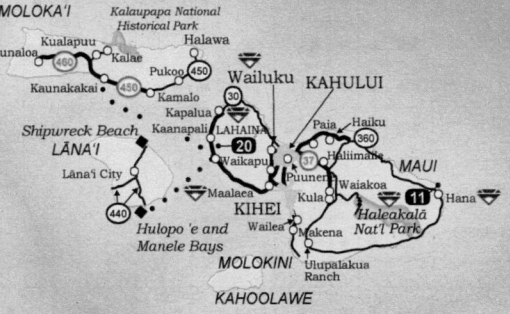

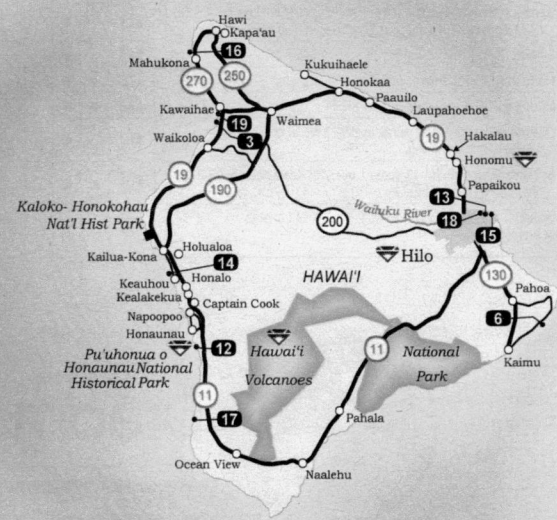

Only places listed in the Attractions
section appear on this map.

See AAA GEM Index

1 See Recreation Areas Chart
on following page

Recreation Areas Chart

The map location numerals in column 2 show an area's location on the preceding map.

	MAP LOCATION	CAMPING	PICNICKING	HIKING TRAILS	BOATING	BOAT RAMP	BOAT RENTAL	FISHING	SWIMMING	PETS ON LEASH	BICYCLE TRAILS	SKIN/SCUBA	VISITOR CENTER	LODGE/CABINS	FOOD SERVICE
NATIONAL PARKS *(See place listings.)*															
Haleakalā **(E-9)** 30,183 acres.			•	•	•					•	•			•	•
Hawai'i Volcanoes **(H-10)** 333,086 acres.			•	•	•					•	•		•	•	•
STATE															
Ahupua'a O Kahana **(G-4)** 5,229 acres n. of Kahana on SR 83. Bodysurfing.	**1**	•	•	•	•	•	•		•	•			•		
Hā'ena **(A-2)** 66 acres near Hā'ena at the west end of SR 560. Snorkeling. *(See Hā'ena p. 64.)*	**2**		•	•				•	•			•			
Hāpuna Beach **(F-10)** 62 acres 2 mi. s. of Kawaihae on SR 19. Bodysurfing. *(See Kawaihae p. 50.)*	**3**		•	•					•					•	
Ka'ena Point **(F-1)** 779 acres in Makua off SR 930. Surfing only for experts. No drinking water. *(See Mokulē'ia p. 167.)*	**4**		•	•				•	•						
Kōke'e **(A-1)** 4,345 acres 15 mi. n. of Kekaha on SR 550. *(See Waimea p. 80.)*	**5**	•	•	•				•					•	•	
MacKenzie **(H-12)** 13 acres 9 mi. n.e. of Kaimu on SR 137. No drinking water.	**6**	•	•					•							
Mālaekahāna **(F-4)** 110 acres 1 mi. n. of Lā'ie off SR 83. Bodysurfing.	**7**	•	•					•	•					•	
Nāpali Coast **(A-1)** 6,175 acres 5 mi. from Hānalei Landing. *(See Hā'ena p. 65.)*	**8**	•	•	•	•			•							
Polihale **(B-1)** 38 acres 5 mi. n. of Mānā.	**9**	•	•					•	•						
Sand Island **(I-4)** 140 acres on Sand Island off SR 92 in Honolulu. Surfing.	**10**	•	•					•	•						
Wai'anapanapa **(E-10)** 122 acres 2.5 mi. n.w. of Hāna via SR 360, then .5 mi. n. on Wai'anapanapa Rd. *(See Hāna p. 91.)*	**11**	•	•	•				•						•	
OTHER															
Hookena **(H-10)** 3 acres 1 mi. s. of Hookena, then 2 mi. w. off SR 11.	**12**	•	•					•	•			•			•
James Kealoha **(G-12)** 3 acres in Hilo off CR 137/370.	**13**		•					•	•			•			
Kahalu'u Beach **(G-10)** 4 acres 5 mi. s. of Kailua-Kona on Ali'i Dr. at Milepost 5. Snorkeling, surfing. *(See Kailua-Kona p. 46.)*	**14**		•						•			•			•
Leleiwi **(G-12)** 2 acres in Hilo off Kalaniana'ole St.	**15**		•					•	•			•			
Māhukona **(F-10)** 3 acres just n. of Māhukona on SR 270.	**16**	•	•					•	•			•			
Miloli'i **(H-10)** 1 acre in Miloli'i off SR 11.	**17**	•	•					•				•			
Onekahakaha **(G-12)** 11 acres in Hilo, 3 mi. e. off Kalaniana'ole St. (SR 19). Snorkeling.	**18**		•					•	•			•			
Spencer Beach **(F-10)** 13 acres 1 mi. s. of Kawaihae off SR 270. Snorkeling. *(See Kawaihae p. 50.)*	**19**	•	•					•	•			•			
Wahikuli Wayside **(D-8)** 8 acres 2.5 mi. n. of Lahaina. Bodysurfing.	**20**		•					•	•	•		•			

Dream. Plan. Go.

TripTik® Travel Planner

AAA.com/ttp

Planning Your Trip

Of all the states in the United States, Hawai'i is perhaps the most individual. Different cultures, races, religions, philosophies and lifestyles not only coexist but also blend. While this is an important part of Hawai'i's appeal, it is the setting that lures millions of vacationers every year. It offers scenery that ranges from tangled jungles to mist-shrouded peaks to sunny beaches. Flowers, palm trees, exotic food and drink—all the accoutrements of the tropics—are present in abundance. There are few who can resist the friendly, welcoming call of *aloha*.

How to Get There

By Air

Direct service to Hawai'i is available on regularly scheduled flights from the U.S. West Coast and from most major cities across the country. Consult your local AAA club for complete information about flight schedules and rates.

By Water

Several cruise lines offer cruises to Hawai'i from various West Coast ports, including Los Angeles and San Diego. Your local AAA club can provide more information.

Weather and Clothing

The semitropical climate of Hawai'i is so equable that the language of the islands has no word for weather. Except in the mountains, temperatures vary little throughout the year. Highs usually range from the mid-70s to the mid-80s; lows fluctuate from the mid-60s to the low 70s. Bring lightweight clothes, a sweater or jacket for the evening, a scarf to combat the trade winds, rainwear and, of course, a bathing suit. The mountaintops of Haleakalā on Maui and Mauna Kea and Mauna Loa on Hawai'i are cold year-round; pack accordingly.

Informality is the rule for day and evening dress. Daytime garb runs the gamut of casual attire—shorts and sandals, shirts and slacks, dresses and bathing suits. The relaxed attitude carries over into evening. Men have their choice of island-made aloha shirts while women may opt for a *mu'umu'u*—long or short, flowing or fitted—which may be worn anywhere.

Note: While the constant breeze might prevent you from feeling the sun's heat, lying on the beach all day can cause serious sunburn and sun poisoning. An effective sunscreen lotion should be part of every beach wardrobe. Look for one that has ingredient(s) to protect against UVA rays and has a high sun protection factor (SPF) against UVB rays.

Import Limitations

Hawai'i enforces a quarantine inspection upon arrival. Importation of fresh fruit, live plants and flowers, plant products and certain meat and food products from the mainland is strictly controlled.

Unless you plan to stay in the islands for 6 months or longer, pets are best left at home. Dogs and cats must undergo a quarantine of up to 120 days for which you pay entry and daily fees. Some dogs and cats may be eligible for the 5-Day-Or-Less quarantine and airport release program; additional fees apply. Information about fruit and animal quarantines may be obtained from the Hawai'i Department of Agriculture in Honolulu.

Shopping

Typical Hawaiian keepsakes include bowls, trays, compartmented servers and decorative objects of rich brown monkeypod or *koa* woods. Other popular island-made souvenirs include such items as perfume, colorful jewelry of seeds or rare black and pink coral, *lauhala* (woven leaf) items, liquors and liqueurs from such plants as ti or passion fruit, jellies and preserves, macadamia nuts, ceramics and *'ukulele*.

Hawai'i's garment industry produces colorful sportswear and *aloha* shirts, beachwear and island outfits such as *holokū, holomū* and *mu'umu'u* for women. Recordings of Hawaiian music, both traditional and contemporary, often are not available on the mainland. Remember that many shops are closed nights and often weekends; only in such urban areas as Waikīkī can you expect extended hours. *For information about shopping on O'ahu, see Shopping p. 127.*

How to See the Islands

Guided sightseeing tours of varying duration are available on the major islands. Modes of transportation include buses, vans, limousines or private vehicles. Arrangements can be made at hotel tour desks and at the AAA Hawai'i office in Honolulu.

Jewelry shopping in Hawai'i

By Air

Numerous airplane and helicopter tours are available. Fares depend upon the duration of the flight, the destination and fuel charges. See individual attraction listings throughout the book. While not all of Hawai'i's air tours are listed, those shown are representative of the choices available. Helicopters tend to offer better views of volcanoes because unlike airplanes, they are often able to hover over the sites. Due to decompression-related sickness, it is recommended that passengers wait 12 to 24 hours after scuba diving before flying; the amount of time is dependent on particular dive factors.

By Land

While a prearranged guided tour can provide a comprehensive introduction to the islands, there is no better way to explore than by private vehicle. The most developed islands have the greatest proportion of paved highways; even so, roads in Hawai'i tend to be less well-marked than those on the mainland. Obtain a current AAA Hawai'i map and acquaint yourself with the route before starting out.

Facilities for rental cars are numerous. Agencies are available at airports on Hawai'i, Kaua'i, Maui and O'ahu, in addition to off-airport locations, especially in Honolulu. Hertz offers discounts to AAA members. Lists of rental agencies are available through hotel information desks. Reservations are recommended to secure lower rates. Be sure you fully understand the terms of the rental contract before you sign it. Full coverage insurance, personal accident insurance and personal effects coverage are available for additional fees. All rental rates are subject to local taxes and surcharges.

Note: Read the section of the rental contract regarding limits of public liability and property damage insurance carefully; only a few companies provide extended coverage.

Island of Hawai'i: A charge is levied for rentals not returned to the original pickup point. Hertz offices are in Hilo, (808) 935-2898; and Kona, (808) 329-3566.

Island of Kaua'i: A Hertz office is in Līhu'e, (808) 245-3356.

Island of Maui: Hertz offices are in Kahului, (808) 893-5200; and Lahaina, (808) 661-4368 or (808) 667-2651.

Island of O'ahu: Hertz offices are in Honolulu, (808) 529-6800; and Waikīkī, (808) 971-3535.

By Water

There are numerous opportunities for seeing Hawai'i by water. Typical craft include catamarans, trimarans, ketches, yachts, sloops, diesel-powered cruisers and even submarines.

Boat tours vary from narrated sightseeing cruises to moonlight sails to interisland trips. Tours range from 1 hour to 2 days, but most trips are half a day or less. Some provide opportunities for swimming, snorkeling, scuba diving, fishing, picnicking or whale watching (in season) and might include cocktails, snacks, meals, entertainment or dancing.

Most trips depart from the docks at the islands' harbors, but some companies operate directly from the beaches in front of a few large hotels. Reservations are required. Most fares include pickup service or minibus transfers to and from departure points.

While it is impossible to list all the boat tours and cruises in Hawai'i, those shown throughout the book are representative of the choices available. For information about complete listings and reservations on any island, contact AAA Hawai'i, the offices of the Hawai'i Visitors and Convention Bureau or the activity desk at your hotel. Local publications found in hotel lobbies also are good sources of information.

Interisland Travel
By Air

Catching a plane to another island is as common to islanders as catching a bus or train is to those on the mainland. Due to decompression-related sickness, it is recommended that passengers wait 12 to 24 hours after scuba diving before flying; the amount of time is dependent on particular dive factors.

Hawaiian, Island Air and Mokulele airlines offer fast and extensive service. One-way flights range in duration from 20 minutes to about an hour. Hawaiian Airlines does not accept cash for in-flight purchases. For additional information, including luggage restrictions, contact Hawaiian Airlines, (800) 367-5320; Island Air, (800) 652-6541 or (800) 323-3345; or Mokulele Airlines, (808) 270-8767 or (866) 260-7070. AAA Hawai'i also provides information and reservations about interisland transportation and fly/drive packages.

By Water

Ferry service is available between Maui and Moloka'i aboard the Maui-Moloka'i Ferry; the trip takes about 90 minutes. A one-way trip is $40; $20 (ages 4-12). Phone (877) 500-6284. Also available is ferry service between Maui and Lāna'i aboard Expeditions' Maui-Lāna'i Ferry; the trip takes about 45 minutes. A one-way trip is $30; $20 (ages 2-11). Phone (800) 695-2624.

Returning to the Mainland

Remember that due to decompression-related sickness, it is recommended that passengers wait 12 to 24 hours after scuba diving before flying; the amount of time is dependent on particular dive factors.

Rice straw products are strictly forbidden entry into the continental United States. Also prohibited are many agricultural products such as corn, sugarcane, fresh fruit and related plants, as these could harbor diseases that might infect plants on the mainland. Department of Agriculture officials inspect all outgoing baggage. Inspections may be done either at interisland flight terminals or at the main airport. Allow ample time for this procedure. Some common items that visitors may mail or take home with them include fresh flowers, *lei,* seashells, pineapples, coconuts, certain seed *lei* and seed jewelry.

Island of Hawai'i

Queen Lili'uokalani Gardens, Hilo

Kīlauea volcano's fiery red lava streams down ocean cliffs. A group of scuba divers watches an underwater ballet performed by massive manta rays. Tourists and locals alike tan their hides on a sun-splashed Kona beach. Hikers in a pristine rain forest admire a postcard-perfect waterfall. At sunset, atop 13,796-foot-high Mauna Kea volcano, photographers aim at pink clouds for their winning vacation shot.

The "Big Island" of Hawai'i has it all. And your biggest headache won't spring from one-too-many mai tais, but rather from planning on how to see it all in one trip. It's not going to happen; this place measures a whopping 4,028 square miles (larger than all the other islands combined). So, slow your roll, and for at least a portion of your stay, let Hawai'i happen to you. Who knows what will lead you to that gorgeous beach absent of people, a surprise sea turtle sighting or that flawless cup of Kona coffee?

Of course, some pre-trip planning is essential, and the first question a Hawai'i Island novice asks is "Where should I stay?" A vast majority of visitors choose hotels and condos on the island's western (leeward) coast, also known as the Kona coast. Why? You can almost always count on warm, sunny weather and the beaches are the island's best. Toss in Hawai'i's main air hub (Kona International Airport), plus the restaurants and shops of the Kailua-Kona area, and *voilà*—you've got tourist central.

On Hawai'i's eastern (windward) coast sits laid-back Hilo, the island's capital city and one of the rainiest spots in the country (an average of 130 inches falls each year). The upside of all that sogginess is a lush mosaic of brilliant green rain forests, tumbling waterfalls and verdant valleys. This is the tropical island paradise of your daydreams, and even if you don't stay here (a vacation rainout is a very real possibility), a day trip is a must.

In the bucket list department, Kīlauea volcano has been erupting intermittently since 1983. If you're lucky and the Hawaiian volcano goddess Pele is cooperating, the sight of blistering hot magma pouring from the earth is one you'll never forget. Should volcanic fireworks elude you, don't dismiss Hawai'i Volcanoes National Park entirely. This beautiful, fascinating park warrants at least 1 full day of exploration.

Sitting atop the "Hawai'i hot spot," the volcanic source of the entire island chain, Hawai'i Island is the state's youngest, feistiest

Hawai'i Attractions

Scale in Miles

6.5 0 6.5

See p. 6 - Map Legend

Alenuihaha Channel

Upolu Airport (UPP)
UPOLU PT
UPOLU POINT RD
Upolu Point
Coast Guard Reserve
KAUHOLA PT
Kapa'au
AKONI PULE HWY
Keokea Beach Park
Pololu Valley
Kapa'a Beach Park
Mahukona Beach Park
Lapakahi State Historical Park
Mahukona
Hawi

POLOLU VALLEY

Kohala

Forest

Na'alapa Stables

Waipi'o Valley Shuttle and Tours

Horseback Above Waipio

Kukuihaele
Kapulena
Haina
Paauhau
Honokaa
Na'alapa Stables

POHAKEA RD
Paauilo
Kukaiau
Laupahoehoe Point Beach Park

Pua Mau Botanic and Sculpture Garden
Pu'ukoholā Heiau National Historic Site
Samuel M Spencer Beach Park
Sunshine Helicopters
Hapuna Beach State Recreation Area
Kawaihae
Anna Ranch Heritage Center

MAMALAHOA

Waimea (Kamuela)

Hawaiian Vanilla Company
Laupahoehoe Train Museum
Ookala
Laupahoehoe

Kalopa State Recreation Area

Laupahoehoe Natural Reserve Area

OLD PUAKO RD
Pupukea Paalaa Uka Mil Road
Waikoloa Village

Dolphin Quest Hawai'i
Blue Hawaiian Helicopters

Kiholo Bay

MANO PT
Kaupulehu

Puu
Puu Anahulu
Waawaa

Hakalau Forest National Wildlife Refuge

Hilo Forest

MAUNA KEA EL 13,796 FT
Mauna Kea Forest Reserve

Kona International Airport at Keahole (KOA)
Cooperative

Game

Game Management Area

DANIEL K INOUYE HWY

Mauna Kea Information Center

Ocean Rider
Big Island Air
Astronaut Ellison S Onizuka Space Center
Kaloko-Honokohau Natl Hist Park
Body Glove Ocean Adventures
Ahu'ena Heiau
KAIMINANI DR
Hawai'i Forest & Trail
Hula Daddy Kona Coffee
MAMALAHOA HWY
Moku'aikaua Church
Holualoa
Hulihe'e Palace
Kailua-Kona
Keauhou Bay
Lava Legends & Legacies - Journeys of the South Pacific Lū'au
Kahalu'u Beach Park
Fair Wind
Sea Quest Rafting Adventures
Kahaluu
Keauhou
Daifukuji Soto Mission
Kainaliu
Greenwell Farms
Hawaii Pack and Paddle
H N Greenwell Store Mus
Kealakekua
Kona Coffee Living History Farm
Captain Cook
Captain Cook Monument
The Amy B H Greenwell
Kealakekua Bay State Historical Park
Ethnobotanical Garden
Napoopoo
Painted Church (St Benedict's Church)

Pohakuloa Training Area Military Reservation

RECOMMENDED FOR FOUR-WHEEL DRIVE VEHICLES ONLY

Mauna Kea Forest Reserve

SADDLE RD
Kipuka
Ainahou Nene Sanctuary
Upper Waiakea Forest Reserve
Puu Makaa Natur Res

Mauna Loa Forest Reserve

SEE KĪLAUEA CALDERA INSET MAP FOR DETAIL

MAUNA LOA TRAIL

Kipukapuaulu

Volcar

Honaunau
Pu'uhonua o Hōnaunau National Historical Park
Hookena Beach Park
Hookena
Keokea

Hakalau Forest National Wildlife Refuge

Mauna Loa EL 13,679 FT

Hawai'i

Volcanoes

National

Kapapala Forest Reserve

Kau

KĪLAUEA EL 4,190 FT
MAUNA IKI TRAIL
HILINA PALI RD
KAU
Volcanoe
Hawai

Kipahoehoe Natural Area Reserve

Park

Puu O Keokeo EL 6,875 FT

Forest

KAU DESERT TRAIL
DESERT
NILIKAKANI POINT

Milolii
Milolii Beach Park

Manuka Natural Area Reserve

Manuka State Wayside
Ocean View

Pahala

Reserve

Punalu'u Black Sand Beach Park

Waiohinu
Whittington Beach Park

Naalehu

KOHALA BLVD
Kula Kai Caverns

SOUTH POINT RD
KA LAE (SOUTH POINT)

KAMILO POINT

Pacific

2867-16   © 2015 HERE

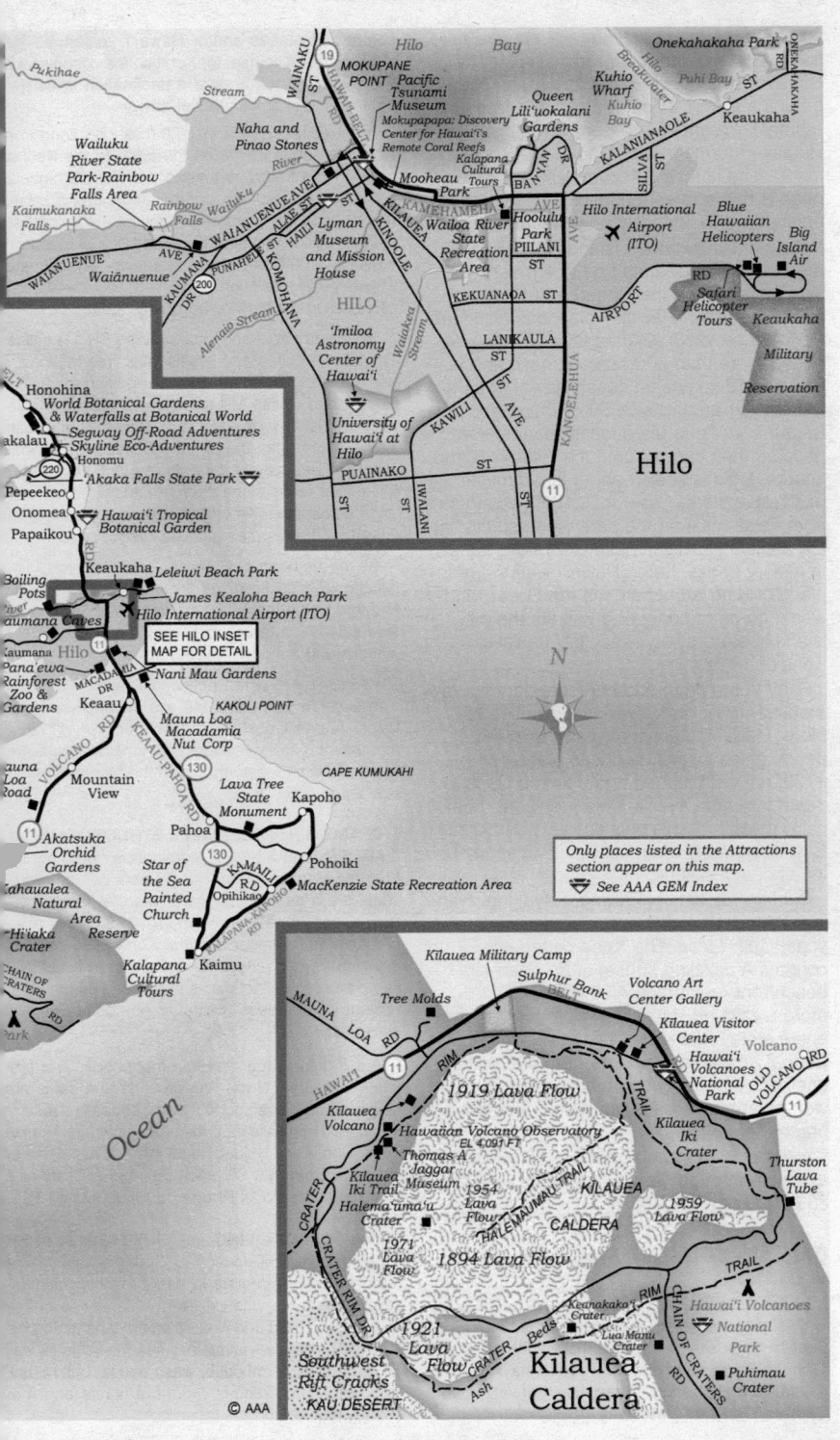

star. It broke the ocean surface about a million years ago and has grown at a steady clip ever since. Five major volcanoes comprise the island. The three oldest and northernmost volcanoes are Kohala (extinct), Hualālai (dormant) and Mauna Kea (dormant). The latter's sometimes snowcapped peak is home to astronomical observatories equipped with seriously powerful telescopes.

Busy making Hawai'i Island even bigger are newcomers Mauna Loa (the most massive mountain on the planet) and Kīlauea, which are within Hawai'i Volcanoes National Park. Since 1983, Kīlauea lava flows have added more than 500 acres of new land to the island's southeast coast. Hawai'i was a tad smaller around A.D. 500, when people from the far-flung Marquesas Islands first paddled their canoes onto the Hawai'i Island shores. Little is known about these mysterious first settlers. About A.D. 1000, voyagers from Tahiti crashed the party and established the ancient Hawaiian culture we read about in history books. Later, Hawai'i was the birthplace of King Kamehameha the Great, who would go on to conquer and unify the other islands before dying peacefully in Kailua-Kona in 1819.

Forty years prior, another legendary figure met his maker on Hawai'i. Only British explorer Capt. James Cook's arrival at the pearly gates wasn't nearly as pleasant. In 1779, natives clubbed and stabbed Cook to death in a fight over a stolen rowboat. Ironically, the site of this ugly scene, Kealakekua Bay, is arguably the most beautiful snorkeling spot in the state.

Surfing. Exceptional diving. Kayaking. Fishing. Hiking. Historic sites. Luxury resorts and spas. Golf. *Lū'au*. The Kona coffee upcountry. A dazzling sunset at an open-air, beachfront restaurant. All this and much more awaits on Hawai'i, a microcosm of the entire state. Just remember, the island is *big*. Budget ample time to drive from one spot to another. And most importantly, leave your worries at home, ease your mind and embrace the *aloha* spirit.

Full-day island and volcano excursions are available through Gray Line; phone (808) 833-3000 or (888) 206-4531.

CAPTAIN COOK (H-10) pop. 3,429, elev. 1,330'
• Attractions map p. 32

One of the largest of the Kona coffee belt towns, Captain Cook sits high above the Pacific along SR 11 in the South Kona district. If you're staying in the Kailua-Kona or Kohala areas, you'll drive through Captain Cook on your way to Hawai'i Island's southern beaches and/or Hawai'i Volcanoes National Park. Of course, for Kona coffee connoisseurs the Captain Cook area is a destination in its own right worthy of at least a half day.

Kona coffee, grown in a 20-mile-long zone from Hōlualoa above Kailua on the north to the Kēōkea area on the south, is among the world's highest-priced java. And with good reason. Kona beans (called "cherries") produce some of the smoothest coffee you'll ever taste. Farms dot the slopes from 1,000 to 2,000 feet above sea level. The climate, with its usual afternoon cloudiness, and the rich volcanic soil make growing conditions ideal.

Roadside farms and shops (along SR 11) sell locally grown coffee and usually offer free tastings; a few of the bigger operations offer guided tours. The Royal Kona Coffee Mill and Museum south of Milepost 107 is a worthwhile stop. Between mileposts 110 and 111, take the turnoff for Nāpo'opo'o Road (on the ocean side of the highway) and you'll find a few coffee farms along the road. Just north of Captain Cook in the town of Kealakekua is the excellent Greenwell Farms *(see attraction listing p. 51)*.

As for the heart of Captain Cook itself, you'll find historic wooden buildings (including the circa-1917 Manago Hotel) that conjure "old Hawaii," plus roadside eateries, a few touristy shops, a couple of gas stations and a modern supermarket.

Kealakekua Bay, an outstanding snorkeling spot a mile below town, was the site of British explorer Capt. James Cook's death on Feb. 14, 1779. A monument marking the spot where native Hawaiians killed him is on the north side of the bay *(see attraction listing p. 55)*.

THE AMY B.H. GREENWELL ETHNOBOTANICAL GARDEN is at 82-6160 Māmalahoa Hwy., across from the Manago Hotel. This 15-acre garden represents the area's vegetation zones that existed before Capt. Cook arrived in 1779. One area preserves the remnants of the Kona Field System, in which stone boundaries separate crop fields. Native plants as well as plants introduced by the Polynesians can be seen. Kamehameha butterflies visit seasonally.

A self-guiding tour app for smartphones and tablets is available. **Note:** The grounds and paths are covered with gravel; good walking shoes are recommended. **Time:** Allow 30 minutes minimum. **Hours:** Tues.-Sun. 9-4. Guided tours at 1. Closed major holidays. **Cost:** $7; $6 (ages 65+); $5 (military with ID); free (ages 0-12). **Phone:** (808) 323-3318. GT

KONA COFFEE LIVING HISTORY FARM is on SR 11 across from Milepost 110. Tours of this 7-acre farm feature interpreters in period clothing demonstrating what life was like for the Japanese coffee farmers who lived and worked on the land during the early 20th century. Visitors can see the fields as well as the original farmhouse, wash house, bathhouse, mills and outbuildings. Various artifacts and machinery also are on the grounds.

Note: Good walking shoes are required due to uneven path conditions that include slight hills and rocks. **Time:** Allow 1 hour minimum. **Hours:** Mon.-Fri. 10-2. Last tour departs 1 hour before closing. Closed major holidays. **Cost:** $15; $13 (ages 62+); $5 (ages 5-17). **Phone:** (808) 323-2006.

THE COFFEE SHACK   808/328-9555

🍷🍷 Sandwiches Pizza. Casual Dining. $10-$14 **AAA Inspector Notes:** This eatery offers an open lanai with drop-dead gorgeous views of the coastline, Kealakekua Bay and coffee trees. Breakfast and lunch is served, including sandwiches, salads and or the sandwiches. During busy times, put your name on the wait list as soon as you arrive. **Features:** patio dining. **Address:** 83-5799 Mamalahoa Hwy 96704 **Location:** On SR 11; between MM 108 and 109. B L 🏧

MANAGO HOTEL RESTAURANT   808/323-2642

🍷 Hawaiian. Casual Dining. $6-$15 **AAA Inspector Notes:** This third-generation-run hotel and restaurant has been serving local families and adventurous travelers since the 1920s. It's known for its remarkable pork chops, which are coated in bread crumbs then fried golden brown. An assortment of fish, including mahi mahi, ono, ahi and butterfish, also is available. Simple preparations and reasonable prices. Each entree includes three small sides served family style. **Features:** beer & wine. **Reservations:** suggested. **Address:** 82-6151 Mamalahoa Hwy 96704 **Location:** On SR 11; between MM 109 and 110. **Parking:** on-site and street. B L D 🏧

HAKALAU (G-12) elev. 151'

WORLD BOTANICAL GARDENS & WATERFALLS AT BOTANICAL WORLD is off SR 19 at Milepost 16, following signs to 31-240 Old Māmalahoa Hwy. Featured on the 300-acre grounds are the Rainbow Walk, filled with 100 species of bromeliads; a wall covered with wild orchids; the Children's Maze; the Honopue Stream and its waterfalls; and the beautiful Kamae'e Falls, reached by a scenic drive. Visitors can also stroll amid trees that grow mangoes, guavas, papayas, pineapples and bananas.

Guided garden and waterfall tours are available by reservation. **Hours:** Daily 9-5:30. **Cost:** Self-guiding tour $15; $7 (ages 13-17); $3 (ages 5-12). Guided tour $57; $33 (ages 5-12). **Phone:** (808) 963-5427 or (888) 947-4753. 🎟

Segway Off-Road Adventures is at World Botanical Gardens & Waterfalls at Botanical World, off SR 19 at Milepost 16, following signs to 31-240 Old Māmalahoa Hwy. Participants may choose from four guided Segway tours ranging from 30 minutes to 3 hours. During the 30-minute Aloha Intro Tour, participants get acquainted with the two-wheeled personal transportation devices before taking a leisurely glide through the botanical gardens. Both the 90-minute Mala Pua Tour and the 3-hour Māmalahoa Tour are easy; the 3-hour off-road Hanapueo Tour is challenging.

Note: Participants must weigh between 70 and 270 pounds and wear closed-toe shoes. Pregnant women and individuals with back injuries or other medical conditions should not ride without consulting a doctor first. **Hours:** Departures daily; times vary. **Cost:** $57-$187. Under 12 are not permitted. Reservations are required. **Phone:** (808) 963-5427 or (888) 947-4753. 🎟

RECREATIONAL ACTIVITIES

Ziplines

- **Zip Isle Zip Line at Botanical World Adventures** is on the World Botanical Gardens & Waterfalls at Botanical World grounds, off SR 19 at Milepost 16, following signs to 31-240 Old Māmalahoa Hwy. **Hours:** Trips depart daily 9-4:30. Phone ahead to confirm schedule. **Phone:** (808) 963-5427 or (888) 947-4753.

LAI NANI RESORT   808/963-5483

fyi Not evaluated. **Address:** 31-212 Hawaii Belt Rd 96710 **Location:** Oceanfront. Off SR 19; at MM 16; 16 mi n of Hilo. Facilities, services, and décor characterize a mid-scale property.

▼GEM HAWAI'I VOLCANOES NATIONAL PARK (H-10)

See also Volcano p. 57
- Hotels p. 39 • Restaurants p. 39
- Attractions map p. 32

Elevations in the park range from sea level at Hōlei Sea Arch to 13,677 ft. at Mauna Loa. Refer to AAA maps for additional elevation information.

Hawai'i Volcanoes National Park is 29 miles southwest of Hilo and 96 miles east of Kailua via SR 11. Established in 1916 (back when Hawai'i was a U.S. territory), the park is one of the planet's most geologically active areas and is home to two of the five volcanoes that comprise the island of Hawai'i: Kīlauea and Mauna Loa. Most Hawai'i Island vacationers spend a hurried day at the park (it's a long drive from the Kona coast resorts), but if you're on the island for a week or more, it's well worth staying a night or two at Volcano House (the park's only hotel) or somewhere in the nearby village of Volcano.

What could warrant spending so much precious tanning time away from the beach? For starters, Kīlauea (at an elevation of 4,091 feet) has been in almost constant eruption along its east rift zone since 1983. Spectacular outbursts with sky-high lava fountains and raging rivers of liquid rock are rare, but even seeing the volcano's normal activity (slowly oozing surface flows) may well be *the* highlight of your trip. That's assuming Kīlauea is cooperating during your visit. The volcano can go months at a time with no visible lava flows.

Mauna Loa, which stands at 13,677 feet above sea level, is the world's most massive active volcano, with an estimated volume of 19,000 cubic miles. Though Mauna Loa hasn't erupted since 1984, it's still an impressive sight and a magnet for hard-core hikers who come to tackle the 19-mile one-way summit trail.

Hawaiian volcanoes are not the pointy conical variety you remember from science class (think Mount Fuji). These are shield volcanoes—massive, broad mounds that typically don't erupt in the mammoth explosions commonly associated with volcanism. In laid-back Hawai'i, even the volcanoes are mellow.

The lava in Hawai'i flows easily and tends to build smooth mountains with shallow summit depressions known as calderas. In the heart of the park, much of the sightseeing and hiking you do will be in and around the main Kīlauea Caldera. On the floor of the caldera's western side, a lava lake roils inside the Halema'uma'u Crater, mythical home of the Hawaiian volcano goddess, Pele. It has been decades since the park service allowed visitors to stand on the rim of the crater and peer into this cauldron of magma. However, even at a distance Halema'uma'u puts on quite a show. By day, you'll see volcanic gas and smoke pour into the sky. At night the fuming crater glows a fiery, ominous red, drawing big crowds to the viewing area at the Thomas A. Jaggar Museum (Kīlauea Overlook and Waldron Ledge are other good vantage points).

In addition to periodic volcanic fireworks, the park will quickly fill your itinerary with its steam vents, walk-through lava tube, caldera overlooks, craters, cinder cones, ancient petroglyphs, lava trees, coastal rock arch and outstanding hiking trails through native rain forests.

General Information and Activities

The park is open daily 24 hours. From the Kailua-Kona area, one-way drive time to the park is about 2.5 hours. Drive time from Hilo averages 45 minutes. Crater Rim Drive, the park's main road, encircles the summit of Kīlauea Caldera. (At press time, 2 miles of Crater Rim Drive downwind of the plume were closed.) Chain of Craters Road intersects with Crater Rim Drive and winds to the coastal areas. All vehicles are restricted to designated roadways; speed limits are posted. There are no car repair facilities within 21 miles of the park, but gas and oil are available 2 miles from Kīlauea Visitor Center in the village of Volcano (from SR 11, take the turnoff for Old Volcano Road). **Note:** The national park site is culturally significant and should be treated with respect.

When hunger strikes, you'll find a restaurant, lounge and prepackaged deli fare (sandwiches and salads) for sale within the park at the Volcano House hotel gift shop near Kīlauea Visitor Center. Just outside the park in the village of Volcano are a handful of eateries (very busy at lunch time) and inns, plus a pair of general stores selling snacks and drinks.

Marked trails crisscross the park and lead to the summit of Mauna Loa and the coastal area of Kīlauea. Back-country camping permits and information about hiking and trail conditions are available at the Visitor Emergency Operations Center, a short drive from Kīlauea Visitor Center (see attraction listing). The park contains several picnic grounds, but fires are permitted only in specified areas. Hunting and trapping are prohibited. See Recreation Areas Chart.

Temperatures are noticeably cooler at higher elevations, and morning and afternoon showers occur frequently. A jacket or sweater and a light raincoat or umbrella are recommended.

ADMISSION to Hawai'i Volcanoes National Park is $10 per private vehicle; $5 per pedestrian or bicyclist; $25 (Hawai'i Tri-park Annual Pass, which includes Haleakalā National Park and Pu'uhonua o Hōnaunau National Historical Park). Admission receipt is good for entry for 7 consecutive days.

PETS must be leashed and attended. They are not allowed on trails on Hilina Pali Road, in Kulanaokuaki Campground or in the backcountry.

COLLECTING rocks and plants, and disturbing archeological sites is prohibited.

ADDRESS inquiries to the Park Superintendent, Hawai'i National Park, P.O. Box 52, Hawai'i National Park, HI 96718-0052. Phone (808) 985-6000 for recorded information and information about lava flow activity.

INSIDER INFO:
Kīlauea Lava Lowdown

"Where do I see lava?" Simple query, but the answer can get complicated, depending on Kīlauea volcano's current activity. Since 1983, Kīlauea has been in a nearly constant state of eruption.

It's been several years since visitors could drive to the end of Chain of Craters Road (within Hawai'i Volcanoes National Park) and witness lava pouring into the Pacific. Today, the action is happening in two locations: on Kīlauea's east rift zone at Pu'u 'Ō'ō vent and at its summit from Halema'uma'u Crater. The Pu'u 'Ō'ō flows are outside the park in a forest reserve, are off-limits to the public, and are currently threatening the town of Pāhoa. The Halema'uma'u eruption is characterized by a lava lake deep within the crater, and while no surface flows are visible here, the reflective glow on the lava during dark hours draws thousands of visitors a day.

The best views of Halema'uma'u Crater are from the Jaggar Museum. For bird's-eye lava views, hop aboard a sightseeing helicopter flight lifting off from nearby Hilo International Airport. Prices are steep, but this is the only way you'll see the beating heart of the fuming Pu'u 'Ō'ō vent. Whatever you choose, a bucket-list experience awaits.

CHAIN OF CRATERS ROAD, within Hawai'i Volcanoes National Park, extends 19 mi. from Crater Rim Dr. at 4,091-foot Kīlauea Summit and ends at a 2003 lava flow. You'll see ancient petroglyphs at the end of the three-quarter-mile Pu'u Loa (Hill of Long Life) Trail; in order to help preserve them, visitors may not disturb them or take rubbings. The road skirts spatter cones, pit craters and recent lava flows as it descends the summit of Kīlauea toward the sea. Mauna Ulu, a large lava shield created by eruptions 1969-74, is visible from an overlook. At the end of the road, where pavement meets the Pacific, you're treated to an excellent view of the 60-foot-tall Hōlei Sea Arch.

Note: Chain of Craters Road dead ends where it's buried by lava from varied flows. Visit the Kīlauea Visitor Center *(see attraction listing)* to check conditions before starting the drive. Restrooms are available, and Volcano House operates a small snack bar at the end of the road. **Hours:** National park daily 24 hours. **Cost:** Included in park admission of $10 (per private vehicle); $5 (per pedestrian or bicyclist); $25 (Hawai'i Tri-park Annual Pass, which includes Haleakalā National Park and Pu'uhonua o Hōnaunau National Historical Park). **Phone:** (808) 985-6000 for recorded park information and information about lava flow activity.

CRATER RIM DRIVE makes an 11-mi. circuit around Kīlauea Caldera within Hawai'i Volcanoes National Park past lava flows, rain forests and craters.

The half-mile, paved Devastation Trail leads through a pumice- and spatter-covered landscape. Thurston Lava Tube was formed when the surface of a lava stream hardened and the molten rock inside flowed away, leaving a tunnel that can be explored for about 500 feet. The parking lot for the 4-mile Kīlauea Iki Trail, one of the park's most popular hikes, is a few minutes' drive southeast of Kīlauea Visitor Center.

Heading west from the visitor center (toward the Thomas A. Jaggar Museum), pull over at the Steam Vents, where rainwater that has seeped into the ground and been heated by hot volcanic rock rises as steam. Across the road, plug your nose for the rotten egg odor of the Sulphur Banks. Along a short, easy boardwalk trail (accessible from either the Steam Vents parking area or the visitor center), volcanic gases spew from the earth amid a landscape painted in colorful sulfur crystals.

Atop 4,078-foot Uwēkahuna Bluff is Hawaiian Volcano Observatory, one of several permanent volcano observatories in the United States; no visitors are allowed inside the observatory.

Note: The western section of Crater Rim Drive (4.7 miles), between the Thomas A. Jaggar Museum and the intersection for Chain of Craters Road, is closed indefinitely because of hazards related to a vent within Halema'uma'u Crater that opened in 2008. Visit the Kīlauea Visitor Center *(see attraction listing)* to check conditions before starting the drive.

Hours: National park daily 24 hours. **Cost:** Included in park admission of $10 (per private vehicle); $5 (per pedestrian or bicyclist); $25 (Hawai'i Tri-park Annual Pass, which includes Haleakalā National Park and Pu'uhonua o Hōnaunau National Historical Park). **Phone:** (808) 985-6000 for recorded park information and information about lava flow activity.

Kīlauea Iki Trail begins at the Kīlauea Iki parking lot on Crater Rim Drive, just s.e. of Kīlauea Visitor Center within Hawai'i Volcanoes National Park. The 4-mile loop trail winds through a lovely fern and 'ōhi'a rain forest before descending some 400 feet to the barren floor of Kīlauea Iki Crater. Crossing the crater floor, keep an eye peeled for steam escaping from cracks in the ground (Kīlauea Iki last erupted in 1959). Save for the 400-foot climb back up to the trailhead, this is an easy-to-moderate trek that'll take around 2.5 hours.

Note: Hikers should expect wet and windy conditions and steep, rocky terrain. Water, snacks, rain gear and sun protection are recommended. **Hours:** National park daily 24 hours. **Cost:** Included in park admission of $10 (per private vehicle); $5 (per pedestrian or bicyclist); $25 (Hawai'i Tri-park Annual Pass, which includes Haleakalā National Park and Pu'uhonua o Hōnaunau National Historical Park). **Phone:** (808) 985-6000.

Thurston Lava Tube is on the east side of Crater Rim Dr. within Hawai'i Volcanoes National Park. From the parking area (often crowded with tour buses), you'll embark on an easy 15- to 20-minute self-guiding walk along a loop trail that starts in the 'ōhi'a forest and continues through this impressive cave-like lava tube. Restrooms and drinking fountains are available at the trailhead. **Hours:** National park daily 24 hours. **Cost:** Included in park admission of $10 (per private vehicle); $5 (per pedestrian or bicyclist); $25 (Hawai'i Tri-park Annual Pass, which includes Haleakalā National Park and Pu'uhonua o Hōnaunau National Historical Park). **Phone:** (808) 985-6000 for recorded park information and information about lava flow activity.

KĪLAUEA VISITOR CENTER, on Crater Rim Dr. within Hawai'i Volcanoes National Park, is the park headquarters and provides literature and displays describing the park and its natural and cultural resources. Displays depict volcanic land formations as well as the plants, animals and people of the volcanic region. A 20-minute film featuring the biology, geology and cultural history of the park is shown on the hour 9-4. An eruption update video is shown on the half-hour.

Park rangers are available to provide eruption updates and answer questions. Detailed hiking trail guide booklets may be purchased in the gift shop. Free ranger-guided activities are posted daily at 9.

Time: Allow 1 hour minimum. **Hours:** Daily 7:45-5. **Cost:** Included in park admission of $10 (per private vehicle); $5 (per pedestrian or bicyclist); $25 (Hawai'i Tri-park Annual Pass, which includes Haleakalā National Park and Pu'uhonua o Hōnaunau National Historical Park). **Phone:** (808) 985-6000.

KĪLAUEA VOLCANO may be reached by SR 11 within Hawai'i Volcanoes National Park and be explored by car and on foot. Kīlauea is so broad and low-profile, unlike your typical cone-shaped volcano, that oftentimes you'll overhear bewildered visitors ask park rangers, "Where's the volcano?" The answer: "You're standing on it." A shield volcano, 4,091-foot-high Kīlauea is crowned by a 400-foot-deep, 3-mile-wide depression known as a caldera. Within Kīlauea Caldera is the Halema'uma'u Crater, the volcano's main vent. March 19, 2008, marked the first explosive Halema'uma'u eruption since 1924. Today, the still-fuming crater contains a boiling lava pond that glows fiery red at night.

The current lava flows, which you'll see pictured on countless tourist brochures, began in 1983 and originate on the volcano's east rift zone at a separate vent named Pu'u 'Ō'ō. This cinder/spatter cone straddles the national park's remote eastern boundary; your best bet for viewing Pu'u 'Ō'ō up close is from a sightseeing helicopter flight. Over the past 30-plus years, lava has buried more than 180 buildings (including the entire town of Kalapana) under 30-plus feet of hardened magma and added more than 500 acres of new coastal land to Hawai'i. Exactly when the current eruption will stop is anyone's guess.

A Kīlauea visit will no doubt inspire many of us to become know-it-all volcanologists for the day. If so, it's critical that you can tell the difference between the volcano's two types of lava. With its silvery, shiny crust, *pāhoehoe* looks smooth, billowy and ropy, like cake batter slowly poured into a pan, while *'a'ā* is rough and jagged (the hardened stuff, guaranteed to shred your Nikes).

Looking back over Kīlauea's last century of volcanic activity, one spectacular event that must be cited is the 1959 Kīlauea Iki eruption. This was a whopper, with lava fountains shooting as high as 1,900 feet (nearly 450 feet higher than the Empire State Building). Today, you can hike the now-cooled Kīlauea Iki Crater from Crater Rim Drive *(see attraction listing).*

Looking forward, there's a new Hawaiian island on the way. About 22 miles south of Kīlauea, and roughly 3,000 feet below sea level, the erupting, submarine Lō'ihi volcano is expected to see the light of day in about 50,000 years. Make your reservations now for the inevitable Lō'ihi Resort, Spa and Golf Club.

Note: Access to the volcano may be restricted at times due to volcanic activity, and roads are subject to closure due to high fire danger or air-quality concerns. **Hours:** National park daily 24 hours. **Cost:** Included in park admission of $10 (per private vehicle); $5 (per pedestrian or bicyclist); $25 (Hawai'i Tri-park Annual Pass, which includes Haleakalā National Park and Pu'uhonua o Hōnaunau National Historical Park). **Phone:** (808) 985-6000 for recorded park information and information about lava flow activity.

KĪPUKAPUAULU is on Mauna Loa Rd. within Hawai'i Volcanoes National Park. A *kīpuka* is an island of older soil and vegetation surrounded by more recent lava flows. A 1.2-mile trail loops through this old-growth forest. **Hours:** National park daily 24 hours. **Cost:** Included in park admission of $10 (per private vehicle); $5 (per pedestrian or bicyclist); $25 (Hawai'i Tri-park Annual Pass, which includes Haleakalā National Park and Pu'uhonua o Hōnaunau National Historical Park). **Phone:** (808) 985-6000 for recorded park information and information about lava flow activity.

MAUNA LOA, adjoining Kīlauea to the west and reached via Mauna Loa Rd. within Hawai'i Volcanoes National Park, is the world's most massive volcano. The summit rises about 56,000 feet above its base (located beneath the floor of the Pacific Ocean) and stands 13,677 feet above sea level. This enormous mountain was built by innumerable lava flows. In the last century, Mauna Loa erupted on an average of once every 3.75 years. The summit is reachable on foot; it is a 19-mile one-way hike from the end of Mauna Loa Road and is typically a 2-day ascent.

One of the more voluminous flows in recent history began in 1950. Very liquid lava escaped from a fissure 13 miles long and reached the sea in less than 3 hours, having advanced at a speed of approximately 3.75 miles an hour. This massive eruption amounted to about 600 million cubic yards of lava, enough to pave a four-lane highway 4.5 times around the world.

With the exception of a brief eruption in July 1975, Mauna Loa waited 34 years before generating another major eruption. On March 25, 1984, Mauna Loa began a 22-day eruption that sent lava flows down its northeast flank from a vent at the 9,400-foot level. The two longest flows extended about 16 miles from the vent. This eruption coincided with yet another eruption of Kīlauea, the first time both volcanoes had erupted simultaneously in 65 years.

Hours: National park daily 24 hours. **Cost:** Included in park admission of $10 (per private vehicle); $5 (per pedestrian or bicyclist); $25 (Hawai'i Tri-park Annual Pass, which includes Haleakalā National Park and Pu'uhonua o Hōnaunau National Historical Park). **Phone:** (808) 985-6000 for recorded park information and information about lava flow activity.

MAUNA LOA ROAD branches off SR 11 opposite Kīlauea Caldera within Hawai'i Volcanoes National Park and reaches an elevation of 6,600 feet. A short turnoff leads to molds of trees formed when lava made a shell around the trunks. A trail at the end of the road passes through mountain parkland and, above 10,000 feet, enters barren lava fields to the summit of Mauna Loa. The trail, one of the island's more difficult hikes, may be closed due to high winds or deep snow. Always check with rangers about current conditions.

Shelters at the 10,000-foot level at Red Hill and near the summit are available by permit on a first-come, first-served basis no more than 24 hours ahead of time. The road may be closed due to high winds or fire danger. The ascent of Mauna Loa can take its toll on the unprepared hiker in the form of severe sunburn, dehydration and acute mountain sickness. **Hikers are required to register at the park's Visitor Emergency Operations Center before starting out for the summit.**

Hours: National park daily 24 hours. **Cost:** Included in park admission of $10 (per private vehicle); $5 (per pedestrian or bicyclist); $25 (Hawai'i ri-park Annual Pass, which includes Haleakalā National Park and Pu'uhonua o Hōnaunau National Historical Park). **Phone:** (808) 985-6000 for recorded park information and information about lava ow activity.

THOMAS A. JAGGAR MUSEUM, 3 mi. w. of Kīlauea Visitor Center on Crater Rim Dr. next to the Hawaiian Volcano Observatory within Hawai'i Volcanoes National Park, is a geological museum dedicated to seismology and volcanology. Inside you'll see several working seismographs and tilt meters hat depict earthquakes as they occur. Videos of ast eruptions of Kīlauea and Mauna Loa run continuously on TV monitors. There's also a computer monitor displaying frequently updated thermal images of Halema'uma'u Crater, taken from the USGS Hawaiian Volcano Observatory webcam.

An adjacent overlook offers excellent views of Kīlauea Caldera and Halema'uma'u Crater. At dusk and into the early evening, this is by far the most popular spot from which to see the fiery red glow of Halema'uma'u. On especially busy nights, parking at he overlook can be a problem. **Time:** Allow 1 hour minimum. **Hours:** Daily 10-8. **Cost:** Included in park admission of $10 (per private vehicle); $5 (per pedestrian or bicyclist); $25 (Hawai'i Tri-park Annual Pass, which includes Haleakalā National Park and Pu'uhonua o Hōnaunau National Historical Park). **Phone:** (808) 985-6000.

VOLCANO ART CENTER GALLERY, next to the Kīlauea Visitor Center within Hawai'i Volcanoes National Park, features fine arts and crafts by Hawai'i artists. Also offered are performances and workshops in Hawaiian culture as well as visual and literary arts. **Hours:** Daily 9-5. Closed Christmas. **Cost:** Included in park admission of $10 (per private vehicle); $5 (per pedestrian or bicyclist); $25 (Hawai'i Tri-park Annual Pass, which includes Haleakalā National Park and Pu'uhonua o Hōnaunau National Historical Park). **Phone:** (808) 967-7565 or (866) 967-7565.

VOLCANO HOUSE   (808)756-9625
▼▼▼ **Historic Hotel** $315-$415 **Address:** 1 Crater Rim Dr 96718 **Location:** Just off SR 11; just past the park's main entry gate. **Facility:** This recently restored historic lodging offers caldera vistas and is located within Hawaii Volcanoes National Park. The primitive cabins managed by the hotel are not AAA inspected or approved. 33 units, some cabins. 2 stories (no elevator), interior corridors. **Terms:** 7 day cancellation notice-fee imposed. **Amenities:** safes. **Dining:** The Rim Restaurant at Volcano House, see separate listing. **Activities:** trails.

🍴 🍸 CALL 🔲 BIZ 📶 ✕ 🐾 📺 💻

WHERE TO EAT

THE RIM RESTAURANT AT VOLCANO HOUSE   808/756-9625
fyi Not evaluated. Creative, island-inspired cuisine that utilizes locally sourced ingredients whenever possible is offered. The dining room window seats offer unobstructed distant views of the Kilauea Caldera. When the volcano is erupting, the nighttime glow offers an amazing perspective, but be sure to make reservations in advance and close to sunset. A prix-fixe lunch is offered. **Address:** 1 Crater Rim Dr 96718 **Location:** Just off SR 11; just past the park's main entry gate; in Volcano House.

HĀWĪ (F-10) pop. 1,081, elev. 590'
• **Attractions map p. 32**

POLOLŪ VALLEY lies e. along the coast, with precipitous scenic gorges extending from the coast to the Kohala Mountains' 5,480-foot summit. **Phone:** (808) 889-6257.

BAMBOO   808/889-5555
▼▼▼ Pacific Rim. Casual Dining. $12-$25 **AAA Inspector Notes:** Historic. Old Hawaiian atmosphere and great food make this a popular choice for locals and tourists visiting the areas art galleries. The Pacific rim influenced menu includes items such as Thai coconut prawns with fresh papaya salsa, Kalua pork and cabbage that is smoked in their own imu (pit), and fresh fish of the day prepared numerous ways such as macadamia nut crusted and fried. Some items for the non-adventurous include burgers with seasonal waffle fries and organic free range teriyaki chicken. **Features:** full bar, Sunday brunch. **Reservations:** suggested. **Address:** 55-3415 Akoni Pule Hwy 96719 **Location:** Center. **Parking:** street only.

🅛 🄳 🐾

SUSHI ROCK   808/889-5900
fyi Not evaluated. While sushi is the focus of this restaurant, they also offer some great salads, sandwiches and dinner entrée choices. **Address:** 55-3435 Akoni Pule Hwy 96719 **Location:** Center.

HILO (G-12) pop. 43,263, elev. 38'
• **Hotels p. 42** • **Restaurants p. 42**
• **Attractions map p. 32**

The Hawai'i Island capital, this beautiful town on the shore of crescent-shaped Hilo Bay sits on the island's eastern side. With its lush tropical surroundings, historic charm, laid-back rhythms and close proximity to Hawai'i Volcanoes National Park (about 30 miles away), Hilo would presumably be a tourist hot spot brimming with resorts and condos. Not so. And the reason can be summed up in one soggy word: rain. It falls here in abundance (about 130 inches per year), and most visitors unwilling to chance a vacation rainout stick to the sunny Kona coast instead.

Even if you don't stay in town, it's well worth spending at least 1 day (preferably 2) exploring Hilo, the Hāmākua Coast to the north, and the Puna area to the south. You'll find a few modern hotels along the Hilo waterfront, as well as smaller motels and B&Bs scattered around town. One-way drive time from Kailua-Kona is roughly 2 hours. Hilo International Airport handles flights to the city. Cruise ships doing the Hawai'i circuit dock 2 miles south of the historic downtown area; take a taxi ($12 to $15) or ask your ship's shore excursion desk about shuttle transportation.

Along downtown's Kamehameha Avenue, colorful historic buildings house souvenir shops, boutiques, jewelers, galleries and restaurants. The area is easily doable on foot, and a bit of exploration will undoubtedly turn up some shopping gems. In the fine art department, check out Dreams of Paradise Gallery (308 Kamehameha Ave. #106), which deals in exceptional works by local painters, sculptors and photographers.

For unique aloha shirts and island wear for women, look no further than the ever-popular Sig Zane (122 Kamehameha Ave., next to the Pacific

Tsunami Museum). All of the clothing is designed by Zane, quality is high, and so are the prices. Basically Books (160 Kamehameha Ave.) is the go-to spot for Hawai'i-related books and maps, including USGS topographic maps for the entire state.

The must-do Hilo Farmers Market takes place daily beginning at 7 a.m. at the corner of Mamo Street and Kamehameha Avenue. The so-called "big days" are Wednesday and Saturday, when the market hosts more than 200 local farmers, florists and crafts dealers and opens an hour earlier. On all market days, the event usually winds down around 4 p.m.

Forgot your toothbrush? Lack a rain jacket? If you need everyday essentials, south of the airport along SR 11 are supermarkets and big-box retailers like Target and Walmart.

Back at the waterfront, outrigger canoes glide across glassy Hilo Bay (protected by a breakwater). Locals and tourists alike stroll along Banyan Drive (the location of Hilo's major hotels), a shady, curving lane lined with more than 50 stately banyan trees. The leafy behemoths were planted in the 1930s, '40s and '50s by visiting celebrities, politicians and other famous folk, and each tree is named for the person who planted it. At the foot of each banyan you'll see wooden signs bearing names like Cecil B. DeMille, Amelia Earhart, Franklin Roosevelt, Babe Ruth, Louis Armstrong and Richard Nixon. Also along Banyan Drive you'll find the pretty Queen Lili-'uokalani Gardens *(see attraction listing)*.

On the north side of town flows the Wailuku River. From the historic downtown area, drive west on Waiānuenue Avenue through residential neighborhoods to see the Boiling Pots pools and Waiānuenue (Rainbow Falls), both of which are in the river's upper reaches *(see attraction listings)*.

Hilo's plentiful rainfall creates ideal agricultural conditions. In addition to sustaining papaya and macadamia nut orchards, the area has become the center of Hawai'i's orchid industry. Akatsuka Orchid Gardens, about 24 miles south in the village of Volcano, produces many types of orchids and other tropical plants and flowers.

In April the ⧬ Merrie Monarch Festival, held at the Edith Kanaka'ole Tennis Stadium and the Afook-Chinen Civic Auditorium, celebrates Hawaiian culture with craft shows, concerts, a parade, a *hula* competition and more.

Big Island Visitors Bureau East Hawai'i Office: 250 Keawe St., Hilo, HI 96720. **Phone:** (808) 961-5797 or (800) 648-2441.

BIG ISLAND AIR departs from Hilo International Airport. Fifty-minute narrated tours include such sights as Kīlauea volcano, north Hilo's waterfalls and the Puna area's rain forest. Stereo headsets are provided.

Note: Due to decompression-related sickness, it is recommended that passengers wait 12-24 hours after scuba diving before flying; the amount of time is dependent on particular dive factors. Ask about possible policies regarding minimum wait time between scuba diving and flying; weight restrictions, weather, cancellation and refund policies; and the minimum and maximum number of passengers for flights. All small aircraft may encounter turbulence. **Hours:** Tours Tues.; phone for departure times. **Cost:** $166.99. Reservations are required. **Phone** (808) 329-4868.

BLUE HAWAIIAN HELICOPTERS departs from Hilo International Airport. The 50-minute Circle of Fire plus Waterfalls Tour features active volcanic areas, lava flows, rain forests and black-sand beaches. Passengers hear music, two-way communication with the pilot, and the pilot's narration via noise-canceling headsets.

Note: Due to decompression-related sickness, it is recommended that passengers wait 12-24 hours after scuba diving before flying; the amount of time is dependent on particular dive factors. Ask about possible policies regarding minimum wait time between scuba diving and flying; weight restrictions, weather, cancellation and refund policies; and the minimum and maximum number of passengers for flights. All small aircraft may encounter turbulence. **Hours:** Daily 7 a.m.-10 p.m. **Cost:** $178-$219 plus applicable fuel surcharge. Reservations are required. **Phone:** (808) 961-5600 or (800) 786-2583. *(See ad on inside front cover.)*

BOILING POTS is about 2 mi. w. of Waiānuenue (also known as Rainbow Falls) via Waiānuenue Ave. at the end of Pe'epe'e Falls Dr. in Wailuku River State Park. As the Wailuku River passes over ancient pool-like lava caves, the water seems to boil. The pools may be viewed from an overlook area; there is no trail access. **Time:** Allow 30 minutes minimum. **Cost:** Free. **Phone:** (808) 961-9540.

⧬ **'IMILOA ASTRONOMY CENTER OF HAWAI'I** is at 600 'Imiloa Pl. in Science & Technology Park on the University of Hawai'i's Hilo campus. The relationship between Hawaiian culture and the universe is showcased through a variety of displays and interactive exhibits, which are written in both English and Hawaiian. The landscaped grounds feature 70 plant varieties either native to the area or brought here by early Polynesians.

Visitors can learn about *hula*, voyaging canoes and the Hawaiian language renaissance as well as the work being done by scientists at Mauna Kea's observatories. The Hawaiian creation chant and the Big Bang Theory, two different but surprisingly similar views about the origins of life, are explored in a theater presentation and with a simulated ascent of Mauna Kea. A planetarium, video presentations and a virtual 3-D space tour also are included.

Time: Allow 2 hours minimum. **Hours:** Tues.-Sun. 9-5. Planetarium shows on the hour noon-3 (also Fri. at 7 p.m. and Sat. at 10 a.m.). Closed Jan. 1, Thanksgiving and Christmas. **Cost:** $17.50; $15.50 (ages 65+ and military with ID); $9.50 (ages

5-12). **Phone:** (808) 969-9700 for recorded information or (808) 969-9703. [GT] [♦]

KALAPANA CULTURAL TOURS departs from Wailoa Harbor. On 2- to 3-hour narrated boat tours of a tropical coastal area, passengers can see whales, spinner dolphins, rare seabirds, old sugar cane mills and interesting caves and coves. If weather permits, they can take a dip in secluded waterfall pools.

Passengers should bring sun protection, 1 liter of water, light snacks, a swimsuit, a towel, a light rain jacket and a camera. Life jackets and additional snacks and beverages are provided. **Hours:** Departures daily at 8 and noon. **Cost:** $125. Reservations are required. **Phone:** (808) 936-0456.

KAŪMANA CAVES, 4.5 mi. s.w. on Saddle Rd. (SR 200) at 1568 Kaūmana Dr., are lava tubes formed by the Mauna Loa eruption of 1881. During its activity this flow came closer to Hilo than during any other on record. Stairs lead down to the cave leading toward Hilo, which can be explored on self-guiding tours for about a half-mile; it ranges 2.5 feet to 5.5 feet high and 10 feet to 50 feet wide.

Note: Visitors should be careful crossing Kaūmana Dr. from the parking area; no traffic signs or crosswalks are available. They should also use caution and watch their footing since the area is often damp and wet with uneven ground. Those entering the cave should have a flashlight and be aware that the area is extremely cramped. The other cave is dangerous and should not be entered. **Hours:** Daily 6 a.m.-11 p.m. **Cost:** Free.

LYMAN MUSEUM AND MISSION HOUSE is at 276 Haili St. The Mission House, completed in 1839, was built for David and Sarah Lyman, a missionary family from New England. The house—reputedly the oldest wood-frame structure on Hawai'i Island—was built with support timbers from local forests and puddle-glass windowpanes. Visitors on a guided tour can view the house's period furnishings, wallpaper and decor.

Next door, the Lyman Museum is a modern museum building built in 1972. Exhibits cover Hawai'i's natural and cultural history. Within the Earth Heritage Gallery are seashell, gem and mineral collections as well as displays about volcanology and Hawai'i's habitats. A special gallery features changing exhibits.

Time: Allow 1 hour minimum. **Hours:** Museum Mon.-Sat. 10-4:30. Guided tours of the Mission House are given Mon.-Sat. at 11 and 2; phone ahead to confirm tour schedule. Closed Jan. 1, Memorial Day, July 4, Labor Day, Thanksgiving and Christmas. **Cost:** $10; $8 (ages 60+); $5 (college students with ID); $3 (ages 6-17); $21 (family). **Phone:** (808) 935-5021.

MAUNA LOA MACADAMIA NUT CORP. is at 16-701 Macadamia Rd. A video describes macadamia nut processing in five languages, and samples of macadamia nuts and chocolate are provided. On weekdays visitors can view the production process from outside balcony windows. **Hours:** Daily 8:30-5. **Cost:** Free. **Phone:** (808) 966-8618 or (888) 628-6256.

MOKUPĀPAPA: DISCOVERY CENTER FOR HAWAI'I'S REMOTE CORAL REEFS is at 76 Kamehameha Ave. Displays, wall panels, interactive exhibits and a three-sided saltwater aquarium showcase the Northwestern Hawaiian Islands, which extend 1,200 miles beyond Kaua'i and now comprise Papahanamokuakea Marine National Monument. Visitors can learn about the animals inhabiting these reefs and tiny islands, as well as the islands' cultural importance and long human history. **Time:** Allow 1 hour minimum. **Hours:** Tues.-Sat. 9-4. Closed major holidays. **Cost:** Free. **Phone:** (808) 933-8180.

NAHA AND PINAO STONES is at 300 Waiānuenue Ave. in front of Hilo Public Library. The Pinao Stone was an entrance pillar of Pinao Temple. The Naha Stone was used as a test of fitness for royalty—reputedly only chiefs of Naha rank were able to move it. Legend says that Kamehameha I lifted the stone and his subsequent reign lent credence to the belief that he who succeeded in performing this feat would be the greatest king. **Hours:** Daily 24 hours. **Cost:** Free.

▼ See AAA listing p. 72 ▼

NANI MAU GARDENS is at 421 Makalika St. The meticulously maintained 20-acre garden is home to a number of native and exotic flowers and plants, including orchids, rare palms and tropical fruits. There's also a Japanese-style bell tower. **Time:** Allow 2 hours minimum. **Hours:** Daily 10-3. **Cost:** $5; $4 (ages 55+); $3 (ages 4-10). **Phone:** (808) 959-3500.

PACIFIC TSUNAMI MUSEUM is at 130 Kamehameha Ave. Educating visitors about the history, science and danger of tsunamis, the museum features exhibits, videos and photographs pertaining to tsunami activity in the Pacific Basin and around the world. Tsunami survivors share their personal stories, and visitors learn how to handle this type of catastrophe should one occur.

Of particular interest are the exhibits about the tsunamis that ravaged Hilo in 1946 and 1960. **Time:** Allow 1 hour minimum. **Hours:** Tues.-Sat. 10-4. Closed Jan. 1, Thanksgiving and Christmas. **Cost:** $8; $7 (ages 60+); $4 (ages 6-17). **Phone:** (808) 935-0926. GT

PANA'EWA RAINFOREST ZOO & GARDENS is s. of Hilo International Airport at jct. SR 11 and Mamaki St. at 800 Stainback Hwy. This 12-acre natural rain forest zoo is home to 75 animal species, including a white Bengal tiger, two-toed sloths and iguanas. A petting zoo and playground also are featured. **Note:** At press time the tiger exhibit was closed for renovations; phone for updates. **Time:** Allow 1 hour minimum. **Hours:** Daily 9-4. Tiger feeding at 3:30. Petting zoo Sat. 1:30-2:30. Closed Jan. 1 and Christmas. **Cost:** Free. **Phone:** (808) 959-9233.

QUEEN LILI'UOKALANI GARDENS, 49 Banyan Dr., is a 30-acre Japanese garden with fish ponds, pagodas and stone lanterns. A bridge crosses to Coconut Island, which has a pavilion and picnic area. **Hours:** Daily 6 a.m.-9 p.m. **Cost:** Free. **Phone:** (808) 961-8311.

SAFARI HELICOPTER TOURS departs from Hilo International Airport's commuter terminal; follow the airport access road off SR 11. Passengers on the 45-minute Volcano Safari Tour hear two-way communication with the pilot via noise-canceling headsets as they view current Kīlauea volcanic activity and destruction from previous lava flows. The 55-minute Deluxe Volcano & Coastline Safari Tour includes the same spectacular views plus views of the waterfalls northwest of Hilo.

Note: Due to decompression-related sickness, it is recommended that passengers wait 12-24 hours after scuba diving before flying; the amount of time is dependent on particular dive factors. Ask about possible policies regarding minimum wait time between scuba diving and flying; weight restrictions; weather, cancellation and refund policies; and the minimum and maximum number of passengers for flights. All small aircraft may encounter turbulence.

Time: Allow 1 hour, 30 minutes minimum. **Hours:** Daily 7:30-5:30. Check-in is 45 minutes prior to departure. Closed Easter and Christmas. **Cost:** Volcano Safari Tour $165. Deluxe Volcano & Coastline Safari Tour $186. Reservations are required. **Phone:** (808) 969-1259 or (800) 326-3356.

WAIĀNUENUE, off Waiānuenue Ave. on Rainbow Dr., has been nicknamed Rainbow Falls. In the morning a rainbow often appears in the mist around the falls. The volume of the falls in Wailuku River State Park dwindles during the dry summer months. **Time:** Allow 30 minutes minimum. **Hours:** Daily dawn-dusk. **Cost:** Free. **Phone:** (808) 961-9540.

CASTLE HILO HAWAIIAN HOTEL   (808)935-9361
Hotel $141-$188 **Address:** 71 Banyan Dr 96720 **Location:** Oceanfront. Jct SR 19 and 11, just nw; on bayfront. **Facility:** 286 units, some efficiencies. 8 stories, interior corridors. **Terms:** 3 day cancellation notice-fee imposed. **Pool(s):** outdoor. **Guest Services:** valet and coin laundry.

DOLPHIN BAY HOTEL   (808)935-1466
Motel $129-$199 **Address:** 333 Iliahi St 96720 **Location:** Just nw of Waianuenue Ave via Keawe St, just past bridge; downtown. **Facility:** 18 kitchen units, some two bedrooms. 2 stories (no elevator), exterior corridors. **Terms:** 10 day cancellation notice. **Guest Services:** coin laundry.

HILO SEASIDE HOTEL   (808)935-0821
Hotel $110-$170
Address: 126 Banyan Way 96720 **Location:** Jct SR 19 and 11, 0.5 mi n on Banyan Dr, then just e. **Facility:** 136 units. 3 stories (no elevator), exterior corridors. **Terms:** cancellation fee imposed. **Pool(s):** outdoor. **Guest Services:** coin laundry. **Featured Amenity:** full hot breakfast.

SHIPMAN HOUSE BED & BREAKFAST   808/934-8002
Historic Bed & Breakfast. Rates not provided. **Address:** 131 Kaiulani St 96720 **Location:** Jct SR 19, just sw on Waianuenue Ave, just nw; downtown. **Facility:** This historic 1899 Victorian B&B features antiques mixed with modern amenities. It's within walking distance of restaurants, museums and the downtown farmers market. Beach gear is provided. 5 units. 2 stories (no elevator), interior corridors. **Terms:** age restrictions may apply.

HILO NANILOA HOTEL   808/969-3333
fyi Not evaluated. **Address:** 93 Banyan Dr 96720 **Location:** 0.5 mi e of jct SR 19 and 11, on bayfront. Facilities, services, and décor characterize a mid-scale property.

WHERE TO EAT

CAFE 100   808/935-8683
Hawaiian. Quick Serve. $4-$10 **AAA Inspector Notes:** Family owned since 1946 and a local favorite, this café specializes in large portions of food served at low prices. Beef stew is the specialty of the house, and many people come for the loco moco served several ways, including spam and teriyaki beef. Sandwiches and daily plate-lunch specials are also available. **Address:** 969 Kilauea Ave 96720 **Location:** Just se of downtown; near south end of Wailoa River State Park; jct Maile St. B L D

CAFE PESTO
808/969-6640

WWW WWW Italian. Casual Dining. $10-$30 **AAA Inspector Notes:** *Historic.* In a historic 1912 building, the café overlooks scenic Hilo Bay. The casual, friendly restaurant features an appealing menu that draws on the cuisines of Italy and Asia with local inspirations. Wood-fired pizzas, calzones and large sandwiches are the signature dishes. The dining room features black-and-white tiled flooring, high ceilings with fans and walls adorned with local artwork. The staff provides efficient and friendly service in the spirit of true Hawaiian hospitality. **Features:** full bar, happy hour. **Reservations:** suggested. **Address:** 308 Kamehameha Ave, Suite 101 96720 **Location:** Facing Hilo Bay; in S. Hata Building. **Parking:** street only. [L] [D]

HILO BAY CAFE
808/935-4939

WWW WWW Continental. Casual Dining. $11-$29 **AAA Inspector Notes:** This contemporary cafe features a range of casual lunch offerings from onion soup, grass-fed beef burgers and pasta to more complex dinner items such as macadamia nut-crusted scallops. **Features:** full bar. **Reservations:** suggested. **Address:** 123 Lihiwai St 96720 **Location:** Jct SR 19, just n. [L] [D] CALL [&M]

KEN'S HOUSE OF PANCAKES
808/935-8711

WWW WWW Breakfast. Casual Dining. $8-$13 **AAA Inspector Notes:** This local landmark has been dishing up diner fare since 1971. Specializing in an extensive breakfast menu that is served all day, diners also will find sandwiches, salads, burgers, fried chicken and steak. **Address:** 1730 Kamehameha Ave 96720 **Location:** Jct SR 19 and 11. [B] [L] [D] [24] CALL [&M]

LE MAGIC PAN
808/935-7777

WWW WWW French. Casual Dining. $10-$15 **AAA Inspector Notes:** French crêpes, as well as salads and soups, are featured at this charming restaurant. French cocktails, wine and beer are available. Live entertainment is offered several days a week. **Features:** full bar. **Address:** 64 Keawe St 96720 **Location:** Downtown. **Parking:** on-site and street. [B] [L] [D] [AC]

PINEAPPLES
808/238-5324

WWW WWW American. Casual Dining. $10-$24 **AAA Inspector Notes:** A fairly new addition to the downtown area, this open-air restaurant is great for people-watching. The mostly American-style menu has many island influences. The fresh catch is always a solid choice and can be ordered as either a sandwich or a coconut-crusted entrée. Live entertainment is offered most nights. **Features:** full bar. **Address:** 332 Keawe St 96720 **Location:** Corner of Keawe and Mamo sts; downtown. **Parking:** street only. [L] [D] [AC]

PONDS
808/934-7663

WWW WWW Steak Seafood. Casual Dining. $14-$36 **AAA Inspector Notes:** Set out over the water, this restaurant offers dining overlooking Ice Pond, a local swimming area, and a koi pond (be sure to ask the waitstaff for fish food to feed the koi). You also can watch the planes coming into the Hilo airport. Aged, flame-broiled steaks and seafood selections such as crab-crusted opakapaka are featured. Sandwiches, burgers and fish and chips prepared with a crispy tempura beer batter are offered at lunch. Live music is performed nightly. **Features:** full bar, Sunday brunch, happy hour. **Reservations:** suggested. **Address:** 135 Kalanianaole Ave 96720 **Location:** Jct SR 19 and 11, just ne; ne of jct Banyan Way. [L] [D] CALL [&M] [AC]

HOLUALOA (G-10) pop. 8,538, elev. 1,388'

HULA DADDY KONA COFFEE is at 74-4944 Māmalahoa Hwy. On guided tours of the coffee orchard and roasting room, visitors learn about the growing, harvesting and roasting processes and can sample a variety of freshly brewed coffees. **Time:** Allow 30 minutes minimum. **Hours:** Mon.-Sat. 10-4. **Cost:** Free. **Phone:** (808) 327-9744 or (888) 553-2339.

HOLUALOA INN
808/324-1121

[fyi] Not evaluated. **Address:** 76-5932 Mamalahoa Hwy 96725 **Location:** Center. Facilities, services, and décor characterize an upscale property.

WHERE TO EAT

HOLUAKOA GARDENS & CAFE
808/322-5072

WWW WWW American. Casual Dining. $12-$32 **AAA Inspector Notes:** The owners have figured out what we want and it's fresh brewed local coffees in the morning, brunch served daily, fresh coffee shop nibbles most of the day and then a bit more upscale dinner with the soft glow of candles. Dining may take place in the vaulted second-floor space with panoramic island views, on the wraparound lanai or out among the trees in the garden. While a bit tricky, there is parking behind the restaurant down a narrow alley. **Features:** full bar, patio dining, Sunday brunch. **Address:** 76-5900 Old Government Rd 96725 **Location:** Center. [B] [L] [D] CALL [&M] [AC]

HONALO (G-10) pop. 2,423, elev. 1,450'
• Attractions map p. 32

DAIFUKUJI SOTO MISSION, 79-7241 Māmalahoa Hwy., is a historic Zen Buddhist temple with two ornate altars. Photography is permitted. **Hours:** Generally open daily 8-5. Phone ahead to confirm schedule. **Cost:** Free. **Phone:** (808) 322-3524.

HŌNAUNAU (H-10) elev. 20'
• Attractions map p. 32

Hōnaunau is best known for its ancient place of refuge *(see Pu'uhonua o Hōnaunau National Historical Park p. 56).*

PAINTED CHURCH (ST. BENEDICT'S CHURCH), off SR 160 at 84-5140 Painted Church Rd., was built in 1899 and continues to hold services. Flamboyant murals depict biblical stories and painted palm fronds and stars adorn the ceiling and upper walls. The first priests, using ordinary house paints, created a way of visually teaching the congregation. If services are in progress visitors should wait until their conclusion to enter. **Time:** Allow 30 minutes minimum. **Hours:** Daily 8-6. **Cost:** Free. **Phone:** (808) 328-2227.

HONOKA'A (F-11) pop. 2,258, elev. 1,114'

Honoka'a (rolling bay) is reminiscent of a Hawaiian plantation village and cowboy town. The region supports such diversified crops as macadamia nuts and tropical fruits, as well as eucalyptus and trees for timber.

Honoka'a is the largest town on Hawai'i Island's Hāmākua Coast. Sugar was king here from the 1870s until the mid-1990s. The industry attracted immigrants and laborers from England, Scotland, China, Portugal, Japan, Puerto Rico and the Philippines, and the town prospered as a trading center and railhead on the line from Hilo. The Honoka'a Sugar Mill operated from 1873 until 1994.

Honoka'a is the place where macadamia nuts were first introduced to Hawai'i. William Purvis, a sugar plantation manager, planted the island's first trees here in 1881. A process to crack the hard nut shell was perfected in the early 1920s, and the territory's first large-scale commercial orchard was planted in 1924.

Central Honoka'a's Mamame Street (SR 240) is lined with plantation-era buildings from the early

1900s, many now housing shops, galleries and eateries. One of the more distinctive is the Honokaʻa Club, built in 1908 as a plantation manager's retreat.

HONOMU (G-12) pop. 509, elev. 300'
• Attractions map p. 32

▼ GEM ‘AKAKA FALLS STATE PARK is 3.6 mi. s.w. at the end of ‘Akaka Falls Rd. (SR 220). In a lush, deep gorge, one of the state's most impressive waterfalls plunges 442 feet into Kolekole Stream. To reach ‘Akaka Falls you'll walk a .4-mile paved loop trail that winds, dips and climbs through a sublime rain forest filled with gurgling streams, tropical plants, bamboo thickets and massive banyan trees. At roughly the halfway mark, a short trail leads to a view of distant Kahuna Falls (bring binoculars), a 300-foot-high cascade that's largely obscured by vegetation.

The main attraction, free-falling ‘Akaka Falls, is most dramatic after a good rainstorm, and at 442 feet, the falls are twice the height of Niagara Falls. The best time for photography is late morning. At a leisurely pace, the entire loop trail will take about 45 minutes. If you're short on time or it's pouring rain (common in the Hilo area), make a left at the trailhead and walk about 800 feet directly to the ‘Akaka overlook. An interpretive kiosk at the trailhead features information about the walk, plants and birds, and cultural history.

Note: Though the entire trail is paved, rain can make the steep staircases and slopes very slick. Use caution. **Time:** Allow 45 minutes minimum. **Hours:** Daily 8:30-5. **Cost:** $5 (per vehicle); $1 (per pedestrian). **Phone:** (808) 961-9540.

RECREATIONAL ACTIVITIES
Ziplines
• **Skyline Eco-Adventures** is at 28-1710 Honomu Rd. **Hours:** Trips depart daily at 10, 11, 1:30 and 2:30; additional tour times may be offered. Phone ahead to confirm schedule. **Phone:** (808) 878-8400 or (888) 864-6947.

THE PALMS CLIFF HOUSE INN   808/963-6076

fyi Bed & Breakfast Did not meet all AAA rating requirements for locking devices in some guest rooms at time of last evaluation on 05/04/2015. **Address:** 28-3514 Mamalahoa Hwy 96728 **Location:** Oceanfront. On SR 19, 13.2 mi n of Hilo between MM 13 and 14 (oceanside). Facilities, services, and décor characterize a mid-scale property.

KAILUA-KONA (G-10) elev. 40'
• Hotels p. 46 • Restaurants p. 47
• Attractions map p. 32

On the island's sunny leeward coast, Kailua-Kona has everything you'd expect to find in a tourist hub: restaurants, shops, tour operators and lodgings galore. At first glance, Kailua-Kona appears to be all souvenir hula dolls, condo complexes and $12 tropical cocktails, but this seaside town played an important role in Hawaiʻi's past and offers some interesting historical sites as well.

About 15 minutes north of town, Kona International Airport receives daily flights from Honolulu and the mainland. Cruise ship passengers disembark at the town's convenient Kailua Pier. The downtown shopping/dining area has a couple of pay parking lots (rates are steep) as well as tough-to-find street parking (watch for posted time limits). Downtown is doable in a half-day. But if you're staying nearby, you'll undoubtedly return to dine at the restaurants.

The heart of town is a roughly .75-mile stretch of Aliʻi Drive, between the Kailua Bay seawall and the Coconut Grove Market Place (at the intersection of Kahakai Road). A good place to start your downtown walkabout is the seaside Kona Inn Shopping Village (75-5744 Aliʻi Dr.), where you'll browse more than 50 specialty shops with items ranging from souvenirs and beachwear to jewelry and fine art.

Nearby are many more shops and open-air eateries, plus the historic Huliheʻe Palace building and Mokuʻaikaua Church (see attraction listings). South on Aliʻi Drive, the shopping/dining area around the Coconut Grove Market Place has a more modern look and feel. And on most nights you'll groove to live street musicians playing their hearts out for tips.

Note: As you motor along narrow Aliʻi Drive, be aware that mornings and afternoons are clogged with roadside joggers. Both pedestrians and motorists alike make all sorts of crazy, unpredictable maneuvers. In other words, pay attention.

Local beaches can't measure up to the idyllic strands along the Kohala Coast or some of the less popular but equally beautiful south island beaches. That said, Kailua-Kona's often-packed Kahaluʻu Beach Park (see attraction listing and Recreation Areas Chart) boasts some of the best snorkeling on the island; scarce parking makes pre-noon arrival a necessity. When the surf's way up, Laʻaloa Beach Park (aka Magic Sands Beach, White Sands Beach and Disappearing Sands Beach) draws daredevil surfers and bodyboarders.

In his old age, Kamehameha I spent much time in Kailua-Kona, a favorite spot of Hawaiian royalty. Ahuʻena Heiau (see attraction listing), near the Kailua Pier, was the seat of government in the early 19th century.

Nowadays, in many ways, this old town is the epitome of garish tourism. Condos on every corner. Chain restaurants transported from Middle America. And enough tacky, made-in-China knickknacks to make your head spin. Yet you can't help but fall a little bit in love with this Hawaiʻi classic, despite the 21st century.

In March, craft beer enthusiasts flock to the Courtyard by Marriott King Kamehameha's Kona Beach Hotel for the ▼ Kona Brewers Festival. This celebration of suds also features food vendors and live entertainment. The ▼ Ironman World Championship, held annually in October, consists of a 2.4-mile ocean swim, a 112-mile bicycle race and a 26.2-mile run. The swim event begins and ends at the Kailua Pier, the bicycle route goes along the Kona coast, and the marathon uses part of the same highway as the bicycle race and concludes on Ali'i Drive in Kailua-Kona.

AHU'ENA HEIAU, on the grounds of the King Kamehameha Kona Beach Hotel near the Kailua Pier, is a temple reconstructed 1812-13 by King Kamehameha the Great. The king lived and conducted government business here until his death in 1819. Visitors may tour the grounds but not enter the temple. *Lū'au* are held at the site.

Note: *Heiau* are culturally significant and should be treated with respect. **Hours:** Grounds daily 9-4. *Lū'au* are held Tues., Thurs. and Sun. at 5. **Cost:** Site free. *Lū'au* $80; $40 (ages 5-12). **Phone:** (808) 326-4969 for lū'au reservations.

ASTRONAUT ELLISON S. ONIZUKA SPACE CENTER is at Kona International Airport at 1 Keāhole Ave. in front of Lobby 1 and Gates 1-5; visitors do not need to be catching a flight to visit the center. The facility honors the state's first astronaut, who perished along with the other six astronauts aboard the space shuttle *Challenger* in 1986. A bronze sculpture and personal belongings showcase Onizuka's life.

Displays and interactive exhibits detail various aspects of the space program, including Apollo missions, the MIR and International space stations, science concepts related to space flight and Hawai'i's role in space exploration. A NASA space suit and a 1972 moon rock can be seen. A 45-seat theater also is included.

Time: Allow 1 hour minimum. **Hours:** Mon.-Sat. 9-3:30. Closed Jan. 1, Thanksgiving and Christmas. **Cost:** $3; $1 (ages 2-12). A fee is charged for parking at the airport. **Phone:** (808) 329-3441.

SAVE **ATLANTIS ADVENTURES:** *ATLANTIS* **SUBMARINES KONA** departs from Kailua-Kona Pier. The company offers narrated underwater voyages during which passengers can see exotic fish, a natural reef and marine animals through large viewing portholes. Including the trip to and from the dive site, the tour lasts about an hour. Whale-watch trips also are offered December through April; exact dates depend on seasonal migratory patterns.

Time: Allow 2 hours minimum. **Hours:** Dives depart daily at 10, 11:30, 1 and 2:30. **Cost:** $115; $48 (ages 4-12). Under 36 inches tall are not permitted. **Phone:** (800) 381-0237.

BIG ISLAND AIR departs from the commuter terminal at Kona International Airport at 73-103 U'u St. Circle Island tours of Hawai'i Island last 1.5 hours and include such sights as Kīlauea volcano, ancient Hawaiian settlements, rain forests, valleys and waterfalls. Pilots provide narration about the land's geography, history, myths and legends. Stereo headsets are provided. A 1.5- to 2-hour Sunset tour also is offered.

Note: Due to decompression-related sickness, it is recommended that passengers wait 12-24 hours after scuba diving before flying; the amount of time is dependent on particular dive factors. Ask about possible policies regarding minimum wait time between scuba diving and flying; weight restrictions; weather, cancellation and refund policies; and the minimum and maximum number of passengers for flights. All small aircraft may encounter turbulence.

Hours: Circle Island tours depart Wed.-Mon. at 7, 9, 11:30 and 2. Sunset tours are offered daily; phone for departure time. Closed Christmas. Phone ahead to confirm schedule. **Cost:** Circle Island tour $334.83. Sunset tour $376.78. Reservations are required. **Phone:** (808) 329-4868.

BODY GLOVE OCEAN ADVENTURES departs from the Kailua Pier at jct. Palani Rd. and Ali'i Dr.; transportation from Waikoloa resorts is available for a fee. Outing options include snorkeling trips, historical cruises to Kealakekua Bay and Captain Cook Monument, and seasonal whale-watch tours.

The whale-watch tours last 2.5 hours, and morning snorkeling trips last 4.5 hours. Refreshments are provided on whale-watch tours; snorkeling cruises include a continental breakfast and a barbecue lunch. A cash bar is available. Dinner and entertainment are provided on the 3-hour historical cruise.

Hours: Whale-watch tour daily at 1 or 2, Dec.-Apr. Morning snorkeling trip daily at 8 or 9. Historical cruise Tues. and Thurs.-Sat. at 4. Phone ahead to confirm schedule. **Cost:** Whale-watch tour $98; $78 (ages 6-17). Morning snorkeling trip $128; $88 (ages 6-17). Historical cruise $118; $88 (ages 6-17). Reservations are recommended. **Phone:** (808) 326-7122 or (800) 551-8911.

FAIR WIND, 6 mi. s. of Kailua-Kona at Keauhou Bay Pier off Ali'i Dr., offers sightseeing and snorkeling cruises aboard the *Fair Wind II*, a catamaran equipped with a waterslide and freshwater showers. Cruises visit Captain Cook Monument *(see attraction listing p. 55).* Snorkeling gear and instruction are provided. The 4.5-hour morning cruise includes breakfast and lunch, and the 3.5-hour afternoon cruise includes a snack. Snuba can be added for an additional fee during the morning cruise.

The luxury catamaran *Hula Kai* takes visitors on sightseeing and snorkeling cruises to remote locations. Snorkeling gear, stand-up paddleboards and instruction are provided. Breakfast and lunch are included in the 5-hour morning cruise. Sea Rockets, underwater propulsion vehicles for snorkelers, can be added for an additional fee. **Time:** Allow 4 hours minimum. **Hours:** *Fair Wind II* morning cruise departs daily at 9. *Fair Wind II* afternoon cruise departs at 2; departure days vary. *Hula Kai* morning cruise departs at 9:30; departure days vary. Phone for Manta Night Snorkel schedule.

Cost: *Fair Wind II* morning cruise $129; $79 (ages 4-12); $29 (ages 0-3). *Fair Wind II* afternoon cruise $79; $49 (ages 4-12). *Hula Kai* morning cruise $149. Manta Night Snorkel trip $109. Minimum age requirements vary by tour. **Phone:** (808) 322-2788 or (800) 677-9461.

HAWAI'I FOREST & TRAIL has various departure points. An interpretive guide leads each of the 15 available 2.5-hour to full-day ecotours. Guests are provided with necessary special gear. Snacks and beverages are provided on shorter trips; full-day trips feature either breakfast and lunch or only dinner. Tour size generally is 4 persons minimum, 10-12 persons maximum. Private and custom tours also are available.

Inquire about weather and refund policies. **Hours:** Daily departure time varies with the tour chosen. **Cost:** $69-$699; $59-$179 (children). Minimum age requirements vary by tour. Reservations are recommended 1 week in advance. **Phone:** (808) 331-8505 or (800) 464-1993.

HULIHE'E PALACE, 75-5718 Ali'i Dr., was built in 1838 and served as home to the Hawaiian monarchy. Today the Daughters of Hawai'i operates and maintains the site as a museum, which houses a collection of artifacts and personal memorabilia of Hawaiian royalty.

Hours: Mon.-Sat. 9-5. Last tour departs 1 hour before closing. Closed major holidays. **Cost:** Guided tours $10; $8 (ages 65+ and Hawai'i residents); free (ages 0-18). Self-guiding tours $8; $6 (ages 65+ and Hawai'i residents); free (ages 0-18). Prices may vary; phone ahead. **Phone:** (808) 329-1877. GT

KAHALU'U BEACH PARK is 5 mi. s. on Ali'i Dr. at Milepost 5. The beach, with an offshore reef, is known for good snorkeling conditions with a large variety of fish in the area. *See Recreation Areas Chart.* **Note:** When there is high surf, rip currents are present. Lifeguards usually are on duty; verify their presence before heading into the water. The beach is somewhat rocky. **Hours:** Daily 6 a.m.-11 p.m. **Cost:** Free. **Phone:** (808) 323-4322. ⊓ ⚐

KAILUA BAY CHARTER CO. INC. offers glass-bottom boat cruises departing from the Kailua Pier at jct. Palani Rd. and Ali'i Dr. across from King Kamehameha Beach Hotel; parking is available at the hotel. Fifty-minute reef tours allow passengers to see underwater fish and coral through large glass windows. **Hours:** Tours depart daily at 11:30 and 12:30. Closed Jan. 1 and Christmas. Phone ahead to confirm schedule. **Cost:** $40; $20 (ages 1-12). Reservations are required. **Phone:** (808) 324-1749.

KONA BREWING CO. is at 74-5612 Pawai Pl. Visitors on a guided 1-hour tour learn about the brewing process, view brewing equipment and sample a selection of fresh brews. **Hours:** Tours daily at 10:30 and 3. A maximum of 15 visitors is permitted on each tour. Closed Christmas. **Cost:** Free. **Phone:** (808) 334-2739. ⊓

LAVA LEGENDS & LEGACIES - JOURNEYS OF THE SOUTH PACIFIC LŪ'AU is at the Royal Kona Resort, 75-5852 Ali'i Dr. After being greeted with a shell *lei*, you can grab a drink, find a seat and listen to live Hawaiian tunes. At sunset, a conch shell is blown and everyone is invited to gather around the

imu (underground oven) to watch the ceremonial uncovering of the roasted pig. You'll then enjoy a buffet of traditional Hawaiian foods while festively costumed dancers and musicians put on a spectacular Polynesian stage show.

Time: Allow 3 hours minimum. **Hours:** Mon.-Wed. and Fri. at 5. Visitors should arrive by 4:45. Closed major holidays. **Cost:** $88; $70 (ages 50+); $41 (ages 6-11). A fee is charged for preferred seating. Reservations are required. **Parking:** $3. **Phone:** (808) 329-3111.

MOKU'AIKAUA CHURCH, 75-5713 Ali'i Dr., was established in 1820 and is the oldest and first-founded Christian church in Hawai'i. The building's stark architectural style reflects the austerity of the New England missionaries. The church, the third built on the site, was constructed by the people of Hawai'i using white coral and lava stone from their former temples, *'ōhi'a* wood from the dormant Mount Hualālai and *koa* wood. **Hours:** Daily 7:30-5:30. **Cost:** Free. **Phone:** (808) 329-0655.

OCEAN RIDER is 1 mi. s. of Kona International Airport at 73-4388 Ilikai Pl., via the Natural Energy Lab road.

Conducted by a professional biologist, the 1-hour Magical Seahorse Tour allows visitors to learn about, view, hold and feed seahorses. The 3-acre oceanfront farm breeds 26 different seahorse species, Hawaiian reef fish and leafy sea dragons. **Time:** Allow 1 hour, 30 minutes minimum. **Hours:** Tours Mon.-Fri. at 10, noon and 2. Arrive 15 minutes before tour. Phone ahead to confirm schedule and prices. **Cost:** Tour $42; $32 (ages 7-12); $30 (ages 3-6). Reservations are recommended. **Phone:** (808) 329-6840.

RECREATIONAL ACTIVITIES
Bicycling

- **Velissimo—Cycling Destinations** tours depart from various locations; bicycles can be rented at 73-5619 Kauhola St. #105. **Hours:** Tours and rentals are available daily. **Phone:** (808) 327-0087.

COURTYARD BY MARRIOTT KING KAMEHAMEHA'S KONA BEACH HOTEL
(808)329-2911

WWWW Hotel $167-$499 **Address:** 75-5660 Palani Rd 96740 **Location:** SR 11 exit Palani Rd (toward ocean), 0.6 mi se; at start of Alii Dr; center; adjacent to pier. **Facility:** 452 units. 6 stories, interior

AAA Benefit: Members save 5% or more!

corridors. **Parking:** on-site (fee). **Amenities:** safes. **Dining:** 2 restaurants. **Pool(s):** outdoor. **Activities:** hot tub, beach access, self-propelled boats, scuba diving, snorkeling, tennis, exercise room, spa. **Guest Services:** valet and coin laundry, boarding pass kiosk, rental car service.

🍽️ 🍸 CALL 🔊M 🛥️ BIZ 📶 ✖️ 🔌 💻 / SOME UNITS HS

HOLIDAY INN EXPRESS HOTEL & SUITES KAILUA-KONA
808/329-2599

WWWW Hotel. Rates not provided. **Address:** 75-146 Palani Rd 96740 **Location:** SR 11 exit Palani Rd (toward ocean), 0.3 mi se on Kuakini Hwy. **Facility:** 75 units. 3 stories, interior/exterior corridors. **Parking:** on-site (fee). **Amenities:** safes. **Pool(s):** outdoor. **Activities:** hot tub, exercise room. **Guest Services:** valet and coin laundry.

🍽️+ CALL 🔊M 🛥️ BIZ HS 📶 ✖️ 🔌 🖼️ 💻

KONA BAY HOTEL (UNCLE BILLY'S)
(808)329-1393

WWW Hotel $109-$129 **Address:** 75-5739 Alii Dr 96740 **Location:** SR 11 exit Palani Rd (toward ocean), 0.8 mi se; center. Facing Kona Inn Shopping Village. **Facility:** 125 units. 4 stories, exterior corridors. **Parking:** on-site (fee). **Terms:** 3 day cancellation notice-fee imposed. **Amenities:** safes. **Pool(s):** outdoor. **Guest Services:** coin laundry.

🍽️+ CALL 🔊M 🛥️ 📶 🔌 ✖️ / SOME UNITS

KONA SEASIDE HOTEL
808/329-2455

WWW Hotel
Rates not provided

Address: 75-5646 Palani Rd 96740 **Location:** SR 11 exit Palani Rd (toward ocean), 0.5 mi se; center. **Facility:** 140 units. 5 stories, interior/exterior corridors. **Parking:** on-site (fee). **Pool(s):** outdoor. **Guest Services:** coin laundry. **Featured Amenity: full hot breakfast.**

SAVE 🍽️+ CALL 🔊M 🛥️ BIZ 📶 ✖️ 🔌 💻

ROYAL KONA RESORT
(808)329-3111

WWW Hotel $139-$270 **Address:** 75-5852 Alii Dr 96740 **Location:** Oceanfront. SR 11 exit Palani Rd (toward ocean), 1.3 mi se; just s of shopping district. **Facility:** 436 units, some two bedrooms. 7 stories, interior/exterior corridors. **Parking:** on-site (fee). **Terms:** check-in 4 pm, 3 day cancellation notice-fee imposed. **Amenities:** safes. **Pool(s):** outdoor. **Activities:** tennis, exercise room, spa. **Guest Services:** valet and coin laundry, boarding pass kiosk.

🍽️ 🍸 CALL 🔊M 🛥️ $HS 📶 ✖️ 🎿 🔌 💻

OUTRIGGER ROYAL SEA CLIFF
808/329-8021

[fyi] **Condominium** Did not meet all AAA rating requirements for locking devices in some guest rooms at time of last evaluation on 04/27/2015. **Address:** 75-6040 Alii Dr 96740 **Location:** 1.8 mi s. Facilities, services, and décor characterize a mid-scale property. The large, well-appointed condos have fully equipped kitchens and private lanais. Some have ocean views.

WHERE TO EAT

BIG ISLAND GRILL
808/326-1153

WW WW Hawaiian. Casual Dining. $10-$26 **AAA Inspector Notes:** Wholesome and affordable family food can be enjoyed in the casual dining area or carried out. Lines are to be expected at peak mealtime hours as this is a favorite among locals and tourists. The open dining room is a bit plain and dated with three windows overlooking parking lots, but the food is fresh and delicious, especially the macadamia nut pancakes served with coconut syrup. Other favorites include the loco moco with spam, chicken katsu and Kalua pork. **Features:** beer & wine. **Address:** 75-5702 Kuakini Hwy 96740 **Location:** Between Henry St and Hanama Pl. B L D

BONGO BEN'S ISLAND CAFE
808/329-9203

WW WW American. Casual Dining. $12-$30 **AAA Inspector Notes:** This downtown spot offers covered outdoor seating for great people-watching and views of the ocean's crashing waves across the street. The fairly large menu is sure to have something to please everyone. The live music will draw you in and the friendly service will bring you back. **Features:** full bar, patio dining, happy hour. **Address:** 75-5819 Alii Dr 96740 **Location:** Downtown. B L D 🎟️

BUNS IN THE SUN
808/326-2774

WW Breads/Pastries Sandwiches. Quick Serve. $5-$11 **AAA Inspector Notes:** Budget-friendly breakfasts and lunches are served all day. A variety of deli sandwiches, fresh breads, pastries and rolls are baked daily. Enjoy 100 percent Kona coffee with your cinnamon roll or grab a smoked Kalua pig sandwich with Swiss cheese, lettuce and tomato on a grilled hoagie roll for your trip to the beach. Guests order at the bakery counter and pick up their food when it is ready to enjoy in the air conditioned room or out on the curbside patio of the shopping plaza. **Address:** 75-5595 Palani Rd 96740 **Location:** SR 11 exit Palani Rd (toward ocean), just w; in Lanihau Center. B L CALL 🔊M

HUGGO'S
808/329-1493

WW WW Pacific Rim. Casual Dining. $24-$36 **AAA Inspector Notes:** Those who want to dine where the locals do should stop by this relaxed restaurant. It's hard to beat the location, which takes full advantage of an oceanfront setting through a casual, open-air dining room with spectacular ocean views. The menu features fresh island fish and certified Angus beef. Huggo's signature teriyaki steak has been served since 1969. Save room for one of the house-made desserts. Live music nightly. **Features:** full bar, happy hour. **Reservations:** suggested. **Address:** 75-5828 Kahakai Rd 96740 **Location:** On Alii Dr, just s of shopping district. **Parking:** on-site and street. D 🎟️

ISLAND LAVA JAVA BISTRO
808/327-2161

WW WW American. Casual Dining. $13-$30 **AAA Inspector Notes:** This is a great option for any meal. With an on-site bakery, locals arrive early for fresh cinnamon rolls or pull-a-parts. Enjoy the house-made granola or a Belgian waffle with bacon and maple syrup. Lunch is casual with some healthy choices, but my favorite is dinner when the lights get turned down, the candles come out and you can dine under the stars while listening to the waves. Fresh pizza dough is made daily. Salads, fresh fish and guava barbecue ribs are offered. BYOB. **Features:** patio dining. **Address:** 75-5799 Alii Dr 96740 **Location:** Center. **Parking:** street only. B L D 🎟️

JACKIE REY'S OHANA GRILL
808/327-0209

WW WW Pacific Rim. Casual Dining. $13-$30 **AAA Inspector Notes:** This restaurant features fresh island-style seafood, steaks and pasta. Prime rib is offered on Friday and Saturday evenings. Pupus are served from 2 to 5 pm Monday through Friday. **Features:** full bar, happy hour. **Reservations:** suggested. **Address:** 75-5995 Kuakini Hwy 96740 **Location:** SR 11 exit Palani Rd (toward ocean), 1.5 mi s. L D

KONA BREWING CO.
808/334-2739

WW Pizza Sandwiches. Casual Dining. $11-$15 **AAA Inspector Notes:** Popular with the local crowd, the casual restaurant is the perfect spot to go for a fun meal and a sampling of some local hand-crafted beers. The menu features hearty portions of simple fare such as sandwiches, finger foods and the ever-popular hand-tossed pizzas. There's a quaint outdoor patio surrounded by tropical foliage and patio umbrellas. The restaurant offers a relaxed yet lively ambience. The service is fast and efficient and the staff is very knowledgeable about the local beers. **Features:** beer only, patio dining. **Address:** 75-5629 Kuakini Hwy 96740 **Location:** From Palani Rd, just n on Kaiwi St, just e on Pawai St. ECO L D CALL 🔊M

KONA INN RESTAURANT
808/329-4455

WW WW Steak Seafood. Casual Dining. $15-$30 **AAA Inspector Notes:** *Historic.* For a taste of Hawai'i's days gone by, visit this historic open-air restaurant. Although the changes have been many since this place originally was built in 1928 as an inn, the nostalgic charm has always remained intact. It has since been converted into a relaxing and charming restaurant. The menu is based on traditional steak and fresh local fish, and there is roasted prime rib of beef on Friday and Saturday. A café menu featuring sandwiches also is available. **Features:** full bar. **Reservations:** suggested, for dinner. **Address:** 75-5744 Alii Dr 96740 **Location:** Oceanfront; at Kona Inn Shopping Village. **Parking:** street only. L D 🎟️

SPLASHER'S GRILL   808/326-2212

💎💎 American. Casual Dining. $12-$25 **AAA Inspector Notes:** This is a solid choice all day long. While there can be a slight wait, the dependable food and great second-floor location with a water view from most tables make it worth a try. The local hotel guests can pack the place first thing in the morning, but tables turn quickly. **Features:** full bar, happy hour. **Address:** 75-5663 Palani Rd 96740 **Location:** Downtown. B L D CALL 🔊M 🎜

SUSHI SHIONO   808/326-1696

💎💎 Japanese Sushi. Casual Dining. $12-$80 **AAA Inspector Notes:** You'll find a wonderful array of sushi dishes, either à la carte or full lunch and dinner plates that include miso soup and rice. Don't worry, there is plenty of free parking in the back. **Features:** full bar, patio dining. **Reservations:** suggested. **Address:** 75-5799 Alii Dr 96740 **Location:** Oceanfront; in Alii Sunset Plaza Mall.

L D CALL 🔊M

THAI RIN RESTAURANT   808/329-2929

💎 Thai. Casual Dining. $9-$35 **AAA Inspector Notes:** Wonderfully tasty Thai dishes are seasoned mild, medium or hot, depending on the diner's preference. Guests can sit on the patio or at a table inside; either offers a great ocean view, as this place is just across the street from a rocky shoreline and its crashing waves. **Features:** beer & wine, patio dining. **Address:** 75-5799 Alii Dr 96740 **Location:** Oceanfront; in Alii Sunset Plaza Mall. L D

KAIMU (H-12) elev. 79'
• Attractions map p. 32

STAR OF THE SEA PAINTED CHURCH is on SR 130 at Milepost 20. Due to a lava flow, the church was moved from Kalapana to its current location in 1990. Built in 1931 by Father Evarist Gielen, the building is adorned with stained-glass windows and colorful religious paintings. **Time:** Allow 30 minutes minimum. **Hours:** Daily 9-4. **Cost:** Free. 🎑

RECREATIONAL ACTIVITIES
Hiking
• **Kalapana Cultural Tours** departs from the headquarters at the southern terminus of SR 137 and offers guided hikes to lava flows. **Hours:** Guided tours are offered daily (lava activity and weather permitting). **Phone:** (808) 936-0456.

KALOKO-HONOKŌHAU NATIONAL HISTORICAL PARK (G-10)
• Attractions map p. 32

About 3 miles north of Kailua-Kona on SR 19, Kaloko-Honokōhau National Historical Park has three entrances: the first off Kealakehe Pkwy., the second near the visitor center and the third on a road called Ala Nui Kaloko. The 1,160-acre park offers a glimpse into the lives of Hawaiian settlers prior to their exposure to Western civilization. Though the area is comprised mostly of infertile lava coastline, settlers managed to thrive off of the available natural resources. They raised and harvested fish, often exchanging their catches for breadfruit, paper mulberry and taro—all products of upland residents. Two impressively designed fish ponds and a fish trap have been preserved. Other archeological features include temple and house platforms, stone walls and a corral. Petroglyphs also can be seen throughout the area.

Blanketed with white coral sand and boasting a *heiau* (temple) at one end, Honokōhau Beach can be accessed via a trail near the visitor center. **Note:** *Heiau* are culturally significant and should be treated with respect.

Among the park's wildlife are sea turtles and Hawaiian monk seals. The Kaloko Fish Pond is home to Hawaiian coots and stilts; during the winter the Aimakapa Fish Pond hosts various migratory birds. The park is ideal for hiking, fishing and snorkeling. Camping is prohibited.

Address inquiries to Kaloko-Honokōhau National Historical Park, 73-4786 Kanalani St. #14, Kailua-Kona, HI 96740.

The park is open daily year-round. The Ala Nui Kaloko gate is open daily 8-5. The visitor center and adjacent parking area are open daily 8:30-4. Free. Phone (808) 326-9057.

KAMUELA—See Waimea p. 61.

KAPA'AU (F-10) pop. 1,734, elev. 407'

Kapa'au lies in Hawai'i Island's Kohala district, not far from the birthplace of King Kamehameha the Great. In 1883 a statue of the king was lost in transit from Paris to Honolulu aboard a ship that caught fire and sank in the South Atlantic. A replica procured with insurance money was installed in front of the Judiciary Building in Honolulu (see King Kamehameha Statue attraction listing in Honolulu p. 136). The original was discovered in a junkyard at Port Stanley in the Falkland Islands; it now surveys the land of the conqueror's birth from a pedestal in Kapa'au.

KAUPULEHU
• Restaurants p. 50

FOUR SEASONS RESORT HUALALAI AT HISTORIC KA'UPULEHU   (808)325-8000

💎💎💎💎💎 Resort Hotel $695-$1695

Address: 72-100 Ka'upulehu Dr 96740 **Location:** Oceanfront. 6 mi n of Kona International Airport on SR 19, 1.3 mi sw. **Facility:** Luxury and exceptional service is the hallmark of this fine, oceanfront hotel featuring a cluster of two-story townhouse buildings set over several manicured acres. 243 units, some two and three bedrooms. 1-2 stories, exterior corridors. **Parking:** on-site and valet. **Terms:** 21 day cancellation notice-fee imposed. **Amenities:** video games, safes. **Dining:** 3 restaurants, also, Beach Tree, ULU Ocean Grill, see separate listings, entertainment. **Pool(s):** heated outdoor. **Activities:** sauna, hot tub, steamroom, cabanas, scuba diving, snorkeling, regulation golf, tennis, recreation programs, kids club, game room, trails, spa. **Guest Services:** complimentary and valet laundry, rental car service.

SAVE 📶 🍴 👷 📺 📶 CALL 🔊M 🛏 📶 BIZ
📶 ✕ 🎜 🔌 🖥 / SOME UNITS 🐾

WHERE TO EAT

BEACH TREE   808/325-8000

▼▼▼ California. Casual Dining. $20-$44 **AAA Inspector Notes:** This casual and family-friendly beach-side restaurant offers cuisine inspired by the flavors of California and Italy. Live entertainment is offered nightly. **Features:** full bar, patio dining. **Address:** 72-100 Ka'upulehu Dr 96740 **Location:** Off SR 19, 6 mi n of Kona International Airport; in Four Seasons Resort Hualalai at Historic Ka'upulehu. **Parking:** on-site and valet.

⊞ Ⓛ Ⓓ 🅺

ULU OCEAN GRILL   808/325-8000

▼▼▼ Pacific Rim Sushi. Fine Dining. $32-$55 **AAA Inspector Notes:** The sounds of crashing waves combine with the smell of salt air to provide a relaxed yet sophisticated essence of the traditional Hawaiian experience. Guests like to start the evening with a cocktail by the open fire pit and watch the sun set. Centered on Pacific fusion cuisine, the menu uses fresh regional ingredients of island fish, meat, produce, herbs and spices. **Features:** full bar, patio dining. **Reservations:** suggested. **Address:** 72-100 Ka'upulehu Dr 96740 **Location:** Off SR 19, 6 mi n of Kona International Airport, 1.3 mi sw; in Four Seasons Resort Hualalai at Historic Ka'upulehu. **Parking:** on-site and valet. ⊞ Ⓑ Ⓓ CALL 🅜 🅺

KAWAIHAE (F-10) elev. 52'
• Attractions map p. 32

With an average annual rainfall of less than 10 inches, this tiny port town at the north end of the Kohala resort area is perhaps Hawai'i Island's driest spot. Protected by a breakwater, the small harbor is home to a handful of fishing and scuba outfitters as well as a sprinkling of shops and restaurants. There's not exactly a *ton* of tourist interest here, though history buffs, take note: Kawaihae was the seat of the Kingdom of Hawai'i for a short time in the 1700s and was the home of King Kamehameha I for a short period. If this piques your interest, check out the Pu'ukoholā Heiau National Historic Site (*see attraction listing*).

What you're *really* here for are the beaches south of town—a few of them among the prettiest and most frequented along the Kohala Coast. Touting typically calm waters and a full host of facilities (bathrooms, showers, picnic tables and lifeguard stations), the northernmost strand, Spencer Beach Park (the access road is off SR 270 between mileposts 2 and 3) is popular with local families (*see Recreation Areas Chart*). A gorgeous, sandy crescent, Mauna Kea Beach lies just south (the access road is off SR 19 at Milepost 68) and is the stuff of glossy coffee-table books. Snorkeling is very good around the rocks to the left. The limited parking situation can be a headache; arrive early.

At SR 19's Milepost 69, take the turnoff for always-busy Hāpuna Beach (*see Recreation Areas Chart*). No parking nightmares here; the lot can accommodate a few hundred cars. This broad, picturesque, half-mile-long golden sand beach has it all: shady picnic areas, snack bars, plenty of elbow room on the shore, rows of tanned hides and fun bodyboarding when the surf's up. For a bit less bustle at an equally beautiful beach, try Waialea Bay (from SR 19, take the turnoff for Puakō Road and follow signs). This is a wonderful beach with a series of sandy, scalloped coves. Snorkeling is decent around the offshore rocks in the middle of the bay, and there's a small rock arch at Waialea's northern end.

PUA MAU BOTANIC AND SCULPTURE GARDEN is at 10 Ala Kahua Dr.; look for Milepost 6 and signs. This 13-acre garden offers designed displays of tropical trees, flowers, shrubs and panoramas of the ocean and mountains. While an aviary houses exotic birds, larger-than-life sculptures of insects and animals dot the landscape.

Note: There are steep hills to climb; visitors should be in reasonably good health. **Time:** Allow 1 hour minimum. **Hours:** Daily 9-4. **Cost:** $15; $13 (ages 65+); $5 (ages 6-16). **Phone:** (808) 882-0888. 🄰

PU'UKOHOLĀ HEIAU NATIONAL HISTORIC SITE is at 62-3601 Kawaihae Rd. Kapoukahi, the famous prophet of Kaua'i, prophesied that Kamehameha would conquer all the islands if he built a large *heiau* (temple) dedicated to his family war god, Kūkā'ilimoku, atop Pu'ukoholā—"whale hill"—at Kawaihae. Pu'ukoholā Heiau was built 1790-91 by thousands of men who passed water-worn lava rocks hand-by-hand in a human chain for 20 miles over the Kohala Mountains from the Pololū Valley. Human sacrifices were offered in the *heiau* to Kūkā'ilimoku. In 1810, through conquest and treaties, Kamehameha the Great unified all the Hawaiian islands and was the revered king.

Featuring activities like *lei* making, quilting and canoe rides, the site's ▼ Ho'oku'ikahi Establishment Day Hawaiian Cultural Festival in August celebrates ancient Hawaiian traditions.

Near the site is Mailekini Heiau, an older temple. During the rule of Kamehameha I, British sailor John Young helped the king convert this temple into a fort. A third temple, Hale o Kapuni, was dedicated to the shark gods. This temple lies just offshore and was last seen in the 1950s. **Note:** *Heiau* are culturally significant and should be treated with respect. **Time:** Allow 30 minutes minimum. **Hours:** Daily 8-4:45. **Cost:** Free. **Phone:** (808) 882-7218.

BLUE DRAGON RESTAURANT   808/882-7771

▼▼ International Fusion. Casual Dining. $17-$38 **AAA Inspector Notes:** Dining and dancing under the stars with live music and palm trees swaying make for a fun and entertaining evening at this restaurant with no roof. Locally influenced menu items with a global twist are the real stars of the show. Recommended are the guava pork chop and the Kauai prawns with chimichurri. Be sure to try one of the creative libations. All desserts are house made. Seating also is available on the back patio away from the music. **Features:** full bar, patio dining. **Reservations:** suggested. **Address:** 61-3616 Kawaihae Rd 96743 **Location:** SR 270; across from Kawaihae Harbor. Ⓓ CALL 🅜 🅺

SEAFOOD BAR & GRILL   808/880-9393

▼▼ Seafood. Casual Dining. $13-$30 **AAA Inspector Notes:** The popular restaurant is worth the drive from Kohala Coast resorts. Guests will find a good variety of fresh local seafood in a relaxed nautical atmosphere. Favorite starters include clam strips, steamers and an always-fresh daily chowder. Among entrées are charbroiled, sauteed or Cajun-style island fish, barbecue ribs, entrée-size salads and Huli-style chicken. Seating is offered in the air-conditioned dining room or a small side covered patio. The staff provides friendly, efficient service. **Features:** full bar, patio dining, early bird specials, happy hour. **Reservations:** suggested. **Address:** 61-3462 Kawaihae Rd 96743 **Location:** On SR 270; at Kawaihae Harbor. Ⓛ Ⓓ

KEALAKEKUA (G-10) pop. 2,019, elev. 1,550'
• Attractions map p. 32

Driving through Kealakekua, one of a string of towns in the Kona coffee belt, you'll find the usual roadside eateries and shops, Kona coffee establishments, high-priced gas stations, recreational outfitters and businesses catering to locals.

Kealakekua takes its name from the "Path of the Gods," two ceremonial *heiau* (temples) that stand along the coast by Kealakekua Bay. **Note:** *Heiau* are culturally significant and should be treated with respect.

The town also is the subject of the famous song "My Little Grass Shack in Kealakekua, Hawai'i," which accomplishes the amazing feat of incorporating *humuhumunukunukuāpua'a* (the Hawai'i state fish) in the lyrics.

The Central Kona Union Church, in town on SR 11, was built of lava rock mortared with lime created by burning coral.

One mile north of Kealakekua in the town of Kainaliu, stop at the Donkey Balls Factory & Store, 79-7411 Māmalahoa Hwy. (SR 11), and appease your sweet tooth with some outrageously delicious macadamia nuts covered in gourmet chocolate. At the back of the store you can watch the treats, which are available in several different flavors, being handmade. If you miss the shop, there's a nearby outlet in downtown Kailua-Kona as well.

GREENWELL FARMS is at 81-6581 Māmalahoa Hwy. (SR 11) between mileposts 111 and 112. Established in the 1850s, one of the Kona region's oldest coffee plantations offers 20-minute guided tours of the coffee orchards and a small processing facility. Before or after the tour, you can sample an array of the farm's 100 percent Kona coffee. **Time:** Allow 30 minutes minimum. **Hours:** Daily 8-5. Last tour departs 1 hour before closing. Closed major holidays. Phone ahead to confirm schedule. **Cost:** Free. **Phone:** (808) 323-2295.

H.N. GREENWELL STORE MUSEUM is on SR 11 between mileposts 111 and 112. Costumed interpreters introduce guests to the daily lives of multi-ethnic ranchers and coffee farmers of the 1890s. **Time:** Allow 30 minutes minimum. **Hours:** Mon. and Thurs. 10-2. Closed major holidays. **Cost:** $7; $3 (ages 5-12). **Phone:** (808) 323-3222.

RECREATIONAL ACTIVITIES
Kayaking
• **Hawaii Pack and Paddle** is at 79-7493 Māmalahoa Hwy. (SR 11). Other activities are offered. **Hours:** Tours depart daily year-round. **Phone:** (808) 328-8911.

ARECA PALMS ESTATE BED & BREAKFAST   (808)323-2276
🛏🛏 **Bed & Breakfast** $135-$155 **Address:** 81-1031 Keopuka Mauka Rd 96750 **Location:** Just s of MM 111; turn up hill across from Pineapple Park Kayak Central. **Facility:** 4 units. 2 stories (no elevator), interior corridors. **Terms:** 2 night minimum stay, age restrictions may apply, 30 day cancellation notice-fee imposed. **Activities:** hot tub. 🏠📶📶🗙🅰🄴

WHERE TO EAT

ANNIE'S ISLAND FRESH BURGERS   808/324-6000
🛏🛏 Burgers. Casual Dining. $14-$19 **AAA Inspector Notes:** As the name implies, the burger is king here. The hand-formed patties are teamed with house-made pickles, organic lettuce and vine-ripe tomatoes and served with hand-cut fries, slaw or purple potato salad. Not in the mood for a burger? Try one of the several salad and sandwich options such as the fresh catch-of-the-day sandwich. Fresh local produce, seafood and grass-fed, island-raised beef are served at this casual spot that offers creative, organic menu items. **Features:** full bar, happy hour. **Address:** 79-7460 Mamalahoa Hwy 96750 **Location:** Center; just s of MM 113; located in the Mango Court Center. Ⓛ Ⓓ

KEEI CAFE AT HOKUKANO   808/322-9992
🛏🛏 Pacific Rim. Casual Dining. $15-$29 **AAA Inspector Notes:** This charming café, facing Highway 11 with a distant ocean view, is located on the second floor of a two-story building. The open-air concept allows a wonderful breeze to flow through the restaurant. There are a few tables on the small lanai. Enjoy the fresh fish catch of the day, pork chops with a pineapple glaze or a juicy burger for lunch. Live music plays five nights a week. Cash only. **Features:** full bar. **Reservations:** suggested. **Address:** 79-7511 Mamalahoa Hwy 96750 **Location:** SR 11, between MM 112 and 113. Ⓓ CALL 🕓Ⓜ 🄰

MI'S ITALIAN BISTRO   808/323-3880
🛏🛏 Italian. Casual Dining. $17-$34 **AAA Inspector Notes:** A convenient place for dinner after a day of snorkeling or touring the coffee farms along the coast, this cozy bistro offers local products such as veal and Meyer lemon piccata and salads prepared with Big Island produce. **Features:** beer & wine. **Reservations:** suggested. **Address:** 81-6372 Mamalahoa Hwy 96750 **Location:** Center. Ⓓ

KEAUHOU (G-10) elev. 13'
• Hotels p. 52
• Attractions map p. 32

SEA QUEST RAFTING ADVENTURES departs Keauhou Bay and offers five different snorkeling adventures. The 3-hour afternoon Captain Cook Express takes passengers to snorkel at Kealakekua Bay, site of the Captain Cook Monument, and allows for exploration of sea caves and lava tubes as well as observation of dolphins and whales; snacks are included. The 4-hour Deluxe Morning Adventure includes additional snorkeling at Hōnaunau Bay, and the 5-hour Expedition South Kona outing includes lunch and yet another snorkeling site. The 5-hour Dolphin Encounter tour includes swimming with wild dolphins; a coral reef snorkel; and lunch. The 1.5-hour nighttime Manta Ray tour includes snorkeling with manta rays; snacks are included. Snorkeling gear, instructions and flotation devices are provided on all three trips.

Note: These tours cannot accommodate pregnant women and people with back problems. Inquire about weather and refund policies. **Hours:** Captain Cook Express tour departs daily at 12:45. Deluxe Morning Adventure tour departs daily at 8. Expedition South Kona tour departs daily at 8:15. Dolphin Encounter tour departs Tues. and Thurs. at 8:15. Manta Ray tour departure times vary seasonally; phone for details. Passengers must check in 15 minutes prior to departure. **Cost:** Captain Cook Express tour $76; $65 (ages 5-12). Deluxe Morning Adventure tour $96; $78 (ages 5-12). Expedition South

Kona tour $114; $93 (ages 5-12). Dolphin Encounter tour $139. Manta Ray tour $89. Under age 5 are not permitted. Reservations are required. **Phone:** (808) 329-7238.

SHERATON KONA RESORT & SPA AT KEAUHOU BAY
(808)930-4900

Hotel
$135-$379

Sheraton HOTELS & RESORTS

AAA Benefit: Members save up to 15%, plus Starwood Preferred Guest® benefits!

Address: 78-128 Ehukai St 96740 **Location:** Oceanfront. SR 11, 1.4 mi sw (toward ocean) on Kamehameha III Rd, 0.7 mi s on Alii Dr, then just w on Kaleiopapa St; watch for Keauhou Bay sign. **Facility:** 509 units. 7 stories, interior/exterior corridors. **Parking:** onsite and valet. **Terms:** 3 day cancellation notice, resort fee. **Amenities:** video games, safes. **Dining:** 3 restaurants, entertainment. **Pool(s):** outdoor. **Activities:** hot tub, cabanas, snorkeling, tennis, recreation programs, kids club, bicycles, game room, exercise room, spa. **Guest Services:** valet and coin laundry, rental car service.

 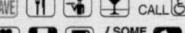

KOHALA COAST

THE FAIRMONT ORCHID, HAWAII
(808)885-2000

Resort Hotel
$400-$3900

Address: One N Kaniku Dr 96743 **Location:** Oceanfront. 19 mi n of Kona International Airport on SR 19, 1 mi w on Mauna Lani Dr, then 1 mi n; in Mauna Lani resort area. **Facility:** This grand, oceanfront hotel features lovely waterfalls and ponds that enhance the manicured grounds. A shoreline trail leads to an adjacent Hawaiian historic site. 540 units. 6 stories, interior corridors. **Parking:** on-site (fee) and valet. **Terms:** 14 day cancellation notice, resort fee. **Amenities:** video games, safes. **Dining:** 3 restaurants, also, Brown's Beach House, see separate listing, entertainment. **Pool(s):** heated outdoor. **Activities:** sauna, hot tub, steamroom, cabanas, self-propelled boats, snorkeling, regulation golf, tennis, recreation programs, kids club, bicycles, exercise room, spa. **Guest Services:** valet laundry, rental car service, area transportation.

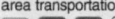      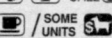

MAUNA LANI BAY HOTEL & BUNGALOWS
(808)885-6622

Resort Hotel
$400-$1800

Address: 68-1400 Mauna Lani Dr 96743 **Location:** Oceanfront. 19 mi n of Kona International Airport on SR 19, 1.8 mi nw; in Mauna Lani resort area. **Facility:** The stunning open-atrium concept of the lobby is the first thing that greets all guests. Looking down from the lobby is a lush garden. 341 units, some houses. 1-6 stories, interior/exterior corridors. **Parking:** on-site (fee) and valet. **Terms:** 14 day cancellation notice, resort fee. **Amenities:** safes. **Dining:** 3 restaurants, also, The CanoeHouse, see separate listing, entertainment. **Pool(s):** heated outdoor. **Activities:** sauna, hot tub, steamroom, cabanas, self-propelled boats, scuba diving, snorkeling, regulation golf, tennis, recreation programs, kids club, bicycles, spa. **Guest Services:** valet and coin laundry, rental car service, area transportation. Affiliated with Preferred Hotels & Resorts.

MAUNA KEA BEACH HOTEL, AUTOGRAPH COLLECTION
808/882-7222

[fyi] Not evaluated. **Address:** 62-100 Mauna Kea Beach Dr 96743 **Location:** Oceanfront. 25 mi n of Kona International Airport on SR 19, just w; in Mauna Kea resort area. Facilities, services, and décor characterize a mid-scale property.

AAA Benefit: Members save 5% or more!

WHERE TO EAT

BROWN'S BEACH HOUSE
808/885-2000

Regional Pacific Rim Fine Dining
$36-$56

AAA Inspector Notes: Attentive and genuine service coupled with the nightly sunset show make for a memorable meal that one would especially enjoy on a special occasion. The open-air restaurant offers an amazing view of the cove beach, ocean and palm-tree-lined shore. Dishes are expertly prepared and presented, especially the creatively prepared selection of fresh, locally caught fish from the Kona coastline such as walu, ahi and ono. **Features:** full bar, patio dining. **Reservations:** suggested. **Address:** One N Kaniku Dr 96743 **Location:** 19 mi n of Kona International Airport on SR 19, 1 mi w on Mauna Lani Dr, then 1 mi n; in Mauna Lani resort area; in The Fairmont Orchid, Hawaii. **Parking:** on-site and valet.

THE CANOEHOUSE
808/885-6622

Pacific Rim. Fine Dining. $36-$48 **AAA Inspector Notes:** On the oceanfront, the restaurant offers fine regional cuisine in a romantic, open-air setting. Torch-lit gardens surround tables bathed in candlelight, and the sounds of crashing waves contribute to an air of tranquility. Servers offer warm Hawaiian hospitality and go out of their way to explain the history and preparation of some of the more traditional menu items. **Features:** full bar, patio dining. **Reservations:** suggested. **Address:** 68-1400 Mauna Lani Dr 96743 **Location:** 19 mi n of Kona International Airport on SR 19, 1.8 mi nw; in Mauna Lani resort area; in Mauna Lani Bay Hotel & Bungalows. **Parking:** on-site and valet.

COAST GRILLE
808/880-1111

Pacific Rim. Fine Dining. $20-$43 **AAA Inspector Notes:** The restaurant features indoor dining as well as open-air candlelight dining on one of the terraces. Spectacular views of the ocean and sunsets are the highlights. The menu highlights include steak and seafood items with a strong focus on regional Hawaiian cuisine. The chef prides himself in an ever-changing menu. Try the oyster bar sampler or the prix fixe menu. **Features:** full bar, patio dining. **Reservations:** suggested. **Address:** 62-100 Kauna'oa Dr 96743 **Location:** 23 mi n of Kona International Airport on SR 19, just w; in Mauna Kea resort area; in Hapuna Beach Prince Hotel at Mauna Kea Resort. **Parking:** on-site and valet.

MANTA & PAVILION WINE BAR
808/882-5707

Pacific Rim. Fine Dining. $38-$52 **AAA Inspector Notes:** What could be more magnificent than a leisurely breakfast or a romantic dinner overlooking Kauna'oa Bay and vast expanse of the Pacific Ocean? The menu strives to feature local produce from area fisherman, farmers and artisans and most often includes seafood, beef, pork and chicken options. Also offered is an extensive selection of wines both by the glass and bottle. For the best view, request a table on the outdoor patio. Be sure and save room for the lilikoi soufflé. **Features:** full bar, patio dining, Sunday brunch. **Reservations:** suggested. **Address:** 62-100 Mauna Kea Beach Dr 96743 **Location:** 25 mi n of Kona International Airport on SR 19, just w; in Mauna Kea resort area; in Mauna Kea Beach Hotel, Autograph Collection.

MONSTERA NOODLES & SUSHI
808/887-2711

Sushi Noodles. Casual Dining. $18-$30 **AAA Inspector Notes:** Japanese-style pub food and sushi made from fresh ingredients are served at this contemporary second-floor restaurant. **Features:** full bar, patio dining. **Address:** 68-1330 Mauna Lani Dr 96743 **Location:** 19 mi n of Kona International Airport on SR 19, 1 mi w; in Shops at Mauna Lani; in Mauna Lani resort area.

RUTH'S CHRIS STEAK HOUSE   808/887-0800

▼▼▼▼ Steak. Fine Dining. $27-$60 **AAA Inspector Notes:** The main fare is steak, which is prepared from several cuts of Prime beef and cooked to perfection, but the menu also lists lamb, chicken and seafood dishes. Guests should come hungry because the side dishes, which are among the a la carte offerings, could make a meal in themselves. **Features:** full bar. **Reservations:** suggested. **Address:** 68-1330 Mauna Lani Dr 96743 **Location:** 19 mi n of Kona International Airport on SR 19, 1 mi w; in Shops at Mauna Lani; in Mauna Lani resort area. [D] CALL[&M]

TOMMY BAHAMA'S TROPICAL CAFE   808/881-8686

▼▼▼▼ Caribbean. Casual Dining. $17-$41 **AAA Inspector Notes:** Located on the second floor, this open-air restaurant offers sweeping views of the mountains and a coastal golf course. Dining on the lanai is an option to catch the sunset. The varied menu includes sandwiches at lunch, entrée salads and fish from the Hawaiian waters prepared with an island flair. **Features:** full bar, patio dining, happy hour. **Reservations:** suggested. **Address:** 68-1330 Mauna Lani Dr 96743 **Location:** 19 mi n of Kona International Airport on SR 19, 1 mi w; in Shops at Mauna Lani; in Mauna Lani resort area. [L] [D] CALL[&M] [ℵ]

KUKUIHAELE (F-11) pop. 336, elev. 30'
• Attractions map p. 32

WAIPI'O VALLEY SHUTTLE AND TOURS, SR 240 to Waipi'o Lookout, offers 90-minute guided tours of the Waipi'o Valley. A four-wheel drive vehicle takes visitors through streams and ponds and past waterfalls, native flora and, sometimes, wild horses. A narrator relates Hawaiian history and legends.

Refunds are not provided if cancellations are made within 24 hours of departure. **Hours:** Tours Mon.-Sat. at 9, 11, 1 and 3. Closed Jan. 1, Thanksgiving and Christmas. **Cost:** $55; $27.50 (ages 3-11). Tickets are available at Waipi'o Valley Artworks. Reservations are recommended. **Phone:** (808) 775-7121.

RECREATIONAL ACTIVITIES
Horseback Riding
• **Horseback Above Waipi'o** is at 48-5416 Kukuihaele Rd. **Hours:** Valley Rim Ride daily at 9 and 1. Hidden Waterfall Ride daily at 9. **Phone:** (808) 775-1007 or (877) 757-1414.

• **Na'alapa Stables** departs from Waipi'o Valley Artworks at 48-5416 Kukuihaele Rd. **Hours:** Guided trips depart Mon.-Sat. at 9:30 and 1. **Phone:** (808) 775-0419.

LAUPAHOEHOE (F-11) pop. 581, elev. 400'
• Attractions map p. 32

Laupahoehoe means "leaf of lava," and that is precisely what the area is: a leaf-shaped peninsula of black lava.

LAUPAHOEHOE POINT BEACH PARK, 1.2 mi. off SR 19 via a narrow winding road, is n. of Pāpa'aloa and Laupahoehoe. The park is on a picturesque peninsula bounded by a spectacular seacoast. There is a monument commemorating the victims of the 1946 tsunami.

Note: Swimming and fishing are not recommended due to the hazardous shoreline and rough surf. With permits, two pavilions are available for day use. **Hours:** Daily 6 a.m.-11 p.m. **Cost:** Park free. A fee is charged for camping. **Phone:** (808) 961-8311. [▲] [⊞]

LAUPAHOEHOE TRAIN MUSEUM is on SR 19 at 36-2377 Māmalahoa Hwy. near Milepost 25. The museum depicts life when railroads were in operation in Hawai'i, 1860s-1950, through photos and memorabilia. The largest line was a passenger/freight line with raw sugar as its main freight; one room is dedicated to sugar trains and plantations.

Video footage from 1916 of a running train can be seen. Also on the premises are a restored boxcar, engine and caboose on track from the rail line. **Time:** Allow 30 minutes minimum. **Hours:** Thurs.-Sun. 10-5, Mon.-Wed. by appointment. Closed major holidays. **Cost:** $6; $5 (ages 60+ and Hawai'i residents); $3 (ages 4-18); $15 (family). **Phone:** (808) 962-6300.

MĀHUKONA (F-10) elev. 33'
• Attractions map p. 32

LAPAKAHI STATE HISTORICAL PARK, on SR 270 (Akoni Pule Hwy.), features remnants of a coastal settlement inhabited at least 600 years ago. Farmers who settled on the mountainside traded with the fishermen living along the shoreline. The remains of houses and canoe sheds as well as a curbed trail that led to the upland fields can be seen along a mile-long interpretive trail. A small visitor center includes exhibits and brochures. Restrooms are available; drinking water is not. **Hours:** Daily 8-4. Closed major holidays. **Cost:** Free. **Phone:** (808) 327-4958. [⊞]

NAALEHU (I-11) pop. 866, elev. 674'

When "towns" are defined as places with post offices, Naalehu, at 19 degrees 3 minutes 40 seconds latitude, is the southernmost town in the United States. Orchards of macadamia nut trees are along the highway west of town. A monkeypod tree planted by Mark Twain (Samuel Clemens) in 1866 stands in the center of the village. Blown down by a hurricane in 1957, the tree has regrown from its original trunk.

South Point, known as *Ka Lae* (The Point) in Hawaiian, is the southernmost point in the 50 states. Archeologists speculate that this is the site where the first Polynesians made landfall in the Hawaiian Islands—sometime between the 1st and 4th centuries—and then a more prominent wave of people came sometime between the 7th and 9th centuries. Here the island's volcanic slope tapers to a broad, windswept cape, where giant waves crash against the lava cliffs and persistent winds shape the few trees able to grow in this environment. About 4 miles west of town off SR 11, a one-lane paved track runs 12 miles to the point; watch for oncoming traffic.

KALAEKILOHANA INN AND RETREAT   (808)939-8052

▼▼▼▼ Country Inn $279-$349 Address: 94-2152 S Point Rd 96772 Location: On SR 11, between MM 69 and 70, 1 mi s. Facility: This is a great base camp for discovering the southern end of the island. The owners consider themselves stewards of the land and are a wealth of historic, cultural and tourism knowledge. 4 units. 3 stories (no elevator), interior corridors. Terms: 2 night minimum stay - seasonal, 30 day cancellation notice-fee imposed. Activities: massage. Guest Services: complimentary laundry.

⓫ 📶 ⊠ 🏋 🕅 ⓩ

WHERE TO EAT

PUNALU'U BAKE SHOP AND VISITOR CENTER   808/929-7343

▼ Breads/Pastries. Quick Serve. $3-$8 AAA Inspector Notes: This is a must-stop on the way to the Hawaii Volcanoes National Park and offers tempting island bakery items such as mango, guava or lilikoi malasadas, sweet breads and sandwiches for lunch. Features: patio dining. Address: 95-5642 Mamalahoa Hwy 96772 Location: Center. ⒷⒷ 🅛 CALL 🔊

NĀPŌʻOPOʻO (H-10) elev. 10'
• Attractions map p. 32

The Hawaiian Islands' first sustained contact with Western civilization took place at Nāpōʻopoʻo and its nearby Hikiau Heiau. A plaque commemorates Hawai'i's first Christian funeral, conducted by Capt. James Cook. Another plaque honors Henry Opukahaia; educated at mission schools in New England, he was influential in having several missionaries sent to educate the natives. Note: Heiau are culturally significant and should be treated with respect.

Because of the clarity of the water and the variety of marine life, Kealakekua Bay (Pathway of the Gods) has been designated a marine preserve.

CAPTAIN COOK MONUMENT, across Kealakekua Bay, is a 27-foot obelisk erected in 1874 near the spot where Capt. James Cook was killed. The spot is marked by a submerged plaque that can be seen through the water, but it is accessible only by boat. Cost: Free. Phone: (808) 961-9540.

OCEAN VIEW (H-10) elev. 1,575'

RECREATIONAL ACTIVITIES
Climbing
• Kula Kai Caverns is at 92-8864 Lauhala Dr. Hours: Daily year-round. Reservations are required. Phone: (808) 929-9725.

PAʻAUILO (F-11) pop. 595, elev. 712'

HAWAIIAN VANILLA COMPANY is at 43-2007 Pa'auilo Mauka Rd. Farm tour participants explore the grounds, watch a video presentation about vanilla farming, and sample vanilla-flavored ice cream and beverages. Luncheon tours include a meal and a trip to the company's mill. Tastings, tea brunches, seminars and classes also are offered.

Note: Luncheon tour participants are advised that the roads to the mill are steep; the walk may be difficult for some. Time: Allow 1 hour minimum. Hours: Farm tours Mon.-Fri. at 1. Luncheon tour Mon.-Fri. at 12:30. Cost: Farm tour $25; $10 (ages 4-12).

Luncheon tour $39; $19.50 (ages 0-11). Reservations are required. Phone: (808) 776-1771. 🕮

PĀHALA (H-11) pop. 1,356, elev. 920'
• Attractions map p. 32

Pāhala is a former sugar mill community containing buildings with false fronts and an air of yesterday. To the east lies Ka'ū Desert, a barren expanse of lava and pumice that reaches from the sea to the rim of Kīlauea Crater.

PUNALUʻU BLACK SAND BEACH PARK, 5 mi. s.w. off SR 11 (the signed entrance road is between mileposts 55 and 56), is perhaps the most easily accessible of Hawai'i Island's black sand beaches, formed when hot lava meets cool ocean water and shatters into tiny pieces. Wave action further pulverizes the black volcanic rock into grains of sand. Backed by tall coconut palms, the crystalline black strand is very popular with day trippers traveling between the Kailua-Kona area and Hawai'i Volcanoes National Park; count on seeing tour buses here.

The shoreline is mostly rocky, and ocean conditions are generally rough (beware of rip currents), but you needn't swim or snorkel far from shore to see the bay's resident green sea turtles. In fact, you'll often find them lazing on the sand, surrounded by groups of camera-happy tourists.

In addition to picnic tables, restrooms and public showers, there's a bungalow with vendors selling snacks, drinks and souvenirs. If the first parking lot you encounter (the north lot) is full, there are more spaces just down the road in the south lot. Note: Green and hawksbill sea turtles are threatened species protected by federal and state laws. Harassing or touching them carries heavy fines. A permit is required for camping and picnic pavilion use. Hours: Daily 6 a.m.-11 p.m. Cost: Park free. A fee is charged for camping. Phone: (808) 961-8311. 🅰 ⛺

PĀHOA (H-12) pop. 945, elev. 655'
• Attractions map p. 32

Pāhoa is in the Puna area, where desolate lava flows form a backdrop for tiny tropical villages. The region retains much of the island's once leisurely approach to life.

In 1955 an eruption in the east rift zone of Kīlauea occurred a few miles from Pāhoa. Lava flows engulfed orchards and sugarcane farms, destroyed one village and reached the edge of another, but evacuation measures prevented loss of life. Six miles of roads were buried; new sections have been cut through the flows.

Winding along the coast south of Kapoho, SR 137 offers views of the rugged cliffs formed when lava flows met the sea. South of Pāhoa, SR 130 passes tropical forests and flower farms interspersed with stark lava formations and small cones that still emit steam and sulfur fumes.

Note: SR 130 between Kīlauea Caldera and the coast has closed because of lava flows between Kalapana and Chain of Craters Road.

LAVA TREE STATE MONUMENT is 3 mi. s.e. off Pāhoa-Pohoiki Rd. (Hwy. 132) in Nānāwale Forest Reserve. Around 1790 an eruption from Kīlauea volcano engulfed a grove of ʻōhiʻa trees in lava. The moisture in the tree trunks chilled and hardened the lava into a rigid shell where each tree stood. The flow of lava then ceased, and the molten portions drained away, leaving the tree molds. A .7-mile loop trail provides views of the lava trees. No drinking water is available. **Time:** Allow 30 minutes minimum. **Hours:** Daily dawn-dusk. **Cost:** Free. **Phone:** (808) 961-9540. 🏕

PAPAIKOU (G-12) pop. 1,314, elev. 220'
• Attractions map p. 32

HAWAIʻI TROPICAL BOTANICAL GARDEN is at 27-717 Old Māmalahoa Hwy. Tickets are purchased at the visitor center; access is through a wrought iron gate across the street. On Hawaiʻi Island's lush windward coast, this botanic garden is one of the finest on the islands. Hand-built by Dan Lutkenhouse, an ex-trucker from San Francisco, Calif., the 17-acre Eden boasts more than 2,000 species of tropical plants, trees and flowers, including an impressive collection of orchids.

A 1.25-mile network of paved paths winds through the garden, where highlights include a serene palm jungle, a koi-filled lily pond, a macaw aviary, monkeypod trees and the lovely, three-tiered Onomea Falls. The grand finale is an overlook of rugged, wave-lashed Onomea Bay.

Time: Allow 2 hours minimum. **Hours:** Daily 9-5. Last admission 1 hour before closing. Closed Jan. 1, Thanksgiving and Christmas. **Cost:** $15; $5 (ages 6-16). **Phone:** (808) 964-5233.

PUʻUHONUA O HŌNAUNAU NATIONAL HISTORICAL PARK
(H-10)
• Attractions map p. 32

Off SR 160, 22 miles south of Kailua-Kona, Puʻuhonua o Hōnaunau, meaning "Place of Refuge of Hōnaunau," is a fun site to explore and as a bonus offers a good Hawaiian history lesson. Established in the 15th century, this is a place modern-day jailbirds wish was still around. The coastal compound was one of Hawaiʻi Island's six sacred spots that provided sanctuary to commoners who broke kapu (religious law). If they could successfully flee to the safety of the puʻuhonua, the offenders would be absolved by a priest and could then return to a "new" life.

The puʻuhonua also provided a safe haven to women, children, the infirm and the elderly seeking protection in time of battle.

You'll begin the park's easy .5-mile self-guiding walking tour at the visitor center, where you're given a handy map/guide. A cellphone tour also is offered. From here you immediately enter the sacred wahi pana (legendary place) through the Royal Grounds. With pretty Hōnaunau Bay to your right and swaying coconut palms all around, it's a lovely setting. Along the path you'll see hale (houses), hālau (open-ended structures) and heiau (temples), as well as a cove that served as a royal canoe landing.

The Royal Grounds (the area reserved for chiefs and their people) and the puʻuhonua are separated by a 1,000-foot-long, 12-foot-high and 17-foot-wide stone Great Wall. At the bay end of the impressive Great Wall, kiʻi (carved wooden statues representing Hawaiian gods) surround the thatched Hale o Keawe temple, which was originally a mausoleum once containing the bones of 23 aliʻi (chiefs). These bones were believed to possess mana (divine or supernatural power) and protect the puʻuhonua.

On the sanctuary side of the Great Wall you'll pass stone heiau, coastal tide pools and a fishpond before returning to the visitor center. If you have time, after hopping back in the car, drive to the far end of the parking lot and turn onto the dirt road that's just left of the visitor center. In a few minutes you'll reach the park's picnic area—a series of tables (with barbecue grills) along the coastline. If you've come in late afternoon, it's a beautiful, tranquil spot to watch the sun sink into the Pacific.

Visitors also can hike 2 miles round-trip on the 1871 Trail to view Kiʻilae Village, which includes abandoned house sites, agricultural features, animal pens and salt vats; a flier is available at the visitor center.

The visitor center has restrooms, a gift shop, a few exhibits and rangers on duty to answer questions. Orientation talks are presented daily at 10:30 and 2:30.

Note: The Royal Grounds area of the park is wheelchair accessible; the visitor center provides big-wheeled "beach" wheelchairs free of charge. Camping is prohibited. Heiau are culturally significant and should be treated with respect. Allow 1 hour minimum. One-way drive time from Kailua-Kona is about 40 minutes.

Address inquiries to the Park Superintendent, Puʻuhonua o Hōnaunau National Historical Park, P.O. Box 129, Hōnaunau, HI 96726.

The 421-acre park is open daily 7 a.m.-dusk. The visitor center is open daily 8:30-4:30. A 7-day pass is $5 per private vehicle; $3 per pedestrian, bicyclist or motorcyclist; free (ages 0-15). A Hawaiʻi Tri-park Annual Pass (includes Haleakalā National Park, Hawaiʻi Volcanoes National Park and Puʻuhonua o Hōnaunau National Historical Park) is $25. Phone (808) 328-2288 or (808) 328-2326.

VOLCANO pop. 2,575
See also Hawai'i Volcanoes National Park p. 35

KILAUEA LODGE AND RESTAURANT (808)967-7366

WWW **Historic Country Inn** $195-$355 **Address:** 19-3948 Old Volcano Rd 96785 **Location:** Jct SR 11 and CR 148, just nw on CR 148, just w. **Facility:** Set in a building originally constructed in 1938, this lodge is located just a mile from the popular Hawai'i Volcanoes National Park, which is a must-see. 16 units, some kitchens, houses and cottages. 1-2 stories (no elevator), interior/exterior corridors. **Terms:** 7 day cancellation notice-fee imposed. **Dining:** Kilauea Lodge Restaurant, see separate listing. **Activities:** hot tub.

WHERE TO EAT

CAFE ONO 808/985-8979

WW Vegetarian Vegan. Casual Dining. $10-$15 **AAA Inspector Notes:** This is a great lunch stop, offering natural foods, when visiting Hawaii Volcanoes National Park. Enjoy the farmhouse or outdoor seating and then go say "hi" to Ernest The Goat on your way to exploring the secret garden. **Features:** patio dining. **Address:** 19-3834 Old Volcano Rd 96785 **Location:** Jct SR 11 and CR 148, just nw on CR 148 (Wright Rd), then just ne.

KILAUEA LODGE RESTAURANT 808/967-7366

WW American. Casual Dining. $21-$49 **AAA Inspector Notes:** Located just a mile from Hawai'i Volcanoes National Park, the charming restaurant serves tasty renditions of European favorites and fresh fish from the Big Island. A cozy, historic fireplace with stones representing 32 countries is the centerpiece. **Features:** full bar, Sunday brunch. **Reservations:** suggested. **Address:** 19-3948 Old Volcano Rd 96785 **Location:** Jct SR 11 and CR 148, just e on CR 148, just s; in Kilauea Lodge and Restaurant.

WAIKOLOA (G-10) elev. 410'
• Restaurants p. 59

A resort area on the western side of Hawai'i Island, Waikoloa is known for its beaches and golf courses.

The Great Waikoloa 'Ukulele Festival, held in March at the Kings' Shops and Queens' Market-Place, features performances by 'ukulele players from around the world. 'Ukulele lessons and give-aways add to the fun.

BLUE HAWAIIAN HELICOPTERS departs from Waikoloa Heliport. Helicopter tours last between 50 minutes and 2 hours and provide views of active volcanic areas, sea cliffs, valleys and waterfalls. Passengers hear music, two-way communication with the pilot, and the pilot's narration via noise-canceling headsets.

Note: Due to decompression-related sickness, it is recommended that passengers wait 12-24 hours after scuba diving before flying; the amount of time is dependent on particular dive factors. Ask about possible policies regarding minimum wait time between scuba diving and flying; weight restrictions; weather, cancellation and refund policies; and the minimum and maximum number of passengers for flights. All small aircraft may encounter turbulence.

Hours: Daily 7 a.m.-10 p.m. **Cost:** $194-$450, plus applicable fuel surcharge. Reservations are required. **Phone:** (808) 886-1768 or (800) 786-2583. *(See ad on inside front cover.)*

SAVE **DOLPHIN QUEST HAWAI'I,** at the Hilton Waikoloa Village, 425 Waikoloa Beach Dr., offers a variety of fun and educational programs that allow visitors of all ages to interact with Atlantic bottlenose dolphins. Programs are led by professional trainers. Most of the encounters take place in shallow water, but some involve swimming and snorkeling in deep water. Photographers stand by to capture highlights of the encounter; photos can be purchased after the program.

Note: Visitors should have their parking tickets validated at Dolphin Quest Hawai'i. Swimsuits and towels are required. Life jackets are provided. Showers are available. Participants may not use a camera during the program, but non-participants may take photos from behind the roped-off area. Inquire about cancellation policies. **Time:** Allow 1 hour minimum. **Hours:** Daily 8:30-5. Participants must arrive 30 minutes before the program begins.

Cost: The 45-minute Encounter Deluxe $260. The 30-minute Encounter $210. The 1.25-hour Kids Quest $220 (ages 5-9). The 10-minute Wee Tots encounter $110 (one adult and one child age 2-4). The 1.75-hour Sea Quest $350. The 45-minute Dolphin Family and Friends encounter $1,400 (family, up to six people). The 5.5-hour Trainer for a Day program $700. Age restrictions vary. Reservations are required. **Phone:** (808) 886-2875 or (800) 248-3316.

HILTON GRAND VACATIONS CLUB AT WAIKOLOA BEACH RESORT
(808)886-8700

Resort Condominium
$349-$649 **Address:** 69-550 Waikoloa Beach Dr 96738 **Location:** 17 mi n of Kona International Airport on SR 19; just w on Waikoloa Beach Dr, 0.6 mi n on Ala Ihi Way, then just e; in Waikoloa Beach resort area. **Facility:** The attractive two-bedroom suites have contemporary décor and spacious lanais. Some offer golf course views and some offer hot tubs. Relax in this quiet setting. 120 condominiums. 3 stories, exterior corridors. **Terms:** check-in 4 pm, 1-7 night minimum stay, cancellation fee imposed. **Amenities:** video games, safes. **Pool(s):** heated outdoor. **Activities:** hot tub, tennis, recreation programs, exercise room. **Guest Services:** complimentary and valet laundry, area transportation.

AAA Benefit: Members save 5% or more!

HILTON WAIKOLOA VILLAGE
(808)886-1234

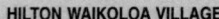

Resort Hotel
$149-$559

Hilton HOTELS & RESORTS

AAA Benefit: Members save 5% or more!

Address: 69-425 Waikoloa Beach Dr 96738 **Location:** Oceanfront. 17 mi n of Kona International Airport on SR 19, 1.2 mi nw; in Waikoloa Beach resort area. **Facility:** This massive property features three separate tower sections where guests can use a tram system or one of the many canal boats to get to each tower. 1240 units, some two bedrooms. 1-6 stories, interior/exterior corridors. **Parking:** on-site (fee) and valet. **Terms:** 1-7 night minimum stay, cancellation fee imposed. **Amenities:** video games, safes. **Dining:** 7 restaurants, also, Kamuela Provision Company, Kirin Chinese Restaurant, see separate listings, entertainment. **Pool(s):** outdoor. **Activities:** sauna, hot tub, steamroom, cabanas, self-propelled boats, scuba diving, snorkeling, miniature golf, tennis, recreation programs, kids club, bicycles, spa. **Guest Services:** valet and coin laundry, rental car service, area transportation. *(See ad p. 53.)*

KINGS LAND, HILTON GRAND VACATIONS CLUB
(808)881-3000

Resort Condominium
$219-$1040

Hilton Grand Vacations

AAA Benefit: Members save 5% or more!

Address: 69-699 Waikoloa Beach Dr 96738 **Location:** 17 mi n of Kona International Airport on SR 19, just w on Waikoloa Beach Dr, 0.6 mi n on Ala Ihi Way, then just w; in Waikoloa Beach resort area. **Facility:** The latest addition to the Waikoloa resort area, this spacious, open-air Hilton set on 30 acres has lush plantation-style public areas. 311 condominiums. 3 stories, exterior corridors. **Terms:** check-in 4 pm, 1-7 night minimum stay, cancellation fee imposed. **Amenities:** video games, safes. **Dining:** entertainment. **Pool(s):** heated outdoor. **Activities:** hot tub, regulation golf, recreation programs, kids club, game room, exercise room. **Guest Services:** complimentary and valet laundry, boarding pass kiosk, area transportation.

WAIKOLOA BEACH MARRIOTT RESORT & SPA

(808)886-6789

Resort Hotel
$199-$549

AAA Benefit: Members save 5% or more!

Address: 69-275 Waikoloa Beach Dr 96738 **Location:** Oceanfront. 17 mi n of Kona International Airport on SR 19, 0.7 mi w; in Waikoloa Beach resort area. **Facility:** Situated near a beautiful bay, this property features expansive manicured grounds and modern guest rooms. There is a slide and two fun pools for families, and an infinity pool for the adults. 555 units. 6 stories, interior corridors. **Parking:** on-site (fee) and valet. **Terms:** 3 day cancellation notice, resort fee. **Amenities:** safes. **Dining:** entertainment. **Pool(s):** heated outdoor. **Activities:** hot tub, cabanas, self-propelled boats, scuba diving, snorkeling, tennis, recreation programs, exercise room, spa. **Guest Services:** valet and coin laundry, boarding pass kiosk, rental car service, area transportation.

LAVA LAVA BEACH CLUB

808/769-5282

[fyi] Not evaluated. **Address:** 69-1081 Ku'uali'i Pl 96738 **Location:** Oceanfront. 17 mi n of Kona International Airport on SR 19, 0.6 mi w on Waikoloa Beach Dr, then just sw; in Waikoloa Beach resort area. Facilities, services, and décor characterize a mid-scale property.

OUTRIGGER FAIRWAY VILLAS

808/886-0036

[fyi] Not evaluated. **Address:** 69-200 Pohakulana Pl 96738 **Location:** 17 mi n of Kona International Airport on SR 19, 0.4 mi w; in Waikoloa Beach resort area. Facilities, services, and décor characterize a mid-scale property. These attractive low-rise condos are surrounded by a golf course, and shops are within walking distance. Guest check-in is at the Kings' Shops, 69-250 Waikoloa Beach Dr., second level, from 9-7.

WHERE TO EAT

KAMUELA PROVISION COMPANY

808/886-1234

Seafood Steak. Fine Dining. $33-$82 **AAA Inspector Notes:** This casual restaurant lets diners sample fresh regional Hawaiian cuisine. The dining room delights with hidden tables overlooking the tropical grounds, pool or waterfalls, as well as the popular outdoor terrace, which affords sweeping views of the ocean. Reserving a table at sunset doesn't guarantee a sunset-view table. Validated parking is offered. **Features:** full bar, patio dining. **Reservations:** suggested. **Address:** 69-425 Waikoloa Beach Dr 96738 **Location:** 17 mi n of Kona International Airport on SR 19, 1.2 mi nw; in Waikoloa Beach resort area; in Hilton Waikoloa Village. **Parking:** on-site (fee) and valet.

KIRIN CHINESE RESTAURANT

808/886-1288

Chinese. Casual Dining. $18-$52 **AAA Inspector Notes:** Between the Ocean and Palace towers at the Hilton Waikoloa Village, this restaurant prepares a fine selection of classic Chinese dishes. The diverse menu offers dim sum luncheons and a wide variety of full-course or a la carte specialties at dinner. Servers gladly answer questions about the options. **Features:** full bar, patio dining. **Reservations:** suggested. **Address:** 69-425 Waikoloa Beach Dr 96738 **Location:** 17 mi n of Kona International Airport on SR 19, 1.2 mi nw; in Waikoloa Beach resort area; in Hilton Waikoloa Village. **Parking:** on-site (fee) and valet.

LAVA LAVA BEACH CLUB

808/769-5282

Seafood Steak. Casual Dining. $13-$37 **AAA Inspector Notes:** Situated on the water's edge at beautiful Anaeho'omalu Bay, this lively open-air restaurant features a farm-to-beach menu with island inspirations. Recommended are the tasty sizzling shrimp and the pineapple fried rice. Be sure to make a reservation to enjoy the sunset, the live music and the hula dancer. **Features:** full bar, patio dining, happy hour. **Reservations:** suggested. **Address:** 69-1081 Ku'uali'i Pl 96738 **Location:** 17 mi n of Kona International Airport on SR 19, 0.6 mi w on Waikoloa Beach Dr, then just sw; in Waikoloa Beach resort area.

MERRIMAN'S MEDITERRANEAN CAFE

808/886-1700

Regional Mediterranean. Casual Dining. $10-$29 **AAA Inspector Notes:** This fun and casual restaurant is the little sister to its location in Waimea. Representative of high-quality delicatessen fare are sandwiches and salads for lunch and pasta, fresh fish of the day and full chicken or steak entrées for dinner prepared with Mediterranean inspiration. **Features:** full bar, patio dining, happy hour. **Address:** 250 Waikoloa Beach Dr 96738 **Location:** Off SR 19, 17 mi n of Kona International Airport, 1.4 mi w; in The King's Shops.

ROY'S

808/886-4321

Pacific Rim Fusion. Fine Dining. $14-$70 **AAA Inspector Notes:** Enjoy fusion of fresh Pacific seafood, French sauces and Asian seasonings. The ever-changing menu has many entrées such as grilled salmon and barbecue lamb rack, and the signature dessert, chocolate soufflé. **Features:** full bar. **Reservations:** suggested. **Address:** 250 Waikoloa Beach Dr 96738 **Location:** 17 mi n of Kona International Airport on SR 19, 0.4 mi w; in The King's Shops; in Waikoloa Beach resort area.

SANSEI SEAFOOD, STEAK & SUSHI BAR

808/886-6286

Pacific Rim Sushi Steak. Casual Dining. $19-$59 **AAA Inspector Notes:** A variety of appetizers and an extensive list of sushi specialty rolls, sashimi, and steak and seafood entrées are served at this casual restaurant. Recommended is the 20-day-aged, bone-in rib-eye steak, seared to order in the restaurant's 1,800-degree broiler. Sushi, appetizers and entrées are half off Sunday-Monday 5-6 pm (first come, first serve) and 25 percent off Tuesday-Saturday 5:30-6 pm. Late-night dining and karaoke is offered Friday-Saturday, 9:30 pm-midnight. **Features:** full bar, early bird specials, happy hour. **Reservations:** suggested. **Address:** 201 Waikoloa Beach Dr, Suite 801 96738 **Location:** Off SR 19, 17 mi n of Kona International Airport, just e on Waikoa Beach Dr; in Queens' MarketPlace.

THE THREE FAT PIGS

808/339-7145

Pacific Rim. Casual Dining. $12-$39 **AAA Inspector Notes:** As one might get from this restaurant's name, pork figures heavy on the menu and anything featuring it is a great choice. To get a good sampling of what the chef can do, maybe stick to small plates with a selection from the charcuterie, some tempura asparagus, the roasted bone marrow and a pub house salad. While the pear brown Betty and adult s'mores make great desserts, try a scoop of the ice cream or sorbet for something lighter and delightful. **Features:** full bar, patio dining. **Reservations:** suggested. **Address:** 69-250 Waikoloa Beach Dr 96738 **Location:** 17 mi n of Kona International Airport on SR 19, 0.4 mi w; in The King's Shops; in Waikoloa Beach resort area.

WAIMEA (F-10) pop. 9,212, elev. 2,669'

Waimea, also called Kamuela to distinguish it from the town of Waimea on Kaua'i, is on the Waimea Plateau. The surrounding region is primarily ranching country.

Two scenic roads lead northwest to Hāwī. SR 270 skirts the coast; SR 250 winds through the Kohala Mountains.

Six miles south, Saddle Road (SR 200) leaves the Māmalahoa Highway and traverses the high pass between Mauna Kea and Mauna Loa. The road has sharp curves and occasional heavy fog, so check conditions locally before starting out.

Guests can dance the *hula* and sample the traditional foods of the islands at the Mauna Kea Hawaiian Lū'au at Mauna Kea Resort's Mauna Kea Beach Hotel on Tuesday and Friday evenings; phone (808) 882-5707.

In February the 🐦 Waimea Cherry Blossom Heritage Festival imbues the island with the heritage of Japan. Celebrants come together for a heritage fair, pageant and coronation ball, as well as demonstrations of the tea ceremony and the Japanese art of flower arranging.

Big Island Visitors Bureau West Hawai'i Office: 68-1330 Mauna Lani Dr., Suite 109B, Kohala Coast, HI 96743. **Phone:** (808) 885-1655 or (800) 648-2441.

ANNA RANCH HERITAGE CENTER is at 65-1480 Kawaihae Rd. Named for late owner and beloved community leader Anna Lindsey Perry-Fiske, the property offers a peek into the lives of an early 20th-century ranching family. Visitors can take a self-guiding grounds tour and watch a blacksmith and a saddle maker at work.

The circa 1910 ranch house, which may be seen only on a guided tour, is furnished in period and contains *koa* wood furniture, family photographs and collections of saddles, millinery and fine china. **Time:** Allow 1 hour minimum. **Hours:** Grounds Tues.-Fri. 10-3. Home tours Tues.-Fri. at 10 and 1; reservations are required. Closed major holidays. **Cost:** Grounds free. Home tour $10. **Phone:** (808) 885-4426.

SUNSHINE HELICOPTERS departs from Hāpuna Heliport at the nearby Hāpuna Beach Prince Hotel; hotel pickup and return is available from all major resorts in the Waikoloa and Kohala Coast area. Narrated helicopter tours of the Hāmākua coastline, hidden valleys and waterfalls are offered. Tours last between 35 minutes and 1 hour, 45 minutes.

Note: Due to decompression-related sickness, it is recommended that passengers wait 12-24 hours after scuba diving before flying; the amount of time is dependent on particular dive factors. Ask about possible policies regarding minimum wait time between scuba diving and flying; weight restrictions; weather, cancellation and refund policies; and the minimum and maximum number of passengers for flights. All small aircraft may encounter turbulence.

Hours: Flights depart daily; phone for schedule. **Cost:** $199-$635, depending on tour, helicopter and seating. Reservations are required. **Phone:** (808) 882-1223 or (800) 469-3000. 🔲

RECREATIONAL ACTIVITIES
Horseback Riding

- **Na'alapa Stables** meets at Kahua Ranch Ltd., 59-564 Kohala Mountain Rd. **Hours:** Guided trips lasting 2.5 hours depart daily at 9 and 1. Trips lasting 1.5 hours depart at 10 and 1:30. **Phone:** (808) 889-0022.

BIG ISLAND BREWHAUS   808/887-1717

♥♥ Mexican. Casual Dining. $7-$12 **AAA Inspector Notes:** Handcrafted beer and soda and a bamboo beer garden are featured at this brewpub. The menu features tasty burritos. Live music is offered three nights a week. **Features:** full bar, patio dining, happy hour. **Address:** 64-1066 Mamalahoa Hwy 96743 **Location:** On SR 190; jct Kamamalu; center. Ⓛ Ⓓ

MERRIMAN'S WAIMEA   808/885-6822

♥♥♥ Pacific Rim. Fine Dining. $11-$49 **AAA Inspector Notes:** The elegant décor, attentive staff and, most importantly, the well-executed menu using locally sourced organic ingredients make for a memorable dining experience. The lunch menu features casual fare. There is a three-course prix fix menu for $69. **Features:** full bar. **Reservations:** suggested. **Address:** 65-1227 Opelo Rd 96743 **Location:** On SR 19, just w of jct SR 190; in Opelo Plaza. Ⓛ Ⓓ Ⓚ

Island of Kaua'i

Kīlauea Lighthouse and Kīlauea Point National Wildlife Refuge, Kīlauea

The popular name for Kaua'i (ka-WA-ee) is "The Garden Isle" due to its lush vegetation and agricultural bounty. Its complete ancient name was *Kaua'i-a-mano-ka-la-ni-po,* "the fountainhead of many waters from on high and bubbling up from below." Fourth-largest and northernmost of the major Hawaiian Islands, Kaua'i was the first to be free of volcanic activity.

Historically, Kaua'i is believed to be the first populated island of the group, with the *Menehune* being the first known settlers. Legend has given these diminutive people many elfin characteristics and supernatural powers. They were supposedly stocky and muscular and 2 to 3 feet tall with unusually large abdomens. Their engineering feats, such as Menehune Ditch near Waimea, were probably the result of industriousness, cooperative working habits and population size, which some estimates place at nearly a half million at one time. The decline and final disappearance of the *Menehune* is still the subject of much speculation.

Kaua'i's distance from the other islands was its saving grace during Kamehameha the Great's conquest of the islands—he never reached it. Possibly foreseeing the inevitable, the king of Kaua'i reluctantly gave Kamehameha the island and its satellite Ni'ihau in 1810.

The remains of an 1817 Russian fort overlooking Waimea Bay are indicative of 19th-century interest in the Sandwich Islands. Christianity arrived somewhat later: Missions were founded at Hānalei and Kōloa in the mid-1800s. It is said that a Union vessel hid in the Wailua River from the Confederate ship *Shenandoah,* which had been dispatched to destroy the northern Pacific whaling fleet.

The first successful sugar plantation in Hawai'i, established at Kōloa in 1835, foreshadowed an economic trend that has continued to the present. Tourism ranks first among the island's industries, with sugar, coffee, beef, papaya and other exotic fruit also important. Kaua'i has the state's only remaining commercial taro fields. High technology and the Pacific Missile Range Facility (PMRF) round out Kaua'i's economic base. A 3,400-acre former sugar plantation is now the largest American coffee plantation; a visitor center welcomes guests. Together these products support the island's population of about 65,000.

About 6 million years ago a single volcano broke the surface of the sea, building upon itself in successive eruptions until it covered

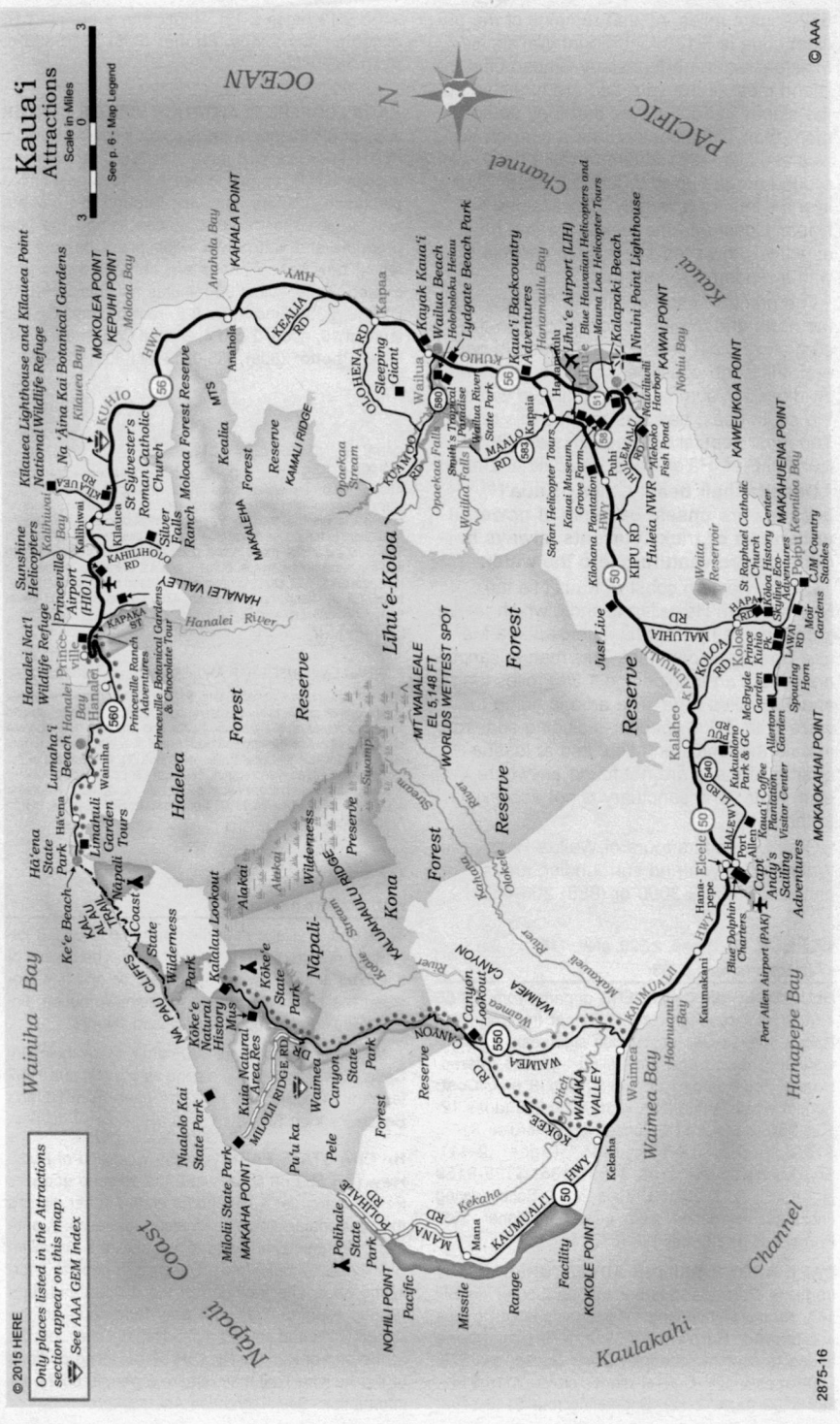

© 2015 HERE

Only places listed in the Attractions section appear on this map.

▽ See AAA GEM Index

Kaua'i Attractions

Scale in Miles
See p. 6 - Map Legend

N

OCEAN

PACIFIC

Kaua'i Channel

Kaua'i

552 square miles. All that remains of the ancient cone is 5,148-foot Mount Wai'ale'ale. Moisture-laden northeasterly winds buffet the island most of the year and are funneled up the slopes in such a way that they dump more than 460 inches of rain a year on Wai'ale'ale. Over time, these torrents have eroded gorges up to 3,000 feet deep. The island's interior is largely inaccessible; the Nāpali Coast and the Alaka'i Swamp have effectively thwarted attempts to encircle it with a modern road system.

The primary resort areas are Princeville to the north, the Wailua coconut coast in the east and Po'ipū on the south coast. In general, the north coast beaches are best for swimming in summer and surfing in winter; the south coast beaches reverse this rule. The most popular safe beaches are Po'ipū, Hānalei Pier, Hā'ena and Kalapaki at Līhu'e.

Despite their beauty, many Kaua'i beaches are unsafe because of powerful undertows or tricky currents; always inquire before venturing into the water.

Off the western coast of Kaua'i lie the Northwestern Hawaiian Islands, which together make up Papahānaumokuākea Marine National Monument. This marine sanctuary covers an archipelago 1,200 miles long and 100 miles wide. The area is home to more than 7,000 species, including seabirds, marine mammals and fish, and at least a quarter of these are not found anywhere else. **Note:** The sanctuary is not accessible to the public.

Gray Line offers tours of Wailua River, Waimea Canyon and surrounding areas; phone (808) 833-3000 or (888) 206-4531.

ELEELE (B-1) pop. 2,390, elev. 118'
• Attractions map p. 63

BLUE DOLPHIN CHARTERS departs from SR 50 s. (toward the ocean) on SR 541 at the Port Allen Harbor Marina Center. Various sightseeing, whale-watching, scuba and snorkeling trips are offered. **Hours:** Tours depart daily 6:30 a.m.-8 p.m. Sunset whale watch (Nov.-Apr.) $75; $70 (ages 12-17); $55 (ages 2-11). Sunset dinner cruise $105; $100 (ages 12-17); $85 (ages 2-11). Snorkeling/scuba tours $139-$185; $129-$159 (ages 12-17); $99-$139 (ages 2-11). Scuba diving (includes instruction and gear) additional $39. **Phone:** (808) 335-5553 or (877) 511-1311.

CAPT. ANDY'S SAILING ADVENTURES departs from the Port Allen Harbor Marina Center on SR 541. Various sightseeing, sailing and snorkeling trips are offered. **Hours:** Daily 7 a.m.-9 p.m. Phone ahead to confirm schedule. **Cost:** Sunset sail $79; $59 (ages 2-12). Sunset dinner cruise $119-$149; $89-$109 (ages 2-12). Snorkeling tour $149-$169;

$109-$119 (ages 2-12). Under age 2 are not permitted on some trips. **Phone:** (808) 335-6833 or (800) 535-0830.

KAUA'I COFFEE PLANTATION VISITOR CENTER is w. on SR 50 then s. on SR 540, following signs to 870 Halewili Rd. With more than 3,100 acres in production, this is reputed to be Hawai'i's largest coffee plantation. Visitors can walk through the orchard and in the visitor center they can sample the final products and watch two video presentations detailing how coffee beans are harvested and processed. **Time:** Allow 30 minutes minimum. **Hours:** Daily 9-5:30, June-Aug.; 9-5, rest of year. Guided tours at 10, noon, 2 and 4. Closed Christmas. **Cost:** Free. **Phone:** (808) 335-0813 or (800) 545-8605. GT

KAUAI ISLAND BREWERY & GRILL · 808/335-0006
American. Casual Dining. $12-$25 **AAA Inspector Notes:** After a day on the water, come on into this open warehouse that stays fairly cool with ocean breezes passing through both sides of open doors. Billed as the "world's westernmost brewery," they usually have eight to ten house-made beers on tap, plus several guest taps. The fairly expansive menu has a great selection of pupus, chicken and fish sandwiches, wraps, burgers and full entrées of island-fresh fish, pork and steak. Don't forget the Kauai sand pie for dessert. **Features:** full bar, happy hour. **Address:** 4350 Waialo Rd 96705 **Location:** Jct SR 50, just s; in Port Allen Marina Center. L D K

PORT ALLEN SUNSET BAR AND GRILL · 808/335-3188
American. Casual Dining. $12-$25 **AAA Inspector Notes:** Locals gather at this casual watering hole to enjoy a bite to eat and some live music on Wednesday, Friday and Saturday. Most people choose to sit out on the covered deck where they can see the distant sunset and watch the local traffic come and go. Get a taste of the local flavors with an island martini. The chef's special catch of the day is always a good choice. **Features:** full bar, happy hour. **Address:** 4353 Waialo Rd, Suite 7A 96705 **Location:** Jct SR 50, just s; in Port Allen Marina Center. L D

HĀ'ENA (A-2) pop. 431, elev. 22'
• Attractions map p. 63

Hā'ena, a village near the north end of SR 56, offers snorkeling, swimming and hiking. The beauty of this area is idyllic rather than majestic and has provided the appealing setting for several motion pictures, including "South Pacific" and "North."

With a depth of about 300 yards, Maniniholo Dry Cave is partially filled with sand as a result of a 1957 tsunami. Visitors can view the cave from Hā'ena Beach Park on SR 560.

HĀ'ENA STATE PARK is at the west end of Kūhiō Hwy. (SR 560). It is said that the volcano goddess Pele's search for a new home ended in her digging the Waikapalae and Waikanaloa wet caves. A path along the shoreline leads to the site of a Hawaiian *hula heiau* (temple). Ke'e Beach is a popular snorkeling spot. The trailhead of the difficult and dangerous Kalalau Trail, the only land route to the remote cliffs and valleys of the Nāpali Coast, begins at the end of Kūhiō Hwy. (SR 560). Hiking portions of the Kalalau Trail may require a permit; phone for information. *See Recreation Areas Chart.*

Note: The park's caves are not safe to enter; view from cave openings. The Kalalau Trail is often muddy and slippery, and hikers should be aware of tree roots, rocks and stream crossings. Flash flooding is possible on the trail. *Heiau* are culturally significant and should be treated with respect. Restrooms and drinking water are available at the park. **Hours:** Daily dawn-dusk. **Phone:** (808) 274-3444. ⊠ 🛆

LIMAHULI GARDEN TOURS is .5 mi. w. of Hā'ena Beach Park on SR 560. This conservation garden offers a close look at native foliage and ancient terraces. The garden lies in a valley surrounded by green cliffs eroded by wind and rain.

Allow 1 hour, 30 minutes for self-guiding tour and 2 hours, 30 minutes for guided tour. **Hours:** Tues.-Sat. 9:30-4. Guided tours Tues.-Sat. at 10. **Cost:** Guided tour $40; $20 (ages 10-12). Self-guiding tour $20; free (ages 0-18 with paying adult). Guided tour not recommended for children under age 10. Reservations are required for the guided tour. **Phone:** (808) 826-1053.

NĀPALI COAST STATE WILDERNESS PARK, on the northwest coast 5 mi. w. from Hānalei Landing, is accessible by the difficult and dangerous 11-mile Kalalau Trail *(see Hā'ena State Park)*. The park includes the coastal area from Hā'ena to Miloli'i Valley as well as the Nu'alolo and Kalalau valley regions, all with small beaches at the base of lava cliffs. Archeological sites of Nu'alolo Kai's and Nāpali's early settlers are along the park's rugged hiking trails; Nu'alolo Kai is accessible only by boat. It is a 2-mile hike to Hanakāpī'ai Valley and Beach. *See Recreation Areas Chart.*

Note: The Kalalau Trail is often muddy and slippery, and hikers should be aware of tree roots, rocks and stream crossings. Flash flooding is possible on the trail. **Due to unpredictable ocean currents, swimming and wading along the Nāpali Coast beaches are not recommended September through May.** Camping permits are required beyond Hanakoa Valley. **Hours:** Daily dawn-dusk. **Cost:** Free. Camping permit $20 per person, per night; $15 (Hawai'i residents). **Phone:** (808) 274-3444. 🅰 ⊠ 🛆

HANALEI (A-2) pop. 450, elev. 13'
• Attractions map p. 63

Hanalei's colorful history embraces whalers and traders who docked at the bustling harbor for supplies. Once supported by the sugar industry, the town is now a visitor center with shops and eateries. Hanalei Valley can be viewed from two lookouts on Kūhiō Highway.

LUMAHA'I BEACH, 2 mi. w. on SR 560, is a small beach along Hanalei Bay where Mitzi Gaynor sudsed her way through "I'm Gonna Wash That Man Right Outa My Hair" in "South Pacific"; it is among the most photographed spots in the islands. **Due to strong currents and undertows, swimming in these waters is dangerous and should not be attempted at any time of the year. Hours:** Daily 24 hours. **Cost:** Free. **Phone:** (808) 245-3971.

HANALEI COLONY RESORT   808/826-6235

fyi Not evaluated. **Address:** 5-7130 Kuhio Hwy 96714 **Location:** 5 mi w on SR 560 to Haena. Facilities, services, and décor characterize a mid-scale property. On the North Shore, this tranquil oceanfront resort offers two-bedroom condos with kitchens.

WHERE TO EAT

BAR ACUDA   808/826-7081

▼▼▼ Mediterranean Small Plates. Fine Dining. $12-$26 **AAA Inspector Notes:** Still the hottest spot on the North Shore, with a refined casual atmosphere in a candlelit room. The tapas are great for sharing and artfully prepared in an open kitchen with a chef's counter for those who enjoy watching the action. Fresh local seafood and meats and organic produce are utilized whenever possible, and the breads are house-made. Reservations are recommended, and many request to be seated on the covered outdoor wraparound porch. **Features:** full bar, patio dining. **Address:** 5-5161 Kuhio Hwy 96714 **Location:** Center. **Parking:** on-site and street. D 🎶

BOUCHONS HANALEI GRILL & SUSHI BAR   808/826-9701

▼▼ Pacific Rim Sushi. Casual Dining. $11-$26 **AAA Inspector Notes:** This restaurant is located on the second floor of the Ching Young Village, so be sure to request a window table for spectacular views of the Hanalei mountains and the cascading waterfalls. The menu is decidedly Pacific, with a little French influence, and has a full sushi bar. This place offers a little something for everyone, along with tasty cocktails served in a relaxed atmosphere. **Features:** full bar, patio dining, happy hour. **Address:** 5-5190 Kuhio Hwy 96714 **Location:** Center. L D CALL 🎶M 🎶

BUBBA'S BURGERS   808/826-7839

▼ Burgers. Quick Serve. $5-$10 **AAA Inspector Notes:** This old-fashioned hamburger place serves 88-percent fat-free Kauai beef, along with hot dogs, fries and milk shakes made with real ice cream. The deck looks out to the street scene. **Address:** 5-5161 Kuhio Hwy 96714 **Location:** Center. **Parking:** on-site and street. L D 🎶

THE HANALEI DOLPHIN RESTAURANT, FISH MARKET & SUSHI LOUNGE   808/826-6113

▼▼ Seafood. Casual Dining. $8-$38 **AAA Inspector Notes:** Located along the banks of the Hanalei River, this is a popular stop with locals and tourists on this side of the island. The décor is simple, the atmosphere relaxed and the food fresh and tasty. Select from an all-day pupu menu or a light lunch menu with dishes such as fish and chips and fin burgers. Dinner entrées include preparations of fish, lobster, chicken or steak, all served with family-style salad and home-made bread. **Features:** full bar, patio dining. **Address:** 5-5016 Kuhio Hwy 96714 **Location:** SR 560; at entrance of town. L D CALL 🎶M 🎶

MEDITERRANEAN GOURMET   808/826-9875

▼▼▼ Mediterranean. Casual Dining. $24-$35 **AAA Inspector Notes:** Mediterranean cuisine with an island flair is prepared with fresh, local ingredients whenever possible. Wonderful ocean views are offered, as is nightly live music. An oceanfront luau is offered on Tuesday and reservations are required. **Features:** full bar, patio dining, Sunday brunch, happy hour. **Reservations:** suggested. **Address:** 5-7132 Kuhio Hwy 96714 **Location:** 5 mi w on SR 560 to Haena; in Hanalei Colony Resort. L D CALL 🎶M

POSTCARDS CAFE   808/826-1191

▼▼▼ Pacific Rim Seafood. Casual Dining. $19-$34 **AAA Inspector Notes:** Island-inspired seafood and organic vegetarian dishes cooked with the freshest ingredients have been served in this charming 1860s-era plantation cottage for more than 15 years. The restaurant opens nightly at 6 pm, and while reservations are recommended they are only accepted for parties of four or more. Smaller parties should arrive early or be prepared for a long wait. Diners have a choice of the covered outdoor porch, enclosed patio or intimate dining room. **Features:** beer & wine, patio dining. **Address:** 5-5075 Kuhio Hwy 96714 **Location:** Center. **Parking:** on-site and street. D CALL 🎶M 🎶

HANAMAULU (B-2) pop. 3,835, elev. 397'
• Attractions map p. 63

RECREATIONAL ACTIVITIES
Tubing
• **Kaua'i Backcountry Adventures** departs from 3-4131 Kūhiō Hwy. Other activities are offered. **Hours:** Tubing trips through an old sugar cane plantation irrigation ditch and tunnel system depart daily on the hour 9-10 and 1-2. Closed half-day Jan. 1 and Thanksgiving, all day Christmas. Phone ahead to confirm schedule. **Phone:** (808) 245-2506 or (888) 270-0555.

HANAPĒPĒ (B-1) pop. 2,638, elev. 20'

Easygoing Hanapēpē has not always been so. In 1924, 20 people died in a fracas between striking sugarcane workers and police. The community is now known for its art galleries and the beauty of its setting. From a vantage point west of town on SR 50 unfolds a vista of Hanapēpē Valley and its taro patches. The rim of Waimea Canyon is visible to the west.

South off Lele Road, the ancient Hawai'i Salt Ponds still are used to produce salt from sea water. In the Kaumakani (windswept) area west of Hanapēpē, the rich, red soil not only produces excellent sugar crops but also gives a red tinge to nearly everything in the vicinity.

KALĀHEO (B-2) pop. 4,595, elev. 700'
• Attractions map p. 63

Kaua'i coffee has supplanted the sugarcane that once was the primary yield of the rolling green valley surrounding Kalāheo. The town is quietly reminiscent of Hawai'i's plantation era.

KUKUIOLONO PARK AND GOLF COURSE, 1 mi. s. off SR 50, following signs, offers Japanese gardens, panoramic ocean and mountain views as well as a collection of legendary stones reputedly gathered and arranged by the *Menehune* people. The park was part of the estate of sugar magnate Walter McBryde, who is buried near the 8th hole of the public golf course. **Hours:** Park daily dawn-dusk. **Cost:** Park free. A fee is charged for the golf course. **Phone:** (808) 332-9151.

KALAHEO INN   808/332-6023
[fyi] Not evaluated. **Address:** 4444 Papalina Rd 96741 **Location:** Jct SR 50, just s. Facilities, services, and décor characterize an economy property.

Ask about on-the-spot
vehicle battery testing
and replacement

BRICK OVEN PIZZA   808/332-8561
▼▼ Pizza. Casual Dining. $10-$32 **AAA Inspector Notes:** This place has been pleasing patrons since 1977 with its hearth-baked pizzas with homemade flavor that come on whole wheat or white crusts. Garlic butter can be brushed onto the edges of the pizza for added flavor. Hot sandwiches and an all-you-can-eat buffet are available on Monday and Thursday nights. **Features:** full bar, happy hour. **Address:** 2-2555 Kaumualii Hwy 96741 **Location:** On SR 50; center. [L] [D]

KALAHEO CAFE & COFFEE CO   808/332-5858
▼▼ ▼▼ American. Casual Dining. $13-$29 **AAA Inspector Notes:** Just 10 minutes from Poipu, this neighborhood cafe serves breakfast favorites, fresh deli sandwiches at lunch and dinner specials featuring island seafood. Dinner is served Wednesday through Saturday. **Features:** beer & wine, patio dining. **Address:** 2-2560 Kaumualii Hwy 96741 **Location:** On SR 50; center.
[B] [L] [D] CALL [M] [K]

KALAHEO STEAK & RIBS   808/332-4444
▼▼ Steak. Casual Dining. $16-$33 **AAA Inspector Notes:** Looking for that classic small-town restaurant with warm décor and a friendly staff that probably knows every local on a first-name basis when they walk through the door? This is it. If not in the mood for a steak, there are several fish, chicken, pasta and pork dishes to provide variety. Homemade potato skins calm the hunger pangs as you decide between the rib-eye steak, roasted prime rib or baby back pork ribs. The Molokai sweet bread pudding with Irish cream sauce is a perfect finish. **Features:** full bar, happy hour. **Address:** 4444 Papalina Rd 96741 **Location:** Jct SR 50, just s. **Parking:** street only.
[D]

THE RIGHT SLICE   808/212-5798
[fyi] Not evaluated. Looking for a local favorite for dessert? Then leave the tourist-crowded beach and head to this little pie shop. The whole pies and slices of tropical delight are prepared like only a local can. A crowd pleaser is the tropical trio with pineapple, mango and candied ginger. **Address:** 2-2459 Kaumualii Hwy 96741 **Location:** Center.

KAPA'A (A-2) pop. 10,699

At the north end of Kaua'i's Coconut Coast, Kapa'a is the island's largest city. It evolved from a string of fishing villages and 1913-1960 it was an important pineapple-canning center. The architecture in Kapa'a's central district, surrounding the junction of SR 56 and CR 581, reflects its role as a plantation town.

RECREATIONAL ACTIVITIES
Horseback Riding
• **Esprit De Corps Riding Academy** is near Kapa'a. **Hours:** Guided horseback ecotours depart daily; phone for schedule. Closed major holidays. **Phone:** (808) 822-4688.

Kayaking
• **Kayak Kaua'i** is at the Wailua River Marina, 3-5971 Kūhiō Hwy. Other activities are offered. **Hours:** Daily 7-5. **Phone:** (808) 826-9844 or (888) 596-3853.

ASTON ISLANDER ON THE BEACH   (808)822-7417
▼▼ ▼▼ Hotel $175-$359 **Address:** 440 Aleka Pl 96746 **Location:** Oceanfront. Jct SR 580, 0.8 mi n on SR 56. Located near Coconut MarketPlace Shopping Center. **Facility:** 118 units. 3 stories (no elevator), exterior corridors. **Terms:** 3 day cancellation notice-fee imposed, resort fee. **Amenities:** video games, safes. **Pool(s):** outdoor. **Activities:** hot tub. **Guest Services:** coin laundry. *(See ad starting on p. 148.)* [icons]

COURTYARD BY MARRIOTT KAUAI AT COCONUT BEACH
(808)822-3455

 Hotel $119–$263 **Address:** 650 Aleka Loop 96746 **Location:** Oceanfront. Jct SR 580, 0.8 mi n on SR 56. Located near Coconut MarketPlace Shopping Center. **Facility:** 311 units. 4 stories, interior corridors. **Parking:** on-site and valet. **Terms:** 7 day cancellation notice, resort fee. **Amenities:** video games, safes. **Pool(s):** outdoor. **Activities:** hot tub, tennis, exercise room, spa. **Guest Services:** valet and coin laundry.

AAA Benefit: Members save 5% or more!

[icons]

KAUAI COAST RESORT AT THE BEACHBOY
808/822-3441

 Condominium. Rates not provided. **Address:** 520 Aleka Loop 96746 **Location:** Oceanfront. Jct SR 580, 0.8 mi on SR 56. Adjacent to Coconut MarketPlace Shopping Center. **Facility:** 108 condominiums. 3 stories (no elevator), interior corridors. **Terms:** check-in 4 pm. **Amenities:** safes. **Dining:** Hukilau Lanai, see separate listing, entertainment. **Pool(s):** heated outdoor. **Activities:** hot tub, bicycles, exercise room, spa. **Guest Services:** complimentary laundry.

[icons]

PLANTATION HALE SUITES
(808)822-4941

Vacation Rental Condominium
$99–$299

Address: 525 Aleka Loop 96746 **Location:** Jct SR 580, 0.8 mi n on SR 56. Located in Coconut MarketPlace Shopping Center. **Facility:** These self-contained, spacious condominium units each have a lanai or patio. Shopping, restaurants and the beach are just a short walk away. 84 condominiums. 2 stories (no elevator), interior corridors. **Terms:** 7 day cancellation notice-fee imposed, resort fee. **Amenities:** safes. **Pool(s):** outdoor. **Activities:** hot tub. **Guest Services:** valet and coin laundry.
(See ad p. 68.)

[icons]

KAUAI SHORES
808/822-4951

(fyi) Not evaluated. **Address:** 420 Papaloa Rd 96746 **Location:** Oceanfront. Jct SR 580, 0.8 mi n on SR 56. Facilities, services, and décor characterize an economy property.

WAIPOULI BEACH RESORT & SPA KAUAI BY OUTRIGGER
808/823-1401

(fyi) Condominium Did not meet all AAA rating requirements for locking devices in some guest rooms at time of last evaluation on 04/30/2015. **Address:** 4-820 Kuhio Hwy 96746 **Location:** Oceanfront. On SR 56; downtown. Facilities, services, and décor characterize a mid-scale property. Luxury awaits at these modern beachfront condos with top-of-the-line appliances. The lush tropical landscaping includes a heated saltwater pool and a meandering lazy river-style pool.

WHERE TO EAT

BRICK OVEN PIZZA
808/823-8561

 Pizza. Casual Dining. $10–$32 **AAA Inspector Notes:** This company has been pleasing patrons since 1977 with its hearth-baked pizzas with homemade flavor that come on whole wheat or white crusts. Garlic butter can be brushed onto the edges of the pizza for added flavor. Hot sandwiches and an all-you-can-eat buffet are featured on Monday and Thursday nights. **Features:** full bar, happy hour. **Address:** 4-361 Kuhio Hwy 96746 **Location:** Jct SR 580, just n on SR 56; just s of Coconut MarketPlace Shopping Center.

[icons] L D CALL

BUBBA'S BURGERS
808/823-0069

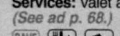 Burgers. Quick Serve. $4–$9 **AAA Inspector Notes:** This old-fashioned hamburger place serves 88-percent fat-free Kauai beef, along with hot dogs, fries and milk shakes made with real ice cream. The deck looks out to the street scene and offers ocean views. **Features:** patio dining. **Address:** 4-1421 Kuhio Hwy 96746 **Location:** Just n on SR 56; in old Kapaa town; across from Kapaa Beach Park. [icons] L D

HUKILAU LANAI
808/822-0600

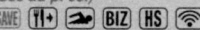
Seafood
Casual Dining
$19–$32

AAA Inspector Notes: With special treats such as 20 great wines for $20-something, nightly pupu creations and savory fresh Kauai cuisine of locally caught fish along with evening entertainment and views of the ocean, this restaurant entices patrons to linger. **Features:** full bar, patio dining, happy hour. **Reservations:** suggested. **Address:** 520 Aleka Loop 96746 **Location:** Jct SR 580, 0.8 mi n on SR 56; in Kauai Coast Resort at the Beachboy. [icons] D CALL

LEMONGRASS GRILL SEAFOOD & BAR
808/821-2888

Seafood. Casual Dining. $15–$27 **AAA Inspector Notes:** Feeling more like a lodge or rustic tavern with wood-paneled walls and varnished wood tables, you have to remind yourself you're right downtown. While the menu leans to seafood with scallops, shrimp, ono and bass, there are several meat choices, including guava barbecue ribs for the land lover along with some curries and a few vegetarian dishes. Relaxed service and nightly entertainment. **Features:** full bar, patio dining. **Address:** 4-871 Kuhio Hwy 96746 **Location:** On SR 56; in Choy Village Shopping Center. [icons] D CALL

OASIS ON THE BEACH
808/822-9332

American. Casual Dining. $13–$32 **AAA Inspector Notes:** The creative menu at this casual oceanfront restaurant features local products and is a fusion of Asian and Hawaiian cuisines. **Features:** full bar, patio dining, Sunday brunch, happy hour. **Reservations:** suggested. **Address:** 4-820 Kuhio Hwy 96746 **Location:** On SR 56; in Outrigger Waipouli Beach Resort & Spa. [icons] L D CALL

OLYMPIC CAFE
808/822-5825

American. Casual Dining. $13–$27 **AAA Inspector Notes:** Centrally located in the heart of downtown, this second-floor restaurant offers great views of the bustling street scene. This is a great place to people-watch and enjoy huge portions of traditional American fare selected from an expansive menu. This place is sure to offer something to please everyone in your group. There's a parking lot behind the building. **Features:** full bar. **Address:** 1354 Kuhio Hwy 96746 **Location:** Center. [icons] B L D CALL

WAHOOO SEAFOOD GRILL & BAR
808/822-7833

Seafood. Casual Dining. $13–$49 **AAA Inspector Notes:** Fresh seafood, steak and pasta dishes are served in a relaxed, island-style setting. Guests would need a snorkel to see more fish. The restaurant is just east of the Coconut Marketplace Shopping Center. **Features:** full bar, patio dining, happy hour. **Reservations:** suggested. **Address:** 4-733 Kuhio Hwy 96746 **Location:** On SR 56 at Pouli Rd. [icons] L D

THE BULL SHED
808/822-3791

(fyi) Not evaluated. It's easy to miss the driveway entrance to this restaurant in the Mokihana condo complex—look for the McDonald's, and it's right across the street. This local favorite has been around since 1973 in the same location. You can gaze out at the ocean while dining. Prices are reasonable for steaks and seafood and a trip to the salad bar. Be sure to arrive early to avoid waiting for a table; the restaurant accepts reservations for large parties only. **Address:** 796 Kuhio Hwy 96746 **Location:** On SR 56.

KAPAIA (B-2) elev. 154'
• Attractions map p. 63

WAILUA FALLS is 3.9 mi. n. off Kūhiō Hwy. on SR 583 (Māʻalo Rd.), following signs. The 80-foot falls figured prominently in the lives of ancient Hawaiian chiefs. More recently, the falls were shown during

A Boutique Hotel in the Heart of Kauai's Royal Coconut Coast

the opening credits of the television show "Fantasy Island." **Hours:** Daily 24 hours. **Cost:** Free. **Phone:** (808) 274-3444.

KĪLAUEA (A-2) pop. 2,803, elev. 300'
• **Attractions map p. 63**

Off the coast of Kīlauea, porpoises, sea turtles, Hawaiian monk seals and humpback whales often are spotted within 100 yards of shore during the winter and spring.

St. Sylvester's Roman Catholic Church, off SR 56, employs unusual architectural styles. The octagonal church, which seats 150, is made of lava rock and wood; its design is similar to that of a theater in the round. The interior frescoes are by noted WPA muralist Jean Charlot, whose works adorn public buildings on the mainland and in Mexico City; phone (808) 822-7900.

KĪLAUEA LIGHTHOUSE AND KĪLAUEA POINT NATIONAL WILDLIFE REFUGE is off Kolo Rd. at the end of Kīlauea Lighthouse Rd. The 52-foot lighthouse was built in 1913 and was in use until 1976. A visitor center showcases the structure's history and lighthouse keepers. The wildlife refuge is home to the Laysan albatross, frigate birds and red-footed boobies. **Time:** Allow 1 hour minimum. **Hours:** Tues.-Sat. 10-4. Closed major holidays. **Cost:** $5; free (ages 0-15). Cash only. **Phone:** (808) 828-1413.

NA 'ĀINA KAI BOTANICAL GARDENS is on SR 56 between mileposts 21 and 22 at 4101 Wailapa Rd.; go .5 mi. e. on Wailapa Rd. to the visitor center entrance. This once-private 240-acre estate is a marvelous tapestry of 12 gardens and wild areas sprinkled with more than 130 life-size, representational and sometimes whimsical bronze sculptures.

Notable features include a three-quarter-acre lagoon with many colorful koi fish; a plant-shaped hedge maze in which unexpected flowers, topiaries and sculptures delight the wanderer; an international desert garden; a plantation of hardwood trees; a bog house; a beachside meadow; and a children's garden. The gardens may be viewed only on guided tours, which are led by knowledgeable guides and range from 90 minutes to 5 hours, depending on the tour.

Picnicking is not permitted. **Time:** Allow 2 hours minimum. **Hours:** Visitor center Tues.-Thurs. 8-5, Fri. 8-1. Formal gardens stroll departs Tues.-Thurs. at 9 and 1, Fri. at 9. Formal and wild forest garden ride departs Tues.-Thurs. at 9:30, Fri. at 9. Formal and wild forest garden stroll and ride departs Tues.-Fri. at 9. Walk on the Wild Side trek departs Tues.-Thurs. at 9:30 (reservations are required). Under the Rainbow family tour departs Tues.-Thurs. at 9:30 and 1:30, Fri. at 9:30. Seasonal Bird Tour departs Wed. at 8:30, Dec.-Apr. Closed Jan. 1, July 4, Thanksgiving, Christmas Eve, Christmas and Dec. 31.

Cost: Formal gardens stroll $35. Formal and wild forest garden ride $50. Formal and wild forest garden

stroll and ride $50. Walk on the Wild Side trek (includes lunch and reusable water bottle) $85. Under the Rainbow family tour $35; $20 (ages 2-12). Seasonal Bird Tour $60. Under age 13 are not permitted except on prearranged family tours. Reservations are strongly recommended. **Phone:** (808) 828-0525.

RECREATIONAL ACTIVITIES
Horseback Riding
• **Silver Falls Ranch** is at 2888 Kamookoa Rd. **Hours:** Guided horseback rides depart daily; phone for schedule. **Phone:** (808) 828-6718.

KŌLOA (B-2) pop. 2,144, elev. 200'
• **Restaurants p. 70**
• **Attractions map p. 63**

Kōloa blossomed after the first sugar mill on the island was erected in 1835. Its port, Kōloa Landing, rivaled Honolulu and Lahaina as a storage depot for whaling ships. The sugar mill no longer exists, and Kōloa, with its false-front buildings, seems a remnant from another time.

Kōloa History Center, in the Waikomo Shops off Kōloa Road, offers a glimpse into the town's past; phone (808) 245-7238.

ALLERTON GARDEN, 4425 Lāwai Rd., 2.5 mi. w. of Spouting Horn, once was part of the private estate of a Chicago businessman. Before that, it was a retreat for Hawai'i's Queen Emma. All tours include a 15-minute bus ride into the garden. Daily tours include a mildly paced 1-mile walk among tropical foliage, fountains, waterfalls and statuary. A Sunset Allerton Estate Tour also is offered.

The 3.5-hour Discovery Tour offers a behind-the-scenes look at conservation and research projects, Allerton Garden's riparian area and McBryde Garden's *(see attraction listing)* rain forest trail and waterfall.

Visitors should wear comfortable walking shoes and bring mosquito repellent, rain or sun protection and bottled water. Camera tripods are not permitted. Allow 2 hours, 30 minutes minimum for the guided tour. **Hours:** Visitor center daily 8-5. Daily tours departs on the hour 9-3. Sunset Allerton Estate Tour is offered Tues.-Sat.; phone for tour times. Discovery Tour is offered Mon., Wed. and Fri.; phone for tour times. Visitors must check in 30 minutes prior to departure.

Cost: Tour $40; $15 (ages 6-12). Sunset Allerton Estate Tour (includes appetizers and beverages) $80; $40 (ages 6-12). Discovery Tour (includes water, juice and snacks) $50; $25 (ages 6-12). Reservations are required. **Phone:** (808) 742-2623. GT

McBRYDE GARDEN is at 4425 Lāwai Rd. A 15-minute bus ride transports visitors to the tropical garden for a 1-mile self-guiding tour. The garden features an extensive collection of native and Polynesian plants, including spice plants, orchids and rare palms. Highlights include the Biodiversity Trail, a stream and the Canoe Garden.

The 3.5-hour guided Discovery Tour offers a behind-the-scenes look at conservation and research projects, McBryde Garden's rain forest trail and waterfall and Allerton Garden's *(see attraction listing)* riparian area.

Guests should wear comfortable walking shoes and bring mosquito repellent, rain or sun protection and water. **Hours:** Self-guiding tour buses depart on the half-hour daily 9:30-3:30. Discovery Tour is offered Mon., Wed. and Fri.; phone for tour times. Visitors must arrive at least 30 minutes prior to bus departure. **Cost:** Self-guiding tour $20; $10 (ages 6-12). Discovery Tour (includes water, juice and snacks) $50; $25 (ages 6-12). Reservations are required for the Discovery Tour. **Phone:** (808) 742-2623. GT

PRINCE KŪHIŌ PARK, 2.5 mi. s.w. on Po'ipū Rd., is a small park with a bust marking the 1871 birthplace of Jonah Kūhiō Kalaniana'ole, born of royal parentage and decreed prince in 1871. He worked to benefit the Hawaiian people and was Hawai'i's delegate to Congress 1902-22. **Hours:** Daily 24 hours. **Cost:** Free. **Phone:** (808) 241-4460.

ST. RAPHAEL CATHOLIC CHURCH is 1 blk. e. of jct. CR 520 and Kōloa Rd., .5 mi. s. on Weliweli Rd., then .5 mi. s. to 3011 Hapa Rd. Founded in 1841, this is the oldest Catholic church on Kaua'i. Its purpose was to serve the mission founded by Father Robert Arsenius Walsh, who received 17 acres of land from King Kamehameha III in 1843. Visitors can view the historic church, original chapel and grottoes. **Hours:** Office Mon.-Fri. 8:30-12:30. Services Mon.-Fri. at 7 a.m., Sat. at 5 p.m., Sun. at 7 and 9:30 a.m. **Cost:** Free. **Phone:** (808) 742-1955.

SPOUTING HORN is near the fire station; at the roundabout turn s.w. onto Lāwai (Beach) Rd. and go 2 mi. to the end of the road. A Welcome to Po'ipū Beach sign points to the spout. A fenced overlook provides viewing of the spout, which is formed when water from incoming waves rushes under a lava shelf and bursts through a small surface opening. A nearby blowhole emits a weird groan that local legend attributes to the hissing of a large lizard trapped within the lava tube.

Whales and dolphins sometimes can be seen from this site. The best time to see dolphins is in the mornings when they are more active. Whale season is generally December through April. **Hours:** Daily 24 hours. Vendors and restrooms are generally available 8-5. **Cost:** Free. **Phone:** (808) 742-7444 or (888) 744-0888.

RECREATIONAL ACTIVITIES
Horseback Riding

- **CJM Country Stables** is at the end of Po'ipū Rd. **Hours:** Maha'ulepu rides depart Mon.-Sat. at 9:30 and 2. Beach picnic rides depart Wed. and Fri. at 1. Closed major holidays. **Phone:** (808) 742-6096.

Ziplines

- **Just Live** is at 3416 Rice St., Suite 504. Other activities are offered. **Hours:** Trips depart Mon.-Sat.; phone for schedule. **Phone:** (808) 482-1295.

BUBBA'S BURGERS   808/742-6900

Burgers. Quick Serve. $4-$9 **AAA Inspector Notes:** This old-fashioned hamburger place serves 88-percent fat-free Kauai beef, along with hot dogs, fries and milk shakes made with real ice cream. The deck looks out to the street scene. **Address:** 2829 Ala Kalanikaumaka 96756 **Location:** In Shops at Kukui'ula Village; at Poipu roundabout. L D K

THE DOLPHIN POIPU   808/742-1414

Seafood. Casual Dining. $8-$38 **AAA Inspector Notes:** Located in a shopping area, this is a popular stop with locals and tourists. The décor is simple, the atmosphere relaxed and the food fresh and tasty. There's an all-day pupu menu or a light lunch menu with dishes such as fish and chips and fin burgers. Dinner entrées include preparations of fish, lobster, chicken and steak. A full selection of fresh sushi also is offered. **Features:** full bar, patio dining. **Address:** 2829 Ala Kalanikaumaka St 96756 **Location:** In Shops at Kukui'ula Village; at Poipu roundabout. L D K

EATING HOUSE 1849   808/742-5000

Pacific Rim. Casual Dining. $15-$40 **AAA Inspector Notes:** This restaurant is conveniently located in a pleasant shopping village, so plan ahead for a pre- or post-dinner stroll. With a great out-of-the-way second-floor location, guests who dine here are treated to a view of sweeping verdant fields and, possibly, a sunset. The rustic dining room feels somewhat like a warehouse with lights and rotating fans overhead. While the entrées are tasty and filling, I would choose to make a meal out of several pupus that can be shared by the table. **Features:** full bar. **Reservations:** suggested. **Address:** 2829 Ala Kalanikaumaka St, Suite A-201 96756 **Location:** At Poipu roundabout; in Shops at Kukui'ula Village. D K

JOSSELIN'S TAPAS BAR & GRILL   808/742-7117

Pacific Rim Small Plates. Casual Dining. $18-$30 **AAA Inspector Notes:** This contemporary dining room affords views of the open kitchen. The tapas creations are made for sharing, so bring lots of friends. The menu leans toward Asian fusion, with duck wontons, hoisin-braised short ribs and most everyone's favorite, the 36-hour braised pork belly. Served tableside, try one of the signature tropical sangrias made with passion fruit rum and lychees. **Features:** full bar, happy hour. **Reservations:** suggested. **Address:** 2829 Ala Kalanikaumaka St 96756 **Location:** In Shops at Kukui'ula Village; at Poipu roundabout. D

LA SPEZIA RESTAURANT AND WINE BAR   808/742-8824

Italian. Casual Dining. $18-$22 **AAA Inspector Notes:** At this interesting location lines form early for the traditional American breakfast. At night it becomes a rustic traditional Italian joint where the pasta is made fresh, the bar is hopping and the owner circulates through the room to make sure all of her patrons are satisfied. Reservations are typically not accepted, so plan to arrive early or expect a wait during the high season. **Features:** full bar, Sunday brunch. **Address:** 5492 Koloa Rd 96756 **Location:** Center. B D

MERRIMAN'S FISH HOUSE   808/742-8385

Pacific Rim Seafood. Fine Dining. $27-$50 **AAA Inspector Notes:** The second-floor location offers views of the distant mountains, ocean and even sunset. Settle back and enjoy; this is a meal that's meant to be savored. With most ingredients sourced from the islands, the fresh flavors enhance each dish. Pick and choose from the daily menu or perhaps the raw bar. For a sampling of appetizers, start with the pupu taster. The wok-charred ahi, salt-and-pepper New York steak and Colorado lamb chops keep the regulars returning. Gluten-free options are available. **Features:** full bar, patio dining. **Reservations:** suggested. **Address:** 2829 Ala Kalanikaumaka St, Suite G-149 96756 **Location:** In Shops at Kukui'ula Village; at Poipu roundabout. D CALL M

MERRIMAN'S GOURMET PIZZA & BURGERS   808/742-8385

▼▼ Burgers Pizza. Casual Dining. $11-$16 **AAA Inspector Notes:** A high-energy kind of place, this restaurant specializes in hand-tossed artisan pizzas, fired in a wood-burning oven, and gourmet burgers that can come with a side of cilantro-garlic fries. Choose a table on the patio and watch the shoppers wander past. **Features:** full bar, patio dining. **Address:** 2829 Ala Kalanikaumaka St, Suite G-149 96756 **Location:** In Shops at Kukui'ula Village; at Poipu roundabout. [L] [D] CALL [M] [X]

TORTILLA REPUBLIC   808/742-8884

▼▼ Mexican. Casual Dining. $16-$30 **AAA Inspector Notes:** The upbeat, casual eatery serves modern food and has a lively margarita bar downstairs and bit more peaceful dining scene upstairs. Plenty of patio seating is available on both levels. Start the meal with a salsa tasting offering three types of salsas with your fresh chips and then proceed to the sizzling jumbo tiger shrimp fajitas or short rib chile verde. **Features:** full bar, patio dining, Sunday brunch, happy hour. **Address:** 2829 Ala Kalanikaumaka St 96756 **Location:** In Shops at Kukui'ula Village; at Poipu roundabout.
[B] [L] [D] [X]

LĪHU'E (B-2) pop. 6,455, elev. 206'

- Hotels p. 74 • Restaurants p. 74
- Attractions map p. 63

County seat of Kaua'i and the neighbor island of Ni'ihau (not open to visitors), Līhu'e also is a cultural and business center. The 872-acre Līhu'e Airport lies about 1.5 miles east.

A number of 19th-century buildings along Rice Street, the main thoroughfare, house stores and offices. The Grove Farm museum, on Nāwiliwili Road, was acquired by George N. Wilcox in 1864 and depicts life on an old sugar plantation. Tours of the plantation home, buildings and grounds are available by appointment up to 3 months in advance; phone (808) 245-3202.

Kaua'i Visitors Bureau: 4334 Rice St., Suite 101, Līhu'e, HI 96766. **Phone:** (808) 245-3971 or (800) 262-1400.

'ALEKOKO FISH POND (Menehune Pond), on Hulemalu Rd. in nearby Niumalu, reputedly was built by the *Menehune,* Hawai'i's legendary "little people" who inhabited Kaua'i before the migrations from the Polynesian islands. It is said that the *Menehune* formed a 25-mile-long human chain and, passing stones to each other, finished the pond in one night. **Hours:** Daily 24 hours. **Cost:** Free.

BLUE HAWAIIAN HELICOPTERS departs from Līhu'e Heliport. Check-in is at Harbor Mall at 3501 Rice St., Unit 107; transportation to and from the airport is provided. Kaua'i's natural features, including Hanapēpē Valley, Waimea Canyon, Nāpali Coast and Mount Wai'ale'ale, are seen on the 50- to 55-minute Eco Adventure Tour. Passengers hear music, two-way communication with the pilot, and the pilot's narration via noise-canceling headsets.

Note: Due to decompression-related sickness, it is recommended that passengers wait 12-24 hours after scuba diving before flying; the amount of time is dependent on particular dive factors. Ask about possible policies regarding minimum wait time between scuba diving and flying; weight restrictions; weather, cancellation and refund policies; and the minimum and maximum number of passengers for flights. All small aircraft may encounter turbulence.

Hours: Tours depart daily on the hour 8-4. **Cost:** $239, plus applicable fuel surcharge. Reservations are required. **Phone:** (808) 245-5800 or (800) 745-2583. **(See ad on inside front cover.)**

KALAPAKĪ BEACH, 2 mi. e. on SR 51 at SR 58, at the left of the harbor, is a popular family spot and good for swimming, windsurfing, boogie boarding and surfing. Surf and sailboat lessons, catamaran cruises, kayak tours and sailboat rentals are available nearby. **Hours:** Daily dawn-dusk. **Cost:** Free. **Phone:** (808) 245-3971.

KAUA'I MUSEUM, 4428 Rice St., is a two-building complex offering exhibits, lectures and demonstrations that relate the history of Kaua'i and Ni'ihau. The Albert Spencer Wilcox Memorial Building, built from lava rock, and the William Hyde Rice Building feature thousands of stone, shell and feather artifacts; textiles; photographs; works of art; and natural-history video presentations.

Hours: Mon.-Sat. 10-5. Guided tours Mon.-Fri. at 10:30. Closed Jan. 1, Memorial Day, July 4, Labor Day, Thanksgiving and Christmas. Phone ahead to confirm schedule. **Cost:** $10; $8 (ages 65+ and Hawai'i residents with ID); $6 (ages 13-17); $2 (ages 6-12). **Phone:** (808) 245-6931. GT

KILOHANA PLANTATION is at 3-2087 Kaumuali'i Hwy. The 105-acre historic plantation and estate boasts a restored 16,000-square-foot Tudor-style mansion, gardens, fruit orchards and animal pastures. A 40-minute train tour on the 2.5-mile Kaua'i Plantation Railway allows visitors to explore island agriculture and feed the livestock.

On a 3-hour, 40-minute combination train-walk tour of Kahuna Nui Valley, participants learn about indigenous plants, eat lunch, and pick and taste fruit right off the trees. The Lū'au Kalamaku features an open bar, a Hawaiian buffet and a theatrical production about the Tahitians' migration to Hawai'i.

Hours: Estate daily 9:30-9. Train tours depart daily on the hour 10-2. Combination train-walk tour is offered Mon.-Fri.; check-in is at 9:30. Lū'au Kalamaku is offered Tues. and Fri.; phone for schedule. **Cost:** Train tour $18; $14 (ages 3-12). Combination train-walk tour $75; $60 (ages 3-12). Lū'au Kalamaku $99.95; $69.95 (ages 7-12); $39.95 (ages 3-6). Estate free. Reservations are required for Lū'au Kalamaku. **Phone:** (808) 245-7245. ⫯

MAUNA LOA HELICOPTER TOURS is at 3501 Rice St., Suite 222-C, in Harbor Mall. The 50- to 60-minute Private Island Tour offers spectacular views from a helicopter with or without doors. Other tours are offered.

Note: Due to decompression-related sickness, it is recommended that passengers wait 12-24 hours after scuba diving before flying; the amount of time is dependent on particular dive factors. Ask about possible policies regarding minimum wait time between scuba diving and flying; weight restrictions; weather, cancellation and refund policies; and the minimum and maximum number of passengers for flights. All small aircraft may encounter turbulence. Passengers should wear long pants, a jacket that closes and glasses or other eye protection; cameras must be secured with a neck or wrist strap, and other personal belongings must be stored under the seat. Validated parking is available at Harbor Mall.

Time: Allow 2 hours minimum. **Hours:** Daily 8:30-4:30. Passengers must check in with a valid photo ID 45 minutes prior to departure time. **Cost:** Private Island Tour $274. Reservations are required. **Phone:** (808) 652-3148.

NĀWILIWILI HARBOR, 2 mi. e. on SR 51 at jct. SR 58, is the island's chief port. The harbor and the nearby airport make Līhu'e a transportation and tour center. The harbor accommodates many cruise ships, and at the water's edge is a huge bulk sugar plant from which raw sugar is shipped directly to the mainland for refining. The harbor was shelled Dec. 31, 1941, but sustained only slight damage. **Phone:** (808) 241-3750.

SAFARI HELICOPTER TOURS departs from Līhu'e Heliport. Check-in is at 3225 Akahi St. Passengers on the 50- to 60-minute Deluxe Waterfall Safari Tour hear narration, music and two-way communication with the pilot via noise-canceling headsets as they glimpse numerous waterfalls, Mount Wai'ale'ale, Waimea Canyon and the Nāpali Coast. The 90-minute Kaua'i Refuge Eco-Tour includes the same spectacular views plus a 30-minute stop at a private botanical preserve where indigenous plants are being sustained.

Note: Due to decompression-related sickness, it is recommended that passengers wait 12-24 hours after scuba diving before flying; the amount of time is dependent on particular dive factors. Ask about possible policies regarding minimum wait time between scuba diving and flying; weight restrictions; weather, cancellation and refund policies; and the minimum and maximum number of passengers for flights. All small aircraft may encounter turbulence.

Time: Allow 2 hours minimum. **Hours:** Daily 7:30-5:30. Passengers must check in 45 minutes prior to departure. Closed Easter and Christmas. **Cost:** Deluxe Waterfall Safari Tour $186. Kaua'i Refuge Eco-Tour $248. Reservations are required. **Phone:** (808) 246-0136 or (800) 326-3356. *(See ad p. 73, p. 41.)*

SUNSHINE HELICOPTERS departs from 3416 Rice St. #203. Narrated tours lasting between 40 and 55 minutes reveal some of the island's most scenic views, including Waimea Canyon, Wailua Falls, Mount Wailaleale and the Nāpali Coast. **Note:** Due to decompression-related sickness, it is recommended that passengers wait 12-24 hours after scuba diving before flying; the amount of time is dependent on particular dive factors. Ask about possible policies regarding minimum wait time between scuba diving and flying; weight restrictions; weather, cancellation and refund policies; and the minimum and maximum number of passengers for flights. All small aircraft may encounter turbulence.

Hours: Flights daily; phone for schedule. **Cost:** $244-$364, depending on tour, helicopter and seating. Reservations are required. **Phone:** (808) 245-8881 or (800) 469-3000.

▼ See AAA listing p. 72 ▼

Safari Helicopters

Only 20% of Kauai is accessible by car. Come on Safari with us and see what every one else is going to be missing.

Safari Helicopters has been a family owned business since 1987, small enough for Preston and his family to be personally involved in every detail and big enough to be the leading innovator in flightseeing in Hawaii. Preston always looked for ways to improve his passenger's overall experience; as a result, he has made his mark on Hawaii's helicopter tour industry by introducing many new innovations. Safari Helicopters is the first tour operator in the State of Hawaii to fly helicopter tours in an air-conditioned ASTAR helicopter dubbed by Preston as the "Cadillac" of sightseeing helicopters. Safari is also the first in Hawaii to offer two-way communication between passengers and pilots featuring Bose® noise cancelling headsets and the first to install and operate an FAA Approved multiple camera video system to record passenger's actual tour with live narration and choreographed music. The newest additions to his helicopters on Kauai are the Super Mega Windows with bottom of the floor to top of the cabin visibility. It is like flying without doors but much safer.

Preston Myers (owner of Safari) aviation career spans more than 40 years, starting with a college degree in aviation, followed by service as a U.S. Naval Aviator during the Vietnam conflict. Preston returned to South East Asia as a civilian and flew for many years with the now famous "Air America" and flew in Laos, Thailand, Cambodia and South Vietnam. Prior to the fall of Saigon, Preston moved to Singapore and flew with various companies that provided helicopter support for oil exploration projects in Borneo, Sumatra, Celebes, Irian Jaya (Dutch New Guinea) and the Andaman Islands of India. In 1987, Preston started Safari Helicopters on Kauai and since then has expanded the company's flight seeing operations and charter operations to the Big Island in Hilo. He retired from the US Naval Reserves as a Commander (O-5) in 1992.

Preston wants Safari passengers to fully enjoy their adventure, but he considers safety of the utmost importance. He holds to the axiom, "there are old pilots and there are bold pilots, but there are no old bold pilots," and he requires that all his pilots adhere to the same high standards of professionalism that he personally carried out over the years.

Scan this tag on your smartphone and start saving today!

AAA members receive a Special Discount
Not available through reservation activity desks. Call Safari direct
Email: info@safarihelicopters.com - Web: www.safarihelicopters.com
808-246-0136 Kauai - **808-969-1259** Hilo
1-800-326-3356 Toll Free
Tours vary depending on weather, 48 hr. cancellation, Weight restrictions apply.

AQUA KAUAI BEACH RESORT   (808)245-1955

Hotel
$189-$540

Address: 4331 Kauai Beach Dr 96766 **Location:** Oceanfront. On SR 56, 2 mi n of airport, just e. **Facility:** 350 units. 2-4 stories, interior corridors. **Parking:** on-site and valet. **Terms:** 3 day cancellation notice-fee imposed. **Amenities:** video games, safes. **Dining:** 2 restaurants, entertainment. **Pool(s):** outdoor. **Activities:** hot tub, tennis, recreation programs, exercise room, spa. **Guest Services:** valet and coin laundry, rental car service, area transportation. (See ad p. 150.)

SAVE ⊕ ❄ 🍴 👙 ✈ CALL ⬇M
🏊 BIZ SHS 📶 ✕ 🎥 🖥

🖥

BANYAN HARBOR RESORT   (808)245-7333

Vacation Rental
Condominium
$119-$235

Address: 3411 Wilcox Rd 96766 **Location:** From airport, 2 mi s on SR 51, just n on Ka'ilikea St, then just w. **Facility:** Within walking distance of a public beach, restaurants and a small shopping mall, the hillside buildings offer many units with water views and lanais. 27 condominiums. 3 stories (no elevator), exterior corridors. **Terms:** check-in 4 pm, 3 day cancellation notice-fee imposed, resort fee. **Pool(s):** heated outdoor. **Activities:** tennis. **Guest Services:** complimentary laundry. (See ad this page.)

SAVE 🏊 BIZ 📶 ✕ 🖥
🖥 🖥 / SOME UNITS 🐾

Request roadside assistance in a click — online or using the AAA or CAA apps

---

KAUA'I MARRIOTT RESORT   (808)245-5050

▼▼▼ **Resort Hotel** $250-$399

AAA Benefit:
Members save 5% or more!

Address: 3610 Rice St 96766 **Location:** Oceanfront. From airport, 2 mi s on SR 51. **Facility:** Guests to this resort will find beautifully maintained grounds, comfortable guest rooms and upgraded bathrooms. Facing Kalapaki Beach, this property features the largest single-level pool in Hawaii. 356 units. 10 stories, interior corridors. **Parking:** on-site (fee) and valet. **Terms:** check-in 4 pm. **Amenities:** safes. **Dining:** Cafe Portofino, Duke's, see separate listings, entertainment. **Pool(s):** heated outdoor. **Activities:** hot tub, cabanas, self-propelled boats, snorkeling, recreation programs, kids club, exercise room, spa. **Guest Services:** valet and coin laundry, boarding pass kiosk, rental car service.

🖥 ⊕ ❄ 🍴 👙 📶 CALL ⬇M 🏊 BIZ HS
📶 ✕ 🎥 🖥 🖥 / SOME UNITS

GARDEN ISLAND INN HOTEL   808/245-7227

fyi **Motel** Did not meet all AAA rating requirements for locking devices in some guest rooms at time of last evaluation on 04/15/2015. **Address:** 3445 Wilcox Rd 96766 **Location:** From airport, 2 mi s on SR 51, just n on Ka'ilikea St, then just e. Facilities, services, and décor characterize an economy property.

KAUAI INN   808/245-9000

fyi Not evaluated. **Address:** 2430 Hulemalu Rd 96766 **Location:** From airport, 2 mi s on SR 51, 0.7 mi sw via Wilcox and Waapa rds, then just n. Facilities, services, and décor characterize an economy property.

WHERE TO EAT

CAFE PORTOFINO   808/245-2121

▼▼ Northern Italian. Casual Dining. $19-$45 **AAA Inspector Notes:** Next to Duke's, the café overlooks beautiful Kalapaki Bay. The highlight of the evening will be the elegant and romantic sound of a harp, which can be heard from the indoor dining room or the outside patio. The dining areas offer a comfortable relaxed setting. The staff will highlight the changing daily specials. The owner is usually on hand to ensure guests are happy and enjoying their evening. Parking at the Marriott is recommended. **Features:** full bar, patio dining. **Reservations:** suggested. **Address:** 3481 Ho'olaule'a Way 96766 **Location:** From airport, 2 mi s on SR 51; in Kaua'i Marriott Resort. **Parking:** on-site and valet. D 🐾

DUKE'S
808/246-9599

▼▼▼ Hawaiian Fusion. Casual Dining. $16-$34 **AAA Inspector Notes:** Pictures and memorabilia of the famous Hawaiian surfer Duke Kahanamoku fill this fun and casual beachfront restaurant. The downstairs level features a light casual menu of appetizers, burgers and salads, and upstairs (5-10 pm only) offers a full menu with fresh fish, steaks, prime rib and great ocean views from many seats. The friendly staff carries out relaxed service. The signature dessert is the hula pie. **Features:** full bar, patio dining, happy hour. **Reservations:** suggested, for dinner. **Address:** 3610 Rice Rd 96766 **Location:** From airport, 2 mi s on SR 51; in Kaua'i Marriott Resort.

🔲 Ⓛ Ⓓ CALL 🔣 Ⓚ

THE FERAL PIG
808/246-1100

▼▼▼ American. Casual Dining. $9-$17 **AAA Inspector Notes:** Serving healthy portions at reasonable prices, this is a great place to grab a bite before an adventure or stop by for a drink and fish tacos to wrap up the day. While traditional breakfast options are offered, dine like a local and try the loco moco (ground beef, eggs, rice and brown gravy). Lunch might be a Kauai-Cubano sandwich or a fresh ground beef burger. Dinner offerings include house-smoked pork loin, seared ahi and Jamaican jerk chicken. Anything with Kalua pork is a winner. **Features:** full bar, patio dining. **Address:** 3501 Rice St 96766 **Location:** From airport, 2 mi s on SR 51. Ⓑ Ⓛ Ⓓ

GAYLORD'S
808/245-9593

▼▼▼▼ American. Fine Dining. $26-$36 **AAA Inspector Notes:** Farm-fresh cuisine and seasonal menus are embraced at this restaurant in the main house of a restored plantation estate. Patrons dine in a casually elegant and tranquil covered courtyard with views of the lush lawns and trees. A few tables are beside a cozy fire pit. **Features:** full bar, patio dining, Sunday brunch. **Reservations:** suggested. **Address:** 3-2087 Kaumuali'i Hwy 96766 **Location:** On SR 50 (Kaumuali'i Hwy), 1 mi w of jct SR 56; at Kilohana Plantation.

Ⓛ Ⓓ CALL 🔣 Ⓚ

HAMURA SAIMIN
808/245-3271

▼ Noodles. Casual Dining. $5-$10 **AAA Inspector Notes:** This is one of those only-in-Hawaii restaurants. In lieu of tables, there is a winding saimin counter where visitors and locals rub elbows as they slurp bowls of steaming-hot Japanese noodles. It's a little tricky to find, but this place merits seeking out. **Address:** 2956 Kress St 96766 **Location:** Jct SR 50, 0.4 mi s on Rice St, then just w (turn at Lee's Furniture store). **Parking:** street only. Ⓛ Ⓓ

JJ'S BROILER RESTAURANT AT KALAPAKI BAY
808/246-4422

▼▼ American. Casual Dining. $12-$42 **AAA Inspector Notes:** At Kalapaki Bay, this restaurant offers casual dining on a patio with views of the bay. The menu features steaks, including a Slavonic-prepared steak, fresh island seafood, prime rib and other island favorites. The staff provides friendly service. **Features:** full bar, patio dining, happy hour. **Address:** 3416 Rice St 96766 **Location:** SR 51; at Anchor Cove Shopping Center. Ⓛ Ⓓ Ⓚ

KAUAI BEER COMPANY
808/245-2337

▼▼ American. Casual Dining. $8-$15 **AAA Inspector Notes:** If you are looking to get away from the resorts and rub elbows with a few locals, here's a fun place that is crafting its own beers with at least six on tap and offering a limited food menu on most evenings. For a real local vibe, Thursdays food options are served fresh and hot from a couple of food trucks. **Features:** beer & wine, patio dining. **Address:** 4265 Rice St 96766 **Location:** Jct SR 50 (Kaumuali'i Hwy), 0.3 mi s. **Parking:** street only. Ⓓ

MARIACHI'S AUTHENTIC MEXICAN CUISINE
808/246-1570

▼▼ Mexican. Casual Dining. $10-$20 **AAA Inspector Notes:** On the second floor of Harbor Mall, this little gem of a restaurant takes great pride in preparing authentic Mexican cuisine with sauces that are whipped up fresh every day. Dine out on the large lanai and enjoy the distant view of Kalapaki Bay. Validated two-hour parking is available. **Features:** full bar, happy hour. **Address:** 3501 Rice St, Suite 205 96766 **Location:** SR 51; in Harbor Mall.

Ⓑ Ⓛ Ⓓ Ⓚ

THE RIGHT SLICE
808/212-8320

fyi Not evaluated. Looking for a local favorite for dessert? Then leave the tourist-crowded beach and head to this little pie shop. It's located in an industrial park but is worth the trek. The whole pies and slices of tropical delight are prepared like only a local can. A crowd pleaser is the tropical trio with pineapple, mango and candied ginger. For me, it's the chocolate macadamia nut. **Address:** 1543 Haleukana St 96766 **Location:** Jct SR 50, 0.4 mi s on Puhl Rd, just w on Hanalima St, then just n.

PO'IPŪ (B-2) pop. 979, elev. 20'
• Restaurants p. 76
• Attractions map p. 63

Po'ipū, the beach area east of Kōloa Landing, is a popular resort and recreation center. The half-mile coastal Māhā'ulepū Heritage Trail affords breathtaking views of the Makawehi Lithified Cliffs; hikers should use caution and watch their footing.

MOIR GARDENS is at 2253 Po'ipū Rd. at the Outrigger Kiahuna Plantation. Alexandra Moir, wife of Kōloa Sugar Plantation manager Hector Moir, began planting her garden after her marriage in 1930. By 1948 it was known internationally as one of the world's best cactus and succulent gardens. Orchids and bromeliads are included. An Italian marble cutting stone once imported for kitchen use has been made into a bench and placed in the gardens. **Time:** Allow 30 minutes minimum. **Hours:** Daily dawndusk. **Cost:** Free. **Phone:** (808) 742-6411.

RECREATIONAL ACTIVITIES
Ziplines
• **Skyline Eco-Adventures** departs from The Shops at Kukui'ula, 2829 Ala Kalanikaumaka St. **Hours:** Trips depart daily at 8, 11 and 2; additional tour times may be offered. Phone ahead to confirm schedule. **Phone:** (808) 878-8400 or (888) 864-6947.

ASTON AT POIPU KAI
(808)742-7424

▼▼▼ Vacation Rental Condominium $275-$679 **Address:** 1775 Poipu Rd 96756 **Location:** 3 mi se of Koloa; in Poipu Beach area. **Facility:** All condos have full kitchens, separate bedrooms, lanais and daily maid service. The five separate condo complexes have a central office check-in building on Poipu Road. 63 condominiums. 2-3 stories (no elevator), exterior corridors. **Terms:** 3 day cancellation notice-fee imposed, resort fee. **Amenities:** safes. **Pool(s):** outdoor. **Activities:** hot tub, tennis. **Guest Services:** complimentary and valet laundry. *(See ad starting on p. 148.)*

🍴 🏊 🅱🅸🆉 📶 ✖ Ⓚ 🛎 🖥 🖨

GRAND HYATT KAUAI RESORT & SPA (808)742-1234

Resort Hotel
$329-$639

GRAND | HYATT

AAA Benefit: Members save 10%!

Address: 1571 Poipu Rd 96756 **Location:** Oceanfront. 3.4 mi se of Koloa; in Poipu Beach area. **Facility:** The resort's luxurious setting on the island's dry side includes a lagoon area and tropically landscaped grounds. Guest rooms feature a large lanai, tasteful appointments and spaciousness. 602 units. 6 stories, interior corridors. **Parking:** on-site (fee) and valet. **Terms:** check-in 4 pm, 3 day cancellation notice-fee imposed, resort fee. **Amenities:** safes. **Dining:** 6 restaurants, also, Dondero's, Tidepools, see separate listings, entertainment. **Pool(s):** heated outdoor. **Activities:** sauna, hot tub, steamroom, cabanas, self-propelled boats, snorkeling, regulation golf, tennis, recreation programs, kids club, bicycles, game room, exercise room, spa. **Guest Services:** complimentary and valet laundry, boarding pass kiosk, rental car service, area transportation.

[SAVE] [ECO] [⟷] [¶¶] [↙] [Y] [🛏] CALL [&M] [≈] [BIZ]
[🛜] [✕] [🖋] [📶] [🖥]

HIDEAWAY COVE POIPU BEACH (808)635-8785

▼▼▼ **Vacation Rental Condominium** $185-$200 **Address:** 2307 Nalo Rd 96756 **Location:** 2 mi se of Koloa on Poipu Rd, just s (toward ocean) on Hoowili Rd, just e on Hoone Rd, then just ne; in Poipu Beach area. **Facility:** Located in a residential neighborhood right next to a AAA-approved Italian restaurant, these wonderful condos range from cozy standard rooms to more spacious two- and three-bedroom units. 7 condominiums. 2 stories (no elevator), exterior corridors. **Terms:** check-in 4 pm, 2 night minimum stay, 60 day cancellation notice-fee imposed, resort fee. **Activities:** beach access. **Guest Services:** complimentary laundry.

[¶¶↦] [BIZ] [🛜] [✕] [📶] [🖥] [🖥]

KIAHUNA PLANTATION & THE BEACH BUNGALOWS BY CASTLE RESORTS (808)742-2200

▼▼ **Vacation Rental Condominium** $161-$282 **Address:** 2253-B Poipu Rd 96756 **Location:** Oceanfront. 2.3 mi se of Koloa; in Poipu Beach area. **Facility:** Spacious one- and two-bedroom units, many with lovely garden views, are offered. Ceiling fans are in both bedroom and living area as there is no air conditioning. All have large decks or patios. 138 condominiums. 2-3 stories (no elevator), exterior corridors. **Terms:** 5 night minimum stay - seasonal, 3 day cancellation notice-fee imposed, resort fee. **Amenities:** safes. **Pool(s):** outdoor. **Activities:** hot tub, snorkeling, tennis, exercise room. **Guest Services:** valet and coin laundry.

[¶¶] [Y] [≈] [BIZ] [🛜] [✕] [𝄞] [📶] [🖥] [🖥]

KIAHUNA PLANTATION RESORT KAUAI BY OUTRIGGER (808)742-6411

▼▼ **Vacation Rental Condominium** $169-$319 **Address:** 2253 Poipu Rd 96756 **Location:** Oceanfront. 2 mi se of Koloa; in Poipu Beach area. **Facility:** Large one- and two-bedroom units with the conveniences of home, all with large decks or patios and many with garden views. Ceiling fans in both bedroom and living area as there is no air conditioning. 172 condominiums. 2-3 stories (no elevator), exterior corridors. **Terms:** 2 night minimum stay - weekends, 7 day cancellation notice-fee imposed, resort fee. **Amenities:** safes. **Dining:** Plantation Gardens, see separate listing. **Activities:** snorkeling. **Guest Services:** valet and coin laundry.

[¶¶] [Y] [🛜] [✕] [𝄞] [📶] [🖥] [🖥]

POIPU SHORES RESORT (808)742-7700

▼▼ **Vacation Rental Condominium** $286-$476 **Address:** 1775 Pe'e Rd 96756 **Location:** Oceanfront. 3 mi se of Koloa on Poipu Rd, just sw; in Poipu Beach area. **Facility:** On a lava-rock coastline, this condo resort, fronting the ocean, offers spacious accommodations. The swimming pool juts out over the lava rock and crashing waves. 18 condominiums. 2-4 stories (no elevator), exterior corridors. **Terms:** 2-4 night minimum stay - seasonal, 3 day cancellation notice-fee imposed, resort fee. **Amenities:** safes. **Pool(s):** heated outdoor. **Guest Services:** complimentary and valet laundry.

[≈] [🛜] [✕] [𝄞] [📶] [🖥] [🖥]

SHERATON KAUAI RESORT 808/742-1661

Hotel
Rates not provided

Sheraton

AAA Benefit: Members save up to 15%, plus Starwood Preferred Guest® benefits!

Address: 2440 Hoonani Rd 96756 **Location:** Oceanfront. 1.8 mi se of Koloa on Poipu Rd, just se; in Poipu Beach area. **Facility:** 394 units. 4 stories, exterior corridors. **Parking:** on-site and valet. **Amenities:** safes. **Dining:** 2 restaurants, entertainment. **Pool(s):** outdoor. **Activities:** hot tub, cabanas, snorkeling, recreation programs, exercise room. **Guest Services:** valet and coin laundry, boarding pass kiosk, rental car service, area transportation.

[SAVE] [ECO] [⟷] [¶¶] [↙] [Y] CALL [&M] [≈] [BIZ] [🛜]
[✕] [🖋] [📶] [🖥] / SOME UNITS [🛏]

KO'A KEA HOTEL & RESORT 808/828-8888

[fyi] Not evaluated. **Address:** 2251 Poipu Rd 96756 **Location:** 2.3 mi se of Koloa; in Poipu Beach area. Facilities, services, and décor characterize a mid-scale property.

KOLOA LANDING AT POIPU BEACH WYNDHAM GRAND RESORT 808/240-6600

[fyi] **Condominium** Did not meet all AAA rating requirements for viewports/peepholes in some guest rooms at time of last evaluation on 05/05/2015. **Address:** 2641 Poipu Rd 96756 **Location:** 2 mi se of Koloa; in Poipu Beach area. Facilities, services, and décor characterize a mid-scale property.

MAKAHUENA AT POIPU 808/742-1155

[fyi] Not evaluated. **Address:** 1661 Pe'e Rd 96756 **Location:** Oceanfront. 3 mi se of Koloa on Poipu Rd, then just sw; in Poipu Beach area. Facilities, services, and décor characterize a mid-scale property. This well-established condo property includes many units with an ocean view.

WHALERS COVE RESORT AT POIPU 808/742-7571

[fyi] Not evaluated. **Address:** 2640 Puuholo Rd 96756 **Location:** Oceanfront. S of Poipu roundabout on Lawai Rd, just s. Facilities, services, and décor characterize a mid-scale property. A peaceful complex located in a residential neighborhood where all of the privately owned condos are fully equipped and have an ocean view. Convenient to shops and restaurants.

◼ WHERE TO EAT ◼

BEACH HOUSE RESTAURANT 808/742-1424

▼▼▼ Pacific Rim. Fine Dining. $14-$40 **AAA Inspector Notes:** This relaxed, open-air restaurant offers a romantic setting with candlelit tables and peaceful ocean views. The menu offers a good selection of regional Hawaiian cuisine prepared with fresh local ingredients. Friendly staffers in aloha attire are knowledgeable about the local seafood and the chef's preparation techniques. They also will assist with wine selections from the extensive list. Reservations are a must for a sunset-view table during the busy season. **Features:** full bar. **Reservations:** suggested. **Address:** 5022 Lawai Rd 96756 **Location:** 2 mi s of Koloa, follow signs to Sprouting Horn; at Lawai Beach. **Parking:** valet only. [L] [D] [𝄞]

BRENNECKE'S BEACH BROILER 808/742-7588

▼▼ American. Casual Dining. $14-$30 **AAA Inspector Notes:** With the dining room on the second floor, this casual beachfront restaurant is ideal for sunset watching. The menu features an all-day selection of pupu (appetizers), salads and burgers, as well as a dinner menu with seafood from the beach. The staff provides friendly, casual service. **Features:** full bar, happy hour. **Reservations:** suggested. **Address:** 2100 Hoone Rd 96756 **Location:** 2 mi se of Koloa on Poipu Rd, just s (toward ocean) on Hoowili Rd; in Poipu Beach area. [L] [D] [𝄞]

CASA DI AMICI 808/742-1555

◆◆ Italian. Casual Dining. $18-$33 **AAA Inspector Notes:** This romantic little restaurant in a residential neighborhood serves fresh, locally caught fish with a heavy Italian influence. There are some unusual risottos flavored with Thai curry or Spanish paella. Finish with the baked Hawaii, a close cousin to the baked Alaska. **Features:** full bar, patio dining. **Reservations:** suggested. **Address:** 2301 Nalo Rd 96756 **Location:** 2 mi se of Koloa on Poipu Rd, just s (toward ocean) on Hoowili Rd, just e on Hoone Rd, then just ne; in Poipu Beach area. [D] CALL ⎍M ⎈

DONDERO'S 808/240-6456

◆◆ Regional Italian. Fine Dining. $16-$42 **AAA Inspector Notes:** A little romance goes a long way, and this charming restaurant has the formula. Patrons dine amid décor reminiscent of old Italy. The staff offers professional, attentive service, and the chef is always willing to make your favorite dishes. **Features:** full bar, patio dining. **Reservations:** suggested. **Address:** 1571 Poipu Rd 96756 **Location:** 3.4 mi se of Koloa; in Poipu Beach area; in Grand Hyatt Kauai Resort & Spa. **Parking:** on-site and valet. ⊞ [D] CALL ⎍M

KEOKI'S PARADISE 808/742-7534

◆◆ Pacific Rim Seafood. Casual Dining. $16-$33 **AAA Inspector Notes:** A tropical waterfall welcomes diners to this casual, open-air dining room, which is filled with lush tropical plants that create a jungle-like atmosphere. The menu features hearty portions of American fare with a variety of fresh local fish, beef and the ever-popular grilled ribs. The hula pie shouldn't be missed. **Features:** full bar, patio dining, early bird specials, happy hour. **Reservations:** suggested. **Address:** 2360 Kiahuna Plantation Dr 96756 **Location:** 2 mi se of Koloa; in Poipu Beach area; at Poipu Shopping Village. [L] [D] ⎈

PLANTATION GARDENS 808/742-2121

◆◆ Pacific Rim. Casual Dining. $25-$37 **AAA Inspector Notes:** Situated in beautiful Moir Gardens, tables are set on verandas for panoramic garden views and the romance of flickering tiki torches. Start your evening by sharing a plate of crab Rangoon or pork pot stickers followed by coconut carrot soup, locally caught grilled or sautéed fish and then, for dessert, a baked Hawaiian that will leave you wanting to lick the plate. **Features:** full bar, patio dining. **Reservations:** suggested. **Address:** 2253 Poipu Rd 96756 **Location:** 2 mi se of Koloa; in Poipu Beach area; in Kiahuna Plantation Resort Kauai by Outrigger. [D] ⎈

RED SALT 808/828-8888

◆◆ ◆◆ Hawaiian Seafood. Fine Dining. $25-$69 **AAA Inspector Notes:** This contemporary restaurant, named after the colored salt on the island, offers up a sophisticated dining experience. A side of red salt is offered along with bread and butter and an amuse-bouche while you wait for your first course. The menu contains many locally sourced options. If you're feeling generous, share a dessert paired with a glass of wine for a sweet ending. Be sure and request a window seat for a view of the swimming pool and distant ocean. **Features:** full bar. **Reservations:** suggested. **Address:** 2251 Poipu Rd 96756 **Location:** 2.3 mi se of Koloa; in Poipu Beach area; in Ko'a Kea Hotel & Resort. **Parking:** valet only. [B] [D] CALL ⎍M

TIDEPOOLS 808/742-1234

◆◆◆ Pacific Rim. Casual Dining. $25-$42 **AAA Inspector Notes:** This thatched-roof, open-air restaurant is surrounded by tropically landscaped grounds with a cascading waterfall and torch-lit fish ponds with resident swans. Candlelit tables and cool ocean breezes lend to a romantic ambience. Service is casual and relaxed. **Features:** full bar, patio dining. **Reservations:** suggested. **Address:** 1571 Poipu Rd 96756 **Location:** 3.4 mi se of Koloa; in Poipu Beach area; in Grand Hyatt Kauai Resort & Spa. **Parking:** on-site and valet. ⊞ [D] ⎈

Ask about AAA/CAA

Associate membership to

share the benefits you value

PRINCEVILLE (A-2) pop. 2,158, elev. 194'
• Restaurants p. 78

PRINCEVILLE BOTANICAL GARDENS & CHOCOLATE TOUR is at 3840 Ahonui Pl. Three-hour guided tours include a walk through gardens, groves and a chocolate orchard; a dark-chocolate tasting; and an explanation of the history, harvesting and production of chocolate.

Note: Tours take place rain or shine; comfortable clothing and footwear are recommended. **Time:** Allow 3 hours minimum. **Hours:** Tues. and Thurs. at 9:30 and 2; Fri. at 9:30. Closed major holidays. **Cost:** $55; $17 (ages 7-16). Reservations are required. **Phone:** (808) 634-5505. [GT]

SUNSHINE HELICOPTERS departs from Princeville Airport, 5-3541 Kūhiō Hwy. Passengers on 40- to 50-minute narrated flights are treated to views of natural areas that can't be explored on foot. The pilot also points out a number of sites featured in Hollywood movies.

Note: Due to decompression-related sickness, it is recommended that passengers wait 12-24 hours after scuba diving before flying; the amount of time is dependent on particular dive factors. Ask about possible policies regarding minimum wait time between scuba diving and flying; weight restrictions; weather, cancellation and refund policies; and the minimum and maximum number of passengers for flights. All small aircraft may encounter turbulence.

Hours: Flights depart daily; phone for schedule. **Cost:** $289-$364, depending on tour and seating. **Phone:** (808) 245-8881 or (800) 469-3000.

RECREATIONAL ACTIVITIES
Horseback Riding

• **Princeville Ranch Adventures** is near Milepost 27 at 5-4280 Kūhiō Hwy. Other activities are offered. **Hours:** Waterfall horseback tours depart Mon.-Sat. at 8 or 9, noon and 1. **Phone:** (808) 826-7669.

THE ST. REGIS PRINCEVILLE RESORT (808)826-9644

◆◆◆ ◆◆◆ Resort Hotel $480-$1200

ST REGIS

AAA Benefit: Members save up to 15%, plus Starwood Preferred Guest® benefits!

Address: 5520 Ka Haku Rd 96722 **Location:** Oceanfront. SR 56 exit Princeville, 2 mi n. **Facility:** On the lush and tropical north side of the island, this hotel cascades down a hillside with ocean and mountain views. 252 units. 11 stories, interior/exterior corridors. **Parking:** valet only. **Terms:** check-in 4 pm, 30 day cancellation notice-fee imposed. **Amenities:** safes. **Dining:** 3 restaurants, also, Kauai Grill, see separate listing, entertainment. **Pool(s):** heated outdoor. **Activities:** sauna, hot tub, steamroom, cabanas, snorkeling, recreation programs, spa. **Guest Services:** valet laundry, area transportation.

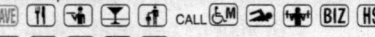

THE WESTIN PRINCEVILLE OCEAN RESORT VILLAS
(808)827-8700

WESTIN HOTELS & RESORTS

Resort Hotel
$300-$1900

AAA Benefit: Members save up to 15%, plus Starwood Preferred Guest® benefits!

Address: 3838 Wyllie Rd 96722 **Location:** Jct SR 56, just nw on Ka Haku Rd, just e. **Facility:** Set along a cliff 200 feet above the Pacific Ocean, the resort features a koi pond and plunge pools. All villas have private lanais and island views. 346 units, some efficiencies and kitchens. 3 stories, interior corridors. **Parking:** on-site (fee) and valet. **Terms:** check-in 4 pm, 3 day cancellation notice-fee imposed. **Amenities:** safes. **Pool(s):** heated outdoor. **Activities:** sauna, hot tub, steamroom, cabanas, recreation programs, exercise room, massage. **Guest Services:** complimentary and valet laundry, area transportation.

SAVE ⊞ 🍴 🛁 🍸 CALL 🔧 🏊 BIZ HS 📶 ✕ 🔌 🖨 📺

C J'S STEAK & SEAFOOD
808/826-6211

◈◈ Steak Seafood. Casual Dining. $8-$32 **AAA Inspector Notes:** This simple steakhouse has been around since 1978. Try their burgers or hot and cold sandwiches for lunch, and for dinner enjoy a variety of steaks. Open for lunch Monday through Friday. **Features:** full bar, patio dining. **Reservations:** suggested. **Address:** 5-4280 Kuhio Hwy 96722 **Location:** On SR 56; in Princeville Shopping Center. L D 🔧

KAUAI GRILL
808/826-9644

◈◈◈ Steak Seafood. Fine Dining. $35-$72 **AAA Inspector Notes:** Described as steak and seafood cuisine, heavy Asian and Hawaiian influences can be seen in dishes like Kona Kampachi with Sugarloaf pineapple, Meyer's rum and wasabi, or grilled pork chop served with smoked chile glaze, baby bok choy and shiitake mushrooms. While the dining room is lovely with a fabric-draped ceiling that mimics a nautilus shell, plan to arrive before sunset as the panoramic ocean view is the sight to enjoy before the Jean-Georges Vongerichten-inspired dishes start arriving. **Features:** full bar. **Reservations:** suggested. **Address:** 5520 Ka Haku Rd 96722 **Location:** SR 56 exit Princeville, 2 mi n; in The St. Regis Princeville Resort. **Parking:** valet only. D CALL 🔧

WAILUA (B-2) pop. 2,254, elev. 13'
• Attractions map p. 63

At the mouth of the Wailua River, Wailua is at the northern edge of a growing resort center that lines the east-central coast. Wailua Falls is southwest of Wailua on SR 583 *(see attraction listing p. 67).*

Wailua Beach extends from 1 block south of jct. SRs 56 and 580 to .5 miles north along SR 56 at the mouth of the river. **Note:** Swimming is not recommended. The water is treacherous in rough weather. The beach is open daily 24 hours. Marina hours vary; phone ahead. Phone (808) 245-3564 for the marine forecast.

Lydgate Beach Park, off SR 56 on Leho Dr., offers a protected swimming area that has been set off from the surrounding dangerous currents and waves with rocks.

HOLOHOLOKŪ HEIAU, on SR 580 w. of jct. SR 56, is a temple restored by Kaua'i Historical Society and Bishop Museum in Honolulu. The site is said to be the oldest *heiau* on the island not built by the *Menehune.* It consists of a semicircle of piled rocks, which looks like a low wall. Outside the enclosure are Royal Birthstones, which women of royal blood were required to reach before giving birth, in order to ensure the child's royal status. Kaumuali'i, the last king of Kaua'i, was born at Holoholokū.

Note: *Heiau* are culturally significant and should be treated with respect. **Hours:** Daily 24 hours. **Cost:** Free. **Phone:** (808) 245-3373.

SLEEPING GIANT, 1 mi. n. of jct. SRs 56 and 580, is a mountain formation resembling a sleeping giant. Several legends and myths are connected to this site. One legend relates that the *Menehune,* trying to awaken the giant to help them repel an invading force, bounced huge rocks off his stomach. Although he did not awaken, the boulders ricocheting into the sea frightened off the invaders. Unfortunately, some rocks bounced into the mouth of the giant, who swallowed them and died. **Hours:** Daily 24 hours. **Cost:** Free.

SMITH'S TROPICAL PARADISE is in the marina area of Wailua River State Park, following signs. Thirty acres of tropical plants, lagoons and a variety of fruit orchards as well as exotic peacocks and other birds are featured. **Time:** Allow 2 hours minimum. **Hours:** Daily 8:30-4. A *lū'au* including a tram ride, cocktails, dinner and a show is held Mon.-Fri. 5-9, June-Aug.; Mon. and Wed.-Fri. 5-9, Feb.-May and Sept.-Oct.; Mon., Wed. and Fri. 5-9, rest of year. Gates open at 7:30, Mar.-Oct.; at 7:15, rest of year for those attending only the *lū'au* show. **Cost:** Gardens $6; $3 (ages 3-12). All-inclusive *lū'au* $88; $30 (ages 7-13); $19 (ages 3-6). *Lū'au* show only $15; $7.50 (ages 3-12). **Phone:** (808) 821-6895.

WAILUA RIVER STATE PARK, along the banks of the Wailua River off Kūhiō Hwy. (SR 56), contains two waterfalls and several park areas with terrain varying from beach to mountain. The first migratory Tahitians reputedly landed at the mouth of the river. Many Hawaiian royalty traced their ancestry to the great chief Puna, who settled in the area and is associated with the first migration from the Marquesas, A.D. 1000 or earlier. *Heiau* (temples) once stretched from the mouth of the river to the top of Mount Wa-i'ale'ale; several can be visited in the park.

Note: *Heiau* are culturally significant and should be treated with respect. **Hours:** Daily dawn-dusk. **Cost:** Free. **Phone:** (808) 274-3444.

Kuamo'o Road (King's Highway), extending 2 mi. along SR 580, .2 mi. w. of SR 56, overlooks the Wailua River. Along SR 580 are two *heiau* (temples). 'Opaeka'a Falls, on SR 580, is a short distance beyond Poli'ahu Heiau. This small, picturesque waterfall gets its name, which means "rolling shrimp," from the shrimp that lay eggs in the many rocky pools at the base of the cascade. **Note:** *Heiau* are culturally significant and should be treated with respect. **Time:** Allow 30 minutes minimum. **Hours:** Daily dawn-dusk. **Cost:** Free. **Phone:** (808) 274-3444.

Smith's Wailua River/Fern Grotto Cruise departs from Wailua River Marina, just w. off SR 56. The 80-minute narrated trip, via the only navigable river in the islands, includes Hawaiian entertainment and passes banks covered with *pandanus* and *hau* trees and *pili* grass, once used for houses. The grotto is a fern-festooned cave with a small waterfall flowing over the top. The abundance of vegetation and the force of the waterfall depend on the annual rainfall.

Hours: Trips depart daily at 9:30, 11, 2 and 3:30. **Cost:** $20; $10 (ages 3-12). **Phone:** (808) 821-6895.

GARDEN LUAU AT SMITH'S TROPICAL PARADISE
808/821-6895

Hawaiian Casual Dining $88

AAA Inspector Notes: Experience an authentic lū'au starting with a stroll through the gardens to the imu pit for the uncovering of the roasted pig, then to the large buffet-style presentation. Afterward, enjoy the international stage show. The lū'au schedule varies throughout the year. Gates open at 4:45 pm in winter and 5 pm in summer. Complimentary shuttle service is provided from nearby Wailua-area hotels. Warm Hawaiian hospitality is offered. **Features:** full bar. **Reservations:** required. **Address:** 174 Wailua Rd 96746 **Location:** Jct SR 580, just s; in Smith's Tropical Paradise Gardens; in Wailua River State Park. D CALL 🕭M 🕮

WAIMEA (B-1) pop. 1,855, elev. 9'
• Hotels p. 80 • Restaurants p. 80

Once the Polynesian capital of Kaua'i, Waimea was the site of Capt. James Cook's first landing in the islands in 1778. The settlement later became a favorite harbor and a main provisioning port for early whalers and traders. Commemorating the arrival of Capt. Cook, February's ▽ Waimea Town Celebration features live entertainment, food and crafts vendors, cultural and sporting events, *lei* and *'ukulele* contests and a rodeo.

South of town are the remains of an 1817 Russian fort. Menehune Ditch, once an aqueduct covering 25 miles along the Waimea River, is said to have been built overnight by the *Menehune*—legendary small people. Visitors can view the 2-foot-high portion of one ditch wall from a location on Menehune Road.

The area from Waimea through Kekaha and Mānā to the Nāpali Cliffs is a hot, dry but fertile plain. Irrigated mainly by mountain water, it produces abundant sugarcane crops. Beyond Mānā private dirt roads run through the cane fields.

The Nāpali Cliffs—sheer cliffs and deep valleys—extend to the water and are accessible only by sea or by foot via the challenging Kalalau Trail. Two beaches with small boat access provide camping and fishing.

KŌKE'E STATE PARK is 15 mi. n. on SR 550, a narrow, winding road requiring cautious driving. The Kalalau and Pu'u O Kila lookouts provide spectacular views of Kalalau Valley and portions of the Nāpali Coast. In a rugged mountainous region, the area is rough and primitive; hiking should not be attempted without proper preparation. Sturdy shoes and comfortable clothing are imperative. Seasonal fishing and hunting are permitted only with a license.

Information about hiking trails is available from the Kōke'e Natural History Museum. *See Recreation Areas Chart.* **Hours:** Daily 24 hours. **Cost:** Day use free. Camping (up to six people) $18; $12 (Hawai'i residents). Each additional person, up to a maximum group size of 10, $3; $2 (Hawai'i residents). **Phone:** (808) 274-3444. 🅰 🎋

Kalalau Lookout, 3 mi. beyond Kōke'e State Park headquarters, overlooks the beautiful Kalalau Valley and the Pacific Ocean 4,000 feet below. Though clouds often obscure the view, they tend to drift through quickly. Nevertheless, it's best to arrive in the morning when the skies are typically clearer.

Demigods were immortal as long as they remained in the shade. Two young demigods joined mortal children playing in the moonlight and became so enthralled with the games that they forgot the time and turned into stone at sunrise. This is the legend of origin of the two small stone figures on a hogback ridge.

Nēnē (Hawaiian geese) frequent the area; be careful when driving near them, as they prefer walking over flying. **Hours:** Daily 24 hours. **Cost:** Free. **Phone:** (808) 274-3444. 🎋

Kōke'e Natural History Museum, 15 mi. n. on SR 550 in Kōke'e State Park, contains exhibits pertaining to plants, birds, animals and the weather as well as stone artifacts found on Kaua'i. **Hours:** Daily 9-4. **Cost:** Donations. **Phone:** (808) 335-9975.

WAIMEA CANYON STATE PARK is 15 mi. on SR 550 adjoining Kōke'e State Park *(see attraction listing).* The Pu'u Hinahina Lookout provides views of Ni'ihau Island and is the trailhead for the popular Canyon Trail. The serpentine lower portion of the highway—Waimea Canyon Drive—requires cautious driving. A short nature trail, the Iliau Nature Loop, can be found between mile markers 8 and 9 on SR 550. No drinking water is available. **Hours:** Daily dawn-dusk. **Cost:** Free. **Phone:** (808) 274-3444. 🎋

Canyon Lookout, at the 3,400-foot level in Waimea Canyon State Park, affords the best view of the 10-mile series of gorges cut into Alaka'i Plateau. Wild goats can be seen on the cliffs. The deep, brilliantly hued gorges are aptly referred to as the "Grand Canyon of the Pacific." **Hours:** Park daily dawn-dusk. **Cost:** Free. **Phone:** (808) 274-3444.

WAIMEA PLANTATION COTTAGES, A COAST MANAGED HOTEL 808/338-1625

🔻🔻 **Vacation Rental Cottage.** Rates not provided. **Address:** 9400 Kaumualii Hwy 96796 **Location:** Oceanfront. Just w on SR 50. **Facility:** The restored, historic 1900s cottages recall Hawaii's plantation era and are furnished with mahogany, wicker and rattan combined with modern amenities on attractively landscaped tranquil grounds. 61 cottages. 1 story, exterior corridors. **Amenities:** safes. **Pool(s):** outdoor. **Guest Services:** complimentary laundry.

🍴 🍸 🛥 BIZ 📶 ✕ 🛏 🖼 ☕ / SOME UNITS 🐾

WEST INN 808/338-1107

fyi Not evaluated. **Address:** 9690 Kaumualii Hwy 96796 **Location:** Center. Facilities, services, and décor characterize an economy property.

WHERE TO EAT

THE LODGE AT KOKE'E 808/335-6061

🔻 American. Quick Serve. $5-$8 **AAA Inspector Notes:** Hot and cold sandwiches and a few light entrées are served in this 1920s lodge. Large picture windows look out to an expansive lawn area. The lilikoi chiffon pie shouldn't be missed. **Features:** full bar, patio dining. **Address:** SR 552 96796 **Location:** Jct SR 50 (Kaumuali'i Hwy) and 550 (Waimea Canyon Dr), 15 mi n on SR 550; in Koke'e State Park. B L

SHRIMP STATION RESTAURANT 808/338-1242

🔻 Specialty. Quick Serve. $6-$13 **AAA Inspector Notes:** This casual eatery prepares Kauai shrimp in a variety of ways, from burgers and tacos to several entrée selections. **Features:** patio dining. **Address:** 9652 Kaumualii Hwy 96796 **Location:** Just e of SR 550 (Waimea Canyon Dr); center. **Parking:** street only.

L 🐾

WRANGLER'S STEAKHOUSE 808/338-1218

🔻🔻 American. Casual Dining. $17-$35 **AAA Inspector Notes:** Wrangler's is a combination restaurant and gift shop. You'll enjoy sandwiches, seafood, house specials and combo plates. Try the 'kau kau' lunch served in the traditional plantation tin for a unique Hawaiian experience. **Features:** full bar, patio dining. **Address:** 9852 Kaumualii Hwy 96796 **Location:** Just w on SR 50 at Halepule Rd. L D

Island of Lāna'i

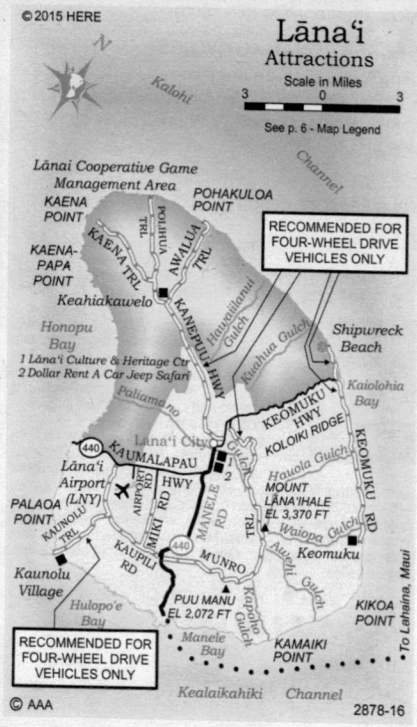

Rocky shoreline of Lāna'i

© 2015 HERE

Lāna'i Attractions

Scale in Miles

See p. 6 - Map Legend

Kalohi Channel

Lānai Cooperative Game Management Area

KAENA POINT

POHAKULOA POINT

KAENA-PAPA POINT

Keahiakawelo

RECOMMENDED FOR FOUR-WHEEL DRIVE VEHICLES ONLY

Honopu Bay

1 Lāna'i Culture & Heritage Ctr
2 Dollar Rent A Car Jeep Safari

Shipwreck Beach

Kaiolohia Bay

Kuahua Gulch

Maunalei Gulch

KAENA TRL

AWALUA TRL

PUHIELELU TRL

KANEPUU HWY

Paliamano

KEOMUKU HWY

KOLOIKI RIDGE

Lāna'i City

KAUMALAPAU

Lāna'i Airport (LNY)

PALAOA POINT

KAUNOLU TRL

Hauola Gulch

MOUNT LĀNA'IHALE EL 3,370 FT

KEOMUKU RD

Waiopa Gulch

Keomuku

Auahi Gulch

AIRPORT RD

MIKI RD

MANELE RD

KAUPILI RD

MUNRO TRL

Kaunolu Village

Hulopo'e Bay

PUU MANU EL 2,072 FT

Kapoho Gulch

KIKOA POINT

Manele Bay

KAMAIKI POINT

RECOMMENDED FOR FOUR-WHEEL DRIVE VEHICLES ONLY

To Lahaina, Maui

© AAA

Kealaikahiki Channel

2878-16

Kidney-shaped Lāna'i is 18 miles long and 13 miles wide. Its reef-fringed north coast lies 9 miles south of Moloka'i; 8 miles of water separate its eastern shore from Maui. The volcanic fires that built it have long been quenched, leaving 3,370-foot Mount Lāna'ihale on the eastern part of the island as a quiet remnant. Abandoned pineapple fields and dry grassland occupy the mostly rolling and open western region.

Lāna'i always has been the least visited of the major islands. One legend holds that for 1,000 years evil spirits occupied the deserted area, then called "The Forbidden Island." Finally the spirits were foiled by a young Hawaiian prince who outwitted them and drove them out.

Today, Lāna'i's breathtaking views of Moloka'i and Maui and its highland ridges covered with patches of wild thimbleberries and Hawaiian gardenias beckon visitors who want to glimpse a paradise untainted by man.

Nearly all of Lāna'i's 3,500 residents live in Lāna'i City. With minimal development and only 30 miles of paved roads, the island is an off-the-beaten-track treasure. Axis deer, feral goats, pronghorn antelope and mouflon as well as pheasants, quail and turkeys are common sights.

HULOPO'E AND MĀNELE BAYS (E-8)

On opposite flanks of a small promontory on the south coast, Hulopo'e Bay and Mānele Bay are approximately 9 miles south of Lāna'i City *(see place listing)* via paved SR 440. Both attractive county parks, they are the recreational focus of Lāna'i. Hulopo'e's white sand beach, the only protected strand on the island, is a favorite place for swimming and bodysurfing.

Under water, the fragile coral and filtered light attract divers. Pu'u Pehe, or Sweetheart Rock, punctuates the sea just off the tip of the peninsula. Just outside Mānele Bay are the Cathedrals. These caverns, accessible only by boat, feature dramatic coral spires rising almost to the water's surface from a depth of 70 feet. The first and second cathedrals are approximately 100 feet long and about two stories tall. Several varieties of fish, shrimp and coral thrive here. Occasionally turtles and spinner dolphins can be seen. **Note:** The coral should not be damaged or removed.

LĀNA'I CITY (D-8) pop. 3,102, elev. 1,620'

• **Attractions map p. 81**

A "company town," Lāna'i City lies almost at the center of the island at the foot of Mount Lāna'ihale. This comfortably cool setting is flanked by towering Norfolk pine trees.

All island roads radiate from Lāna'i City. Area hotels provide regular shuttle service around the island, but many of the best sites can be reached only by four-wheel-drive vehicles. For information about rental cars phone (808) 565-7227; maps, up-to-date information about trail conditions and suggested itineraries also are available. Do not attempt to leave paved roads on Lāna'i in any vehicle other than one equipped with four-wheel drive. Because all sites are remote, make sure you have sufficient food and beverage with you.

Scenic Kuamalapau Harbor, about 7.5 miles west of town via SR 440, is Lāna'i's main commercial seaport. The fishing is terrific here, and so are the views. Access to the harbor is limited, however, and there are no nearby facilities.

KEAHIAKAWELO, 7 mi. n.w. on Polihua Rd., is also known as Garden of the Gods. It is in a windswept area of the island where erosion has carved an assortment of pinnacles and buttes. Low morning or evening light accentuates the odd formations. Legend has it that the area was once the site of a magical battle between the sorcerers of Lāna'i and Moloka'i.

Beyond Keahiakawelo, the road becomes increasingly rough and ends at the westernmost tip of the island, Ka'ena Point. Polihua Beach, on the northern coast, is accessible only via Keahiakawelo. The area is known for its nesting turtles; visitors should view them from afar and not disturb them.

Polihua Road is a dirt road that should be attempted only during good weather and only in a four-wheel-drive vehicle. Strong currents make swimming dangerous and ill-advised. Cost: Free. **Phone:** (808) 565-7600.

LĀNA'I CULTURE & HERITAGE CENTER is at 730 Lāna'i Ave. The center has a wealth of artifacts, photos, documents, memorabilia and well-done exhibits that focus on the settlement of the island, the plantation and ranching eras, and the people who contributed to the island's growth. **Time:** Allow 30 minutes minimum. **Hours:** Mon.-Fri. 8:30-3:30, Sat. (also day before Thanksgiving, Christmas Eve and Dec. 31) 9-1. Closed Jan. 1, Thanksgiving and Christmas. **Cost:** Free. **Phone:** (808) 565-7177.

MUNRO TRAIL, leaving SR 440 about .5 mi. n., is a 12.8-mile loop that travels through rain forest to 3,370-foot Mount Lāna'ihale, Lāna'i's highest peak. On a clear day, six islands are visible from the summit. The trail ends at SR 440 south of Lāna'i City.

About a mile from SR 440, the road passes some fortifications where, in 1778, warriors attempted to fend off an invasion by a force from the island of Hawai'i. New Zealand naturalist George Munro introduced much of the vegetation in the early 20th century. Nearby, a trail leads to an overlook of 2,000-foot-deep Hauola Gulch. South of Lāna'ihale Overlook the extremely rough 'Awehi Trail leaves the Munro Trail and switchbacks down the steep windward slope near the site of Naha, an old Hawaiian village. **Note: The road is extremely rough in places and requires a four-wheel-drive vehicle. Phone:** (808) 565-7600.

RECREATIONAL ACTIVITIES

Jeep Tours (Self-driving)

- **Dollar Rent A Car Jeep Safari** is at 1036 Lāna'i Ave. **Hours:** Daily 7-7. **Phone:** (808) 565-7227, ext. 1.

FOUR SEASONS RESORT LANA'I AT MANELE BAY (808)565-2000

fyi

Resort Hotel

$750-$25000

Under major renovation, scheduled to be completed December 2015. **Last Rated:** ♦♦♦♦ **Address:** 1 Manele Bay Rd 96763 **Location:** Oceanfront. From airport, 3 mi e on Kaumalapau Hwy to Lana'i City, 6 mi s on SR 440. **Facility:** This newly enhanced resort provides panoramic ocean views atop rugged lava cliffs and white sand beaches. Accommodations are highly crafted and culturally contextual, giving a nod to Hawaiian aesthetics. 217 units. 2 stories, exterior corridors. **Parking:** on-site and valet. **Terms:** 21 day cancellation notice-fee imposed. **Amenities:** safes. **Dining:** Nobu Lana'i, One Forty, see separate listings, entertainment. **Pool(s):** heated outdoor. **Activities:** sauna, hot tub, steamroom, cabanas, scuba diving, snorkeling, regulation golf, tennis, recreation programs, kids club, bicycles, game room, trails, exercise room, spa. **Guest Services:** valet laundry, area transportation.

SAVE CALL BIZ HS / SOME UNITS

HOTEL LANA'I 808/565-7211

fyi Not evaluated. **Address:** 828 Lanai Ave 96763 **Location:** Center. Facilities, services, and décor characterize a mid-scale property.

WHERE TO EAT

BLUE GINGER CAFE
808/565-6363

Breads/Pastries. Casual Dining. $5-$15 **AAA Inspector Notes:** The varied menu features local favorites such as saimin, mahi mahi sandwiches, salads, stir-fry dishes and delicious pastries. The popular eatery offers daily lunch specials, too. **Features:** patio dining. **Address:** 409 7th St 96763 **Location:** Center; across from Dole Park. **Parking:** street only. [B] [L] [D]

LANAI CITY GRILLE
808/565-7211

American. Casual Dining. $28-$40 **AAA Inspector Notes:** Located in what was once a 1920s plantation home, this restaurant serves dishes with an island flair. The rotisserie chicken is their signature dish. **Features:** full bar. **Reservations:** suggested. **Address:** 828 Lanai Ave 96763 **Location:** Center; in Hotel Lana'i. [D]

NOBU LANA'I
808/565-2832

Pacific Rim. Fine Dining. $26-$52 **AAA Inspector Notes:** Contemporary Pacific Rim and Peruvian-Japanese fusion cuisine are offered at this restaurant with modern décor and a sushi bar. Lounge tables outside make for a perfect setting to sip cocktails and sample a wide variety of dishes with friends. **Features:** full bar, patio dining. **Reservations:** suggested. **Address:** 1 Manele Bay Rd 96763 **Location:** From airport, 3 mi e on Kaumalapau Hwy to Lana'i City, 6 mi s on SR 440; in Four Seasons Resort Lana'i at Manele Bay. **Parking:** on-site and valet. [D] CALL [M]

ONE FORTY
808/565-2000

Steak. Fine Dining. $24-$58 **AAA Inspector Notes:** This romantic open-air restaurant allows warm Hawaiian breezes to surround guests as they dine. Floor-to-ceiling doors open to the terrace with distant views of the ocean. Fresh seafood and steaks utilizing seasonal, local products are at the heart of the menu. **Features:** full bar, patio dining. **Reservations:** suggested. **Address:** 1 Manele Bay Rd 96763 **Location:** From airport, 3 mi e on Kaumalapau Hwy to Lana'i City, 6 mi s on SR 440; in Four Seasons Resort Lana'i at Manele Bay. **Parking:** on-site and valet. [B] [D] CALL [M]

PELE'S OTHER GARDEN
808/565-9628

Italian Deli. Casual Dining. $8-$20 **AAA Inspector Notes:** A deli by day and bistro by night, this restaurant serves salads and sandwiches for lunch and several pasta selections and gourmet pizzas at dinnertime. **Features:** beer & wine, patio dining, happy hour. **Reservations:** suggested. **Address:** 811 Houston St 96763 **Location:** Jct 8th St; center; across from Dole Park. **Parking:** street only. [L] [D]

LANAI OHANA POKE MARKET
808/559-6265

[fyi] Not evaluated. The freshest poke (raw fish), prepared several different ways, is just about all that can be found here except for the daily lunch specials and poke bowls. Patrons order takeout or dine at the outdoor picnic tables. Arrive early as they sometimes run out. **Address:** 834-A Gay St 96763 **Location:** Jct 8th St, just s; center.

SHIPWRECK BEACH (D-8)
• Attractions map p. 81

Over the centuries, trade winds through the Pailolo Channel between Moloka'i and Maui, as well as currents and coral reefs, have made Shipwreck Beach—also known as Kaiolohia—the graveyard of many ships. A decommissioned World War II concrete-and-steel Liberty Ship oil tanker mournfully looms over Lāna'i reef, on which it was intentionally grounded as an economical means of disposal. **The roads to the east and west of the beach are extremely rough and require a four-wheel-drive vehicle.**

Shipwreck Beach is considered an excellent place for beachcombing and shore fishing. **Strong currents make swimming in the area extremely hazardous.**

KEOMUKU, 6 mi. s.e., is a ghost town. The village was a flourishing sugar community until 1901, when stones from the nearby Kahe'a Heiau (temple) allegedly were used in the building of Maunalei Sugar Co.'s railroad. The water at the mill turned brackish, and the village had to be abandoned.

Petroglyphs can be seen on the large stones near the site of the *heiau*, but visitors should not disturb them or take rubbings. **Note:** *Heiau* are culturally significant and should be treated with respect. **The road is extremely rough in places and requires a four-wheel-drive vehicle. Hours:** Daily dawn-dusk. **Cost:** Free. **Phone:** (808) 565-7600.

Island of Maui

Haleakalā National Park

In Hawai'i, appetizers are called *pūpū*. If Maui were on a menu, it would surely be the ultimate *pūpū* sampler platter. Each Hawaiian island has its specialties, but people who know Maui know "The Valley Isle" has it all.

For starters, the beaches are some of the most beautiful in the state and are often ranked among the best on the planet. Looking for rain forest and waterfalls? The famous Hāna Highway is hands down the ultimate jungle adventure drive in Hawai'i. Volcano? Maui has one of those, too. Sure, it hasn't oozed lava in more than 200 years, but watching the sunrise from atop 10,023-foot-high Haleakalā is an ethereal experience you won't soon forget.

Sunsets are best viewed from Maui's leeward shore, where you'll find the bulk of the island's lodgings. Resorts and condos line west Maui's palm-fringed coast from the old whaling port of Lahaina north to Kapalua. Just beyond it, sea life teems beneath the surface of Honolua Bay, a snorkeling favorite and a magnet for surfers during big winter swells. West Maui also claims Kā'anapali Beach, a resort-backed strand that caters to sun-and-fun seekers with lively restaurants, bars and shops.

Lahaina, once the capital of Kamehameha the Great's Hawaiian kingdom, is now the west side's go-to town for tourist-geared dining, shopping and nightlife. While some gripe Lahaina has become a tacky tourist trap, naysayers are outnumbered by those who champion Lahaina's intriguing art galleries, top-flight restaurants and wonderful old wooden buildings with fascinating histories to match.

West Maui's dramatic backdrop, Mauna Kahalewai (the summit is 5,788-foot Pu'u Kukui), is the older of the two volcanoes that formed the island. The 7-mile-wide isthmus that links it to Haleakalā in the south usually is credited with giving Maui the nickname "The Valley Isle."

At the western foot of hulking Haleakalā lies south Maui, the leeward shore's other resort area. With affordable condos and hotels in the town of Kīhei and swank digs (think Fairmont and Four Seasons) in Wailea, the area attracts a mix of middle-class travelers, high-income honeymooners and moneyed duffers who tee off at some of the country's finest golf courses. The swimming and sunbathing along this coast are outstanding. And the snorkeling rarely disappoints, especially at the off-shore sunken crater of Molokini, where visibility averages 150 eye-popping feet.

Six miles off Maui's southwest coast is the

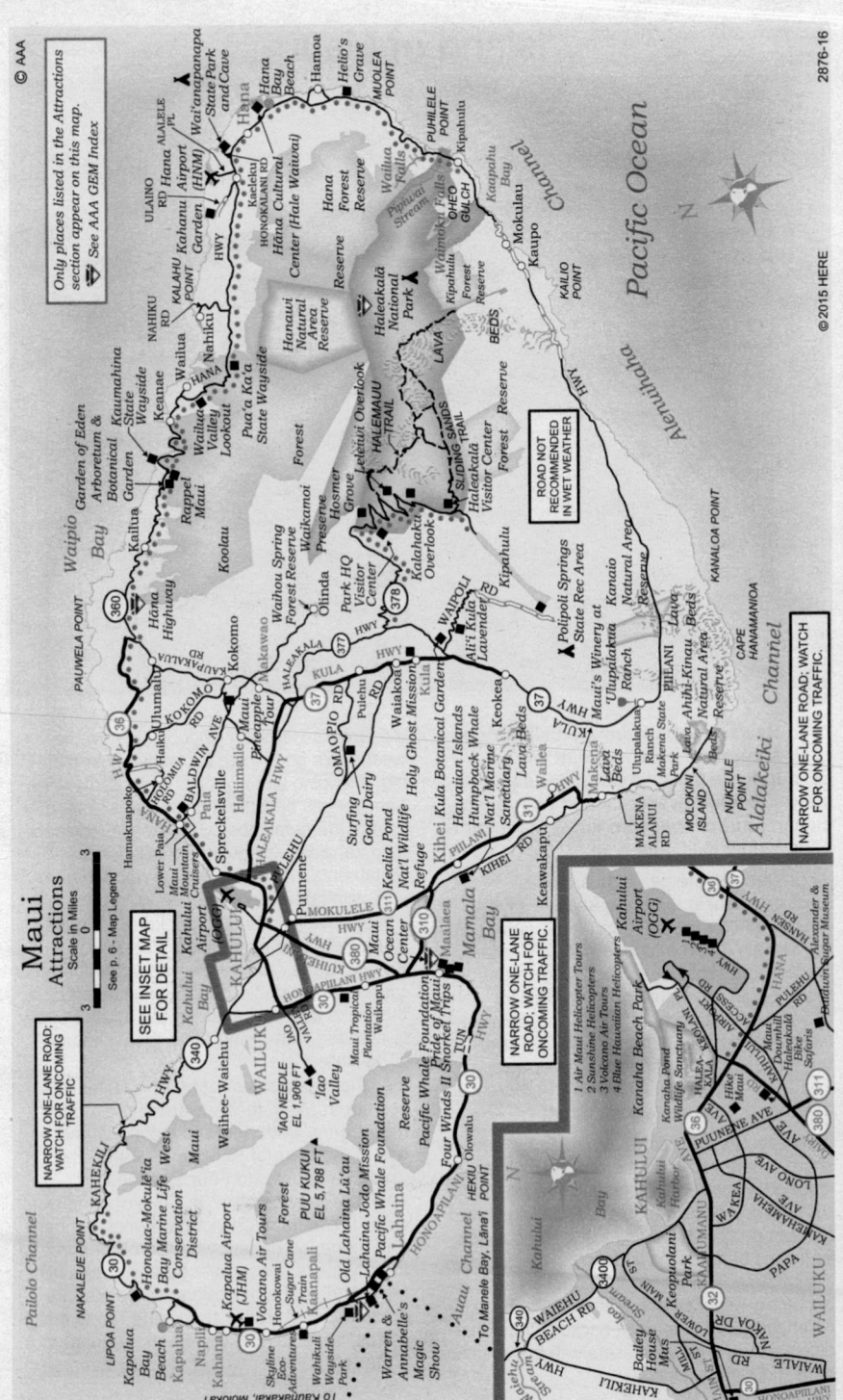

Only places listed in the Attractions section appear on this map.

See AAA GEM Index

Maui
Attractions
Scale in Miles
See p. 6 - Map Legend

SEE INSET MAP FOR DETAIL

ROAD NOT RECOMMENDED IN WET WEATHER

NARROW ONE-LANE ROAD; WATCH FOR ONCOMING TRAFFIC.

NARROW ONE-LANE ROAD; WATCH FOR ONCOMING TRAFFIC.

NARROW ONE-LANE ROAD; WATCH FOR ONCOMING TRAFFIC.

Pacific Ocean

2876-16

© 2015 HERE

▼ *See AAA listing p. 105* ▼

45-square-mile island of Kahoʻolawe. Between the early 1940s and 1990 it was used as a U.S. Navy bombing range. A restoration and revegetation process is expected to take 200 years to complete. Ownership of the island was returned to the state of Hawaiʻi in 2003, but the site is not open to the general public at this time.

Hawaiian trade winds cool Maui's windward east coast and the north shore of the isthmus, where many of the island's 145,000 residents dwell in the towns of Wailuku and Kahului. Just southwest, mammoth Haleakalā rises from the central flatlands, its summit typically crowned with a halo of clouds.

The volcano's vast northern slope is called Upcountry. A land of rolling hills, grassy ranches, yuppie enclaves and old *paniolo* (Hawaiian cowboy) towns, Upcountry is Maui's high-altitude answer to the tropical beach stereotypes of tourist brochures. On the opposite side of Haleakalā, where the southeastern flank meets the sea, rain forest greenery abounds in the form of Hāna and the lush ʻOheʻo Gulch.

On paper Maui is flawless, but in reality the island faces the inevitable problems that come with a steady stream of more than 2 million visitors a year. Traffic in west Maui can slow to a maddening crawl during commute hours. And finding parking at popular beaches can sometimes result in a frustrating, fruitless search, especially in peak summer months.

Island residents take it all in stride, though, and so should you. The people of Maui are friendly and low-key and move at a laid-back "Hawaiʻi time" pace. If you've come to truly relax, it's wise to follow their lead. Locals often say "*Maui nō ka ʻoi*," which means "Maui is the best." Is it? Considering the beauty found throughout the Hawaiian Islands, that's a tough call. But one thing is certain: Arriving at your conclusion is a fine way to spend a vacation.

Gray Line offers sightseeing tours; phone (808) 833-3000 or (888) 206-4531.

HAIKU (D-9) elev. 486'

RECREATIONAL ACTIVITIES

Climbing

- **Rappel Maui** departs from the Garden of Eden Arboretum & Botanical Garden, 10600 Hāna Hwy. Pickup service is available at the park-and-ride commuter lot at jct. SRs 310 and 30 near Maʻalaea. **Hours:** The 6.5-hour tours depart daily at 8, 9:30 and 11:30. **Phone:** (808) 270-1500.

HAʻIKU PLANTATION INN   808/575-7500

[fyi] Not evaluated. **Address:** 555 Haiku Rd 96708 **Location:** From Hana Hwy, just se. Facilities, services, and décor characterize an economy property.

HALEAKALĀ NATIONAL PARK
(E-9)

- **Attractions map p. 86**

Elevations in the park range from sea level at ʻOheʻo to 10,023 ft. at the summit of Puʻu ʻulaʻula. Refer to AAA maps for additional elevation information.

From Kahului, follow SRs 36, 37, 377 and 378 sequentially to the park headquarters on SR 378. The 27-mile drive through plantations and ranch land (watch for stray cattle) reaches an elevation of 7,000 feet at the headquarters.

Called "the House of the Sun," the park encompasses the summit of Haleakalā, Kīpahulu Valley and the ʻOheʻo area near Hāna. The dormant Haleakalā is on the upper slopes and makes up all of east Maui. Although many refer to the feature at the top of Haleakalā as a "crater," it is actually a valley formed by erosion. The reddish hues of cinder cones and black lava flows characterize the scenic landscape.

Among the park's wildlife is the state bird, the rare *nēnē* (Hawaiian goose), which was reintroduced to the island in 1962 and might be seen around the eastern section of the erosional valley and near park headquarters. Native plants include the unusual *ʻāhinahina* (silversword).

Visibility varies during the day but is sometimes best before mid-morning, when the valley usually is free of clouds, and in the late afternoon and evening. Cloudy conditions prevail during midday but frequently improve for short periods, permitting at least partial views of the valley. Mornings are best for viewing Kahoʻolawe, Lānaʻi and west Maui. Weather permitting, afternoons offer the best conditions for photographing the area.

Drivers returning downhill from the summit should brake carefully, drive in low gear to prevent brake failure and stay within speed limits to avoid accidents.

Weather changes rapidly at high elevations on Haleakalā. Temperatures usually range between 35 and 70 degrees Fahrenheit but can be below freezing at any time of the year when the wind chill factor is taken into account. Intense sunlight, thick clouds, heavy rain and high winds are possible daily. **Note:** If it is raining anywhere on the island, watch for flash floods. Hikers and swimmers should evacuate an area immediately when streams appear to swell; flash floods rise quickly, creating hazardous conditions. Do not cross ropes or railings. Check at park visitor centers for weather and stream conditions prior to entry.

Note: Gasoline and food are not available. **Rental car contracts prohibit driving beyond the ʻOheʻo Gulch on Piʻilani Hwy. (CR 31). West of**

Kīpahulu this road is not recommended for travel, particularly in wet weather. The road is narrow and has sharp curves; a four-wheel-drive vehicle may be necessary after heavy rains. Allow 3 hours minimum. Phone (808) 944-3756 for the Maui weather forecast.

General Information and Activities

The park grounds are open daily 24 hours, except during extreme weather conditions. Park Headquarters Visitor Center is open daily 8-3:45.

SR 378 continues past the Park Headquarters Visitor Center 10 miles to the visitor center on the western rim of Haleakalā valley and climbs to the summit. There are 30 miles of well-marked hiking and horseback riding trails in the valley area; there are no roads other than SR 378. The trails are rough in spots, and since the temperature on Haleakalā averages 30 degrees cooler than at sea level, hikers should dress accordingly. High elevations might pose a problem to those with heart, high blood pressure or respiratory conditions.

Several operators offer guided horseback trips into the valley.

There are numerous opportunities for bicycling down Haleakalā. **Note:** Due to safety concerns, no commercial bike tours are currently operating within the park. Phone the park for additional details.

Haleakalā Visitor Center, 10 miles past headquarters on the western rim of the valley, has exhibits and interpretive panels pertaining to geology and natural and cultural history. The center is open daily dawn-3. Nature talks are given daily. The Pu'u 'ula'ula (Red Hill) shelter/overlook on the summit offers views of the neighboring islands and is open daily 24 hours. *See Recreation Areas Chart.*

ADMISSION (valid for 3 days) is $10 per private vehicle; $5 per pedestrian, bicyclist or motorcyclist; $25 (Hawai'i Tri-park Annual Pass, which includes Haleakalā National Park and Pu'uhonua o Hōnaunau National Historical Park).

ADDRESS inquiries to the Superintendent, Haleakalā National Park, P.O. Box 369, Makawao, HI 96768; phone (808) 572-4400.

HALEAKALĀ SUMMIT DISTRICT covers a major portion of Haleakalā National Park. Haleakalā is an enormous volcano 10,023 feet above sea level. Streams eroded deep valleys into its flanks during a long period of volcanic inactivity. Subsequent lava flows spread over the valley floors and formed a new floor, which is punctuated with cinder cones up to 900 feet high. The most recent volcanic activity was 200-400 years ago at a low elevation near Wailea.

Hours: Park open daily 24 hours, except during extreme weather conditions. Park Headquarters Visitor Center daily 8-3:45. **Cost:** Included in 3-day park pass of $10 (private vehicle); $5 (pedestrian, bicyclist or motorcyclist). **Phone:** (808) 572-4400.

Kalahaku Overlook, 2 mi. below the Haleakalā Visitor Center in Haleakalā National Park, is at an elevation of 9,324 feet and affords panoramas of the valley's cinder cones. Protected by a rock wall, some rare 'āhinahina (silverswords) grow just below the parking area. **Hours:** Park open daily 24 hours, except during extreme weather conditions. Park Headquarters Visitor Center daily 8-3:45. **Cost:** Included in 3-day park pass of $10 (private vehicle); $5 (pedestrian, bicyclist or motorcyclist). **Phone:** (808) 572-4400.

Kawilinau, near the valley's center in Haleakalā National Park, is 65 feet deep and may be observed from the rim. The head of the Sliding Sands Trail is at Haleakalā Visitor Center on the valley rim. This difficult trail begins with a steep descent to the crater floor. The trail skirts, but does not enter, the pit. **Note:** Wear sturdy shoes and carry sufficient water. Free trail maps are available at all visitor centers.

Hours: Park open daily 24 hours, except during extreme weather conditions. Park Headquarters Visitor Center daily 8-3:45. **Cost:** Included in 3-day park pass of $10 (private vehicle); $5 (pedestrian, bicyclist or motorcyclist). **Phone:** (808) 572-4400.

Leleiwi Overlook is 6 mi. above the Park Headquarters Visitor Center in Haleakalā National Park and can be reached after a short walk from the Leleiwi parking lot. At an elevation of 8,840 feet, the overlook offers an almost surreal view of the valley. In late afternoon it is possible on rare occasions to see "The Specter of the Brocken," a phenomenon in which a person's shadow is projected onto the heavy cloud layer in the valley; the image is encircled by a rainbow. It is named for Mt. Brocken in Germany, where the phenomenon also occurs.

Hours: Park open daily 24 hours, except during extreme weather conditions. Park Headquarters Visitor Center daily 8-3:45. **Cost:** Included in 3-day park pass of $10 (private vehicle); $5 (pedestrian, bicyclist or motorcyclist). **Phone:** (808) 572-4400.

The Silversword Loop, accessed by a 4.7-mi. hike from the park road on the Halemau'u Trail in Haleakalā National Park, encircles an area covered with unique 'āhinahina (silverswords). The spheres of silvery dagger-shaped leaves are endemic to higher elevations on Haleakalā Volcano. When in full bloom during summer, they can attain a height of 6 feet. Silverswords also can be seen near the Park Headquarters Visitor Center and at the summit.

Allow 6-8 hours for the 9.4-mile round-trip hike. Free trail maps are available at all visitor centers. **Hours:** Park open daily 24 hours, except during extreme weather conditions. Park Headquarters Visitor Center daily 8-3:45. **Cost:** Included in 3-day park pass of $10 (private vehicle); $5 (pedestrian, bicyclist or motorcyclist). **Phone:** (808) 572-4400.

HOSMER GROVE, just northwest of Park Headquarters Visitor Center in Haleakalā National Park, was the site of an experimental planting of temperate-climate trees around 1910. A half-mile nature trail points out the differences between introduced vegetation and rare native plants. This also is an excellent area for bird-watching.

Hours: Park open daily 24 hours, except during extreme weather conditions. Park Headquarters Visitor Center daily 8-3:45. **Cost:** Included in 3-day park pass of $10 (private vehicle); $5 (pedestrian, bicyclist or motorcyclist). **Phone:** (808) 572-4400.

KĪPAHULU DISTRICT is 10 mi. s. of Hāna on CR 31 in Haleakalā National Park. This verdant landscape offers streamside trails and immersion in the east Maui coast's rain forest. The region receives more than 300 inches of rain annually. When weather permits, swimming in the cool lower pools of 'Ohe'o Gulch *(see Hāna Highway attraction listing p. 91)* is popular. This series of terraced rocky pools, descending to the shoreline and strung together by cascades, is officially called the Pools of 'Ohe'o. It also is known by its more exotic nickname, "the Seven Sacred Pools."

To reach the pools, follow the easy half-mile Kuloa Loop Trail, which begins near the visitor center parking lot. Pīpīwai Trail crosses CR 31, travels up the gulch and follows the south side of the Pīpīwai Stream, leading to an overlook of Makahiku Falls. From there, another 1.5-mile uphill trek across the countryside and through a serene bamboo forest leads to 400-foot-high Waimoku Falls. This is widely considered Maui's premier rain forest hike.

Note: If it is raining anywhere on the island, watch for flash floods. Hikers and swimmers should evacuate an area immediately when streams appear to swell; flash floods rise quickly, creating hazardous conditions. Do not cross ropes or railings. Check at park visitor centers for weather and stream conditions prior to entry. Gas, food, lodging and potable water are not available. **Rental car contracts prohibit driving beyond the 'Ohe'o Gulch on Pi'ilani Hwy. (CR 31). West of Kīpahulu this road is not recommended for travel, particularly in wet weather. The road is narrow and has sharp curves; a four-wheel-drive vehicle may be necessary after heavy rains.**

Hours: Park grounds daily 24 hours, except during extreme weather conditions. Kīpahulu Visitor Center daily 9-5. **Cost:** Included in 3-day park pass of $10 (private vehicle); $5 (pedestrian, bicyclist or motorcyclist). **Phone:** (808) 248-7375.

RECREATIONAL ACTIVITIES
Horseback Riding
- **Pony Express Tours** is 2.5 mi. e. off SR 377 on SR 378 (Haleakalā Hwy.). **Hours:** Haleakalā Ranch tours depart daily; phone for schedule. **Phone:** (808) 667-2200.

Ziplines
- **Skyline Eco-Adventures** departs from 2.5 mi. e. off SR 377 on SR 378 (Haleakalā Hwy.). **Hours:** Trips depart daily 8:30-3:30. Phone ahead to confirm schedule. **Phone:** (808) 878-8400 or (888) 864-6947.

HĀLI'IMAILE (D-9) pop. 964, elev. 1,001'
- **Attractions map p. 86**

MAUI PINEAPPLE TOUR departs from Hui No'eau Visual Arts Center, 2841 Baldwin Ave. During a tour of the processing plant, visitors learn how pineapple is processed and packaged; on a drive through the fields, they learn about planting and harvesting techniques. Each visitor can taste several varieties straight from the field and will receive a boxed, airport-ready pineapple to take home.

Note: Sandals are not permitted. Comfortable, closed-toe shoes; hats and sunscreen are recommended. **Time:** Allow 1 hour, 45 minutes minimum. **Hours:** Tours depart daily at 9 and 11:45. Visitors must arrive 15 minutes prior to departure. Closed major holidays. Phone ahead to confirm schedule. **Cost:** $65; $55 (ages 5-12). Tour with lunch $85; $75 (ages 5-12). Under age 5 and pregnant women are not permitted. Reservations are required. **Phone:** (808) 665-5491. GT 🍽

HALI'IMAILE GENERAL STORE RESTAURANT   808/572-2666
▼▼▼ Pacific Rim. Fine Dining. $20-$42 **AAA Inspector Notes:** Well worth the drive "upcountry," this restaurant is renowned for its regional Hawaiian cuisine. This former general store nurtures a friendly, bustling atmosphere and is a great place to relax and enjoy a fine meal. Lunch is served weekdays only. **Features:** full bar. **Reservations:** suggested. **Address:** 900 Hali'imaile Rd 96768 **Location:** SR 37, 1 mi e on SR 371 (Hali'imaile Rd). L D

HĀNA (E-10) pop. 1,235, elev. 98'
- **Hotels p. 92** • **Restaurants p. 92**
- **Attractions map p. 86**

Hāna is rich in legend and history. It was built on an ancient battleground where chiefs from the island of Hawai'i attempted to wrest control from Maui warriors. Helio's Grave, 8 miles south, commemorates the 19th-century chieftain who converted more than 4,000 islanders to Catholicism.

Kamehameha's favored wife, Ka'ahumanu, was born in a cave at the foot of Ka'uiki Hill, a cinder cone formed during one of Maui's most recent volcanic eruptions. The cave is marked by a plaque near the lighthouse and can be seen from a short trail that begins at Hāna Bay's pier and ends at scenic Red Sand Beach. Blanketed with burnt-red cinder from Ka'uiki Hill, this remote pocket beach is a popular clothing-optional spot. **Note:** The trail to the beach is steep and slippery, and no lifeguards are available; visitors should exercise caution. State law officially prohibits nudity on public beaches.

Before World War II Hāna was a busy sugar port. After the war, cane fields gave way to pasture for beef cattle and the town developed into a trade center for surrounding ranches.

Established in 1910, the Hasegawa General Store in the center of town is one of few stores of its type remaining in the islands. Wananalua Congregational Church was built in 1838 of lava rock held together by a cement of pulverized coral rock. The 119-acre Hāna Airport is about 3 miles northwest of town.

Below Hāna, CR 31 follows the coast to the 'Ohe'o Gulch in Haleakalā National Park *(see Hāna Highway attraction listing)*. **Rental car contracts prohibit driving beyond the 'Ohe'o Gulch on Pi'ilani Hwy. (CR 31). West of Kīpahulu this road is not recommended for travel, particularly in wet weather. The road is narrow and has sharp curves; a four-wheel-drive vehicle may be necessary after heavy rains.** Washouts may be encountered between Kīpahulu and 'Ulupalakua Ranch *(see place listing p. 107)* during the rainy seasons.

HĀNA BAY BEACH, n. of town, is a small black-sand public swimming area with picnic facilities and a pavilion. **Hours:** Daily 7 a.m.-10 p.m. **Cost:** Free. **Phone:** (808) 248-7022.

HĀNA CULTURAL CENTER (HALE WAIWAI), 4974 Uakea Rd., just above Hāna Bay off SR 360, contains photographs, tools and other artifacts illustrating local history. A replica of a Hawaiian living compound is composed of cooking, sleeping, meeting and canoe huts. The site also includes one of the oldest historical buildings in Maui, currently being used as the Hāna District Courthouse. **Hours:** Mon.-Thurs. and select Fri. 10-4. Closed Jan. 1, Thanksgiving and Christmas. Phone ahead to confirm schedule. **Cost:** Donations. **Phone:** (808) 248-8622.

HĀNA HIGHWAY (SRs 36 and 360) runs from Kahului to Hāna. This road winds through brushy ravines, bamboo forests, hamlets and fishing settlements, past gorges and waterfalls. Visitors can view Twin Falls (past Milepost 2) at Ho'olawa Bridge, Painted Bark Eucalyptus Trees (Milepost 7), and Ke'anae Arboretum (past Milepost 16) which features hiking trails and picnic tables. Lookouts at Ke'anae (Milepost 17) and Wailua (past Milepost 19) peninsulas offer panoramas of taro fields.

Note: No gasoline is available between Pā'ia and Hāna. Although the entire road is paved and well-marked, the first 30 miles from Kahului cover a narrow section with 600 curves and 54 one-lane bridges. The approximate one-way driving time between Kahului and Hāna is 3.5 hours; the round trip takes a full day. Beyond Hāna is the 'Ohe'o Gulch with its terraced rock-bound pools cascading into the ocean. The paved road to the pools is narrow, winding and bumpy; the pavement ends 2.5 miles past the pools and a gravel road continues 16 miles (a 90-minute drive). **Rental car contracts prohibit driving beyond 'Ohe'o on Pi'ilani Hwy. (CR 31). West of Kīpahulu this road is not recommended for travel, particularly in wet weather. The road is narrow and has sharp curves; a four-wheel-drive vehicle may be necessary after heavy rains.**

Garden of Eden Arboretum & Botanical Garden is just past Milepost 10 on SR 360 (Hāna Hwy.). Flowers, trees, waterfalls and peacocks can be seen in this 27-acre drive-through arboretum. The garden restores natural ecosystems and promotes Hawai'i's indigenous species, but exotic plants plucked from the South Pacific and various rain forests around the world also can be found. More than 500 botanically labeled plants are featured. Two miles of walking trails wind through the site and offer scenic jungle, waterfall and ocean views.

Time: Allow 1 hour minimum. **Hours:** Daily 8-4 (may be closed on very rainy days). **Cost:** $15; $10 (military and students with ID). **Phone:** (808) 344-8600. 🎡

Kahanu Garden is just past Milepost 31 on Hāna Hwy., then 1.5 mi. n. to 650 Ula'ino Rd. Plants from the Pacific Islands are featured on 122 acres. The garden is said to have the largest known collection of breadfruit cultivars, a chief South Pacific food source. Pi'ilanihale Heiau also is on the grounds. **Note:** *Heiau* are culturally significant and should be treated with respect. **Time:** Allow 1 hour minimum. **Hours:** Self-guiding tours Mon.-Fri. 9-4, Sat. 9-2. Guided tours Mon.-Tues. and Thurs.-Fri. at 10 and noon. Closed major holidays. **Cost:** Self-guiding tour $10; free (ages 0-12). Guided tour $25; free (ages 0-12 when accompanied by paying adult). Reservations are required for guided tours. **Phone:** (808) 248-8912.

Kaumahina State Wayside, just past Milepost 12 on Hāna Hwy., offers coastline views of Honomanū Bay and the Ke'anae Peninsula. The 7.8-acre forested area contains some flamboyant plants. No drinking water is available. **Cost:** Free. 🎡

Pua'a Ka'a State Wayside, .6 mi. past Milepost 22 on Hāna Hwy., is a mountain area with a small waterfall and a natural pool. No drinking water is available. **Cost:** Free. 🎡

Wailua Valley Lookout, .9 mi. past Milepost 18 on Hāna Hwy., has a sweeping vista of the fertile peninsula with its green flat lands of taro and banana groves. No drinking water is available. **Cost:** Free.

WAI'ANAPANAPA STATE PARK AND CAVE is about 2.5 mi. n.w. via SR 360, then about .5 mi. n. at the end of Honokalani Rd.; the route is narrow and winding. The small Honokalani Black Sand Beach is composed of small, smooth lava pebbles. A coastal trail leads to a small sea arch, sea caves, blowholes and seaside lava tubes. Various trails lead past temple ruins and a *hala* forest. *See Recreation Areas Chart.*

Note: Visitors should use caution while exploring the sea arch, sea caves, blowholes and seaside lava tubes. Wear walking shoes and bring water. **Hours:** Daily dawn-dusk. **Phone:** (808) 984-8109.

WAILUA FALLS, 8 mi. s. on SR 31, drops 200 feet into Wailua Gulch and is most impressive in morning sunlight. The water comes from Haleakalā to a grove of *kukui,* also known as candlenut trees. Hawaiians once strung the quarter- to half-dollar-sized *kukui* nuts on sticks and burned them as torches. The smaller Kanahualui Falls are just down the road. **Phone:** (808) 270-7845.

TRAVAASA HOTEL HANA   (808)248-8211

Resort Hotel
$450-$1300

Address: 5031 Hana Hwy 96713 **Location:** Oceanfront. At south edge of village (SR 360), follow business route. **Facility:** In a tranquil setting, the property features spacious guest rooms with no televisions or radios to distract from the peaceful ambiance. Some cottages offer spectacular ocean views and decks. 71 units, some cottages. 1 story, exterior corridors. **Parking:** on-site and valet. **Terms:** check-in 4 pm, 10 day cancellation notice, resort fee. **Amenities:** safes. **Dining:** Kaʻuiki Dining Room, see separate listing, entertainment. **Pool(s):** heated outdoor. **Activities:** hot tub, steamroom, snorkeling, tennis, recreation programs, bicycles, exercise room, spa. **Guest Services:** complimentary laundry, area transportation.

[icons]

HANA KAI MAUI   808/248-8426

fyi Not evaluated. **Address:** 4865 Uakea Rd 96713 **Location:** Jct SR 360 (Hana Hwy) 0.5 mi s. Facilities, services, and décor characterize a mid-scale property.

WHERE TO EAT

HANA RANCH RESTAURANT   808/248-8211

American. Casual Dining. $8-$22 AAA Inspector Notes: If you're making the drive to Hana, this is a convenient spot located near the Travaasa Hana on SR 360. Enjoy a quick bite and enjoy ocean views from the patio or come inside for dinner later on. The takeout window accepts lunch orders daily between 11 am and 4 pm. **Features:** full bar, patio dining, happy hour. **Address:** 5031 Hana Hwy 96713 **Location:** At south edge of village (SR 360), follow business route. [L] [D] CALL [icons]

KAʻUIKI DINING ROOM   808/248-8211

Pacific Rim. Casual Dining. $16-$40 AAA Inspector Notes: Considered one of the best places to eat in town, this lovely open-air restaurant offers gentle breezes and distant views of the ocean. Background music from the bar sets the scene as guests settle in to enjoy the imaginative and inventive kitchen creations. This is a great spot for special occasions and for those who have just finished the drive to Hana. **Features:** full bar, patio dining. **Reservations:** suggested. **Address:** 5031 Hana Hwy 96713 **Location:** At south edge of village (SR 360), follow business route; in Travaasa Hotel Hana. **Parking:** on-site and valet. [B] [L] [D] CALL [icons]

KĀʻANAPALI (D-8) pop. 1,045, elev. 5'
• Attractions map p. 86

Kāʻanapali is part of the resort area that lines the wide 4-mile-long curve of Kāʻanapali Beach, one of the better beaches on the island. No lifeguards are available. The north end of the beach is sandier and has fewer reefs. Nāpili Bay is north along SR 30. Molokaʻi and Lānaʻi are visible across the intervening channels.

Information and reservations for local cruises, tours, fishing charters and other activities are available from Beach Activities of Maui on Kāʻanapali Beach. Beachfront hotels offer snorkel equipment rental.

Shopping: Whalers Village, off SR 30 in the Kāʻanapali Beach Resort area, is a large complex of shops and dining spots with open-air displays reflecting Maui's whaling era; phone (808) 661-4567.

RECREATIONAL ACTIVITIES
Ziplines
• **Skyline Eco-Adventures** departs from the Fairway Shops at 2580 Kekaʻa Dr., just s. of SR 30. **Hours:** Trips depart daily on the hour 7-2. **Phone:** (808) 878-8400 or (888) 864-6947.

ASTON AT PAPAKEA RESORT   (808)665-0880

Vacation Rental
Condominium
$269-$859

Address: 3543 Lower Honoapiilani Rd 96761 **Location:** Oceanfront. SR 30 exit Lower Honoapiilani Rd, just nw; in North Kaanapali Beach resort area. **Facility:** A 13 acre resort with tropical landscaping and koi ponds where units range from studios with kitchens to multi-bedroom condos with private lanais, daily maid service and in-room washer/dryers. 130 condominiums. 4 stories, exterior corridors. **Terms:** 3 day cancellation notice. **Amenities:** video games, safes. **Pool(s):** outdoor, heated outdoor. **Activities:** hot tub, tennis, recreation programs. **Guest Services:** complimentary laundry. *(See ad starting on p. 148.)*

[icons]

ASTON AT THE WHALER ON KAANAPALI BEACH
                                     (808)661-6000

Vacation Rental
Condominium
$345-$1065

Address: 2481 Kaanapali Pkwy 96761 **Location:** Oceanfront. SR 30 exit Kaanapali Pkwy, just nw; in Kaanapali Beach resort area. Adjacent to Whalers Village Mall. **Facility:** Featured at this condo complex is tropical landscaping and koi ponds as well as many spacious rooms, possibly among the largest on Maui. Most units, many recently renovated, offer ocean views. 135 condominiums. 12 stories, interior corridors. **Parking:** on-site (fee). **Terms:** check-in 4 pm, 2 night minimum stay - weekends, 3 day cancellation notice, resort fee. **Amenities:** safes. **Pool(s):** heated outdoor. **Activities:** sauna, hot tub, snorkeling, tennis, exercise room, spa. **Guest Services:** valet and coin laundry. *(See ad starting on p. 148.)*

[icons]

ASTON KAANAPALI SHORES   (808)667-2211

Address: 3445 Lower Honoapiilani Rd 96761 **Location:** Oceanfront. SR 30 exit Lower Honoapiilani Rd, just nw; in North Kaanapali Beach resort area. **Facility:** This oceanfront high-rise condo complex offers a few hotel-style rooms without cooking facilities, an efficiency studio and one- to two-bedroom units with full kitchens. 386 condominiums. 4-9 stories, interior/exterior corridors. **Parking:** on-site (fee). **Terms:** 3 day cancellation notice, resort fee. **Amenities:** video games, safes. **Pool(s):** heated outdoor. **Activities:** sauna, hot tub, scuba diving, snorkeling, tennis, recreation programs, exercise room, massage. **Guest Services:** valet and coin laundry. *(See ad starting on p. 148.)*

Vacation Rental
Condominium
$269-$1119

[icons]

ASTON MAHANA AT KAANAPALI   (808)661-8751

Vacation Rental Condominium $339-$899 Address: 110 Kaanapali Shores Pl 96761 **Location:** Oceanfront. SR 30 exit Lower Honoapiilani Rd, just nw, then just sw; in North Kaanapali Beach resort area. **Facility:** Overlooking beautiful Kaanapali Beach, this condo complex features studios, one- and two-bedroom suites, all with full kitchens and washer/dryer units. 121 condominiums. 12 stories, exterior corridors. **Terms:** 3 night minimum stay, 3 day cancellation notice-fee imposed, resort fee. **Amenities:** video games, safes. **Pool(s):** heated outdoor. **Activities:** hot tub, tennis. **Guest Services:** complimentary laundry, boarding pass kiosk. *(See ad starting on p. 148.)*

[icons]

HONUA KAI RESORT & SPA   (808)662-2800

Resort
Condominium
$374

Address: 130 Kai Malina Pkwy 96761 **Location:** Oceanfront. SR 30 exit Kai Malina Pkwy, just w; in North Kaanapali Beach resort area. **Facility:** Featured is upscale, spacious one-, two- and three-bedroom suites with very large lanais, each with glass railings so the view is not obstructed. 628 condominiums. 10 stories, interior corridors. **Parking:** on-site and valet. **Terms:** check-in 4 pm, 21 day cancellation notice-fee imposed, resort fee. **Amenities:** safes. **Dining:** Duke's Beach House, see separate listing. **Pool(s):** heated outdoor. **Activities:** hot tub, cabanas, scuba diving, snorkeling, recreation programs, exercise room, spa. **Guest Services:** valet and coin laundry, boarding pass kiosk.

HYATT REGENCY MAUI RESORT & SPA   (808)661-1234

Resort Hotel
$199-$549

HYATT REGENCY

AAA Benefit: Members save 10%!

Address: 200 Nohea Kai Dr 96761 **Location:** Oceanfront. SR 30 exit Kaanapali Pkwy, just w, then just s; in Kaanapali Beach resort area. **Facility:** The lovely resort is on several acres of manicured grounds. A gorgeous beach, spectacular waterfalls and serene ponds are among its features. 806 units, some two and three bedrooms. 10 stories, interior/exterior corridors. **Parking:** on-site (fee) and valet. **Terms:** check-in 4 pm, 3 day cancellation notice-fee imposed, resort fee. **Amenities:** video games, safes. **Dining:** 4 restaurants, also, Japengo - Maui, see separate listing, entertainment. **Pool(s):** heated outdoor. **Activities:** sauna, hot tub, steamroom, cabanas, scuba diving, snorkeling, tennis, recreation programs, kids club, game room, exercise room, spa. **Guest Services:** valet and coin laundry, rental car service, area transportation.

SHERATON MAUI RESORT & SPA   (808)661-0031

Resort Hotel
$299-$679

Sheraton

AAA Benefit: Members save up to 15%, plus Starwood Preferred Guest® benefits!

Address: 2605 Kaanapali Pkwy 96761 **Location:** Oceanfront. SR 30 exit Kaanapali Pkwy, just nw; in Kaanapali Beach resort area. **Facility:** A historic lava rock called Black Rock is the site of a ceremonial cliff-diving tradition at sunset. 508 units. 2-6 stories, interior/exterior corridors. **Parking:** on-site (fee) and valet. **Terms:** 3 day cancellation notice-fee imposed, resort fee. **Amenities:** safes. **Dining:** 4 restaurants, entertainment. **Pool(s):** outdoor. **Activities:** hot tub, cabanas, scuba diving, snorkeling, tennis, recreation programs, exercise room, spa. **Guest Services:** valet laundry, rental car service, area transportation.

THE WESTIN KAʻANAPALI OCEAN RESORT VILLAS   (808)667-3200

Resort Hotel
$359-$679

WESTIN
HOTELS & RESORTS

AAA Benefit: Members save up to 15%, plus Starwood Preferred Guest® benefits!

Address: 6 Kai Ala Dr 96761 **Location:** Oceanfront. SR 30 exit Kai Ala Dr, just w. **Facility:** Situated on 27 beachfront acres, this property offers several attractive pool areas and koi ponds. All units have a washer and dryer. 1021 kitchen units. 6 stories, interior corridors. **Parking:** on-site (fee) and valet. **Terms:** check-in 4 pm, 3 day cancellation notice-fee imposed, resort fee. **Amenities:** safes. **Dining:** 2 restaurants, also, Pulehu, an Italian Grill, see separate listing, entertainment. **Pool(s):** heated outdoor. **Activities:** hot tub, cabanas, scuba diving, snorkeling, tennis, recreation programs, kids club, playground, exercise room, spa. **Guest Services:** valet and coin laundry, boarding pass kiosk, area transportation. *(See ad p. 103.)*

ROYAL LAHAINA RESORT   808/661-3611

[fyi] Not evaluated. **Address:** 2780 Kekaa Dr 96761 **Location:** SR 30 exit Kai Ala Dr, just sw; in North Kaanapali Beach resort area. Facilities, services, and décor characterize a mid-scale property.

WHERE TO EAT

C J'S DELI & DINER   808/667-0968

American. Quick Serve. $8-$19 **AAA Inspector Notes:** Patrons can surf the web wirelessly while enjoying their meal. Those planning to head to the beach or take the long drive to Hana might pick up the Hana box lunch, the ideal take-out meal. Don't forget the fresh-baked pies for dessert. **Features:** patio dining. **Address:** 2580 Keka'a Dr, Suite 120 96761 **Location:** SR 30 exit Keka'a Dr; in Kaanapali Fairway Shops. [B] [L] [D]

DUKE'S BEACH HOUSE   808/662-2900

Hawaiian Fusion. Casual Dining. $13-$33 **AAA Inspector Notes:** Pictures and memorabilia of the famous Hawaiian surfer Duke Kahanamoku fill the fun and casual beachfront restaurant. The staff carries out relaxed service. The Ohia bar serves a lighter casual menu, while the dining room offers a full menu with fresh fish, steaks and a braised pork shank. Live music is offered most evenings. **Features:** full bar, patio dining, early bird specials, happy hour. **Reservations:** suggested. **Address:** 130 Kai Malina Pkwy 96761 **Location:** SR 30 exit Kai Malina Pkwy, just w; in North Kaanapali Beach resort area; in Honua Kai Resort & Spa. **Parking:** on-site and valet. [B] [L] [D] [AC]

HULA GRILL   808/667-6636

Pacific Rim. Casual Dining. $13-$32 **AAA Inspector Notes:** This popular establishment presents a menu of regional Hawaiian cuisine. Several types of fresh, local fish are prepared in a variety of styles. A more casual menu is available on the terrace. Be sure to try the Baked Hawaii, their signature dessert that's a take on a baked Alaska. The open dining room and patio provide romantic sunset views of the ocean and surrounding islands. Live hula entertainment is featured nightly. **Features:** full bar, patio dining, happy hour. **Address:** 2435 Kaanapali Pkwy, Bldg P 96761 **Location:** In Whalers Village; in Kaanapali Beach resort area. [L] [D] [AC]

JAPENGO - MAUI
808/667-4796

▼▼▼ Pacific Rim Sushi. Casual Dining. $22-$40 **AAA Inspector Notes:** This restaurant offers Pacific Rim and Southeast Asian cuisine in a contemporary setting. Located on the lobby level of the hotel but set on a rise overlooking the lush tropical grounds, cascading waterfalls, sandy beach and breaking surf, it's a great place to catch the sunset. And the food's great, too. Duck pot stickers, prawn and mango salad and hoisin-glazed pork ribs are on the menu. A sushi bar and complimentary valet parking are available. **Features:** full bar, patio dining, happy hour. **Address:** 200 Nohea Kai Dr 96761 **Location:** SR 30 exit Kaanapali Pkwy, just w, then just s; in Kaanapali Beach resort area; in Hyatt Regency Maui Resort & Spa. **Parking:** on-site and valet. 🍴 D CALL ♿M

JAVA JAZZ
808/667-0787

▼▼ American. Casual Dining. $10-$31 **AAA Inspector Notes:** Funky is the best way to describe the café, which has a full menu of soups, salads, burgers and sandwiches. Breakfast is served all day. At dinner there are pasta and nightly entrée selections. The cozy and eclectic décor lines the walls. Those looking for a great cup of soup and a good cuppa joe need look no further. **Features:** full bar, patio dining, Sunday brunch, happy hour. **Address:** 3350 Lower Honoapiilani Rd, Suite 203 96761 **Location:** SR 30 exit Honoapiilani Rd, just e; in Honokowai Marketplace. B L D CALL ♿M

LEILANI'S ON THE BEACH
808/661-4495

▼▼ American. Casual Dining. $12-$34 **AAA Inspector Notes:** First- and second-floor dining rooms are decorated in a casual Polynesian style, and are open to ocean breezes and provide lovely sunset views. Fresh local fish is thoughtfully prepared in a variety of ways. Also available are grilled steaks, shellfish and kiawe wood-smoked ribs and chicken. Hula pie is the signature dessert. **Features:** full bar, patio dining, early bird specials, happy hour. **Reservations:** suggested. **Address:** 2435 Kaanapali Pkwy 96761 **Location:** In Whalers Village; in Kaanapali Beach resort area. L D 🍴

MAUI FISH & PASTA
808/662-0668

▼▼ American. Casual Dining. $13-$28 **AAA Inspector Notes:** A great choice all day long, with traditional American dishes served with a touch of the islands. A breakfast treat is deep-fried stuffed Hawaiian sweet bread with berry compote and whipped coconut cream. For lunch, maybe a little lighter with grilled catch of the day and a Caesar salad. Dinner starts with grilled monster prawns on Kula corn ravioli, herb grilled tender pork chops and a fresh Kula apple-banana cream tart for dessert. Request a table closer to the windows for an ocean view. **Features:** full bar, early bird specials, happy hour. **Address:** 2435 Kaanapali Pkwy 96761 **Location:** SR 30 exit Kaanapali Pkwy, just nw; in Whalers Village; in Kaanapali Beach resort area. B L D 🍴

PULEHU, AN ITALIAN GRILL
808/667-3200

▼▼▼ Italian. Casual Dining. $20-$42 **AAA Inspector Notes:** Pulehu, in the Hawaiian language, means "grilled or cooked over an open flame." Here you will find contemporary cuisine, including pasta specialties and pizzas cooked in a wood-stone oven. A few tables overlook the koi ponds in the open-air dining room at this upscale but casual spot. **Features:** full bar, patio dining. **Reservations:** suggested. **Address:** 6 Kai Ala Dr 96761 **Location:** SR 30 exit Kai Ala Dr, just w; in The Westin Ka'anapali Ocean Resort Villas. **Parking:** on-site and valet. *(See ad p. 103.)* 🍴 D CALL ♿M 🍴

ROY'S
808/669-6999

▼▼▼ Pacific Rim Fusion. Fine Dining. $16-$55 **AAA Inspector Notes:** Enjoy fusion of fresh Pacific seafood, French sauces and Asian seasonings. The ever-changing menu has many entrées such as grilled salmon and barbecue lamb rack, and the signature dessert, chocolate soufflé. **Features:** full bar, happy hour. **Reservations:** suggested. **Address:** 2290 Kaanapali Pkwy 96761 **Location:** SR 30 exit Kaanapali Pkwy, just nw; on the grounds of the Kaanapali Golf Course. 🍴 L D CALL ♿M

KAHANA

NOELANI CONDOMINIUM RESORT
(808)669-8374

Vacation Rental Condominium
$145-$209

Address: 4095 Lower Honoapiilani Rd 96761 **Location:** Oceanfront. SR 30 exit Akahele St; in Kahana Beach resort area. **Facility:** Situated on lovely grounds, these oceanfront accommodations range from studios to three-bedroom suites. Each unit features a full kitchen, stereo and large lanai. 44 condominiums. 2-3 stories (no elevator), exterior corridors. **Terms:** 3 night minimum stay - seasonal and/or weekends, 30 day cancellation notice. **Amenities:** safes. **Pool(s):** outdoor, heated outdoor. **Activities:** hot tub, limited exercise equipment, massage. **Guest Services:** complimentary laundry.

SAVE 🏊 📶 ✕ 🏋 🛄 🖼 🍴

ROYAL KAHANA MAUI BY OUTRIGGER
(808)669-5911

▼▼ Vacation Rental Condominium $99-$295 **Address:** 4365 Lower Honoapiilani Rd 96761 **Location:** Oceanfront. SR 30 exit Hoohui Rd; in Kahana Beach resort area. **Facility:** On the beach, this complex offers prime views of the ocean. Choose from studio units and one- or two-bedroom condos with full kitchens. All units have a washer/dryer. 236 condominiums. 12 stories, exterior corridors. **Terms:** 2 night minimum stay, 7 day cancellation notice-fee imposed, resort fee. **Amenities:** safes. **Pool(s):** heated outdoor. **Activities:** exercise room. **Guest Services:** complimentary laundry.

🏊 BIZ 📶 ✕ 🛄 🖼 🍴

WHERE TO EAT

MAUI BREWING CO.
808/669-3474

▼▼ American. Casual Dining. $12-$25 **AAA Inspector Notes:** Check out the newest brewpub on the island. It has become a favorite of locals and tourists alike. To accompany the huge selection of house-made beers, there are several sliders, burgers, sandwiches and adult grilled cheese, not to mention pizzas, meatloaf and jambalaya. Purchase a growler and take some beer back to your condo or hotel. **Features:** full bar, happy hour. **Address:** 4405 Honoapiilani Hwy, Suite 217 96761 **Location:** SR 30 exit Hoohui Rd, just nw; in Kahana Gateway Shopping Center. L D CALL ♿M

KAHULUI (D-9) pop. 26,337, elev. 40'
- Restaurants p. 96
- Attractions map p. 86

Kahului is the island's main seaport and site of its only airport capable of handling jet traffic. A modern commercial city with residential areas, schools and shopping centers, it abuts Wailuku *(see place listing p. 110)*. All interisland freight passes through Kahului's protected harbor, where large freighters take aboard sugar, pineapples and other cargo to ship to the mainland. About 3 miles east of town is the 1,391-acre Kahului Airport.

Hāna Highway (SRs 36 and 360) is a 52-mile winding road between Kahului and Hāna. Numerous waterfalls, hidden trails and fern-lined pools border the narrow road *(see attraction listing p. 91)*.

Shopping: Maui Mall, 70 E. Ka'ahumanu Ave., offers more than 45 shops and eateries.

AIR MAUI HELICOPTER TOURS, at Kahului Heliport, Hangar 110, offers several narrated tours over the island of Maui. Passengers may glimpse waterfalls, rain forests and valleys as well as the West Maui Mountains and Haleakalā Crater. Tours last between 30 and 65 minutes. A 2-hour combination flight and zipline tour also is offered.

Note: Due to decompression-related sickness, it is recommended that passengers wait 12-24 hours after scuba diving before flying; the amount of time is dependent on particular dive factors. Ask about possible policies regarding minimum wait time between scuba diving and flying; weight restrictions; weather, cancellation and refund policies; and the minimum and maximum number of passengers for flights. All small aircraft may encounter turbulence.

Hours: Daily 7-5. **Cost:** $175-$499, plus applicable fuel surcharge. Fares may vary; phone ahead. Reservations are required. **Phone:** (808) 877-7005 or (877) 238-4942.

BLUE HAWAIIAN HELICOPTERS departs from Kahului Airport. Helicopter tours range from 30 minutes to 2 hours and provide views of Maui's mountains, valleys, rain forests, waterfalls and cliffs. Moloka'i can be seen on one of the tours. Passengers hear music, two-way communication with the pilot, and the pilot's narration via noise-canceling headsets.

Note: Due to decompression-related sickness, it is recommended that passengers wait 12-24 hours after scuba diving before flying; the amount of time is dependent on particular dive factors. Ask about possible policies regarding minimum wait time between scuba diving and flying; weight restrictions; weather, cancellation and refund policies; and the minimum and maximum number of passengers for flights. All small aircraft may encounter turbulence.

Hours: Daily 7 a.m.-10 p.m. **Cost:** $148-$550, plus applicable fuel surcharge. Reservations are required. **Phone:** (808) 871-8844, or (800) 745-2583 from the mainland. *(See ad on inside front cover.)*

KANAHĀ BEACH PARK is .2 mi. n. of Kahului Airport. Calm, protected, warm waters and light onshore winds make this beach a popular windsurfing and fishing spot. **Hours:** Daily dawn-dusk. **Cost:** Free. **Phone:** (808) 270-7389. 🏕️

KANAHĀ POND WILDLIFE SANCTUARY, 1.5 mi. s.w. of Kahului Airport at jct. SRs 36 and 37, provides an observation booth for viewing migratory ducks, endangered Hawaiian coots and stilts, and other birds. **Hours:** Observation booth daily dawn-dusk. Full sanctuary access available Mon.-Fri. 8-3, Sept.-Mar. **Cost:** Free. **Phone:** (808) 984-8100.

SUNSHINE HELICOPTERS, departing from Kahului Heliport, Hangar 107, offers narrated helicopter tours of the Maui coastline, Haleakalā's vast moonlike crater, the Hāna rain forest, the 'Ohe'o Gulch and coastline waterfalls. Tours last between 40 and 70 minutes.

Note: Due to decompression-related sickness, it is recommended that passengers wait 12-24 hours after scuba diving before flying; the amount of time is dependent on particular dive factors. Ask about possible policies regarding minimum wait time between scuba diving and flying; weight restrictions; weather, cancellation and refund policies; and the

minimum and maximum number of passengers for flights. All small aircraft may encounter turbulence.

Hours: Flights depart daily; phone for schedule. **Cost:** $260-$495, depending on tour, helicopter and seating. Reservations are required. **Phone:** (808) 871-0722 or (800) 469-3000.

VOLCANO AIR TOURS departs Kahului Airport Commuter Airlines Terminal. These 2-hour tours aboard nine-passenger, twin-engine airplanes fly over the spectacular scenery of Maui and Hawai'i Island. Some of the many dramatic sights are lava flows in an active volcano area on Hawai'i Island and cascading waterfalls. All seats are window seats.

Note: Due to decompression-related sickness, it is recommended that passengers wait 12-24 hours after scuba diving before flying; the amount of time is dependent on particular dive factors. Ask about possible policies regarding minimum wait time between scuba diving and flying; weight restrictions; weather, cancellation and refund policies; and the minimum and maximum number of passengers for flights. All small aircraft may encounter turbulence.

Hours: Afternoon flights daily; phone for schedule. Office hours 7 a.m.-9 p.m. Arrive at the terminal 15 minutes before departure. **Cost:** $385, plus applicable taxes. Reservations are required. **Phone:** (808) 877-5500.

RECREATIONAL ACTIVITIES
Bicycling

- **Maui Downhill Haleakalā Bike Safaris** provides pickup service at hotels and condominiums. **Hours:** Tours depart daily; phone for schedule. **Phone:** (808) 871-2155, or (800) 535-2453 off Maui.

Hiking

- **Hike Maui** departs from the park-and-ride commuter lot on Kuihelani Hwy. (SR 380) just s. of SR 311. Other activities are offered. **Hours:** Waterfall and rain forest tours daily; phone for schedule. **Phone:** (808) 879-5270 or (866) 324-6284.

COURTYARD BY MARRIOTT - MAUI KAHULUI AIRPORT
(808)871-1800

Hotel
$218-$395

COURTYARD
Marriott

AAA Benefit: Members save 5% or more!

Address: 532 Keolani Pl 96732 **Location:** Jct Kuihelani (SR 380) and Haleakala hwys; just sw of airport. **Facility:** 138 units, some kitchens. 4 stories, interior corridors. **Parking:** on-site (fee). **Terms:** 3 day cancellation notice. **Pool(s):** heated outdoor. **Activities:** hot tub, exercise room. **Guest Services:** valet and coin laundry, boarding pass kiosk, area transportation.

MAUI SEASIDE HOTEL (808)877-3311

Hotel
$140-$200

Address: 100 W Kaahumanu Ave 96732 **Location:** Waterfront. Jct Lono and W Kaahumanu (SR 32) aves. On Kahului Bay. **Facility:** 185 units. 2-3 stories, interior/exterior corridors. **Parking:** on-site (fee). **Terms:** cancellation fee imposed. **Pool(s):** outdoor. **Guest Services:** coin laundry. **Featured Amenity:** full hot breakfast.

SAVE ✈ ⏹ CALL &M ☕ BIZ
📶 ✕ 🔋 💻

WHERE TO EAT

MARCO'S GRILL & DELI 808/877-4446

Italian. Casual Dining. $8-$21 **AAA Inspector Notes:** An Italian feel punctuates this casually upbeat dining room, in which diners can choose from a full range of American and Italian specialties. **Features:** full bar. **Address:** 444 Hana Hwy 96732 **Location:** Corner of Hana Hwy (SR 36) and Dairy Rd (SR 380).

B L D CALL &M

KAPALUA (D-8) pop. 353, elev. 267'
• Attractions map p. 86

HONOLUA-MOKULĒ'IA BAY MARINE LIFE CONSERVATION DISTRICT is off SR 30, just past Milepost 32. The district is composed of twin horseshoe-shaped bays separated by a rocky point. Mokulē'ia Bay, which is not visible from the road, is accessible via the concrete steps near the parking area. A favorite among snorkelers, the bay is relatively small with a sandy pocket beach. On the west side, a small stream empties into the ocean.

Less than a mile east of Mokulē'ia Bay on SR 30 is a dirt trail that leads to the slightly larger Honolua Bay. The beach is covered in a jumble of smooth, rounded boulders, and an intermittent stream drains into the sea. Snorkelers can spot coral, sea turtles and a variety of fish. **Note:** Swimming is not recommended at either beach during the winter months when high surf is common. Parking is available only along the highway. **Time:** Allow 2 hours minimum. **Hours:** Daily dawn-dusk. **Phone:** (808) 243-5294. 🏧

KAPALUA BAY BEACH is off SR 30, then about 1 mi. n.w. on Office Rd. and about .8 mi. w. on Lower Honoapi'ilani Hwy. This is a quiet beach with dependably calm surf and decent underwater scenery at the far north end of the bay near the rocky point. Restrooms and outdoor showers are located near the parking lot. **Hours:** Daily dawn-dusk. **Cost:** Free. 🏧

VOLCANO AIR TOURS departs Kapalua West Maui Airport, located on Akahele St. near Lahaina. These 2-hour, 15-minute tours aboard nine-passenger, twin-engine airplanes fly over the spectacular scenery of Maui and Hawai'i Island. Some of the many dramatic sights are lava flows in an active volcano area on Hawai'i Island and cascading waterfalls. All seats are window seats.

Note: Due to decompression-related sickness, it is recommended that passengers wait 12-24 hours after scuba diving before flying; the amount of time is dependent on particular dive factors. Ask about possible policies regarding minimum wait time between scuba diving and flying; weight restrictions; weather, cancellation and refund policies; and the minimum and maximum number of passengers for flights. All small aircraft may encounter turbulence.

Hours: Morning flights daily; phone for schedule. Office hours 7 a.m.-9 p.m. Arrive at the terminal 15 minutes before departure. **Cost:** $425, plus applicable taxes. Reservations are required. **Phone:** (808) 877-5500.

MONTAGE KAPALUA BAY 808/662-6500

Resort Hotel. Rates not provided. **Address:** One Bay Dr 96761 **Location:** Oceanfront. SR 30 exit Office Rd, just n to Lower Honoapiilani Rd, then just nw; in Kapalua resort area. **Facility:** Featuring cascading pools and expansive tropical grounds, this property offers luxurious, spacious suites. All suites have lanais, the perfect place to relax. Each unit offers at least two bedrooms with all the comforts of home. 50 kitchen units, some two and three bedrooms. 4-7 stories, exterior corridors. **Parking:** valet only. **Amenities:** safes. **Dining:** 2 restaurants, entertainment. **Pool(s):** heated outdoor. **Activities:** sauna, hot tub, steamroom, scuba diving, snorkeling, kids club, bicycles, lawn sports, spa. **Guest Services:** complimentary and valet laundry, area transportation.

⏹ 🛁 🍸 CALL &M ☕ 🏋 BIZ 📶 ✕ 🔋
📠 💻

THE RITZ-CARLTON, KAPALUA   (808)669-6200

Resort Hotel
$559-$919

AAA Benefit:
Unequaled service at special member savings!

Address: One Ritz-Carlton Dr 96761 **Location:** Oceanfront. SR 30 exit Office Rd; in Kapalua resort area; on northwest shore. **Facility:** This waterfront property indulges you in the pure luxury, from its wonderfully decorated rooms and spa-like bathrooms to its lush and expansive grounds. 463 units, some two bedrooms. 9 stories, interior corridors. **Parking:** on-site (fee) and valet. **Terms:** check-in 4 pm, 21 day cancellation notice-fee imposed, resort fee. **Amenities:** safes. **Dining:** 3 restaurants, also, The Beach House, Kai Sushi, see separate listings. **Pool(s):** heated outdoor. **Activities:** sauna, hot tub, steamroom, cabanas, self-propelled boats, scuba diving, snorkeling, tennis, recreation programs, kids club, playground, spa. **Guest Services:** valet laundry, area transportation. *(See ad this page.)*

WHERE TO EAT

THE BEACH HOUSE   808/669-6200

American. Casual Dining. $14-$33 **AAA Inspector Notes:** This relaxing spot faces a secluded public beach with views of the island of Moloka'i. It's accessible through the elegant grounds of the Ritz-Carlton resort. Lighter fare is served, with burgers, fresh fish, baby back ribs, appetizers and salads sharing space on the menu. It is a long hike to and from the restaurant, but patrons too full to tackle the hill can request a shuttle cart back to the hotel. **Features:** full bar, patio dining, happy hour. **Address:** One Ritz-Carlton Dr 96761 **Location:** SR 30 exit Office Rd; in Kapalua resort area; on northwest shore; in The Ritz-Carlton, Kapalua. **Parking:** on-site and valet.

Visit AAA.com/searchfordiscounts to save

on travel, shopping, dining and attractions

KAI SUSHI   808/669-6200

Sushi. Casual Dining. $12-$30 **AAA Inspector Notes:** Located just off the lobby of The Ritz-Carlton, Kapalua, this dining venue is decorated in rich earth tones and elements that mimic the Hawaiian life. Diners get an incredible view of the elegant swimming pool and distant ocean from this lofty perch. The restaurant has a sushi bar where patrons can watch and interact with chefs as they enjoy sushi, sashimi and other fine cuisine. **Features:** full bar. **Reservations:** suggested. **Address:** One Ritz-Carlton Dr 96761 **Location:** SR 30 exit Office Rd; in Kapalua resort area; on northwest shore; in The Ritz-Carlton, Kapalua. **Parking:** on-site and valet.

MERRIMAN'S KAPALUA   808/669-6400

Seafood. Fine Dining. $36-$65 **AAA Inspector Notes:** The spectacular view of the Pacific Ocean, elegant décor, attentive staff and above all—the well-executed menu that uses farm-to-table organic ingredients—make for a memorable dining experience. **Features:** full bar, patio dining, happy hour. **Address:** One Bay Club Pl 96761 **Location:** SR 30 exit Office Rd, 0.7 mi n, 0.5 mi w on Lower Honoapiilani Rd, then just n; in Kapalua resort area. **Parking:** valet only.

PINEAPPLE GRILL   808/669-9600

Pacific Rim. Casual Dining. $10-$40 **AAA Inspector Notes:** This air-conditioned restaurant with expansive windows overlooks the gorgeous sprawling golf course and the tennis courts. Creative Pacific Island cuisine is served along with a selection of 30 wines by the glass. **Features:** full bar, patio dining, Sunday brunch, happy hour. **Reservations:** suggested, for dinner. **Address:** 200 Kapalua Dr 96761 **Location:** SR 30 exit Kapalua, just s on Office Rd, then e on Kapalua Dr; in the Bay Golf Course clubhouse at Kapalua Resort.

THE PLANTATION HOUSE RESTAURANT   808/669-6299

Pacific Rim. Casual Dining. $20-$42 **AAA Inspector Notes:** Located on a magnificent golf course, the hillside clubhouse features a wonderful restaurant that offers panoramic views of the ocean and golf course. From 8 am to 3 pm daily, patrons can explore the breakfast and lunch menus; in the evenings, the food offerings are served with some of Maui's best sunset views. This is a delightful stop for those touring the west side of the island. **Features:** full bar, patio dining. **Reservations:** required, for dinner. **Address:** 2000 Plantation Club Dr 96761 **Location:** Off SR 30, on Plantation Golf Course, follow signs.

▼ See AAA listing this page ▼

SANSEI SEAFOOD RESTAURANT & SUSHI BAR
808/669-6286

▼▼▼ Japanese Sushi. Casual Dining. $16-$34 **AAA Inspector Notes:** This upbeat, welcoming restaurant is a popular addition to the island's dining scene. The menu centers on fine cuisine, including many sushi choices. Late-night karaoke is offered Thursday and Friday nights until 1 am. A largely discounted happy hour in the early evening draws in plenty of locals and resort-goers alike. **Features:** full bar, patio dining, happy hour. **Reservations:** suggested. **Address:** 600 Office Rd 96761 **Location:** SR 30 exit Office Rd, just n. [D] CALL [&M]

KĪHEI (E-9) pop. 20,881, elev. 7'
- Restaurants p. 100
- Attractions map p. 86

On Māʻalaea Bay, at the north end of the swath of white sand beach that outlines Maui's southwestern coast, Kīhei is the more affordable half of the south Maui resort area; the ritzy Wailea neighborhood is down the road. South Kīhei Drive is the town's main commercial thoroughfare. The nightlife here is surpassed only by the scene up in Lahaina.

Kīhei also is the location of the state's only known Canadian-style totem pole—a monument to George Vancouver, who supposedly landed here in the early 19th century. Nearby Mai Poina ʻOe Iaʻu Beach Park is a popular spot for whale watching December through April.

Kealia Pond National Wildlife Refuge, on SR 311 north of Kīhei, protects a 691-acre saltwater wetland, one of the few remaining in Hawaiʻi. The refuge is home to endangered native water birds, and hosts migratory ducks and shorebirds August through April. It provides habitat for Hawaiian stilts, coots and herons, and the adjacent Kealia Beach is a nesting ground for the endangered hawksbill turtle. Visitors should view the turtles from afar and not disturb them.

Within the refuge is the 2,200-foot-long Kealia Coastal Boardwalk, which offers in-depth learning opportunities via observation and interpretive exhibits; phone (808) 875-1582.

HAWAIIAN ISLANDS HUMPBACK WHALE NATIONAL MARINE SANCTUARY is at 726 S. Kīhei Rd. Two-thirds of the North Pacific humpback whale population migrates from Alaska to Hawaiian waters from October through April to calve, nurse and breed. The sanctuary also is home to an array of marine animals, corals and plants, some of which are not found anywhere else on Earth. Facilities house hands-on exhibits and allow for lectures.

Adjacent to the sanctuary is Kalepolepo County Park as well as the ancient royal Kōʻieʻie Fish Pond, dating at least to the 1400s. Children can wade and swim in the pond. **Time:** Allow 30 minutes minimum. **Hours:** Mon.-Fri. 10-3; closed federal and state holidays. Whale lectures Tues. and Thurs. at 11; phone for evening lecture times. **Cost:** Donations. **Phone:** (808) 879-2818 or (800) 831-4888. 🅰️

HALE KAMAOLE
(808)879-2778

▼▼▼ **Vacation Rental Condominium** $168-$315 **Address:** 2737 S Kihei Rd 96753 **Location:** SR 31 (Piilani Hwy) exit Keonekai St, just w, then just s. **Facility:** This set of condos is located across the street from the family-friendly Kamaole Beach III. Each unit features a private lanai. 32 condominiums. 2-3 stories, exterior corridors. **Terms:** off-site registration, 4-10 night minimum stay - seasonal, cancellation fee imposed, resort fee. **Amenities:** safes. **Pool(s):** heated outdoor. **Activities:** beach access, tennis. **Guest Services:** complimentary laundry.

🛶 📶 ❌ 🛅 🖥️ 💻

HALE PAU HANA RESORT
(808)879-2715

Vacation Rental Condominium $180-$550

Address: 2480 S Kihei Rd 96753 **Location:** Oceanfront. SR 31 (Piilani Hwy) exit Alanui Ke Alii Rd, just w, then just s. **Facility:** One of very few area complexes located right on the beach, every condo unit at this property has amazing ocean views. There's a high-rise tower and two-story, low-rise units. 65 condominiums. 2-7 stories, exterior corridors. **Terms:** 4-7 night minimum stay - seasonal, 30 day cancellation notice-fee imposed. **Amenities:** safes. **Pool(s):** heated outdoor. **Guest Services:** coin laundry.

[SAVE] 🍴 🛶 [BIZ] 📶 ❌ 🛅 🖥️ 💻

KIHEI AKAHI
(808)879-2778

▼▼▼ **Vacation Rental Condominium** $139-$315 **Address:** 2531 S Kihei Rd 96753 **Location:** SR 31 (Piilani Hwy) exit Alanui Ke Alii Rd, just w, then just s. **Facility:** These moderately priced condos are located on the south end of town across the street from Kamaole Beach II, one of Kihei's sunniest beaches. Every unit has a washer/dryer and private lanai. 43 condominiums. 6 stories, exterior corridors. **Terms:** 4-10 night minimum stay - seasonal, cancellation fee imposed, resort fee. **Amenities:** safes. **Pool(s):** outdoor. **Activities:** beach access, tennis. **Guest Services:** complimentary laundry.

🍴 🛶 📶 ❌ 🛅 🖥️ 💻

MANA KAI MAUI RESORT-CONDOMINIUM RENTALS HAWAII
(808)879-2778

▼▼▼ **Vacation Rental Condominium** $145-$578 **Address:** 2960 S Kihei Rd 96753 **Location:** Oceanfront. SR 31 (Piilani Hwy) exit Kiohana Dr, just n. **Facility:** Set on an expansive beach with good snorkeling at the south end of town, this complex offers fully equipped condos with large lanais and ocean views. Standard hotel-style rooms lack the lanais and view. 9 units, some condominiums. 8 stories, exterior corridors. **Terms:** off-site registration, 4-10 night minimum stay - seasonal, cancellation fee imposed, resort fee. **Amenities:** safes. **Dining:** Five Palms Beach Grill, see separate listing. **Pool(s):** heated outdoor. **Activities:** snorkeling. **Guest Services:** coin laundry.

🍴 🍸 CALL [&M] 🛶 [BIZ] 📶 ❌ 🛅 🖥️ 💻 / SOME UNITS [🅰️]

MANA KAI MAUI RESORT-MANA KAI MAUI HOTEL, LLC
(808)879-1561

▼▼▼ Vacation Rental Condominium $206-$605

Address: 2960 S Kihei Rd 96753 **Location:** Oceanfront. SR 31 (Piilani Hwy) exit Kiohana Dr, just n. **Facility:** Set on an expansive beach with good snorkeling at the south end of town, this complex offers fully equipped condos with large lanais and ocean views. Standard hotel-style rooms lack the lanais and view. 47 condominiums. 8 stories, exterior corridors. **Terms:** 30 day cancellation notice-fee imposed. **Amenities:** safes. **Dining:** Five Palms Beach Grill, see separate listing. **Pool(s):** heated outdoor. **Activities:** snorkeling. **Guest Services:** coin laundry, boarding pass kiosk.

(See ad p. 99.)

[SAVE] 🍴 🍸 CALL [&M] 🛶 📶 ❌ 🛅 🖥️ 💻

MAUI COAST HOTEL 808/874-6284

 **Hotel.** Rates not provided. **Address:** 2259 S Kihei Rd 96753 **Location:** SR 31 (Piilani Hwy) exit Alanui Ke Alii Rd, just w, then just n. **Facility:** 265 units. 7 stories, interior corridors. **Amenities:** safes. **Dining:** 2 restaurants, entertainment. **Pool(s):** outdoor. **Activities:** hot tub, tennis, bicycles, exercise room. **Guest Services:** complimentary laundry, rental car service, area transportation.

Ask about on-the-spot

vehicle battery testing and replacement

MAUI KAMAOLE (808)879-2778

Vacation Rental Condominium
$196-$420

Address: 2777 S Kihei Rd 96753 **Location:** SR 31 (Piilani Hwy) exit Keonekai St, just w, then just s. **Facility:** These modern and very spacious condos are located across the street from Kamaole Beach III. With its lifeguard station and large sandy beach, it's a great place for you to bring the family. 137 condominiums. 2 stories (no elevator), exterior corridors. **Terms:** 4-10 night minimum stay - seasonal, cancellation fee imposed, resort fee. **Amenities:** safes. **Pool(s):** outdoor, heated outdoor. **Activities:** hot tub, beach access, tennis. **Guest Services:** complimentary laundry.

▼ See AAA listing p. 98 ▼

WHERE TO EAT

CAFE O'LEI 808/891-1368
▼▼▼▼ Pacific Rim. Casual Dining. $17-$29 **AAA Inspector Notes:** This wonderful seafood, sushi and steak restaurant prepares lunches of specially made sandwiches such as macadamia nut-crusted breast of chicken and roasted fresh Maui vegetables in virgin oil with mild goat cheese. The dinner choices are more upscale, with lots of local fish and offerings from the large fresh sushi bar. A "keiki" (kid's) menu appeals to the little ones. **Features:** full bar. **Reservations:** suggested. **Address:** 2439 S Kihei Rd, Suite 201-A 96753 **Location:** South end of town; in Rainbow Mall. L D

FIVE PALMS BEACH GRILL 808/879-2607
▼▼▼▼ Pacific Rim. Casual Dining. $24-$58 **AAA Inspector Notes:** Dine in the open-air dining room or on the large lanai that affords views of the island of Kaho'olawe. Fresh fish from the Hawaiian waters are prepared several different ways. Sunset specials are available. **Features:** full bar, patio dining, happy hour. **Reservations:** suggested, dinner. **Address:** 2960 S Kihei Rd 96753 **Location:** SR 31 (Piilani Hwy) exit Kiohana Dr, just n; in Mana Kai Maui Resort-Mana Kai Maui Hotel, LLC. B L D CALL

FRED'S MEXICAN CAFE 808/891-8600
▼▼▼ Mexican. Casual Dining. $9-$25 **AAA Inspector Notes:** This colorful open-air cafe offers a variety of Mexican dishes, including enchiladas, burritos and sizzling fajitas. The ocean views are a bonus. **Features:** full bar, patio dining, happy hour. **Address:** 2511 S Kihei Rd 96753 **Location:** SR 31 (Piilani Hwy) exit Alanui Ke Alii Rd, just w, then just s. B L D

JOY'S PLACE 808/879-9258
▼ Deli Vegan. Quick Serve. $7-$12 **AAA Inspector Notes:** Vegetarians, vegans and anyone else craving a healthy meal can find it at the small delicatessen-style eatery. Selections include hearty homemade sandwiches and soups made from organically grown, low-fat, low-salt, wheat-free ingredients. Many stop at this spot across the street from Kalama Park to grab a picnic lunch. **Address:** 1993 S Kihei Rd 96753 **Location:** Corner of S Kihei and Auhana rds; in Island Surf Building. **Parking:** street only. B L

MAUI THAI BISTRO 808/874-5605
▼▼ Thai. Casual Dining. $10-$19 **AAA Inspector Notes:** This comfy eatery features delicious food. Selections worth noting include spicy shrimp, chicken topped with coconut-peanut sauce and served over rice, and traditional spring rolls. A selection of vegetarian dishes also is available. Thai wall hangings enhance the simple décor. **Address:** 2439 S Kihei Rd 96753 **Location:** South end of town; in Rainbow Mall. L D

SANSEI SEAFOOD RESTAURANT & SUSHI BAR
808/879-0004
▼▼ Pacific Rim Sushi. Casual Dining. $16-$30 **AAA Inspector Notes:** In a small shopping complex, this casual restaurant entices guests not only with Pacific Rim sushi and seafood but also with free karaoke from 10 pm to 1 am Thursday through Saturday. This place is popular with locals, and sometimes there's a wait for a table. The creations from the kitchen are delightful to look at and even better to eat. **Features:** full bar, early bird specials. **Reservations:** suggested. **Address:** 1881 S Kihei Rd, Suite KT-116 96753 **Location:** Jct Halelani Pl; in Kihei Town Center. D CALL

SARENTO'S ON THE BEACH 808/875-7555

▼▼▼▼▼
Italian
Fine Dining
$26-$49
AAA Inspector Notes: The sounds of the ocean accent the modern, upscale décor of this beachfront dining room, which features an innovative menu of fine Italian and Continental cuisine. The team approach to service works well, as the staff highlights the chef's menu creations and tempts diners with daily selections. The most popular time is sunset, just as the restaurant opens, and reservations for this time of night are a must. **Features:** full bar, patio dining, happy hour. **Reservations:** suggested. **Address:** 2980 S Kihei Rd 96753 **Location:** SR 31 (Piilani Hwy) exit Kiohana Dr, just n; in Maui Oceanfront Days Inn. **Parking:** valet only.
 B D CALL

KULA (E-9) pop. 6,452, elev. 2,493'
• Attractions map p. 86

A belt of land ranging between 2,000 and 4,000 feet on the broad western slope of Haleakalā forms the distinct Maui Upcountry district. Highway 37 connects a string of up-country towns from Pukalani to 'Ulupalakua Ranch. Chinese and Portuguese immigrants settled here in the late 19th and early 20th centuries, establishing small farms on the fertile soils. The Kula district produces much of Hawai'i's fresh vegetables, including carrots, cauliflower, cabbage, lettuce, tomatoes and onions.

Kula is renowned for its flowers, especially carnations, chrysanthemums and the exotic protea. The University of Hawai'i's Maui Agricultural Research Center, off Copp Road on Mauna Place, is a noted protea research and development facility. The first plants were imported from Australia in 1965. Today there are more than 60 nurseries raising protea. The research center's grounds are open to the public; restrooms are not available. Phone (808) 878-1213.

ALI'I KULA LAVENDER is just e. off SR 37 (Kula Hwy.) on SR 377 (Kekaulike Ave.), then .5 mi. e. to 1100 Waipoli Rd. (On Waipoli Rd., pass the cattle guard and follow signs to parking area.) The garden includes more than 45 lavender varieties. Tours introduce visitors to lavender and products that can be made from it.

Note: The tour route traverses uneven ground, a hillside and gravel paths. Comfortable walking shoes are recommended. The garden is located at a 4,000-foot elevation; the temperature is likely to be cooler here than in other island areas.

Time: Allow 1 hour minimum. **Hours:** Grounds daily 9-4. Thirty-minute walking tour departs at 9:30, 10:30, 11:30, 1 and 2:30. Phone for other tour schedules. Closed Thanksgiving and Christmas. **Cost:** $3. Walking tour $12. Reservations are recommended. **Phone:** (808) 878-3004.

HOLY GHOST MISSION is e. of SR 37 (Kula Hwy.) at 4300 Lower Kula Rd. This octagonal church, built 1894-95 by Father James Beissel and his largely Portuguese parishioners, features an ornate hand-carved wooden altar and stations of the cross built in Austria and installed in 1897. **Hours:** Daily 8-6. **Cost:** Donations. **Phone:** (808) 878-1261.

KULA BOTANICAL GARDEN, on SR 377 (Kekaulike Ave.) just n. of Waipoli Rd., has paved paths that wind through 8 acres of tropical and semitropical plantings and alongside a stream and koi pond. The reception center provides excellent views of the island. **Hours:** Daily 9-4. **Cost:** $10; $3 (ages 6-12). **Phone:** (808) 878-1715.

O'O FARM is at 651 Waipoli Rd. On a 3.5-hour tour of this 8.5-acre farm, visitors learn about organic and biodynamic agricultural practices and are given the opportunity to harvest their own fruits and vegetables. A farm-to-table chef prepares and serves a gourmet lunch using the gathered items, and freshly roasted coffee is offered. Visitors are welcome to bring their own alcoholic beverages.

Note: Comfortable walking shoes, a light jacket and sun protection are recommended. **Hours:** Tours depart Mon.-Wed. at 10:30. Closed major holidays. **Cost:** $58; $29 (ages 5-12). Reservations are required. **Phone:** (808) 667-4341. 🍴

SURFING GOAT DAIRY is w. off SR 37 (Kula Hwy.) at 3651 Omaopio Rd. between mileposts 9 and 10. Twenty-minute casual tours provide an overview of the dairy farm. Visitors can sample goat cheese, learn about the goats and how they are milked and view the cheese-making area. A hands-on Evening Chores and Milking tour also is available.

Closed-toe shoes are recommended. The parking lot is surfaced with gravel. **Hours:** Mon.-Sat. 9-5, Sun. 9-2. Casual tours depart every 30 minutes Mon.-Sat. 10-3, Sun. 10-1. Evening Chores and Milking tour departs Mon.-Sat. at 3:15. **Cost:** Casual tour $12; $8 (ages 2-12). Evening Chores and Milking tour $17; $14 (ages 2-12). **Phone:** (808) 878-2870.

KULA LODGE & RESTAURANT   808/878-1535
▼▼ ▼▼ American. Casual Dining. $15-$38 **AAA Inspector Notes:** On the road to Haleakala in an area known as Upcountry Maui, this restaurant is a convenient stop and the panoramic views of west Maui are spectacular. Private canopied tables on the garden terrace, weather permitting, are delightful with a stream running right by the tables. Burgers, sandwiches and several entrée selections are available in half portions. Gourmet hand-tossed pizzas are baked outside in a kiawe wood-fired brick oven. **Features:** full bar, patio dining. **Reservations:** suggested. **Address:** 15200 Haleakala Hwy 96790 **Location:** From SR 37, 5.3 mi se on SR 377.
Ⓑ Ⓛ Ⓓ CALL ⓛM 🄰

LAHAINA (D-8) pop. 11,704, elev. 20'
• Hotels p. 102 • Restaurants p. 104
• Attractions map p. 86

On the northwest coast 22 miles from Wailuku *(see place listing p. 110),* Lahaina was once the whaling capital of the mid-Pacific. The warm waters are a haven for humpback whales, which come from the Arctic to mate and bear their young off the coasts of Maui, Moloka'i and Lāna'i. From December through May the whales, now protected from hunters, can be seen swimming and leaping.

The town name, which means "cruel sun," comes from a description by a Hawaiian chief with a balding pate who was trekking across the mountain slopes behind the village. Today Lahaina bustles with tourists who come to browse the countless souvenir shops, clothing boutiques and art galleries lining Front Street, the town's main drag. Lahaina also boasts the highest concentration of restaurants and bars on the island. Street parking is scarce, but there are several pay lots in the area; watch for signs along Front Street.

The fertile land and abundant freshwater springs so appealed to Kamehameha the Great that he established his capital on Maui after his conquest of the islands. Hawai'i's first constitution was drafted in

Lahaina in 1840. The 1859 courthouse near the harbor, built with coral and lava blocks taken from the ruins of Kamehameha III's rarely used palace, was declared the finest government building in the islands at the time.

Hale Pa'ahao (Stuck-in-Irons House) on Prison Street was a wooden jailhouse surrounded by a thick wall built from coral and lava blocks from the demolished Old Fort 1852-53. Its primary use was to hold drunken sailors until they were bailed out by their captain. The 1834 Baldwin Home at the corner of Front and Dickenson streets contains furnishings, photos, medical books and records from the missionary era.

Other historic structures are the 1828 Waine'e Church, said to be the oldest stone church on the islands, and the 1831 Lahainaluna High School, considered the oldest secondary school in the United States west of the Rocky Mountains. The school contains Hale Pa'i, a coral-block print shop where the first Hawaiian-language newspaper was printed.

Maui Theatre, at 878 Front St., features a 75-minute theatrical production called "'Ulalena." The word refers to a wind that is unique to Maui and a twilight rain that is red and yellow in color. Traditional Hawaiian chants, sounds and dances combine with acrobatic feats and haunting music to tell the history and legends of Maui. The show begins with the stories of the islands' mythic creation as well as the various people who reached them, including Polynesians, Capt. James Cook and more recent inhabitants. Portrayals of mythology, village life, Hawaiian monarchy and nature are featured. Special effects, lighting and surround sound add to the experience. Phone (808) 856-7900.

Lahaina Visitor Center: 648 Wharf St., Lahaina, HI 96761. **Phone:** (808) 667-9193 or (888) 310-1117.

Self-guiding tours: The Lahaina Historic Trail (Ala Mo'olelo O Lahaina) consists of 62 historic sites, 30 bronze interpretive signs along Front Street, 10 interpretive plaques on buildings and the remains of the Lahaina Walking Tour numbered signs. Maps are available at the visitor center in the Old Lahaina Courthouse at 648 Wharf St. A descriptive brochure can be obtained from the Baldwin Home at the corner of Front and Dickenson streets.

[SAVE] **ATLANTIS ADVENTURES:** *ATLANTIS* SUBMARINES LAHAINA departs from Lahaina Harbor (Slip 18). Check-in is at the Pioneer Inn on Front St. The company offers 1-hour narrated underwater voyages during which passengers can see exotic fish, a sunken Carthaginian ship and marine animals through large portholes. Whale-watch trips also are offered December through April; exact cruise dates are dependent on seasonal whale migratory patterns. **Time:** Allow 2 hours minimum. **Hours:** Dives depart daily on the hour 9-2. **Cost:** $115; $48 (ages 4-12). Under 36 inches tall are not permitted. **Phone:** (800) 381-0237.

BANYAN TREE PARK, next to Old Lahaina Courthouse across from Lahaina Harbor, marks the center of town. Planted in 1873 by the sheriff of the town, this 60-foot tree is the largest on the islands. It shades more than two-thirds of an acre and measures one-fourth of a mile in circumference. Local vendors display their arts and crafts in the park most weekends. **Hours:** Daily 6 a.m.-midnight. **Cost:** Free. **Phone:** (808) 667-9193.

THE LAHAINA CRUISE CO., which departs from Lahaina Harbor, offers whale-watch trips. The 2-hour excursions include narration by a trained naturalist. Snorkeling cruises to Lāna'i (June-November), ferry service and day excursions to Moloka'i, and sunset dinner and cocktail cruises also are offered. **Hours:** Whale-watch trips depart daily at 7:30, 9:45, noon and 2:15, mid-Dec. to early May. **Cost:** Whale-watch trips $17.95-$34.95; free (ages 0-6 and one child age 7-12 per paying adult); $15.95-$20.95 (each additional child age 7-12). **Phone:** (808) 661-6165.

LAHAINA JODO MISSION, off Front St. at 12 Ala Moana St., features a large Buddha statue as well as a three-tiered pagoda, temple and sacred bell. Visitors are not permitted inside the shrines. **Hours:** Grounds daily dawn-dusk. **Cost:** Free. **Phone:** (808) 661-4304.

OLD LAHAINA LŪʻAU, 1251 Front St. in Lahaina Cannery Mall, offers visitors an introduction to Hawaiian history and culture through traditional food, music and dance. The site provides a view of the ocean at sunset.

The evening begins with Hawaiian music and demonstrations by islanders of traditional island arts and crafts. The focus is then moved toward the edge of the ocean where a pig is removed from the *imu,* an underground oven. The feast includes a variety of traditional Hawaiian cuisine. The evening is concluded with a production that showcases the history of Hawaiians. The story begins with the early Polynesian migration to the Hawaiian Islands, and the progression of *hula* from ancient times to the present is featured.

Time: Allow 3 hours minimum. **Hours:** Grounds open daily at 5:15 p.m., Oct.-Mar.; at 5:45, rest of year. Phone ahead to confirm schedule. **Cost:** $105; $75 (ages 3-12). Prices may vary; phone ahead. Reservations are required. **Phone:** (808) 667-1998 or (800) 248-5828.

PACIFIC WHALE FOUNDATION tours depart from slips 1 and 4 at Lahaina Harbor; check-in is at the foundation's store at 612 Front St. Whale-watch tours offer the opportunity to see humpback whales that migrate here in winter and spring. Throughout the tours marine naturalists describe whale behavior to passengers. Underwater hydrophones provide an opportunity to listen to the whales' songs. Dolphin watches, snorkeling tours to Molokini and Lāna'i, stargazing cruises and sunset dinner cruises also are available.

Time: Allow 2 hours minimum. **Hours:** Whale-watch tour departs several times daily, late Nov. to mid-May. Other tours are available year-round; phone for schedule. Passengers must check in 45 minutes prior to departure. **Cost:** Whale-watch tours start at $25.95; $18.95 (ages 0-12); free (one child age 0-6 per paying adult). Reservations are required. **Phone:** (808) 249-8811 or (800) 942-5311.

SUGAR CANE TRAIN is off SR 30, with stations in Lahaina at 975 Limahana Pl. and in Puʻukoliʻi on Puʻukoliʻi Rd. This authentic 1890s narrow-gauge sugarcane railroad travels between Lahaina and Puʻukoliʻi, providing a panoramic view of the ocean, Lāna'i, Moloka'i and the Kāʻanapali resort area. The 12-mile round-trip takes 70 minutes.

Note: At press time, tours were temporarily suspended and were expected to resume in late 2015. Phone for updates and to confirm schedule and fare information. **Time:** Allow 1 hour, 30 minutes minimum. **Hours:** Sightseeing trains leave Puʻukoliʻi Mon.-Fri. 10:15-3:15 and leave Lahaina 11:05-4. The last departure from Lahaina is one-way. **Cost:** Round-trip sightseeing tour $22.95; $15.95 (ages 3-12). **Phone:** (808) 661-0080.

WARREN & ANNABELLE'S MAGIC SHOW, 900 Front St., is a 2-hour comedy-magic show involving some audience interaction. The evening begins with optional dining and cocktails. A valid photo ID is required. **Time:** Allow 4 hours minimum. **Hours:** Mon.-Sat. at 5 and 7:30. **Cost:** Show $64. Show with heavy appetizers, dessert, two cocktails and gratuity $104.50. Under 21 are not permitted. **Phone:** (808) 667-6244.

WO HING MUSEUM, 858 Front St., was built in the early 1900s and was the fraternal meeting hall for the Chinese Wo Hing Society. The restored temple exhibits rare Chinese artifacts and memorabilia from the turn of the 20th century, when many Chinese emigrants lived and worked in Lahaina. The only public Taoist altar on Maui is upstairs. The adjacent cookhouse presents films of Hawai'i made by Thomas Edison in 1898 and 1906 and a short documentary on the history of the Chinese in Hawai'i.

Hours: Daily 10-4. Last admission 15 minutes before closing. **Cost:** (Includes admission to the Baldwin Home, 120 Dickenson St.) $7; $5 (ages 65+ and military with ID); free (ages 0-12). Children must be with an adult. **Phone:** (808) 661-5553.

BEST WESTERN PIONEER INN   (808)661-3636

Hotel
$170-$200

AAA Benefit: Save 10% or more every day and earn 10% bonus points!

Address: 658 Wharf St 96761 **Location:** SR 30, w on Dickenson St (toward ocean), just s on Front St; jct Hotel St. **Facility:** 34 units. 2 stories (no elevator), interior corridors. **Pool(s):** outdoor. **Guest Services:** valet laundry.

SOMETHING SUITE
EVERYDAY

Invigorating experiences await you at the AAA Four Diamond Westin Kāʻanapali Ocean Resort Villas. Recharge yourself at our all-suite property, where signature luxuries of a Westin resort blend perfectly with the comforts of an island home. From the Heavenly® Bed and award-winning Spa Helani, to world-class restaurants and lagoon-style swimming pools, every amenity here is thoughtfully designed to uplift your senses and make your stay truly memorable.

AAA Members can save 5-20% off our best available rate every day of the week.

TO RECEIVE YOUR AAA DISCOUNT, PLEASE CALL 866.716.8112 OR 808.921.4654 OR VISIT US AT WESTINKAANAPALI.COM

AAA
Four Diamond
Award

THE WESTIN
KAʻANAPALI
OCEAN RESORT VILLAS

LAHAINA INN (808)661-0577

▼▼ Vintage Hotel $99-$275 **Address:** 127 Lahainaluna Rd 96761 **Location:** SR 30, just w on Lahainaluna Rd (toward ocean). **Facility:** This delightful little inn, originally built in 1938 as a general store, is located in the heart of historic Lahaina with some of the rooms featuring a small balcony overlooking the street. 12 units. 2 stories (no elevator), interior corridors. **Parking:** on-site (fee). **Terms:** 3 day cancellation notice-fee imposed. **Amenities:** safes. **Dining:** Lahaina Grill, see separate listing.

THE PLANTATION INN 808/667-9225

[fyi] Not evaluated. **Address:** 174 Lahainaluna Rd 96761 **Location:** SR 30, just w on Lahainaluna Rd (toward ocean). Facilities, services, and décor characterize a mid-scale property.

WHERE TO EAT

ALOHA MIXED PLATE 808/661-3322

▼▼ Hawaiian. Casual Dining. $5-$17 **AAA Inspector Notes:** A Hawaiian tradition, this restaurant's namesake refers to a dish comprised of a huge plateful of rice, macaroni salad and a choice of meat or fish. Try their Kalua pig dishes that are cooked in a special underground oven called an imu. Guests sit outside under the stars and with the sound of the water and the nearby lū'au. **Features:** full bar, patio dining, happy hour. **Address:** 1285 Front St 96761 **Location:** SR 30 exit Front St; oceanfront; across from Lahaina Cannery Mall.

CHEESEBURGER IN PARADISE 808/661-4855

▼▼ Burgers Sandwiches. Casual Dining. $10-$18 **AAA Inspector Notes:** Cheeseburgers are the house specialty at this casual and rustic beach house, where live music adds to the festive atmosphere most nights. **Features:** full bar, patio dining, happy hour. **Address:** 811 Front St 96761 **Location:** Center; oceanfront. **Parking:** street only.

FLEETWOOD'S ON FRONT ST. 808/669-6425

▼▼ American. Casual Dining. $16-$32 **AAA Inspector Notes:** In the heart of downtown, this second-floor location named after Mick has great ocean and sunset views. Try and arrive before the sun goes down to enjoy a cocktail at the rooftop bar. They offer a decidedly American menu with all the classics but add a little excitement with a Harley Davidson hog burger that costs just shy of $39,000. My waiter swears they have sold three; after all, the gourmet burger comes with a custom Harley. If you want cheese with that burger, add $1. **Features:** full bar, patio dining, happy hour. **Address:** 744 Front St 96761 **Location:** SR 30, just w on Dickenson St (toward ocean), just n. **Parking:** street only.

FRIDA'S 808/661-1287

▼▼ Mexican Seafood. Casual Dining. $10-$25 **AAA Inspector Notes:** Go for the great menu that has some Central and South American influences and be wowed by the fantastic oceanfront location. Fish figures heavily into a lot of the dishes, but go ahead and start with the cheesy goodness of queso fundido or, on a hot afternoon, maybe the refreshing fresco salad. Fresh fish, oysters, scallops, calamari and octopus are featured ingredients in several dishes. Did someone say Baja fish tacos with cabbage and jalapeño tartar? **Features:** full bar. **Reservations:** suggested, dinner. **Address:** 1287 Front St 96761 **Location:** SR 30, just w on Kapunakea St (towards ocean). **Parking:** valet and street only.

GERARD'S 808/661-8939

▼▼▼ Traditional French. Fine Dining. $39-$75 **AAA Inspector Notes:** This restaurant features local ingredients done in classic style. The emphasis is on locally caught seafood and good choices include Hawaiian snapper and the longtime-favorite ahi tartare with Maui taro chips. Enjoy dining on the large veranda or inside with the air-conditioning. There's complimentary parking in the gravel lot beside the restaurant, but be sure to get a parking pass from the staff. **Features:** full bar, patio dining. **Reservations:** suggested. **Address:** 174 Lahainaluna Rd 96761 **Location:** SR 30, just w on Lahainaluna Rd (toward ocean); in The Plantation Inn.

HARD ROCK CAFE 808/667-7400

▼▼ American. Casual Dining. $12-$28 **AAA Inspector Notes:** Rock 'n' roll memorabilia decorates the walls of the popular theme restaurant. Live music on the weekends contributes to the bustling atmosphere. On the menu is a wide variety of American cuisine—from burgers and sandwiches to seafood, steaks and pasta. **Features:** full bar, patio dining. **Address:** 900 Front St, B-7 96761 **Location:** Corner of Papalaua St. [SAVE] [L] [D] CALL

HONO 808/667-9390

▼▼▼ Seafood Pizza. Casual Dining. $15-$45 **AAA Inspector Notes:** The first thing you'll notice as you walk through the front door of this bright and airy restaurant is the oceanfront panoramic view, which locals and tourists alike admire as they enjoy cocktails or a light early supper as the sun sets. The restaurant's name is Hawaiian for "turtle" and those lucky enough to score an oceanfront table will be entertained as the live sea turtles fight the crashing surf in search of food just feet away. Diners of all ages will find something to love on this menu. **Features:** full bar, happy hour. **Reservations:** suggested, dinner. **Address:** 1295 Front St 96761 **Location:** SR 30, just w on Kapunakea St (towards ocean). **Parking:** valet and street only.

KIMO'S 808/661-4811

▼▼ Seafood Steak. Casual Dining. $12-$34 **AAA Inspector Notes:** Overlooking Lahaina Harbor, the casual restaurant is particularly romantic for diners who visit during the gorgeous sunsets. Fresh local fish is prepared in a variety of ways. Also on the menu are prime steaks, shellfish and Kiawe wood-smoked ribs and chicken. **Features:** full bar, patio dining, happy hour. **Reservations:** suggested. **Address:** 845 Front St, Suite A 96761 **Location:** SR 30, just w on Lahainaluna Rd (toward ocean), just n. **Parking:** street only.

KOBE JAPANESE STEAK HOUSE 808/667-5555

▼▼ ◆ Japanese Steak. Casual Dining. $15-$60 **AAA Inspector Notes:** Here, a complimentary tour of the kitchen isn't necessary; just gather around the sizzling grill and watch the Japanese chef prepare your order teppanyaki style and put on an exceptionally skilled cooking show to boot. Seating for each cooking station is for eight. A sushi bar is on the opposite side of the restaurant. **Features:** full bar, early bird specials. **Reservations:** suggested. **Address:** 136 Dickenson St 96761 **Location:** SR 30, just w (toward ocean).

LAHAINA FISH COMPANY 808/661-3472

▼▼ Seafood Steak. Casual Dining. $10-$36 **AAA Inspector Notes:** Overlooking Lahaina Harbor, the open dining room offers lovely sunset views in addition to wonderfully fresh, locally caught fish. Fresh homemade pastas, hand-carved steaks and local poultry also are available. At lunchtime, sandwiches and baskets are served in a casual environment on the first floor. Dinner is served on the second floor. **Features:** full bar, patio dining, happy hour. **Reservations:** suggested. **Address:** 831 Front St 96761 **Location:** SR 30, just w on Lahainaluna Rd (toward ocean), just n. **Parking:** street only.

LAHAINA GRILL 808/667-5117

▼▼▼▼

New American Fine Dining $31-$55

AAA Inspector Notes: Enjoy a fresh, fine dining experience where the creative cuisine can best be described as a combination of New America-, Southwest- and Asia-inspired. A friendly, capable waitstaff attends to patrons in the upscale dining room, which exudes a Cape Cod ambience. Patrons should use the pay parking lots, as street parking is hard to find. **Features:** full bar. **Reservations:** required. **Address:** 127 Lahainaluna Rd 96761 **Location:** SR 30, just w on Lahainaluna Rd (toward ocean); in Lahaina Inn. **Parking:** street only. *Menu on AAA.com* [D]

LAHAINA PIZZA CO. 808/661-0700

▼▼ Italian. Casual Dining. $13-$18 **AAA Inspector Notes:** Since 1994, this place has been serving not just great deep-dish pizza but also a selection of Italian dishes. Its second-floor location is great for gazing at the harbor, people-watching or just plain noshing. **Features:** full bar. **Address:** 730 Front St 96761 **Location:** SR 30, w on Dickenson St (toward ocean), just n. **Parking:** street only.

LEODA'S KITCHEN AND PIE SHOP 808/662-3600

▼▼ Breads/Pastries Sandwiches. Casual Dining. $9-$15 **AAA Inspector Notes:** A convenient stop between Lahaina and Kihei to grab a quick cooked-to-order lunch or a bite to go as you head to the nearby beaches. Fresh, build-your-own sandwiches, savory meat pies, fish sandwiches and a variety of burgers are offered, but those who return do it for the delectable pies. I enjoyed a savory Kula corn pie with my sandwich and a decadent chocolate macadamia nut pie for dessert. Using the freshest local ingredients, everything tastes like it came from mama's kitchen. **Address:** 820 Olowalu Village Rd 96761 **Location:** 6 mi se on SR 30.

LONGHI'S LAHAINA 808/667-2288

WW American. Casual Dining. $20-$50 **AAA Inspector Notes:** Along the waterfront, the restaurant offers two floors of covered open-air seating. Menus are verbally described to diners. Highlights include fresh seafood, fine-cut steaks and a variety of homemade pasta dishes. Desserts are worth the splurge. Guests can park at various pay lots and enjoy the walk; street parking is limited but valet parking is available at dinnertime. **Features:** full bar, patio dining, happy hour. **Reservations:** suggested. **Address:** 888 Front St 96761 **Location:** SR 30, just w on Papalaua St (toward ocean). **Parking:** valet and street only. [B] [L] [D] [Ⓚ]

MOOSE MCGILLYCUDDY'S PUB & CAFE-LAHAINA 808/667-7758

WW WW American. Casual Dining. $9-$18 **AAA Inspector Notes:** The casual eatery serves hearty portions of fun fare. From burgers and entrée salads to steaks and seafood, the choices are sure to satisfy. The atmosphere is loud, bustling and often lively during the famous 3 to 6 pm happy hour. Many tables in the second-floor location overlook busy Front Street, allowing for great people-watching. **Features:** full bar, happy hour. **Address:** 844 Front St 96761 **Location:** SR 30, just w on Lahainaluna Rd (toward ocean), just n; town center; 2nd Level Mariner's Alley. **Parking:** street only.

[B] [L] [D]

PACIFIC'O 808/667-4341

WWW Pacific Rim. Casual Dining. $29-$46 **AAA Inspector Notes:** In the 505 Front Street shopping area on the south side of town, the restaurant features lunch and dinner preparations of Pacific cuisine. In addition to fresh local seafood prepared in innovative ways, the menu lists lamb, beef, pork, pasta and duck. The shrimp wontons are the signature appetizer. Overlooking the ocean, the open dining room features contemporary Hawaiian decor. Patio dining is enhanced by torchlight. **Features:** full bar, patio dining. **Reservations:** suggested. **Address:** 505 Front St 96761 **Location:** SR 30, w on Shaw St (toward ocean). **Parking:** on-site (fee) and street.

[L] [D] CALL [Ⓜ]

RUTH'S CHRIS STEAK HOUSE 808/661-8815

WWW Steak. Fine Dining. $27-$60 **AAA Inspector Notes:** The main fare is steak, which is prepared from several cuts of Prime beef and cooked to perfection, but the menu also lists lamb, chicken and seafood dishes. Guests should come hungry because the side dishes, which are among the a la carte offerings, could make a meal in themselves. **Features:** full bar. **Reservations:** suggested. **Address:** 900 Front St 96761 **Location:** SR 30, just w on Papalaua St (toward ocean). **Parking:** street only. [D] CALL [Ⓜ]

MALA OCEAN TAVERN 808/667-9394

[fyi] Not evaluated. This is probably some of the best "tavern" food you'll find on Maui, and it comes with a great oceanfront view. Locals know to arrive early for a good seat at sunset. While the menu is decidedly heavy on seafood, there are Mediterranean influences in several dishes and a few beef and chicken selections for the land lover. **Address:** 1307 Front St 96761 **Location:** SR 30, just w on Kapunakea St (towards ocean).

MĀ'ALAEA (E-8) pop. 352, elev. 10'
- Restaurants p. 106
- Attractions map p. 86

Mā'alaea has been an important small boat harbor since the early 1950s. Its docks host numerous charter fishing and sightseeing operators. Mā'alaea Beach, accessible at several spots along SR 310, curves 3 miles east to Kīhei. Typical afternoon breezes make this a popular windsurfing area.

FOUR WINDS II SNORKEL TRIPS, departing from Slip 80 at Mā'alaea Harbor, offers 5-hour morning and 3.5-hour afternoon snorkeling cruises aboard the catamaran *Four Winds II*. Passengers can enjoy the vessel's large decks, spacious cabin, glass-bottom viewing room and waterslide. Cruises go to Molokini Crater or Coral Gardens, weather permitting. Humpback whales are often seen December through April.

Hours: Cruises depart daily at 7:30 and 1:30. Arrive 30 minutes before departure. **Cost:** Morning trip (includes snorkeling gear, breakfast, lunch and beverages) $98; $68 (ages 3-12). Afternoon trip (includes snorkeling gear and beverages) $49; $39 (ages 3-12). Optional lunch on afternoon trip $7.50. Reservations are required. **Phone:** (808) 879-8188 or (800) 736-5740. *(See ad p. 87.)*

MAUI OCEAN CENTER, 192 Mā'alaea Rd. (SR 30) at Mā'alaea Harbor, is a state-of-the-art aquarium. Living coral, colorful tropical reef fish, large open-ocean fish, sharks, green sea turtles, stingrays, eels and sea jellies are some of the indigenous marine life displayed. An acrylic tunnel takes visitors through a 750,000-gallon exhibit, giving the illusion of being under the sea.

The Marine Mammal Discovery Center features interpretive stations as well as displays about humpback whales, monk seals and dolphins. Presentations by ocean naturalists are given throughout the day.

Hours: Daily 9-6, July-Aug.; 9-5, rest of year. **Cost:** $25.95; $22.95 (ages 65+); $18.95 (ages 3-12). Weekly pass $34.50; $31.50 (ages 65+); $23.50 (ages 3-12). Audio guide rental $3; $8 (family rate for up to 6 guides). **Phone:** (808) 270-7000. [Ⓣ]

PACIFIC WHALE FOUNDATION tours depart from Mā'alaea Harbor; check-in is at the Mā'alaea Harbor Shops (across from Maui Ocean Center) on Mā'alaea Rd. (SR 30). Whale-watch tours offer the opportunity to see humpback whales that migrate here in winter and spring. Throughout the tours marine naturalists describe whale behavior to passengers. Underwater hydrophones provide an opportunity to listen to the whales' songs. Dolphin watches, snorkeling tours to Molokini and Lāna'i, stargazing cruises and sunset dinner cruises also are available.

Time: Allow 2 hours minimum. **Hours:** Whale-watch tour departs several times daily, late Nov. to mid-May. Other tours are available year-round; phone for schedules. Passengers must check in 45 minutes prior to departure. **Cost:** Whale-watch tours start at $25.95; $18.95 (ages 0-12); free (one child age 0-6 per paying adult). Reservations are required. **Phone:** (808) 249-8811 or (800) 942-5311.

ISLAND SANDS RESORT (808)879-2778

WW WW Vacation Rental Condominium $168-$320 **Address:** 150 Hauoli St 96793 **Location:** Oceanfront. From airport, follow signs to SR 30 towards Lahaina, exit Ma'alaea Harbor Village, just sw on Ma'alaea Rd, then just se. **Facility:** The one- and two-bedroom condos overlook Ma'alaea Bay and harbor. All units have a washer/dryer. 14 condominiums. 6 stories, exterior corridors. **Parking:** street only. **Terms:** 4-10 night minimum stay - seasonal, cancellation fee imposed, resort fee. **Amenities:** safes. **Pool(s):** heated outdoor. **Guest Services:** complimentary laundry.

[icons]

WHERE TO EAT

BUZZ'S WHARF RESTAURANT   808/244-5426

♥♥ Seafood Steak. Casual Dining. $8-$29 **AAA Inspector Notes:** This restaurant is located at the Ma'alaea Harbor where you can enjoy spectacular views of the bay and South Maui coastline. The menu features a wide variety of fresh fish, including catch-of-the-day specials. Lighter lunch fare includes pasta and sandwiches. Dinner entrées include New York or choice rib-eye steaks, with prime rib served every Friday and Saturday night. It's worth a visit just for the views. **Features:** full bar. **Reservations:** suggested, for dinner. **Address:** Ma'alaea Bay Harbor 96793 **Location:** Just off SR 30; facing Ma'alaea Harbor. [L] [D]

MAKAWAO pop. 7,184

MAKAWAO GARDEN CAFE   808/573-9065

♥♥ American. Casual Dining. $8-$14 **AAA Inspector Notes:** Spend the day exploring Makawao or stop by after a morning trip up the volcano to discover this hidden gem shoehorned between two stores. Lunch is served on an open-air patio, weather permitting. More than likely the owner or her daughter will be your waitress as you decide between the bacon and Brie sandwich on a baguette or a quinoa salad with grilled eggplant, red peppers and crumbled goat cheese. The menu focuses primarily on sandwiches and salads with there being no bad choice. **Features:** patio dining. **Address:** 3669 Baldwin Ave, Suite 1101 96768 **Location:** Jct Naku St; center. **Parking:** street only. [L] [Ⓚ]

MAKAWAO STEAK HOUSE   808/572-8711

♥♥ Steak. Casual Dining. $18-$35 **AAA Inspector Notes:** If for nothing more than to experience the classic décor, friendly service and tasty food, this steakhouse is worth a special drive up country. Start at the all-you-can-eat salad bar and then settle into your rosy-pink prime rib with au jus and huge baked potato. If they're serving the tres leches cake with the fresh strawberries, don't pass it up, it's definitely worth the added calories. **Features:** full bar. **Address:** 3612 Baldwin Ave 96768 **Location:** Jct Naku St; center. **Parking:** street only. [D]

MARKET FRESH BISTRO   808/572-4877

♥♥ American. Casual Dining. $14-$25 **AAA Inspector Notes:** Market-fresh organic ingredients are locally sourced and prepared the same day. You can enjoy your meal in the European-style courtyard surrounded by blooming tropical plants. Hearty breakfasts and light refreshing lunches are the staple, but the real thrill comes on Wednesday and Thursday nights when they also serve dinner. The Thursday-night showcase is a seven-course tasting menu served at a communal table. **Features:** beer & wine, patio dining. **Address:** 3620 Baldwin Ave 96768 **Location:** Jct Naku St; center. **Parking:** street only. [B] [L] [D]

MĀKENA (E-9) pop. 99, elev. 11'
• Attractions map p. 86

Mākena Landing was an important port in the late 19th and early 20th centuries, shipping cattle to Honolulu. Trade patterns shifted to other ports and by the mid-1920s Mākena languished.

Keawala'i Congregational Church, at the south end of Mākena Bay, features 3-foot-thick lava rock walls mortared with burnt coral lime. The church was erected in 1855, although the congregation dates to 1832.

Mākena State Park is 1.5 miles south on Mākena Road. The half-mile long golden strand of Big Beach, also known as Oneloa, is one of Maui's finest. The 360-foot cinder cone of Pu'u Ola'i guards its northern flank. A short trail leads over the lava headland at the north end of the beach to Little Beach, a popular clothing-optional spot. **Note:** State law officially prohibits nudity on public beaches.

MAKENA BEACH & GOLF RESORT   (808)874-1111

♥♥♥♥ Resort Hotel $329-$925 **Address:** 5400 Makena Alanui 96753 **Location:** Oceanfront. From end of SR 31, 2.9 mi s. **Facility:** This 1,800-acre resort is on tropical landscaped grounds. Enjoy open public areas and an atrium courtyard with fish-filled ponds and waterfalls. Rooms have either a mountain or water view. 310 units. 7 stories, exterior corridors. **Parking:** on-site and valet. **Terms:** 3 day cancellation notice-fee imposed. **Amenities:** video games, safes. **Dining:** 4 restaurants. **Pool(s):** heated outdoor. **Activities:** hot tub, cabanas, scuba diving, snorkeling, regulation golf, tennis, recreation programs, bicycles, lawn sports, exercise room, massage. **Guest Services:** valet and coin laundry, rental car service, area transportation.

[ECO] [⫟] [📶] [Ⲩ] CALL [&M] [🛏] [BIZ] [HS] [📶] [✕]
[🎥] [📶] [💻] /SOME UNITS [📷]

MOLOKINI ISLAND (E-8)
• Attractions map p. 86

A popular snorkeling and diving spot, Molokini is an inactive sunken volcanic cinder cone 3 miles off Maui's south shore. The horseshoe-shaped islet is a designated marine-life preserve that embraces a tropical ecosystem complete with colorful fish, eels and turtles. The south side of Molokini provides divers a nearly vertical wall while the protected interior offers a safe location for snorkeling. Molokini, designated a State Marine Life and Bird Conservation District, is nearly barren except for some vegetation and the ever-present bird population. Landing on this small island is prohibited.

Morning and afternoon snorkel and dive charters depart from Lahaina Harbor and the Mā'alaea Harbor loading dock. Powerboat rentals are available in harbor areas. **Note:** Very strong currents between Maui and Molokini make it very dangerous to attempt to kayak to the island.

NAPILI

NAPILI SUNSET   (808)669-8083

♥♥♥ Vacation Rental Condominium $180-$510 **Address:** 46 Hui Dr 96761 **Location:** Oceanfront. SR 30 exit Napilihau St, just w, then 0.5 mi ne on Lower Honoapiilani Rd, then just nw; in Napili Bay resort area. **Facility:** This complex offers three buildings, two of which are on the beach. The privately owned older condos include studios and one- and two-bedroom units, some with ceiling fans only. Murphy beds are in studios. 42 condominiums. 2 stories (no elevator), exterior corridors. **Terms:** check-in 4 pm, 15 day cancellation notice-fee imposed. **Amenities:** safes. **Pool(s):** heated outdoor. **Guest Services:** coin laundry.

[🛏] [BIZ] [HS] [📶] [✕] [📶] [🖥] [💻] /SOME UNITS [Ⓚ]

WHERE TO EAT

THE GAZEBO RESTAURANT   808/669-5621

♥♥ Breakfast. Casual Dining. $9-$20 **AAA Inspector Notes:** Located poolside and overlooking the ocean, this wildly popular modest restaurant serves macadamia-nut pancakes and omelets at breakfast and big salads, sandwiches and burgers at lunch. The line forms early for breakfast; expect up to a 45-minute wait while enjoying the ocean view. The fried rice makes for a fantastic alternative breakfast. **Features:** patio dining. **Address:** 5315 Lower Honoapiilani Rd 96761 **Location:** SR 30 exit Napilihau St, just w, then 0.5 mi ne; in Napili Shores Resort; in Napili Bay resort area. [B] [L] [Ⓚ]

Pick up colorful, top-quality travel guides and atlases at AAA/CAA offices

SEA HOUSE RESTAURANT   808/669-1500

♦♦♦ ♦♦♦ Pacific Rim. Casual Dining. $11-$45 **AAA Inspector Notes:** This restaurant lures guests from miles away with its great food and beachfront setting. The décor and service is casual. On the menu are creative entrées and salads, as well as delicious desserts. Entertainment is provided nightly in the lounge. **Features:** full bar, patio dining, early bird specials, happy hour. **Reservations:** suggested. **Address:** 5900 Lower Honoapiilani Rd 96761 **Location:** SR 30 exit to Napilihau St, just w, then 1 mi n; in Napili Kai Beach Resort. B L D Ⓚ

PĀ'IA (D-9) pop. 2,668, elev. 230'
• Attractions map p. 86

RECREATIONAL ACTIVITIES
Bicycling
• **Maui Mountain Cruisers,** 381 Baldwin Ave., offers van pickup service at area hotels. **Hours:** Tours depart daily. **Phone:** (808) 871-6014.

PAIA INN   808/579-6000

ⓕⓨⓘ Not evaluated. **Address:** 93 Hana Hwy 96779 **Location:** Center. Facilities, services, and décor characterize a mid-scale property. Complimentary beach gear is provided to guests of this inn located just a short walk away from the beach. Limited on-site parking is available and additional options are a block away.

WHERE TO EAT

DAZOO   808/579-9999

♦♦♦ Small Plates Breads/Pastries. Casual Dining. $12-$20 **AAA Inspector Notes:** Take a short walk down Baldwin Avenue to find this delightful café where the food is always fresh and you can buy a sweet from the adjoining bakery to take home. It's recommended you park in the public lot and walk as street parking can be limited. Serving brunch on Saturday and Sunday. **Features:** full bar, Sunday brunch. **Address:** 71 Baldwin Ave 96779 **Location:** SR 36 (Hana Hwy), just e. **Parking:** street only. D CALL Ⓚ Ⓜ

MAMA'S FISH HOUSE   808/579-8488

♦♦♦ ♦♦♦ Pacific Rim Seafood. Fine Dining. $38-$58 **AAA Inspector Notes:** Polynesian-style décor is the hallmark in this restaurant's open dining rooms, where you'll savor the freshest fish (the menu even prints where it was caught and the fisherman who caught it) such as grilled Maui he'e (octopus) caught by Cliff Chow freediving near Kuau Cove. Menu items are prepared in an island style with organic, locally grown produce. In business for more than three decades, this beachfront setting has satisfied guests for years. **Features:** full bar, patio dining. **Reservations:** required. **Address:** 799 Poho Pl 96779 **Location:** 1.5 mi e on SR 36 (Hana Hwy), at MM 8. **Parking:** valet only. L D Ⓚ

PAIA FISH MARKET   808/579-8030

♦♦♦ Seafood. Quick Serve. $9-$19 **AAA Inspector Notes:** Located on a busy street corner, this popular spot is on the road to Hana and is known for its fresh fish burgers. You also might want to try the mahi mahi fish plate. Check out the food being devoured as you make your way past satisfied diners to the back of the room; place your order at the counter and then grab any available seat at the communal tables. **Features:** beer & wine. **Address:** 100 Hana Hwy 96779 **Location:** Jct Baldwin Ave; center. **Parking:** street only.
L D Ⓚ

PU'UNĒNĒ (D-9) elev. 76'
• Attractions map p. 86

ALEXANDER & BALDWIN SUGAR MUSEUM is 1.5 mi. s. of Kahului via Mokulele Hwy. (SR 311), to 3957 Hansen Rd. Next to the 1902 Pu'unēnē Mill, the museum documents the history and heritage of the sugar industry and the multiethnic plantation lifestyle that it engendered on Maui. Its six rooms showcase the importance of geography, water, labor and plantation life. Artifacts, photos, scale models and mill equipment are displayed.

Time: Allow 30 minutes minimum. **Hours:** Daily 9:30-4:30. Last admission 30 minutes before closing. Closed major holidays. Phone ahead to confirm schedule. **Cost:** $7; $5 (ages 60+); $2 (ages 6-12); free (ages 0-5, and active and retired military and their immediate dependents with ID). **Phone:** (808) 871-8058.

'ULUPALAKUA RANCH (E-9) elev. 1,916'
• Attractions map p. 86

WINERIES
• **Maui's Winery at 'Ulupalakua Ranch** is on SR 37. **Hours:** Daily 10-5:30. Tours are given daily at 10:30 and 1:30. **Phone:** (808) 878-6058 or (877) 878-6058. ⒼⓉ

WAIKAPU (D-8) pop. 2,965, elev. 400'
• Attractions map p. 86

MAUI TROPICAL PLANTATION, 1 mi. s. on SR 30 between mileposts 2 and 3 at 1670 Honoapi'ilani Hwy., offers 40-minute narrated tram tours of its 60 acres. Guides describe how sugarcane, bananas, macadamia nuts and other products contribute to the state's economy. Indoor agricultural exhibits also are presented. **Hours:** Grounds daily 9-5. Trams depart on the hour 10-4. **Cost:** Tram tour $16.50; $6.25 (ages 3-12). Grounds free. **Phone:** (808) 244-7643 or (800) 451-6805. ▪

Take Your *Imagination* to New Destinations

Use AAA Travel Guides online to explore the possibilities.

Go to AAA.com/travelguide today.

WAILEA (E-9) pop. 5,938, elev. 117'
• Attractions map p. 86

On Maui's southwest shore, the long, gradual lower slopes of Haleakalā meet the sea. In the late 19th century this coastline was part of the sprawling Makee Ranch, raising sugar cane and cattle. Today, Wailea (meaning "water of Lea," the Hawaiian goddess of canoe makers) is one of the world's more exclusive resort enclaves, a planned community cushioned in manicured landscaping.

Wailea's 2-mile shoreline features five pocket beaches of golden sand framed by dark lava rock. All beaches are open to the public. The Wailea Point Coastal Trail leads north from Polo Beach (off Kaukahi St.) to Mōkapu Beach. Interpretive signs identify the coastal flora. Views extend across the sea to Molokini, Kahoʻolawe and Lānaʻi. Whales are often seen December through April.

Wailea's three golf courses are legendary, ranking among the best in the country. Tennis is another popular sport. The Wailea Tennis Club boasts a 1,000-seat stadium. Other recreational activities include swimming, snorkeling, scuba diving, sailing, windsurfing and kayaking. Wailea's major resorts also have full spa facilities.

The 🎬 Maui Film Festival at Wailea, held in June, features film premieres, celebrity appearances and Hawaiian food and dance.

Shopping: The Shops at Wailea, 3750 Wailea Alanui Dr., offers more than 70 stores, boutiques, galleries and restaurants. The complex, set amid landscaped courtyards, reflects 19th-century territorial architecture. Shops include Banana Republic, Gap, Louis Vuitton and Tiffany & Co. Most shops are open daily 9:30-9. Phone (808) 891-6770.

ANDAZ MAUI AT WAILEA RESORT   (808)573-1234

Hotel
$399-$999

ANDAZ.

AAA Benefit: Members save 10%!

Address: 3550 Wailea Alanui Dr 96753 **Location:** Oceanfront. From end of SR 31, 0.5 mi n. **Facility:** Guests are welcomed to this tranquil property by walking over a koi pond and into a giant Zen garden. The rooms are minimalist but still offer many luxuries. 297 units, some two and three bedrooms. 2-7 stories, interior/exterior corridors. **Parking:** valet only. **Terms:** check-in 4 pm, 3 day cancellation notice-fee imposed, resort fee. **Amenities:** safes. **Dining:** Ka'ana Kitchen, Morimoto Maui, see separate listings, entertainment. **Pool(s):** heated outdoor. **Activities:** sauna, hot tub, steamroom, kids club, exercise room, spa. **Guest Services:** valet and coin laundry, area transportation.

[icons] SAVE 🍴 🛎 🍸 ➿ BIZ HS 🛜 ✕ 🎥 🖥 / SOME UNITS 🐾 🚐 🖥

Stay connected with #AAA
and #CAA on your favorite
social media sites

THE FAIRMONT KEA LANI, MAUI   (808)875-4100

Resort Hotel
$549-$7000

Address: 4100 Wailea Alanui Dr 96753 **Location:** Oceanfront. From end of SR 31, 0.7 mi s. **Facility:** This majestic, stark-white, Mediterranean-style building stands out among the lush Hawaiian foliage. Inside you'll find wonderfully large one-bedroom suites, each with a separate sitting area. 450 units, some two bedrooms, three bedrooms and kitchens. 2-7 stories, interior/exterior corridors. **Parking:** on-site (fee) and valet. **Terms:** check-in 4 pm, 21 day cancellation notice-fee imposed, resort fee. **Amenities:** safes. **Dining:** 3 restaurants, also, Nick's Fishmarket Maui, see separate listing, entertainment. **Pool(s):** heated outdoor. **Activities:** hot tub, steamroom, cabanas, snorkeling, recreation programs, kids club, bicycles, lawn sports, exercise room, spa. **Guest Services:** complimentary and valet laundry, rental car service, area transportation.

[icons] SAVE ECO 🍴 🛎 🍸 📶 CALL 🅼 ➿ BIZ sHS 🛜 ✕ 🎥 🖥 📠 🖥 / SOME UNITS 🐾

FOUR SEASONS RESORT MAUI AT WAILEA
(808)874-8000

Resort Hotel
$599-$1849

Address: 3900 Wailea Alanui Dr 96753 **Location:** Oceanfront. From end of SR 31, 0.5 mi s. **Facility:** Known for luxury, this property does not disappoint. The oceanfront resort cascades from hilltop to ocean on terraces with lush manicured landscaping. Guest rooms feature luxurious amenities. 380 units, some two and three bedrooms. 7-8 stories, interior corridors. **Parking:** on-site and valet. **Terms:** 21 day cancellation notice-fee imposed. **Amenities:** safes. **Dining:** Ferraro's Bar e Ristorante, Spago, see separate listings, entertainment. **Pool(s):** heated outdoor. **Activities:** hot tub, steamroom, cabanas, self-propelled boats, scuba diving, snorkeling, tennis, recreation programs, kids club, game room, lawn sports, spa. **Guest Services:** valet laundry, rental car service, area transportation.

[icons] SAVE 🍴 🛎 🍸 📶 CALL 🅼 ➿ 🚶 BIZ HS 🛜 ✕ 🎥 🖥 🖥 / SOME UNITS 🐾 🖥

GRAND WAILEA, A WALDORF ASTORIA RESORT
(808)875-1234

Resort Hotel
$309-$1624

WALDORF ASTORIA
HOTELS & RESORTS

AAA Benefit: Members save 5% or more!

Address: 3850 Wailea Alanui Dr 96753 **Location:** Oceanfront. From end of SR 31, just s. **Facility:** Lush, tropical landscaped grounds, waterfalls and ponds surround the buildings set on 40 acres. There's an expansive system of pools and a waterslide for both adults and children to enjoy. 780 units, some two bedrooms. 7 stories, interior/exterior corridors. **Parking:** valet only. **Terms:** 1-7 night minimum stay, cancellation fee imposed. **Amenities:** video games, safes. **Dining:** 5 restaurants, also, Humuhumunukunukuapua'a, see separate listing, entertainment. **Pool(s):** heated outdoor. **Activities:** sauna, hot tub, steamroom, cabanas, scuba diving, snorkeling, recreation programs, kids club, bicycles, game room, spa. **Guest Services:** valet laundry, rental car service, area transportation.

[icons] SAVE ECO 🍴 🛎 🍸 CALL 🅼 ➿ 🚶 BIZ HS 🛜 ✕ 🎥 🖥 🖥 / SOME UNITS 🖥

HOTEL WAILEA

♦♦♦ ♦♦♦ **Hotel** $499-$799 **Address:** 555 Kaukahi St 96753 (808)874-0500
Location: SR 31 (Piilani Hwy) exit Wailea Ike Dr, just w, just s on Kalai Waa St, then just e. **Facility:** Set on a hillside with ocean views and lush tropical landscaping, each unit is a one-bedroom suite with a private lanai. The rooms feature high-quality kitchens and ample seating. 72 units, some efficiencies. 2 stories, exterior corridors. **Parking:** on-site and valet. **Terms:** 14 day cancellation notice-fee imposed, resort fee. **Amenities:** safes. **Dining:** Capische?, see separate listing. **Pool(s):** heated pool. **Activities:** hot tub, cabanas, snorkeling, recreation programs, lawn sports, exercise room. **Guest Services:** valet laundry, area transportation.

🍴 ⛄ 🍸 🏊 HS 📶 ✕ 🛗 🖼 🖥

WAILEA BEACH MARRIOTT RESORT & SPA

(808)879-1922

Resort Hotel
$299-$779

AAA Benefit:
Members save 5% or more!

MARRIOTT

Address: 3700 Wailea Alanui Dr 96753 **Location:** Oceanfront. From end of SR 31, 0.5 mi n. Located by The Shops at Wailea. **Facility:** Surrounded by water on three sides, this property situated on 22 landscaped acres of tropical gardens and walking paths offers breathtaking views. Guest rooms feature modern luxuries and large lanais. 541 units. 3-8 stories, interior/exterior corridors.
Parking: on-site (fee) and valet. **Terms:** check-in 4 pm, 7 day cancellation notice, resort fee. **Amenities:** safes. **Dining:** 3 restaurants, entertainment. **Pool(s):** outdoor, heated outdoor. **Activities:** hot tub, steamroom, cabanas, scuba diving, snorkeling, exercise room, spa. **Guest Services:** valet and coin laundry, boarding pass kiosk, rental car service, area transportation.

  🍴 ⛄ 🍸 CALL 📶 🏊 BIZ SHS 📶
✕ 🐾 🛗 🖥 / SOME UNITS 🖼

OUTRIGGER PALMS AT WAILEA

808/879-5800

fyi Not evaluated. **Address:** 3200 Wailea Alanui Dr 96753. Facilities, services, and décor characterize a mid-scale property. All of these contemporary one- and two-bedroom units include an air conditioner in the master bedroom, a washer and dryer, and two bathrooms. Landscaped grounds surround the property.

WAILEA BEACH VILLAS

808/891-4500

fyi Not evaluated. **Address:** 3800 Wailea Alanui Dr 96753 **Location:** Oceanfront. From end of SR 31, 0.5 mi n. Facilities, services, and décor characterize an upscale property. On expansive tropical grounds, these luxurious accommodations feature a great room with an open floor plan and a spacious lanai.

WHERE TO EAT

CAPISCHE?

808/879-2224

♦♦♦ Italian. Fine Dining. $35-$55 **AAA Inspector Notes:** Italian-American fusion food is prepared using classical French techniques with local fresh ingredients utilized whenever possible. Dine on the lanai for sunset ocean views or in the romantic garden setting. **Features:** full bar. **Reservations:** suggested. **Address:** 555 Kaukahi St 96753 **Location:** SR 31 (Piilani Hwy) exit Wailea Ike Dr, just w, just s on Kalai Waa St, then just e; in Hotel Wailea. D CALL 📶

FERRARO'S BAR E RISTORANTE

808/874-8000

♦♦♦ Italian. Fine Dining. $29-$56 **AAA Inspector Notes:** With an outdoor patio setting and romantic views of the ocean, the ideal time to enjoy dinner at this family-oriented restaurant is right at sunset, just as the tiki torches are being lit and, in the background, the native tradition of blowing the conch shell bids goodbye to yet another day. The menu focuses on fresh ingredients and rustic Italian fare. Signature lunch dishes include wood-oven pizza and Dungeness crab panini while dinner guests enjoy lobster risotto and homemade ravioli. **Features:** full bar, patio dining. **Reservations:** suggested. **Address:** 3900 Wailea Alanui Dr 96753 **Location:** From end of SR 31, 0.5 mi s; in Four Seasons Resort Maui at Wailea. **Parking:** valet only. 🍴 L D CALL 📶 🐾

GANNON'S

808/875-8080

♦♦♦ Hawaiian Seafood. Fine Dining. $20-$50 **AAA Inspector Notes:** This restaurant has some of the best modern Hawaiian cuisine and incredible views. Request a table on the deck for a panoramic view of the rolling golf greens and brilliant ocean waters. Try to arrive early for a beverage at The Red Bar and catch up on the day's events. Fish is the real strength of the menu with miso-glazed walu, pecan-crusted mahi mahi and grilled ahi. Other options include tandoori loin of lamb and braised short ribs. I start my meal with shrimp-stuffed crab cakes. **Features:** full bar, patio dining, happy hour. **Address:** 100 Wailea Golf Club Dr 96753 **Location:** From Wailea Alanui Dr, just e on Wailea Ike Dr, just s; at Wailea Golf Course. **Parking:** on-site and valet. B L D CALL 📶

HUMUHUMUNUKUNUKUAPUA'A

808/875-1234

♦♦♦♦ Regional Pacific Rim. Casual Dining. $28-$64 **AAA Inspector Notes:** This thatched-roof restaurant is named for Hawaii's state fish. Patrons can ask the hostess to point it out, as it may be swimming nearby. The open-air restaurant is perched above a saltwater lagoon and the sounds of the nearby ocean can be heard. On the menu are many local favorites, including ahi and sashimi. **Features:** full bar, patio dining, happy hour. **Reservations:** suggested. **Address:** 3850 Wailea Alanui Dr 96753 **Location:** From end of SR 31, just s; in Grand Wailea, A Waldorf Astoria Resort. **Parking:** valet only. D 📶

JOE'S IN WAILEA

808/875-7767

♦♦♦ American. Casual Dining. $20-$38 **AAA Inspector Notes:** Perched on a hillside with glass on three sides, you might feel like you're dining in a tree house. Casual dining and tasty down-home food is served with a sunset view. The owner's favorite is the meatloaf served with whipped potatoes and baby carrots. Others enjoy the grilled ahi with jalapeño cream sauce, pumpkin seed-crusted catch of the day or fried chicken and waffles. Vegetarian and gluten-free menus also are offered. It's just up the hill from the Shops at Wailea. **Features:** full bar, patio dining. **Address:** 131 Wailea Ike Pl 96753 **Location:** From Wailea Alanui Dr, just e on Wailea Ike Dr, just n; above the Wailea Tennis Club. **Parking:** on-site and street. D 📶

KA'ANA KITCHEN

808/573-1234

♦♦♦♦ American. Fine Dining. $20-$45 **AAA Inspector Notes:** Sharing fresh, innovative farm-to-table cuisine is what this restaurant is all about, as Ka'ana means 'to share' in Hawaiian. The centerpiece is a hibachi grill, which makes for an entertaining dining experience. **Features:** full bar, patio dining. **Reservations:** suggested, dinner. **Address:** 3550 Wailea Alanui Dr 96753 **Location:** From end of SR 31, 0.5 mi n; in Andaz Maui at Wailea Resort. **Parking:** valet only. B D CALL 📶

LONGHI'S WAILEA

808/891-8883

♦♦ Italian. Casual Dining. $15-$50 **AAA Inspector Notes:** This casual restaurant features open-air seating in a comfortable setting. Menu offerings are designed to satisfy the heartiest of appetites. Local island seafood shares menu space with made-to-order pasta and local farm vegetables. The steamed artichoke appetizer is finished with melted butter. This place is known for its starter of complimentary focaccia. **Features:** full bar, patio dining, happy hour. **Reservations:** suggested. **Address:** 3750 Wailea Ala Nui Dr 96753 **Location:** Jct Wailea Ike Dr; in The Shops at Wailea, lower level. B L D CALL 📶 🐾

MONKEYPOD KITCHEN BY MERRIMAN

808/891-2322

♦♦ Regional American. Casual Dining. $13-$36 **AAA Inspector Notes:** Fresh island fish, hand-tossed pizzas and more than 35 on-tap, handcrafted microbrews are available at this casual spot. You'll find a variety of homemade cream pies on the dessert menu. Most options include ingredients from local farms. The outdoor lanais offer ocean and sunset views. **Features:** full bar, patio dining, happy hour. **Address:** 10 Wailea Gateway Pl, Unit B-201 96753 **Location:** South end of Pi'ilani Hwy; in Wailea Gateway Center. L D CALL 📶

MORIMOTO MAUI   808/243-4766

▼▼▼ Japanese Fusion. Casual Dining. $36-$146 **AAA Inspector Notes:** Acclaimed chef Morimoto, of "Iron Chef" fame, beautifully marries local ingredients with traditional Japanese cuisine. The food is art on a plate and tastes as good as it looks. The Morimoto sashimi is a perfect dish for those who love fresh fish and want to sample some exotics. While the pork gyoza also is phenomenal, it appeals to the land lovers with a rich pomodoro sauce and a bacon foam. The atmosphere is busy and trendy while still offering a relaxing beachfront experience. **Features:** full bar, patio dining. **Reservations:** suggested. **Address:** 3550 Wailea Alanui Dr 96753 **Location:** From end of SR 31, 0.5 mi n; in Andaz Maui at Wailea Resort. **Parking:** valet only. [L] [D] CALL ⑤M

NICK'S FISHMARKET MAUI   808/879-7224

▼▼▼ Seafood Steak. Fine Dining. $29-$55 **AAA Inspector Notes:** A lovely location on the grounds of the Fairmont Kea Lani Hotel is only the beginning of the dining experience. Diners will delight in the highly trained staff offering suggestions from the menu as well as the wonderful feel of the warm tropical evening created by the outdoor terrace, candlelit tables and views of the tiki torch-lit grounds. Complimentary valet parking is offered. **Features:** full bar, patio dining, happy hour. **Reservations:** suggested. **Address:** 4100 Wailea Alanui Dr 96753 **Location:** From end of SR 31, 0.7 mi s; in The Fairmont Kea Lani, Maui. **Parking:** on-site and valet.

[D] CALL ⑤M [AC]

RUTH'S CHRIS STEAK HOUSE   808/874-8880

▼▼▼ Steak. Fine Dining. $27-$60 **AAA Inspector Notes:** The main fare is steak, which is prepared from several cuts of Prime beef and cooked to perfection, but the menu also lists lamb, chicken and seafood dishes. Guests should come hungry because the side dishes, which are among the a la carte offerings, could make a meal in themselves. **Features:** full bar, happy hour. **Reservations:** suggested. **Address:** 3750 Wailea Alanui Dr 96753 **Location:** Jct Wailea Ike Dr; in The Shops at Wailea, upper level. [D] CALL ⑤M

SPAGO   808/879-2999

▼▼▼ ▼▼▼ Pacific Rim. Fine Dining. $39-$64 **AAA Inspector Notes:** Wolfgang Puck's signature restaurant, this contemporary dining room offers spectacular ocean views from its second-floor outdoor terrace. For a prime seating location, a reservation is essential. The innovative menu draws from the islands with local fish-of-the-day catches as well as mainland staples such as steak, chicken and pork, tempting both the locals and tourists to stop for dinner. Free valet parking is available. **Features:** full bar, patio dining. **Reservations:** suggested. **Address:** 3900 Wailea Alanui Dr 96753 **Location:** From end of SR 31, 0.5 mi s; in Four Seasons Resort Maui at Wailea. **Parking:** valet only. ▣ [D] CALL ⑤M

TOMMY BAHAMA'S TROPICAL CAFE   808/875-9983

▼▼▼ Caribbean. Casual Dining. $24-$44 **AAA Inspector Notes:** Located inside the upscale Wailea shopping center on the second floor, Tommy Bahama's offers a tropical theme throughout with a menu to match. Try the soups, salads and sandwiches for lunch or a nice selection of entrées at dinner. Dining on the terrace is an option. When you're done eating, stop in at the Tommy Bahama store right next door. **Features:** full bar, patio dining, happy hour. **Reservations:** suggested. **Address:** 3750 Wailea Alanui Dr 96753 **Location:** Jct Wailea Ike Dr; in The Shops at Wailea, upper level.

[L] [D] CALL ⑤M [AC]

WAILUKU (D-9) pop. 15,313, elev. 331'
• Attractions map p. 86

In 1824, 9 years before the first missionaries set foot in Wailuku, a Chinese man named Hungtai built a sugar mill. The industry took hold, and 124 years later the dominant company, Hawai'i Commercial & Sugar Co., sold three-bedroom houses in neighboring Kahului (see place listing p. 94) to its employees for $7,250. Thus was born the dual community of Wailuku-Kahului.

Because their common boundary is indistinguishable, the two cities at the northern shore of the isthmus are sometimes referred to as Maui's twin cities. The older of the two and the county seat, Wailuku is on the slopes of the mountains overlooking the harbor.

Displays relating to the history of Haleki'i Heiau and Pihana Heiau (temples) are north of Wailuku above Paukūkalo Bridge. **Note:** *Heiau* are culturally significant and should be treated with respect.

Maui Visitors and Convention Bureau: 1727 Wili Pa Loop, Wailuku, HI 96793. **Phone:** (800) 525-6284.

BAILEY HOUSE MUSEUM, 2375-A Main St., was built in 1833 as the Wailuku Female Seminary. Pre-contact Hawaiian artifacts, missionary-era furnishings and paintings by Edward Bailey are displayed. **Hours:** Mon.-Sat. 10-4. Closed major holidays. **Cost:** $7; $5 (ages 60+); $2 (ages 7-12). **Phone:** (808) 244-3326.

'ĪAO VALLEY is at the end of winding 'Īao Valley Rd. In this densely forested cul-de-sac, whose walls are almost a mile high, Kamehameha I trapped and destroyed the defending army of the Maui king. A sign and changing profile indicate rock formations in the shape of past dignitaries. The valley is within West Maui Forest Reserve, which encompasses most of the island's western peninsula. Bring mosquito repellent. Restrooms are available; drinking water is not. **Hours:** Daily 7-7. **Cost:** $5 (per private vehicle). **Phone:** (808) 984-8100.

'Iao Needle, in 'Iao Valley State Monument, is a rock formation blanketed with vegetation and rising more than 1,200 feet above the floor of 'Iao Valley. A shelter and botanical garden are found along the paved .6-mile path. Bring mosquito repellent. **Hours:** Daily 7-7. **Cost:** $5 (per private vehicle). **Phone:** (808) 984-8100.

Kepaniwai Park, 870 'Iao Valley Rd., contains the Heritage Gardens, a group of pavilions built as tributes to the ethnic groups who settled the island. Bring mosquito repellent. **Hours:** Daily 7-7. **Cost:** Free. **Phone:** (808) 270-7230. 〔𝍂〕

PRIDE OF MAUI departs from the main loading dock at 101 Mā'alaea Boat Harbor Rd., off SR 30. A 5-hour morning snorkeling cruise aboard this 65-foot catamaran takes passengers to Molokini and then to Turtle Reef, where green sea turtles often nest. A light breakfast and a barbecue lunch are provided. The boat has restrooms, heated freshwater showers and a glass-bottom slide. Whale-watch, sunset and afternoon snorkeling cruises also are offered.

Visitors must park in the designated parking area behind the aquarium. Sunscreen and a towel are recommended. Scuba gear, snuba gear and camera rentals are available. **Hours:** Morning snorkeling cruise departs daily at 8. Passengers must check in 30 minutes prior to departure. **Cost:** Morning snorkeling cruise $101; $67 (ages 3-12). Reservations are required. **Phone:** (808) 242-0955 or (877) 867-7433. 〔🍴〕

THE OLD WAILUKU INN AT ULUPONO   (808)244-5897
▽▽▽ **Historic Bed & Breakfast** $165-$195 **Address:** 2199 Kahookele St 96793 **Location:** From airport, 4 mi w on SR 32 W through historic Wailuku, just s on SR 30 (High St), then just e; street entrance is the third street on the left (across from Wailuku Elementary School). Located in "Old Wailuku" residential area. **Facility:** Old Hawaii pervades this 1924 inn, where heirloom elements are complemented by modern amenities. 10 units. 2 stories (no elevator), interior corridors. **Terms:** 2 night minimum stay, 61 day cancellation notice-fee imposed. 〔HS〕 〔📶〕 〔✕〕 〔▯〕

Island of Moloka'i

Kamakou Preserve, Kaunakakai

On Moloka'i's north shore, velvety green sea cliffs plunge into the wild blue Pacific. On the island's lush east side, a one-lane road, devoid of traffic, climbs past sweeping coastal vistas, then snakes through misty rain forest on its way to the waterfall-laced Hālawa Valley. Moloka'i's arid western region is rife with picture-perfect beaches, and it's not uncommon to find them deserted at 2 p.m. on a Sunday.

The island's unspoiled beauty is astonishing. Even more amazing is the fact that tiny Moloka'i, clearly visible from neighboring Maui, has failed to register on most tourists' radar. Talk to any local and they'll tell you that's exactly how they like it.

"The Friendly Isle" is just that—a place where everyone seemingly knows everyone and greets one another with hugs and a hearty "A*loha*" in the cramped isles of the Friendly Market, one of the few grocery stores on the island. Reports of tourists being greeted with "stink eye" are largely myth. The people of Moloka'i are warm and welcoming, so long as you haven't come to buy oceanfront property or break ground on a new mega resort.

In Hawai'i, Moloka'i's anti-development attitude is legendary. In 2008 the Moloka'i Ranch company, the island's largest private land owner and operator of The Lodge at Moloka'i Ranch, lost a long battle to develop luxury homes at pristine Lā'au Point—land held sacred by island residents, 50 percent of whom claim native Hawaiian ancestry. Defeated, frustrated and in a reported financial hole, Moloka'i Ranch closed the existing lodge, leaving the island with only one traditional hotel.

Moloka'i's human history stretches back to the mid-seventh century when settlers from the Marquesas Islands landed on the shores of Hālawa Bay. Over the next 1,200 years the population ebbed and flowed. From the 1860s through the 1940s, Moloka'i saw an influx of leprosy patients who'd been banished to the island's remote Kalaupapa Peninsula (also called Makanalua Peninsula), now a National Historical Park. In the early 20th century the rise of the pineapple industry triggered a financial boom that lasted well into the 1970s. Today the economy is supported primarily by agriculture, hunting, fishing and tourism.

Moloka'i, the legendary child of the goddess Hina and the god of creation Wakea, is 260 square miles of dramatic topographic contrasts. Rolling rangelands, windswept beach dunes and rocky shoreline coves

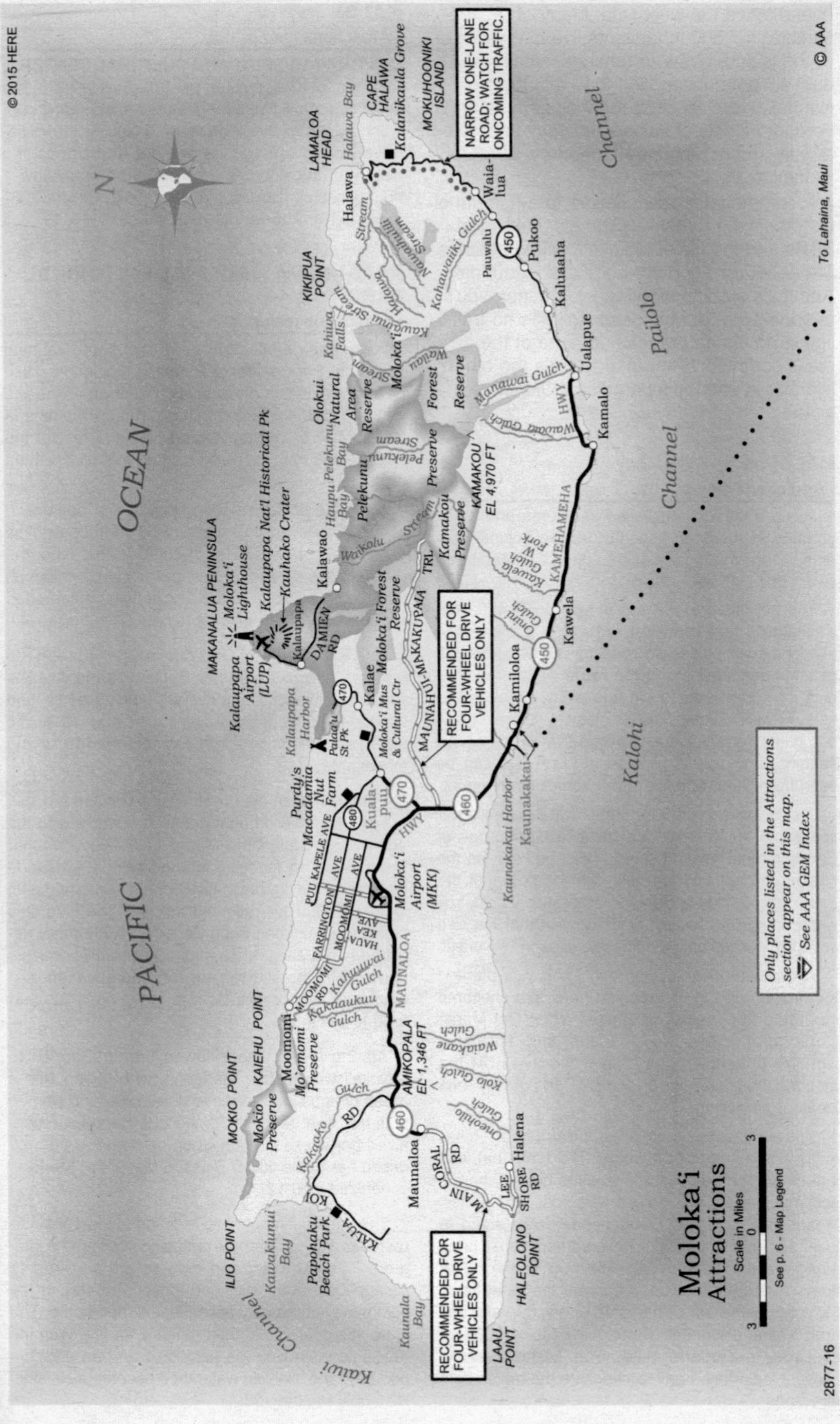
Molokaʻi
Attractions
Scale in Miles
3 0 3
See p. 6 - Map Legend
© 2015 HERE
© AAA
2877-16
PACIFIC
OCEAN
Kalohi
Channel
Pailolo
Channel
Kaiwi
Channel
N
NARROW ONE-LANE ROAD; WATCH FOR ONCOMING TRAFFIC.
RECOMMENDED FOR FOUR-WHEEL DRIVE VEHICLES ONLY
RECOMMENDED FOR FOUR-WHEEL DRIVE VEHICLES ONLY
Only places listed in the Attractions section appear on this map.
See AAA GEM Index
To Lahaina, Maui
MAKANALUA PENINSULA
Molokaʻi Lighthouse
Kalaupapa Nat'l Historical Pk
Kauhako Crater
Kalaupapa Airport (LUP)
Kalaupapa
Kalaupapa Harbor
Kalawao
DAMIEN RD
Molokaʻi Forest Reserve
Palaaʻu St Pk
Kalae
Molokaʻi Mus & Cultural Ctr
Purdy's Macadamia Nut Farm
Kualapuu
Molokaʻi Airport (MKK)
Kaunakakai
Kaunakakai Harbor
Kamiloloa
Kawela
KAMEHAMEHA HWY
Kamalo
Ualapue
Kaluaaha
Pukoo
Pauwalu
Waialua
Halawa
Halawa Bay
CAPE HALAWA
LAMALOA HEAD
Kalanikaula Grove
MOKUHOOHIKI ISLAND
KIKIPUA POINT
Olokui Natural Area Reserve
Molokaʻi Forest Reserve
Pelekunu Preserve
Pelekunu Bay
Haupu Bay
Kamakou Preserve
KAMAKOU EL 4,970 FT
MAUNAHUI-MAKAKUPAIA TRL
MAUNALOA HWY
AMIKOPALA EL 1,346 FT
Maunaloa
Moomomi
Moʻomomi Preserve
KAIEHU POINT
MOKIO POINT
Mokio Preserve
ILIO POINT
Kawakiuʻui Bay
Papohaku Beach Park
KALUAKOI RD
Halena
HALEOLONO POINT
LAAU POINT
Kaunala Bay
MAIN CORAL RD
LEE SHORE RD
FARRINGTON AVE
PUU KAPELE AVE
MOOMOMI AVE
HAUAKEA AVE
MOOMOMI RD
450
460
470
480

characterize the west side. Many of Moloka'i's 7,500 inhabitants live in the center of the island, home to ranches, small residential communities and the main town of Kaunakakai. The often rainy eastern half is a verdant mosaic of valleys, soaring cliffs, waterfalls and mountains—topped by 4,961-foot Kamakou Peak.

Accommodations are limited to a handful of condominium rental resorts, a sprinkling of B&Bs and the Hotel Moloka'i. Island eateries are generally good but not exactly abundant. And if it's sizzling nightlife you're after, you'll need to swim to Maui. Moloka'i has no traffic lights, no canned *aloha* and none of the crass commercialism that plagues the other islands. In short, it's paradise, "Old Hawai'i" style.

HĀLAWA (D-8) elev. 280'
• Attractions map p. 113

Ruins of several Hawaiian structures and burial grounds, half hidden beneath profuse tropical vegetation, are the legacy of the 45-foot tsunami that swept into Hālawa in 1946.

The only road to Hālawa is paved SR 450 from Kaunakakai *(see place listing p. 115).* It follows the fishpond-scalloped south coast for 30 miles; **no gas or oil is available along the route.** As the road begins to climb away from the sea, turtle-shaped Mokuho'oniki Island is visible offshore. Once a practice bombing range during World War II, it's now a seabird sanctuary. A glimpse of Maui also can be seen from Hālawa; it is 8 miles across the channel.

Just before the road begins its twisting 3-mile descent into the valley is Kalanikāula Grove, one of Hawai'i's more revered spots. It can be seen on the hillside. Ancient tradition held that the power of the *kukui,* also called candlenut tree because its oily fruit was burned for candles, was so great that the tree could be touched only with the intercession of a priest.

The revered *kahuna* (priest) Lanikāula planted the grove, and the gray-barked trees that sheltered his home now guard his grave. When Del Monte Corporation wanted to clear the land, Hawaiian workers refused to chop down the trees. At the mouth of the valley is a beach park and grassy area ideal for picnicking.

Moa'ula Falls and pool are approximately 2 miles away at the head of the valley. The trails that lead into the valley are accessible only to hikers who are accompanied by tour guides who possess permits. Mosquito repellent is recommended. According to local superstition, would-be swimmers must bring along a ti leaf to throw into the pool. If the ti leaf floats, it is safe to swim; if it sinks, the giant lizard Mo'o will come out of his cave under the falls and drag swimmers under. Hīpuapua Falls, a 500-foot cascade, is a quarter-mile north. Visitors should allow at least half a day to negotiate the trail in both directions.

KALAE (D-7) elev. 1,368'
• Attractions map p. 113

MOLOKA'I MUSEUM AND CULTURAL CENTER is 2 mi. n.e. of Kualapu'u on SR 470. Built in 1878, this small sugar mill has been restored to operating condition. Much of the equipment, including the mule-driven cane crusher, is original and traces the history of sugar crops on Moloka'i. **Time:** Allow 1 hour minimum. **Hours:** Mon.-Sat. 10-2. **Cost:** $5; $1 (ages 5-18). **Phone:** (808) 567-6436. 🎫

KALAUPAPA NATIONAL HISTORICAL PARK (D-7)
• Attractions map p. 113

Kalaupapa settlement and Kalaupapa National Historical Park are on Kalaupapa Peninsula (also called Makanalua Peninsula), which juts from the center of Moloka'i's north coast. The peninsula is a low tongue of lava separated from the rest of the island—and the world—by a 1,660-foot bluff and an arc of heavy breakers.

Because of its isolation, Kalaupapa became a place of exile for those afflicted with leprosy (now called Hansen's disease) in 1866. At that time, the disease was spreading throughout the Hawaiian islands, and a colony of the afflicted was established at Kalaupapa in an attempt to contain the disease.

In 1873 Belgian Catholic priest Joseph de Veuster, known as Father Damien, arrived at the settlement. Instead of staying 3 months as he had intended, he spent the remaining 16 years of his life here, establishing order and ministering to the inhabitants.

Father Damien died of Hansen's disease in 1889, but his example brought many new workers to the settlement. Called the Martyr of Moloka'i, Father Damien left an indelible impression that extended far beyond the shores of his adopted island home. In October 2009 he received the Catholic Church's highest honor when Pope Benedict XVI formally declared him a saint. More than 500 Hawai'i residents traveled to the Vatican for the canonization ceremony in St. Peter's Square, capping a 33-year road to sainthood.

Among those who followed Father Damien to Moloka'i was Mother Marianne, who, along with a group of nuns, ministered to girls and young women until her own death in 1918. Pope Benedict recognized her works in 2005 when he beatified her and raised her to the title of Blessed Marianne. She was canonized in 2012.

The introduction of sulfone drugs in the 1940s arrested many cases and eventually eliminated contagion. There have been no new admissions to Kalaupapa since 1969, and those who stay in the community do so only because it is their home. The state has guaranteed their tenancy for life. With the residents' approval, the peninsula and an adjacent portion of the Waikolu watershed became a National Historical Park in 1980.

Getting to the settlement can be half the experience since the only access is by commercial air, walking or muleback tours. Tours include Judd Park, Kalaupapa village and the site of the original settlement, Kalawao. At the latter is St. Philomena's Church, repaired and expanded by Father Damien, and a spectacular view of the rugged northeast coast. Moloka'i Lighthouse, near the tip of the peninsula, sends its powerful beacon far out to sea.

Air service is provided by Makani Kai Air, (808) 834-5813 or (877) 255-8532; phone for departure details. Ground access is provided by Moloka'i Mule Ride; phone (808) 567-6088 or (800) 567-7550. Damien Tours offers guided tours of Kalaupapa; phone (808) 567-6171. A combination mule ride and guided tour is available, as are combination packages with air fare from other islands.

A permit from the Department of Health is required to visit Kalaupapa. Visitors' selected commercial tour company will handle the permit arrangements for all day trips. Overnight trips are not permitted unless visitors personally know a resident who is willing to sponsor them and apply for their permit. Visitors must be at least 16 years old. Park open daily. Commercial tours operate Mon.-Sat.; closed Jan. 1, Thanksgiving and Christmas. For more information phone Kalaupapa National Historical Park, (808) 567-6802.

KAMALŌ (D-8) elev. 5'
• Attractions map p. 113

Kamalō is about 10 miles east of Kaunakakai, at the southernmost point on the island. Close to the highway on the ocean side is St. Joseph Church, a frame chapel built by Father Damien in 1876. A small monument a mile east marks the spot where in 1927 Emory Bronte and Ernest Smith concluded the first civilian trans-Pacific flight in the brushy arms of a *kiawe* grove.

KAUNAKAKAI (D-7) pop. 3,425, elev. 5'
• Attractions map p. 113

Kaunakakai is the "metropolis" of Moloka'i. Ala Malama, the 3-block-long commercial section, resembles an Old West movie set with its false-front buildings that house general stores, markets and restaurants. Boutiques feature local arts and crafts. The wharf, reaching a half-mile into the harbor, is the mooring for charter fishing, diving and cruise boats.

Just west of the wharf, Malama Cultural Park is the site of the summer home of Kamehameha V, who reigned 1863-72; he is the Hawaiian monarch most closely identified with Moloka'i. One of the king's projects was the planting of 1,000 coconut palms. Several hundred remain at the Kapuāiwa grove, about 2 miles west where SR 460 curves northward away from the coast. Visitors should be wary of falling coconuts.

Maunahui Road (a jeep road), 3.7 miles north off SR 460, runs 9 miles east to the sandalwood measuring pit, dug to match a ship's hull in size and shape. In the early 19th century, Hawaiian chiefs and laborers measured cut wood in the pit before selling it by the shipload to foreign traders.

Note: Because Maunahui Road is rough, visitors using it should travel either by foot or by four-wheel-drive vehicle. Use caution, especially when it rains.

Two miles farther the road ends at Waikolu Valley Lookout. From this 3,600-foot vantage point a vista extends down the emerald cleft to the sea. Morning trips are best; clouds often obscure the view after late morning or early afternoon. From here you can hike into Kamakou Preserve, a 2,774-acre rain forest with numerous hiking trails. Insect repellent and rain gear are recommended.

To the east, Kamehameha V Highway (SR 450) runs along the reef-lined south coast. Moloka'i's reef system is purported to be the largest in the United States. Along this coastline are the remnants of ancient Hawaiian fishponds, which once numbered almost 60. The semicircular ponds, enclosed by coral and basalt walls, were built between the 14th and 18th centuries to provide a supply of fresh mullet. Several have been restored and are being used for fish farming.

Two ponds have been made national historical landmarks: Keawanui covers almost 55 acres, and 'Ualapu'e covers 22 acres. An occasional patch of taro, the main ingredient of *poi*, a Hawaiian staple, clings to terraced hillsides. The road passes through several small towns en route to its terminus at Hālawa *(see place listing p. 114)*.

Moloka'i Visitors Bureau: P.O. Box 960, Kaunakakai, HI 96748. **Phone:** (808) 553-3876 or (800) 800-6367.

HOTEL MOLOKAI 808/553-5347
[fyi] Not evaluated. **Address:** 1300 Kamehameha V Hwy 96748 **Location:** Oceanfront. SR 460 and 450, 8.5 mi e of airport. Facilities, services, and décor characterize an economy property.

MOLOKAI SHORES 808/553-5954
[fyi] Not evaluated. **Address:** 1000 Kamehameha V Hwy 96748 **Location:** Oceanfront. SR 460 and 450, 8 mi e of airport. Facilities, services, and décor characterize an economy property. The property offers an expansive lawn and an oceanfront pool.

WHERE TO EAT

MOLOKAI PIZZA CAFE 808/553-3288
▼ Pizza. Family Dining. $10-$25 **AAA Inspector Notes:** Since 1992, this family-friendly restaurant has been offering sandwiches, burgers and a few entrées, along with thick- and thin-crust pizzas. **Features:** patio dining. **Address:** 15 Kaunakakai Pl 96748 **Location:** Center; at MM 0. [L] [D]

KUALAPU'U (D-7) pop. 2,027, elev. 878'
• Restaurants p. 116
• Attractions map p. 113

The reservoir just west of the community is the terminus of the Moloka'i Irrigation Project, which brings, via aqueduct and a 5-mile-long tunnel through the mountains, water from the rain-soaked Waikolu Valley to the dry central plain.

PĀLĀA'U STATE PARK, about 3 mi. n. off SR 470, is 233 acres overlooking Kalaupapa Peninsula. Some 1,600 feet below the overlook, which is reached by a short trail, is Father Damien's Kalaupapa *(see Kalaupapa National Historical Park p. 114)*. The Moloka'i Mule Barn on SR 470 is the departure point for guided tours that transport visitors to Kalaupapa by mule train. Just below the park, the 3-mile, 26-switchback Kalaupapa Trail begins its descent to the leaf-shaped Kalaupapa Peninsula.

No drinking water is available. **Hours:** Daily 24 hours. **Cost:** Day use free. A fee is charged for camping. **Phone:** (808) 567-6923. 🅐 ⛱

PURDY'S MACADAMIA NUT FARM is 1.5 mi. e. on SR 480, then n. on Lihi Pali Ave. Guided tours of the 50-tree orchard, which was planted in the 1920s, include explanations of macadamia nut production and harvesting. Visitors learn how to crack the nuts and are invited to sample macadamia nut blossom honey. **Hours:** Tues.-Fri. 9:30-3:30, Sat. 10-2. Phone ahead to confirm schedule. **Cost:** Free. **Phone:** (808) 567-6601.

ESSENCE OF OHANA — 808/567-9490

🐦 Coffee/Tea. Quick Serve. $4-$10 **AAA Inspector Notes:** Offering more than just coffee, this convenient stop also serves tasty light sandwiches, flatbread pizzas and bakery goods. Diners order at the counter, then eat on the porch. **Address:** 1630 Farrington Ave 96757 **Location:** Jct SR 470; in Coffees of Hawaii Plantation.

Ⓑ Ⓛ 🍴

MAUNALOA (D-7) pop. 376
• Attractions map p. 113

The largest settlement on the western end of the island, Maunaloa was the company town for the Dole pineapple plantation until 1975, when the operation shut down. Maunaloa lies close to the Kaluako'i Resort at Pāpōhaku Beach, which offers golfing, camping and a large public beach. The beach covers some 3 miles and offers wide stretches of beautiful sand. There are no lifeguards, though, and the currents, undertow and high surf

(especially in winter) can be dangerous; always use caution.

Blending agricultural history and tourism, re-created plantation buildings sell the works of local artisans. Among the shops and restaurants is a kite factory—the only original plantation building—that offers free kite-flying lessons in a nearby field.

Southwest of town, a dirt road off Mokio Street leads to Hale O Lono Harbor, the starting point for two popular canoe races to O'ahu: the women's 🦅 Na Wahine O Ke Kai in September and the men's 🦅 Moloka'i Hoe Outrigger Canoe Championship in October.

Note: Because of poor road conditions, nighttime travel on the dirt road is not recommended.

PŪKO'O (D-8) elev. 20'
• Attractions map p. 113

Above Pūko'o in Mapulehu Valley is 'Ili'ili'ōpae Heiau ("Temple of the Shrimp"). With a platform measuring 320 by 120 feet, it is the largest *heiau* on Moloka'i and one of the largest of its kind in the state. The *heiau* may have been the site of human sacrifices.

'Ili'ili'ōpae is said to have been built in the 13th century by the *Menehune*, legendary people who were 2 to 3 feet tall and had large abdomens. The *Menehune* formed a line across the island from Wailau and passed the building stones to the site hand over hand. Legend has it that each worker's reward was one freshwater shrimp, hence the *heiau's* name. The route of the *Menehune* line became the Wailau Trail, once a major link to the outside world for taro villages tucked into the coves of the inaccessible Pali Coast.

The owners welcome the public to hike to 'Ili'ili'ōpae Heiau, but visitors must check in at the Moloka'i Visitors Bureau for parking instructions. Phone the Moloka'i Visitors Bureau at (808) 553-3876 for further information. Hikers should wear grip-soled shoes as the pathway to the *heiau* is challenging and often slippery. **Note:** *Heiau* are culturally significant and should be treated with respect.

Island of O'ahu

Sunset at Kapi'olani Regional Park, Honolulu

O'ahu is nicknamed "The Gathering Place," and the name is apt. In addition to its residents—nearly 70 percent of the population of all of the islands combined—a million visitors a year land on O'ahu, then proceed to explore the other islands. To many, O'ahu *is* Hawai'i. Hawai'i's capital, Honolulu, with its commerce, industry and celebrated Waikīkī resort beach, is the heart of both the island and the state.

Honolulu is a true melting pot of people; Polynesian, Chinese, Japanese, European and native ancestry all are represented in an array of shopping, entertainment and cuisine. While the city looks to the future, it celebrates Hawai'i's past with cultural, historical and educational attractions.

Yet O'ahu offers more than just a booming metropolis. Other aspects of the island—wide-open spaces, spectacular vistas and uncrowded beaches—are found "over the *pali*," which encompasses the windward coast, along the deserted stretches of wild-surf beach on the north coast and among the quiet fields of the central plateau. The pace of life in these regions is more leisurely. Many islanders enjoy the best of both worlds, residing on the windward side and commuting to work in Honolulu.

O'ahu covers 597 square miles and comprises two parallel mountain ranges: the older Wai'anae on the west coast and the younger Ko'olau along the windward shore. Flowing lava from the Ko'olau eventually reached the eroded Wai'anae slopes, linking the ridges into a single isle. The highest peak on the island is 4,046-foot Ka'ala Peak in the Wai'anae; 3,150-foot Pu'u Konahuanui tops the Ko'olau. Pineapples flourish on the intervening plateau, the fertile, well-watered Leilehua Plain.

There was little evidence of O'ahu's importance during the early years of exploration. Capt. James Cook spotted the island during his first voyage (1778), but O'ahu remained undisturbed until Kamehameha I, in the process of conquering the archipelago, invaded it in 1795. The king's trade with the outside world brought attention to Honolulu Harbor, which now handles millions of tons of freight a year. Deep Pearl Harbor, similarly important for military reasons, is the hub of a group of military installations that compose almost 25 percent of O'ahu's acreage.

Commercial, governmental and military jobs are the primary economic force. Army, Navy, Air Force, Marine Corps and Coast Guard installations employ thousands, and federal expenditure ranks first as a source of

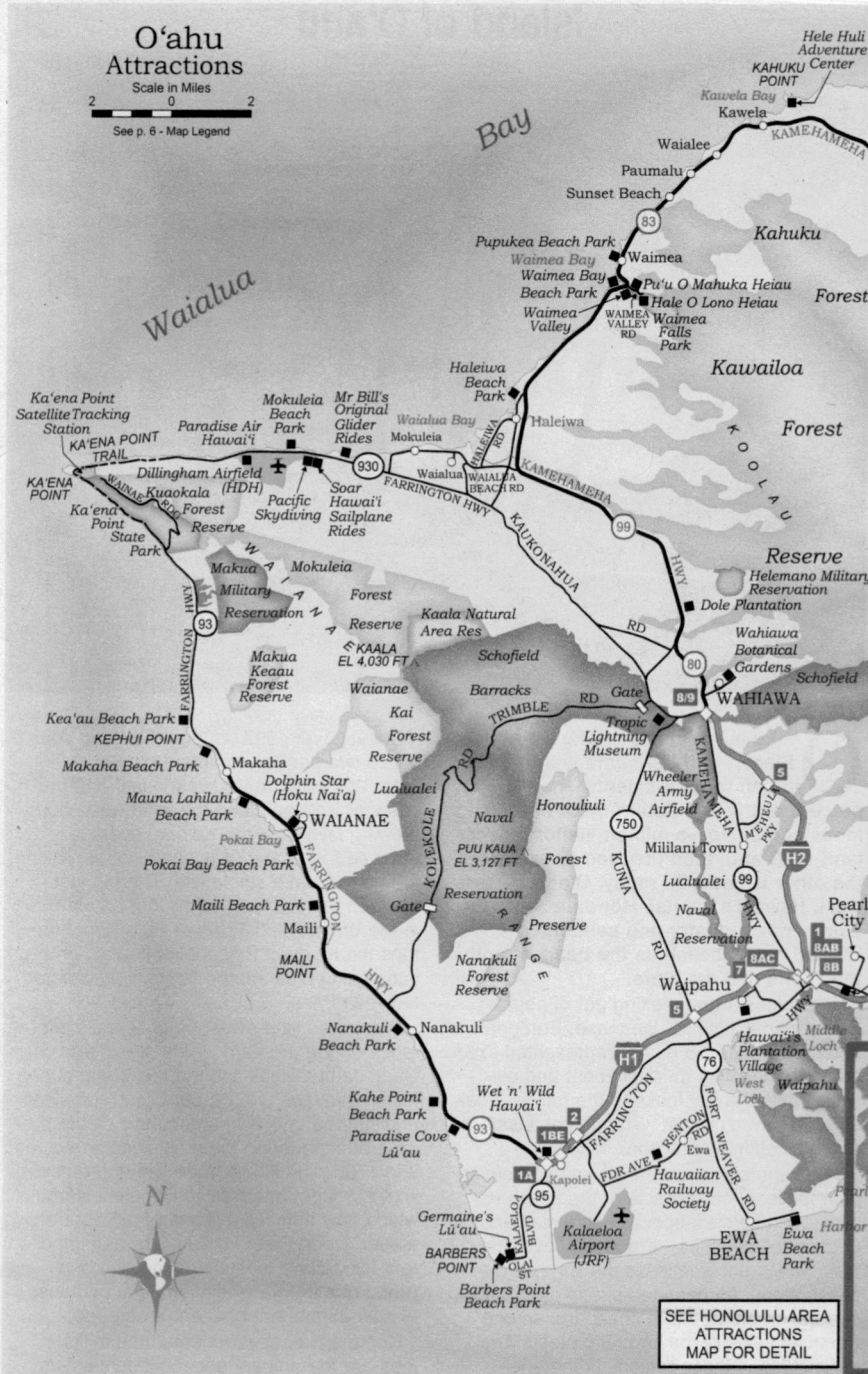

Oʻahu Attractions

Scale in Miles

2 0 2

See p. 6 - Map Legend

SEE HONOLULU AREA ATTRACTIONS MAP FOR DETAIL

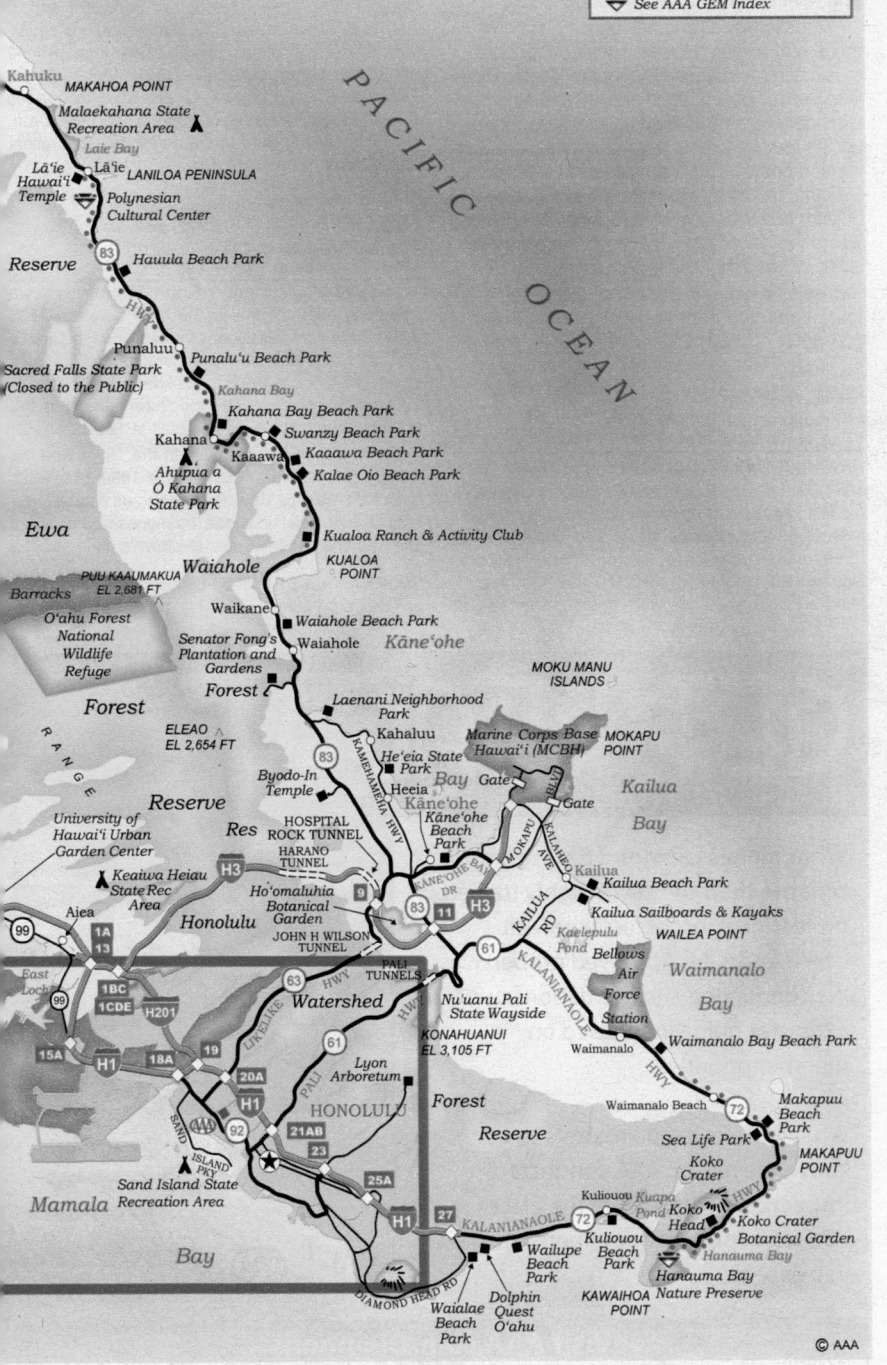

© 2015 HERE

Only places listed in the Attractions section appear on this map.
◆ See AAA GEM Index

the island's—and the state's—revenue. Tourism is a close second. Although the pineapple industry began on O'ahu, it is small and relatively unimportant economically.

Recreationally, O'ahu has become synonymous with surfing. Movies, television, popular music and more have brought the Banzai Pipeline, Sunset Beach, Waimea Bay and other legendary North Shore spots into living rooms across the nation and beyond. World-class surfing and bodysurfing championships are held at Mākaha and other beaches. While these are only for professionals, there are plenty of places where less proficient surfers can perfect their skills. Windsurfing also is popular.

Gray Line offers a variety of sightseeing tours departing from Waikīkī; phone (808) 833-3000 or (888) 206-4531.

'EWA (H-3) elev. 49'
- Attractions map p. 118
- Part of Honolulu area — see p. 122

HAWAIIAN RAILWAY SOCIETY is off SR 76 at 91-1001 Renton Rd. This open-air museum preserves the island's railroad heritage. Static displays of historic rolling stock include steam and diesel locomotives, passenger cars, boxcars and flatcars. Narrated 90-minute train rides to Kahe Point are offered on Sundays; rides with an ice cream stop in Ko Olina are offered on Saturdays. Phone for information about weekday rides.

Time: Allow 1 hour minimum. **Hours:** Grounds Sun. 11:30-5. Train rides depart Sun. at 1 and 3, Sat. at 3; arrive at least 30 minutes before departure. Closed Christmas Eve and Christmas. Phone ahead to confirm schedule. **Cost:** Grounds free. Train ride $12; $8 (ages 2-12 and 62+); free (ages 0-1 on lap). Train ride in parlor/observation car, available second Sun. of the month by reservation, $25. **Phone:** (808) 681-5461. ♿

HALE'IWA (F-2) pop. 3,970, elev. 20'
- Attractions map p. 118
- Part of Honolulu area — see p. 122

Midway along O'ahu's North Shore, Hale'iwa (meaning home of the frigate bird) dates to 1832 when Protestant missionaries established the area's first church. After Queen Lili'uokalani donated a seven-dial clock in 1892, it was known as the Queen Lili'uokalani church. The clock remains, but the present church structure was built in 1961.

The O'ahu Railroad arrived in the 1890s and the island's first hotel was built here in 1899. Hale'iwa's harbor on Waialua Bay offers deep-sea fishing charters. Quaint, eclectic shops, boutiques and galleries line Kamehameha Avenue, the town's main street.

WAIMEA VALLEY is at 59-864 Kamehameha Hwy., across from Waimea Bay. This 1,875-acre historical

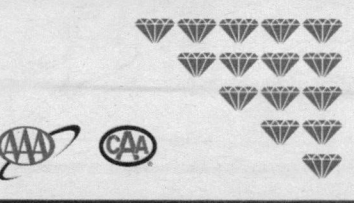

nature park re-creates ancient Hawaiian culture. A paved .75-mile-long pathway traverses the valley and leads to Waimea Falls. If you can't or don't want to make the walk, you can opt for a one-way or round-trip shuttle ride.

Off the main path are 35 themed gardens featuring 5,000-plus different plants from Hawai'i and other parts of the world. Hale O Lono Heiau, a sacred outdoor place of worship built between 1470 and 1700 and dedicated to the Hawaiian god Lono, also is on the grounds.

You can participate in activities like coconut-frond weaving, *lei*-making, *hula* lessons, storytelling and cultural hikes and learn how to play ancient Hawaiian games. You can also take a dip in a 30-foot-deep natural pool at the base of Waimea Falls (weather permitting). Flotation devices are available for rent, and there's a changing facility.

Note: Visitors are prohibited from smoking; picking and eating fruit, nuts and seeds; drinking from the stream; feeding and approaching the peacocks; and swimming anywhere other than in the Waimea Falls pool. Visitors may enter the pool only after asking permission from the lifeguard and should not swim if they have wounds or open sores. Pets (except service dogs) are not permitted. *Heiau* are culturally significant and should be treated with respect. Closed-toe shoes, insect repellent and sunscreen are recommended. Restrooms are available in the visitor center; portable toilets are available elsewhere. Snacks are available at the visitor center and at Waimea Falls.

Time: Allow 3 hours minimum. **Hours:** Daily 9-5. Activities daily 10-4. Closed Jan. 1, Thanksgiving and Christmas. **Cost:** $16; $12 (ages 60+); $10 (military and Hawai'i residents with ID); $8 (ages 4-12 and military ages 60+ with ID); $6 (military children ages 4-12); $100 (family, two adults and up to six children ages 0-17). Round-trip shuttle fare $6. One-way shuttle fare $4. **Phone:** (808) 638-7766.

CHOLO'S HOMESTYLE MEXICAN RESTAURANT & MARGARITA BAR 808/637-3059

Mexican. Casual Dining. $8-$17 **AAA Inspector Notes:** This charming open-air eatery serves island-fresh fish tacos, quesadillas, fajitas and enchiladas. Colorful décor creates a festive atmosphere. **Features:** full bar, patio dining. **Address:** 66-250 Kamehameha Hwy 96712 **Location:** Historic center; in North Shore Marketplace.

HALEIWA JOE'S SEAFOOD GRILL 808/637-8005

Seafood. Casual Dining. $13-$35 **AAA Inspector Notes:** This is a great family-friendly option for those looking for fresh food at a reasonable price. Small- and big-plate options are available. Recommendations include the crunchy coconut shrimp, battered in tempura then dusted with coconut and lightly fried and served with a scrumptious plum-and-honey-mustard dipping sauce. The crab and avocado salad also is a menu highlight. It is served on romaine lettuce with carrots, shaved Parmesan cheese and a creamy homemade peppercorn dressing. **Features:** full bar, patio dining, happy hour. **Address:** 66-011 Kamehamaha Hwy 96712 **Location:** Jct SR 99, 1.4 mi n on SR 83; center; near the historic bridge.

JAMESONS BY THE SEA 808/637-6272

Seafood. Casual Dining. $22-$38 **AAA Inspector Notes:** This restaurant features fresh seafood with a beautiful sunset view of the marina from across the street. Although it's a bit pricey for what you get, the familiar choices are welcome for families with young children. An older 1970s tropical vibe is felt with the potted palms, pink-and-green color scheme and laminate wood-paneled walls. There is a nice gift shop to browse through while you wait. **Features:** full bar, patio dining, Sunday brunch, happy hour. **Reservations:** suggested. **Address:** 62-540 Kamehameha Hwy 96712 **Location:** Jct SR 99, 1.5 mi n on SR 83; center.

MATSUMOTO SHAVE ICE 808/637-4827

Specialty. Quick Serve. $3-$4 **AAA Inspector Notes:** Since 1951, this store has been serving shaved ice or 'snow cones' with homemade syrups. Sit in the courtyard and enjoy this taste treat on a warm day. It's open daily from 9-6. **Address:** 66-087 Kamehameha Hwy 96712 **Location:** In historic Haleiwa; center.

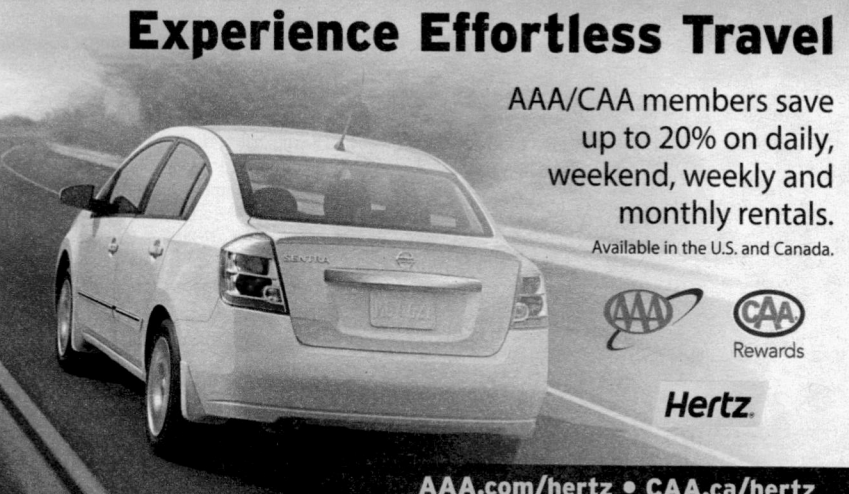

Honolulu

Then & Now

Mix Boston, Las Vegas, Manila, Singapore and Tokyo, put the combination in a natural setting straight out of a painting by Paul Gauguin, add the scent of ginger flowers and the rush of freeway traffic, and you have Honolulu. Capital of Hawai'i and O'ahu's largest city, it is a fascinating combination of East and West, frenetic and laid-back, old and futuristic.

In the Hawaiian language, Honolulu means "sheltered bay." The harbor—negotiated by freighters, luxury liners and even a sampan fishing fleet—remains at the heart of old downtown. And Honolulu's Waikīkī neighborhood, a surfer's paradise flaunting idyllic sun-kissed beaches, is among the largest resort destinations in the Pacific, its surplus of seaside hotels and restaurants offering respite to countless vacationers.

Centuries before the first lodging (the Moana Surfrider, built in 1901) materialized in Waikīkī, Kamehameha the Great, the *ali'i* (chief) of the island of Hawai'i, landed at Maunalua Bay. Intent on conquering and unifying all of the islands, Kamehameha achieved his goal in 1810. Under his careful watch, a trade network between Hawai'i and Asia, carried out by sea-hardy Westerners, emerged.

Kamehameha I died in 1819, the same year whaling ships hailing from New England began utilizing the southeastern O'ahu settlement as a way station. As taverns and brothels proliferated near the waterfront to meet the needs of rough-and-tumble sailors, a completely disparate group of New Englanders—Christian missionaries set on ending the "heathen" ways of the Hawaiians—began arriving in Honolulu.

Chinatown has a diverse restaurant scene

Eventually, the religious leaders' influence with the Hawaiian monarchy pushed the whalers out. Honolulu became the permanent seat of government in 1845, and from that point the history of the city and the islands as a whole merged. A new Hawai'i surfaced—one centered on a then-booming sugar industry—with many of the missionaries' business-minded sons among the wealthiest and most powerful residents. Brought in to work on the sugar (and later, pineapple) plantations, Chinese, Japanese, Portuguese, Puerto Rican, Korean and Filipino laborers settled here, further contributing to the varied cultural heritage of Hawai'i.

Present-day Honolulu stretches along the narrow coastal plain between eastward Koko Head and the necklace of military reservations at Pearl Harbor, an area visited by those seeking out traces of the "date which will live in infamy," Dec. 7, 1941. Vestiges of the missionary

(Continued on p. 123.)

Fast Facts

ABOUT THE CITY

POP: 390,738 ▪ **ELEV:** 21 ft.

MONEY

SALES TAX: Hawai'i has an excise tax of 4 percent (4.712 percent in Honolulu) on most goods and services. Honolulu has a lodging tax of 9.25 percent; rental cars are subject to state tax and a road tax of approximately $3 per day.

WHOM TO CALL

EMERGENCY: 911

POLICE (non-emergency): (808) 529-3111

TEMPERATURE: (808) 973-4380

HOSPITALS: The Queen's Medical Center, (808) 538-9011 ▪ Straub Clinic & Hospital, (808) 522-4000.

WHERE TO LOOK AND LISTEN

NEWSPAPERS: The major newspaper is the *Honolulu Star-Advertiser.*

RADIO: Honolulu radio station KHNR (690 AM) is a popular news/talk radio station ▪ KHPR (88.1 FM) and KIPO (89.3 FM) are members of National Public Radio.

VISITOR INFORMATION

Hawai'i Visitors and Convention Bureau: 2270 Kalākaua Ave., Suite 801, Honolulu, HI 96815. **Phone:** (808) 923-1811 or (800) 464-2924.

The bureau offers tour information, brochures and maps Mon.-Fri. 8-4:30, except holidays.

Spotlight and *This Week* magazines print tourism-oriented information that is helpful to visitors. These free publications are available at most concierge desks and in magazine racks along the street.

TRANSPORTATION

AIR TRAVEL: Busy Honolulu International Airport (HNL) is *the* gateway to the state. Just across Keehi Lagoon off H-1, next to Joint Base Pearl Harbor-Hickam, the airport is served by most domestic and many foreign passenger carriers, as well as interisland and commuter lines.

The average cab fare from the airport to Waikīkī is $40-$45; limousines average about $115.

RENTAL CARS: Hertz, (800) 654-3080, offers discounts to AAA members and has several area locations: the airport, (808) 529-6800; Kahala Hotel & Resort, (808) 735-8983; Hyatt Regency Waikīkī Beach Resort & Spa, (808) 971-3535; Hilton Hawaiian Village Waikīkī Beach Resort, (808) 973-3535; Waikīkī Beach Marriott, (808) 924-1681; Imperial Hotel, (808) 922-3331; Honolulu Pier, (808) 778-2956; and Pagoda Hotel, (808) 942-5626.

TAXIS: The largest companies serving the island are TheCAB, (808) 422-2222 ▪ and Charley's Taxi & Tours, (808) 531-1333.

Prices may be calculated from a base fare of $3.10 with an additional charge of 40c per additional eighth of a mile, or at a rate of $3 per mile in addition to a pickup fee. There may be an additional charge of $4.50 per oversized item (e.g., surfboard or bicycle). Prices vary per company.

PUBLIC TRANSPORTATION: "TheBus" offers transportation around the island. The base fare is $2.50; $1.25 (ages 6-17); $1 (ages 65+ and the physically impaired). Exact change is required. Transfers are free for a second bus only but must be requested when boarding and are good only for 2 hours. A 4-day pass, which provides unlimited rides, is $35 and may be purchased at TheBus Pass Office at the Kalihi Transit Center at the intersection of Middle Street and Kamehameha Highway and at select ABC Stores locations. Phone (808) 848-5555 for route and schedule information. A free time schedule usually is available at the headquarters, at libraries or at any City Hall. Guides for sightseeing via TheBus are sold at most area stores, but visitors should phone ahead to verify information.

(Continued from p. 122.)
era can be seen downtown, while the Chinatown district, which for a time recalled the bawdiness of Honolulu's whaling years in its now-defunct red-light district, creates an exotic atmosphere with open-air *lei* stands and herb shops.

Honolulu fuses the spirit of the Hawaiian people with tastes, ideals and styles borrowed from Asia, Europe and North America. While watching a dazzling island sunset, you may find yourself enthralled by the sweet murmur of a *'ukulele,* a classically Hawaiian instrument derived from the Portuguese

braginha. And, armed with a set of chopsticks in the city's diverse restaurant scene, it's easy to taste the abundance of ethnic influences.

Even the two capitol buildings on the island contrast with and synthesize the essence of their periods in a uniquely Hawaiian way. Marvel over 'Iolani Palace, the only example of American Florentine architecture in the world, before admiring its 20th-century replacement, the Hawai'i State Capitol, which showcases many of the Hawaiian Islands' striking natural aspects. Situated between the two structures is a statue of the beloved Queen Lili-'uokalani, the kingdom's last reigning monarch.

Must Do: AAA Editor's Picks

- Head to one of O'ahu's most beautiful beaches at **Kailua Beach Park**, hop on a bodyboard and ride the gentle waves; the azure waters also attract kayakers, parasailers and windsurfers. Tree-shaded areas and covered pavilions provide respite from the sun.

- Brave the crowds on narrow, 2-mile-long **Waikīkī Beach** and spread a towel on your little sliver of sand in preparation for catching some serious rays. Admire the surfers waiting for the perfect wave, and pay tribute to Duke Kahanamoku—the Honolulu native who popularized the sport of surfing in the early 20th century—by placing a *lei* on his statue.

- Stand on the deck of the 🤿 USS *Arizona* **Memorial** and reflect upon the events of Dec. 7, 1941, when Japanese bombers sank the ship, killing 1,177 sailors and propelling the United States into World War II. Recall other important aspects of that war at two nearby monuments: The 🤿 **Battleship *Missouri* Memorial** preserves "Mighty Mo," on whose deck Japan signed the treaty ending the war, and the 🤿 **USS *Bowfin* Submarine Museum and Park** honors the "silent service" and the crews who served valiantly on those underwater vessels.

- Suit up with fins, a mask and a snorkel—all of which you can rent on the cheap from nearby vendors—and swim with colorful tropical fish in **Hānauma Bay;** the shallow waters are especially appealing to newbie snorkelers.

- Lace up your sneakers (or hiking boots) and trek to the 760-foot summit of **Diamond Head State Monument**, an ancient volcanic crater, where you'll be treated to spectacular 360-degree vistas of Waikīkī. The hike is very steep and you'll need to bring drinking water and sun protection, but the breathtaking views make the effort worthwhile.

- Play a round at **Ko Olina Golf Club,** a scenic course distinguished by its 12th hole, which leaves a beautiful impression with a drive-through waterfall just below the elevated tee box; the challenging 18-hole course ranks high on many "best of" golfing lists.

- When the surf's up at **Waimea Bay,** marvel at the audacity of the surfers who fearlessly take on the awe-inspiring waves, which can reach heights of up to 30 feet. The waves are most pronounced in winter; in summer the water is much calmer and the beach is great for swimming and sunbathing.

- Taste unusual foods, listen to the sounds of the barkers and browse the many peculiar items at the open-air **Aloha Stadium Swap Meet & Marketplace** on the grounds of Aloha Stadium on Wednesday, Saturday and Sunday when more than 400 vendors gather to sell an array of eclectic goods.

- Follow the **Mānoa Falls Trail,** an easy 1.6-mile round-trip hike that traces Waihī Stream and winds through a bamboo forest and the verdant vines, ferns and trees of a rain forest en route to the scenic falls. Choose your footwear carefully, as the trail can be quite muddy and rocky.

- Haggle for bargains in **Chinatown,** where you can find beautiful calligraphy, pungent spices, gold jewelry and handmade *lei*. See what's fresh at a produce, fish or meat market; find colorful trinkets in a souvenir shop; step into a bakery and satiate your sweet tooth; or treat yourself to some dim sum as you immerse yourself in the cultural traditions of not just China but also Vietnam, Japan, Korea, the Philippines, Thailand and Laos.

- Scan the impressive panorama of the windward side of O'ahu from the **Nu'uanu Pali State Wayside**—just be sure to hold on tight to your belongings when doing so. On exceptionally windy days the trade winds are so strong you can actually lean against them. It was at Nu'uanu Pali—a 1,200-foot-high gap flanked by 2,000- to 3,000-foot cliffs—that Kamehameha the Great scored a decisive victory in the conquest of O'ahu.

Hit the links at Ko Olina Golf Club

Honolulu 1-day Itinerary

AAA editors suggest these activities for a great short vacation experience. Those staying in the area for a longer visit can access a 3-day itinerary at AAA.com/TravelGuide.

Morning

- Pay homage to the 3,581 Americans killed or wounded at **Pearl Harbor** on Dec. 7, 1941, when the Japanese launched a surprise assault on the U.S. naval base and its Pacific Fleet. After the early morning strike, a dozen U.S. ships were either sunken or beached and more than 300 U.S. aircraft had either suffered damages or been destroyed.

- Whether you choose to drive or take TheBus (direct routes are Nos. 20 or 42 from Waikīkī and Nos. 20, 42 or 52 from the Ala Moana Center or downtown) to Pearl Harbor, arrive early—some 5,000 somber tourists visit the area daily. Several sites present artifacts from the battle, while interpretive programs and dramatic multimedia displays and films document the "Day of Infamy." Just offshore is the striking ⌖ **USS *Arizona* Memorial;** the white linear structure traverses the final resting place for most of the 1,177 crew members who perished after a devastating armor-piercing bomb hit the battleship. At the ⌖ **Battleship *Missouri* Memorial** you walk the decks of the "Mighty Mo," where, in 1945, Japanese representatives signed an official surrender agreement ending the Second World War. Visitors to the ⌖ **USS *Bowfin* Submarine Museum and Park** discover what life was like for the 80 men stationed on this underwater vessel, launched exactly a year after the Pearl Harbor attack. The park also encompasses a waterfront memorial to World War II's fallen submariners.

Afternoon

- Head to **Nico's Pier 38**, a low-key, waterfront eatery where you can savor a hearty, skillfully prepared meal for less than you might expect thanks to the restaurant's proximity to a fish auction. (It's right next door, so whether you come for breakfast or lunch, Nico's is likely to be packed with ravenous auction workers and fishermen.) Hailing from Lyon, France, chef Nicholas Chaize serves up such Hawaiian staples as the plate lunch, infusing dishes typical to the locale with a dash of French gusto. For an afternoon visit, there's no better choice than the furikake pan-seared ahi, though chef Chaize's juicy, hand-packed double cheeseburger is hard to pass up, even at a place known for its floppingly fresh seafood.

- Explore downtown Honolulu, where cultural and historic sites are clustered together amid gleaming skyscrapers and tall, bending palm trees. Walk through the **Cathedral of Our Lady of Peace** to admire its vibrant stained-glass windows; or browse the metalwork, oil paintings and crafts displayed at the **Hawai'i State Art**

Tour the royal 'Iolani Palace

Museum (HiSAM). Then, tour **'Iolani Palace,** the country's only official royal residence. After being deposed by those in support of Hawai'i's annexation by the United States, Queen Lili'uokalani, the last reigning monarch of the Kingdom of Hawai'i, was imprisoned there in 1893. An accomplished musician and songwriter, she composed about 165 songs while confined within an austere room on the second floor of this otherwise opulent palace. Today a bronze statue of the revered ruler stands between the palace and another architectural gem, the ⌖ **Hawai'i State Capitol.**

Evening

- Leave the flip-flops behind and indulge yourself in paradise. The top-notch chefs at **Bali Steak & Seafood, La Mer** and **Orchids** will ensure you're well-fed on your vacation, preparing such dishes as hot and sour eggplant ravioli, steamed Manila clams and Kobe-style beef with bordelaise sauce. No matter where you choose to dine, book early, and, of course, request a table with a view. Refined elegance and heavenly Waikīkī scenery await you at Bali, a AAA Four Diamond restaurant inside the oceanfront **Hilton Hawaiian Village Waikīkī Beach Resort**. La Mer, a AAA Five Diamond restaurant, and the Four Diamond Orchids present arresting seascapes at the **Halekulani** hotel. Enjoy a cup of pressed Kona coffee with dessert in one of the chic lodging's distinctive dining rooms, then move to the Lewers Lounge for cocktails and classic tunes.

Top Picks for Kids

Under 13

- Ever met a bleeding-heart dove? How about a prehensile-tailed skink? These fascinating critters are among the 900-plus species of mammals, birds and reptiles that call **Honolulu Zoo** home. You can see giraffes, rhinos and zebras in the African Savanna exhibit and get up close and personal with barnyard animals in the petting area.

- At **Hawai'i Children's Discovery Center** kids explore science and culture through role-playing and, well, just *playing*. They can crawl through a digestive system, be a veterinarian, enjoy tea and dim sum in Chinese garb and fly an airplane—all in one day.

- If you happen to be in town on a Friday, Saturday or Sunday from late May to early July, head to Aloha Stadium for some good old-fashioned fun at the ⌇ **50th State Fair**. Try your luck at the games; nosh on cotton candy, funnel cakes and fried Twinkies (just steer clear of the spinning Super Sizzler for a little while afterward); and ooh and ahh at the amazing European-style circus acts.

Teens

- Hop on a horse, ATV, Swiss Army vehicle or catamaran at **Kualoa Ranch & Activity Club** in **Ka'a'awa**. See where "Jurassic Park," "50 First Dates" and other Hollywood blockbusters were filmed, take in terrific views of the Pacific Ocean and the Kualoa Mountains, meander through tropical gardens and unwind on a secluded beach.

Hānauma Bay Nature Preserve

- For once, the phrase "go take a hike" won't trigger a series of eye rolls and deep sighs—as long as it's clear that **Diamond Head State Monument** is the destination. Though it's steep, the trail from the crater interior to the 760-foot-high summit is only .8 miles long, and the reward—a breathtaking 360-degree view encompassing Honolulu and the Pacific—is worth every step.

All Ages

- Immerse yourself in the distinctive culture of Hawai'i at a *lū'au*, a family-friendly picnic feast featuring an unbeatable blend of traditional foods like *kalua* pig and *poi* (a taro-root dish) and Polynesian entertainment ranging from the *hula* to the Samoan fire-knife dance. *Lū'au* are offered at various locations, but you can't go wrong with **Germaine's Lū'au** or **Paradise Cove Lū'au** in **Kapolei**.

- What do you get when you cross a false killer whale with an Atlantic bottlenose dolphin? A wholphin, that's what. Take a gander at this unique hybrid at **Waimānalo**'s **Sea Life Park**, a watery world inhabited by dolphins, penguins, sea lions, seabirds, stingrays, sharks and sea turtles. Be sure to check the schedule for the always-amusing shows and feedings.

- For a history lesson that won't bore the brood to tears, pay a visit to the ⌇ **Battleship *Missouri* Memorial**, anchored at **Pearl Harbor**. A walk on the decks—particularly the Surrender Deck—is an unforgettable experience, and a tour of Mighty Mo's realistically re-created interior makes it easy to imagine what life was like for crew members.

- With its rainbow of reef residents, ⌇ **Hānauma Bay Nature Preserve** is a snorkeler's paradise. Rent some gear and prepare to rub fins with exotic fish that are anything but camera shy. Can't swim? No biggie. The water is so crystal-clear that you can spot sea creatures right from the shoreline. Arrive early, though—the more crowded the water gets, the cloudier it gets.

- Refuel at Pacific Beach Hotel's **Oceanarium Restaurant**, whose atmosphere is as delightful as its menu. Where else can you devour succulent crab legs or prime rib while watching hundreds of kaleidoscopic fish swim around a three-story, 280,000-gallon aquarium? If the fishes' feeding time happens to be the same as yours, you're in for a real treat.

- Gentle waves and lots of lifeguards make 2-mile-long **Waikīkī Beach** one of the safest stretches of sand on O'ahu. Families flock here to indulge in an enticing array of activities, including sailing, swimming, sunbathing and sandcastle-sculpting. If you've never tried surfing before, this is *the* place to do so. You can sign up for lessons or rent a board without an instructor.

Arriving
By Car

The major approach route to this long, narrow city on the south coast of O'ahu is the H-1 freeway, which begins near Barbers Point Naval Air Station at an interchange with the west-coast Farrington Highway (SR 93). It skirts Pearl Harbor, connecting with the H-2 freeway and the Kamehameha Highway (SR 99) from central O'ahu near Pearl City, and continues toward the capital.

From the vicinity of Aloha Stadium there is a choice between shorter, less-traveled SR 78 and H-1, which offers quick access to Joint Base Pearl Harbor-Hickam and Honolulu International Airport.

From the airport eastbound Nimitz Highway (SR 92) parallels H-1, becoming Ala Moana Boulevard at Honolulu Harbor, then Kalākaua Avenue in the Waikīkī area.

The approach from Koko Head is via SR 72, the Kalaniana'ole Highway, which blends into the Lunalilo Freeway, as H-1 is called in the immediate vicinity of downtown Honolulu.

Only two roads actually enter Honolulu from "over the *pali*." Pali Highway (SR 61) and Likelike Highway (SR 63) both use tunnels to carry motorists across the Ko'olau Range from the windward (northeastern) coast. They interchange with H-1 at Bishop Street and Kalihi Street, respectively.

A third highway, H-3, which offers spectacular views of the island's windward side, connects Kailua and Kāne'ohe to Pearl City via a tunnel.

Getting Around

Because of the irregular shape of O'ahu, compass directions seem confusing and are seldom used. In their place is an effective method of defining location based on island landmarks. *Ma kai* is toward the sea; *ma uka* is inland or toward the mountains or upland. *'Ewa* is used for toward the west, and "Diamond Head" for toward the east. "Windward" refers to the windward, or northeastern, coast.

Streets follow the dictates of geography. Those running *ma kai-ma uka* are numbered from the ocean toward the mountains. Nu'uanu Avenue divides the "North" and "South" designations used on the main thoroughfares and some parallel streets.

Moving inland, the primary *ma uka-ma kai* thoroughfares in Honolulu proper are Ala Moana Boulevard (SR 92), Kapi'olani Boulevard, King Street (one-way *diamondhead)*, Beretania Street (one-way *'ewa)* and H-1. In the Waikīkī area the main stem is Kalākaua Avenue, running one-way *diamondhead;* Ala Wai Boulevard carries traffic back toward Honolulu. Most intersecting streets are one way in alternating directions.

The downtown speed limit, unless otherwise posted, is 25 mph; on major one-way thoroughfares it's 35 mph. Unless a sign prohibits it, turning right at a red light after coming to a complete stop is legal. Turning left from one one-way street onto another is allowed if specifically signed. Pedestrians always have the right-of-way, particularly at marked crosswalks; however, both pedestrians and drivers should remain alert.

Driving during rush hours, about 6 to 9 a.m. and 3 to 6:30 p.m., should be avoided. Crossing a solid white line is prohibited—and the law is strictly enforced. Do not honk the horn except in an emergency.

Parking

In addition to the parking facilities provided by hotels, there are privately operated and municipal parking garages and lots. Rates vary widely with the location, but $42 a day is typical. There also is some on-street parking, but this might be hard to find, particularly in the vicinity of Ala Moana Center.

Shopping

Honolulu's several strikingly designed complexes offer shoppers everything from toothpaste to precious black coral and from tube socks to *mu'umu'u.* Music, dance and other entertainment are frequent added incentives.

Ala Moana Center, at 1450 Ala Moana Blvd. across from the park of the same name *(see attraction listing p. 131),* is the largest shopping mall in both Honolulu and the state. Amid gardens, pools, fountains and sculpture, some 220 stores sell products from the entire Pacific area, and a variety of dining spots satisfy hungry shoppers. The department stores—Macy's, Neiman Marcus, Nordstrom and Shirokiya—balance the center's establishments of *haute couture* (think Balenciaga and Escada), as

Shop and dine at Ala Moana Center

Take the kids to the 50th State Fair

well as other upscale establishments like Fendi, Louis Vuitton and Tiffany & Co. Bloomingdale's will be part of a multilevel, 650,000-square-foot expansion that is scheduled to open in late 2015.

Across from Kewalo Basin at Ala Moana Boulevard and Ward Avenue is another Honolulu hallmark, **Ward Centers**. Its contemporary complexes house about 175 specialty stores and restaurants. Ward Entertainment Center boasts a 16-screen movie theater. **Koko Marina Center**, 7192 Kalaniana'ole Hwy. near Hānauma Bay, offers a number of shops and eateries as well as water sports rentals.

Downtown Honolulu, like mainland cities, has been experiencing some urban revitalization. One successful result was the conversion of **Fort Street** into an attractive pedestrian shopping mall. **Chinatown** is a 15-block area bounded by N. Beretania Street, N. Nimitz Highway, River Street and Bethel Street; the proudest development of its renovation is **Cultural Plaza**, where Chinese shops and restaurants showcase the multicultural character of Hawai'i.

One of Honolulu's most recognized landmarks is the centerpiece of the **Aloha Tower Marketplace**, on the waterfront off Ala Moana Boulevard. This 10-story tower, built in 1926, was for decades the tallest building in the city. Residents would line up along the docks and welcome the sailing ships and big steamers with a *hula* dance, music performances and flower *lei*. Today the tower can still be seen from the water, and the observation decks on the top floor provide a scenic view of the Honolulu skyline. The surrounding marketplace includes about 30 shops and dockside restaurants.

In Waikīkī, the most concentrated shopping district is **Kalākaua Avenue**, which extends from downtown Honolulu all the way to the end of Kapi-'olani Park. The **Royal Hawaiian Center**, 2201 Kalākaua Ave., is the area's answer to Ala Moana Center. Stretching three blocks and four stories, the center has more than 110 shops, restaurants and services. Chanel, Gucci and Yves Saint Laurent are among the tony retailers along **Luxury Row**, 2100 Kalākaua. There are 150-plus establishments at the **Waikīkī Shopping Plaza**, 2250 Kalākaua Ave.

Other Waikīkī area temptations are the slick three-level **Pualeilani Atrium Shops** complex at the Hyatt Regency Waikīkī Beach Resort & Spa, 2424 Kalākaua Ave.; **King's Village**, 131 Kaiulani Avenue, which resembles Hawai'i in the 1890s and boasts some 45 shops and restaurants; and **Rainbow Bazaar**, which brings items from Polynesia, Japan and Southeast Asia to the grounds of Hilton Hawaiian Village Waikīkī Beach Resort.

Yet more shopping and dining opportunities are found at the nearly 8-acre **Waikīkī Beach Walk** on Lewers Street, which intersects with Kalākaua Avenue. [SAVE] **Hard Rock Cafe**, at the corner of Beach Walk and Kalākaua, is *the* place to go for rock 'n' roll merchandise.

Aloha Stadium Swap Meet & Marketplace, at Aloha Stadium, offers great bargains Wed. and Sat.-Sun. 8-3 (on Sun. the swap meet opens at 6:30; the marketplace opens at normal time). Admission is $1; free (ages 0-11).

Two large suburban shopping centers are **Kahala Mall**, beyond Diamond Head via H-1 at 4211 Waialae Ave., and **Pearlridge Center**, at Pearl City via Kamehameha Highway. Kahala's more than 90 specialty shops and eateries are anchored by Macy's. At the Pearlridge, a monorail connects the center's two buildings which house more than 170 stores, restaurants and services that are anchored by Macy's and Sears. **Waikele Premium Outlets**, off H-1 exit 7 in Waipahu, has 50 stores, including Coach, Michael Kors and OshKosh B'gosh.

Most of O'ahu's shopping centers open daily at 9 a.m.; closing times vary.

Nightlife

Running the gamut from flip-flop-friendly beachfront bars to pulsing dance clubs to classy cocktail lounges, Honolulu's countless nighttime entertainment options satisfy just about any whim. Picking up a local calendar or chatting with your hotel concierge is a good way to find out what's going on after dark on any given day, but do read on for a sampling of what the city has to offer.

Waikīkī, with its abundance of drink-dispensing hotels, restaurants and stand-alone establishments, is *the* place to shake things up when the sun goes down. If a quintessentially Hawaiian nightlife experience is on your wish list, make your way to **Duke's** at Outrigger Waikiki Beach Resort (2335 Kalākaua

Ave., Suite 116). Complemented by rustling palms and glowing tiki torches, the casual open-air restaurant/bar is almost always packed with patrons—and for good reason. The views of the ocean and Diamond Head State Monument are stunning, and the live Hawaiian music can't be beat; phone (808) 922-2268.

If you're looking—and willing to pay—for a more upscale, intimate Waikīkī nightspot, head to Haleku-lani hotel's chic, dimly lit **Lewers Lounge** (2199 Kalia Rd.). The plush seating and dark wood paneling and flooring help create the perfect ambience for sipping fabulous cocktails and soaking up live jazz tunes. A dress code is enforced, so you'll have to leave the shorts and flip-flops behind; phone (844) 288-8022.

You'll also have to dress to impress and fork over some mad cash if you want to party at **Addiction Nightclub** in The Modern Honolulu (1775 Ala Moana Blvd.). Open Thursday through Saturday, this sleek, colorful, high-energy club has velvet ropes, VIP tables, an amazing overhead light fixture, and DJs who keep the house and hip-hop beats going until the wee hours of the morning; phone (808) 943-5800.

Diverse droves of night owls flock to Chinatown, where barhopping is a breeze thanks to the cluster of establishments along Hotel Street. At trendy, up-beat **Bar 35** (35 N. Hotel St.), beer connoisseurs and amateurs alike can belly up to the red bar or sink into a comfy couch and take their pick of 200-plus concoctions from 20 different countries. Happy hour at this happening hangout runs from 4 until 10 on weeknights and is exceptionally "happy" during themed events and DJ and band performances; phone (808) 537-3535.

Just a hop, skip and jump away from Bar 35 is **The Manifest** (32 N. Hotel St.), a bookstore turned bar hailed for its impressive selection of whiskeys. The high ceilings, exposed brick walls, concrete floors and bar top, recycled furniture and interesting artwork give the place an artsy, industrial feel that's far more San Franciscan than it is Hawaiian. During late-night hours, The Manifest typically trades its laid-back vibe for a club-like one; phone (808) 744-8238.

Why not add a delightful dose of art and culture to your evening out? During **First Friday Honolulu** art walks, held the first Friday of every month, a number of Chinatown watering holes, eateries, galleries and boutiques feature special activities, entertainment and art exhibits.

Big Events

Dancing, music, crafts and demonstrations at several venues citywide help promote harmony between Hawaiians and people of the Asia-Pacific region during the ⇌ **Honolulu Festival** in March. The celebration wraps with the Grand Parade, which wends down Kalākaua Avenue. April's ⇌ **Hawai'i International Film Festival Spring Showcase** presents a menu of independent and foreign films.

In May Kalākaua Avenue is packed with Spam lovers during ⇌ **Waikīkī Spam Jam,** a street festival that celebrates the canned luncheon meat with a cook-off, games and live entertainment. During the ⇌ **Memorial Day Ceremonies** at the **National Memorial Cemetery of the Pacific (Punchbowl Cemetery),** members of the armed forces pay tribute to soldiers who sacrificed their lives for their country.

Aloha Stadium welcomes the entertainment, cultural and educational displays, food, games and rides of the ⇌ **50th State Fair** from late May through early July. Orchids add a splash of color to the agricultural exhibits at this popular event.

The ⇌ **King Kamehameha Celebration and Floral Parade** kicks off with the draping of 13-foot *lei* on the statue of King Kamehameha I on June 11, the state holiday. The event continues on the following Saturday with a floral parade, entertainment and partying in the streets of Waikīkī. In late June dancers from Japan, the mainland United States and Hawai'i swivel, swirl and sway during the ⇌ **King Kamehameha Hula Competition,** held at the **Neal S. Blaisdell Center.**

The ⇌ **Aloha Festivals**—a huge-scale celebration that incorporates parades, *lū'au,* pageants and entertainment on six islands in September—exposes participants to Hawaiian history and traditions, including food, music, dance and art.

A pair of outrigger canoe races—the September ⇌ **Na Wahine O Ke Kai** for women and the October ⇌ **Moloka'i Hoe Outrigger Canoe Championship** for men—challenge rowers to navigate the

See the island from a sailboat

Catch a game at Aloha Stadium

40-plus-mile route across the Ka'iwi Channel from Moloka'i to Waikīkī.

In October the ⚔ **Hawai'i International Film Festival** screens hundreds of productions, focusing particularly on Asian, Pacific Island and U.S. features, documentaries and videos.

The soul-stirring sounds of taps hang in the air during ⚔ **Pearl Harbor Day Commemoration** ceremonies on December 7 at the **Pearl Harbor Memorial Museum & Visitor Center.** Floral offerings, a rifle salute and a wreath presentation also honor those who perished during the attack.

A thrill for the tens of thousands who lace up their sneakers as well as the cheering spectators who line the route, the ⚔ **Honolulu Marathon** covers 26.2 miles on its way to **Kapi'olani Regional Park** on the second Sunday in December.

In late December the ⚔ **Sheraton Hawai'i Bowl** pits a Conference USA team against a Mountain West team; the postseason game is held at Aloha Stadium.

Sports & Rec

Swimming, surfing, snorkeling and **sailing** focus, of course, on the beaches, of which **Waikīkī Beach** is primary. Beginning at Kūhiō Beach, just *diamondhead* (east) of Kapahulu Avenue, it runs the length of the peninsula to the Hilton Hawaiian Village Waikīkī Beach Resort.

Waikīkī is one of the safest beaches on the island, with lifeguards overseeing the activities and beachboys coaching surfing or taking passengers out to run the breakers in an outrigger canoe. Surfboards also can be rented without an instructor.

Concessions often are connected with the hotel facing that strip of beach.

Sailing is a good way to see the island. Honolulu Sailing Company, (808) 239-3900, offers charters, instruction and cruises. Honolulu is also a center for **hang gliding.**

Scuba diving and snorkeling are particularly rewarding in O'ahu's clear waters. Equipment can be rented by divers who have a certification card, or instruction can be taken at one of several dive shops. Hawaiian Diving Adventures, (808) 232-3193, offers both scuba diving and snorkeling trips.

Deep-sea fishing is excellent, particularly during the marlin and tuna runs in late spring and summer. Boats can be chartered for a full or half-day at **Kewalo Basin** at the foot of Ward Street. One company that offers fishing charters is SportFish Hawai'i, (877) 388-1376.

Foremost among nonaquatic sports in Honolulu is **jogging.** It would seem from the number of entrants in the Honolulu Marathon (roughly 30,000) that almost everyone does it. One heavily frequented route encircles **Kapi'olani Park**; you can learn of others by visiting one of the many shops that cater to runners' needs.

Hiking also is possible within sight of the city; trails traverse **Round Top Forest Reserve**. Certain trails, particularly those in areas farther from the city, might be frequented by undesirables. Prospective hikers should first obtain information about safety and trail conditions, and trail maps from the Division of Forestry and Wildlife, 1151 Punchbowl St., Room 325, Honolulu, HI 96813; phone (808) 587-0166. Free park information brochures can be obtained from the Division of State Parks, 1151 Punchbowl St., Room 310, P.O. Box 621, Honolulu, HI 96809; phone (808) 587-0300.

Touring the island on a **bicycle** or taking a short ride through Waikīkī can be a rewarding experience. **Horseback riding** can be enjoyed at **Kualoa Ranch & Activity Club**, (808) 237-8515 or (800) 231-7321 *(see attraction listing under Ka'a'awa p. 163).*

Golf is both pleasant and challenging on O'ahu's numerous courses. While some are open only to club members, others are open to visitors by agreement with their hotel. Of the public courses, **Ala Wai** is the closest and therefore has the longest wait to tee off; **Hawai'i Kai** and **Olomana** also are popular.

College and high school athletes play **baseball, football** and **basketball** in the **Neal S. Blaisdell Center**, the **Aloha Stadium** or The University of Hawai'i at Mānoa's **Les Murakami Stadium**. Sports events and schedules appear in the daily newspapers.

Performing Arts

Although most visitors do not come to Honolulu to attend a play or symphony concert, the city offers both.

Hawai'i Performing Arts Company presents a season of Broadway and off-Broadway plays at

Mānoa Valley Theatre on E. Mānoa Road; **Diamond Head Theatre**, an established amateur group, does likewise at Makapu'u and Alohea avenues near Diamond Head. The **dance and drama departments of the University of Hawai'i** give productions in **Kennedy Theatre** on the East-West Center campus.

The **Hawai'i Opera Theatre** performs in the concert hall at the **Neal S. Blaisdell Center** at Ward Avenue and King Street; the season runs October through April. The Neal S. Blaisdell Center's arena is the scene of concerts by pop stars. A bronze sculpture of Elvis Presley adorns the front of the arena, which hosted the music legend's 1973 concert that was aired in more than 40 countries. Films and a concert series are presented at the **Honolulu Museum of Art** *(see attraction listing p. 135)*. Movie houses are found throughout the city; some offer only Chinese and Japanese films.

The daily papers and the calendar section of the monthly magazine *Honolulu* carry comprehensive listings of cultural events.

Every week the **Urasenke Foundation of Hawai'i** at 245 Saratoga Rd. presents public demonstrations of the traditional **Japanese tea ceremony** known as *Chado,* or the Way of Tea. Rooted in Zen Buddhism, the centuries-old ritual is an important part of Japanese culture. Visitors to the foundation watch a 15-minute video before witnessing this simple yet profound ceremony; admission is by donation and reservations are recommended. Phone (808) 923-3059.

INSIDER INFO:
Go O'ahu Card

Go O'ahu Card is an all-access pass offering admission to 34 O'ahu attractions, including the Polynesian Cultural Center, Sea Life Park, the USS *Bowfin* Submarine Museum and Park, and a catamaran cruise. The card is purchased by the day (1, 3, 5 or 7 days that are valid for 2 weeks) and is priced as low as $39 per day (based on a 7-day card). Go O'ahu Card is available online or at the Diamond Head Vacations Desk in two Honolulu hotels: the Coconut Hotel Waikīkī (450 Lewers St.) and the Castle Waikīkī Shore (2161 Kalia Rd.).

 ATTRACTIONS

Honolulu

ALA MOANA BEACH PARK is entered from the east via Atkinson Dr.; the west entrance is on Ala Moana Blvd. and Kamakee St. The 76-acre park includes a reef-protected beach with lifeguards, tennis courts and shaded picnic areas. While this generally is a safe area for swimming, tidal changes and winds can create strong currents. Aina Moana (Magic Island), at the east end, provides a close look at bay activities and an encompassing view of the Waikīkī shoreline. **Hours:** Daily 4 a.m.-10 p.m. **Cost:** Free. **Phone:** (808) 768-3003.

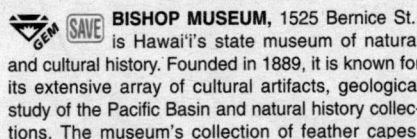 **BATTLESHIP *MISSOURI* MEMORIAL—** see Pearl Harbor p. 168.

BISHOP MUSEUM, 1525 Bernice St., is Hawai'i's state museum of natural and cultural history. Founded in 1889, it is known for its extensive array of cultural artifacts, geological study of the Pacific Basin and natural history collections. The museum's collection of feather capes, helmets, *kāhili* (royal feather standards) and other articles of Hawaiian art is reputed to be one of the finest in the world.

The Richard T. Mamiya Science Adventure Center explores Hawai'i's volcanology, oceanography and ecology. Visitors can operate underwater robots and go inside a re-created volcano and lava tube. The Castle Memorial Building contains hands-on exhibits relating to Pacific culture, science and nature. The J. Watumull Planetarium showcases the Pacific sky. Daily educational programs include storytelling, garden tours and lava shows.

Hours: Wed.-Mon. 9-5. Closed Christmas. **Cost:** $19.95; $16.95 (ages 65+); $14.95 (ages 4-12); $12.95 (military and Hawai'i residents with ID). **Phone:** (808) 847-3511.

CATHEDRAL OF OUR LADY OF PEACE, 1184 Bishop St., was built in 1843 on the site of Hawai'i's first Catholic mission, founded in 1827. Blessed Damien was ordained here on May 24, 1864. It is the only church in the United States to have had a King (Kamehameha III) present for the laying of its cornerstone, and its 1846 clock is said to be the oldest clock in the state. **Hours:** Office Mon.-Fri. 8-5. Phone for mass schedule. **Cost:** Free. **Phone:** (808) 536-7036.

THE CATHEDRAL OF ST. ANDREW (Episcopal), S. Beretania and Queen Emma sts., was founded by King Kamehameha IV and Queen Emma. Construction began in 1862. Stone was brought from Normandy, and the cathedral is said to be the only example of French Gothic-style architecture in Hawai'i. **Hours:** Office Tues.-Fri. 9-5. **Cost:** Free. **Phone:** (808) 524-2822.

DOLPHIN QUEST O'AHU, at The Kahala Hotel & Resort, 5000 Kahala Ave., offers a variety of fun and educational programs that allow visitors of all ages to touch, feed and play with dolphins in the resort's natural lagoons. Programs are led by professional trainers. Photographers stand by to capture highlights of the encounter; photos can be purchased later.

After the program visitors are welcome to hang out at the resort's beach (but they may not use the pool, beach chairs or cabanas). **Note:** Visitors should park in The Kahala Hotel & Resort's parking lot and have their parking tickets validated at Dolphin Quest O'ahu. Swimsuits and towels are required. Life jackets are provided. Participants may

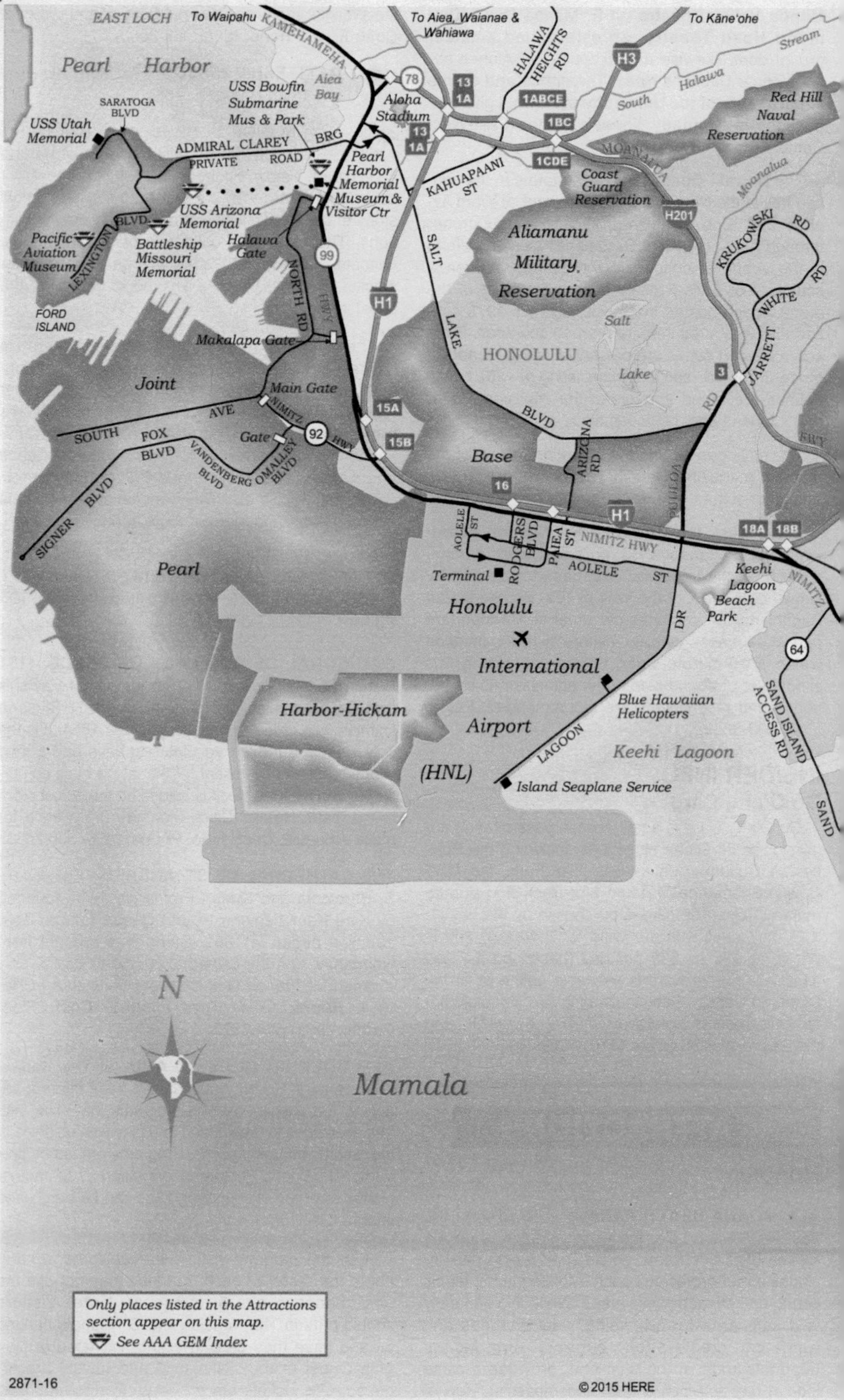

EAST LOCH

To Waipahu

KAMEHAMEHA

To Aiea, Waianae & Wahiawa

To Kāne'ohe

Pearl Harbor

USS Bowfin Submarine Mus & Park

Aiea Bay

HALAWA HEIGHTS RD

South Halawa

Stream

H3

SARATOGA BLVD

USS Utah Memorial

Aloha Stadium

78

13 1A

1ABCE

1BC

MOANALUA

Red Hill Naval Reservation

ADMIRAL CLAREY BRG

PRIVATE ROAD

Pearl Harbor Memorial Museum & Visitor Ctr

13 1A7

1CDE

Coast Guard Reservation

Moanalua

KRUKOWSKI RD

USS Arizona Memorial

KAHUAPAANI ST

H201

Pacific Aviation Museum

BLVD

Halawa Gate

LEXINGTON

Battleship Missouri Memorial

NORTH RD

99

Aliamanu Military Reservation

WHITE RD

JARRETT

FORD ISLAND

H1

SALT

Salt Lake

RD

Makalapa Gate

HONOLULU

3

Joint

Main Gate

LAKE

Lake

BLVD

Base

Pearl

SOUTH

AVE

FOX BLVD

NIMITZ

15A

92 HWY

15B

ARIZONA RD

H1

Gate

VANDENBERG BLVD

O'MALLEY BLVD

16

SIGNER BLVD

AOLELE ST

ROGERS BLVD

PAIEA ST

NIMITZ HWY

18A 18B

NIMITZ

Terminal

Honolulu

AOLELE ST

Keehi Lagoon Beach Park

64

International

DR

Blue Hawaiian Helicopters

SAND ISLAND ACCESS RD

Harbor-Hickam

Airport

(HNL)

LAGOON

Keehi Lagoon

SAND

Island Seaplane Service

N

Mamala

Only places listed in the Attractions section appear on this map.

▽ See AAA GEM Index

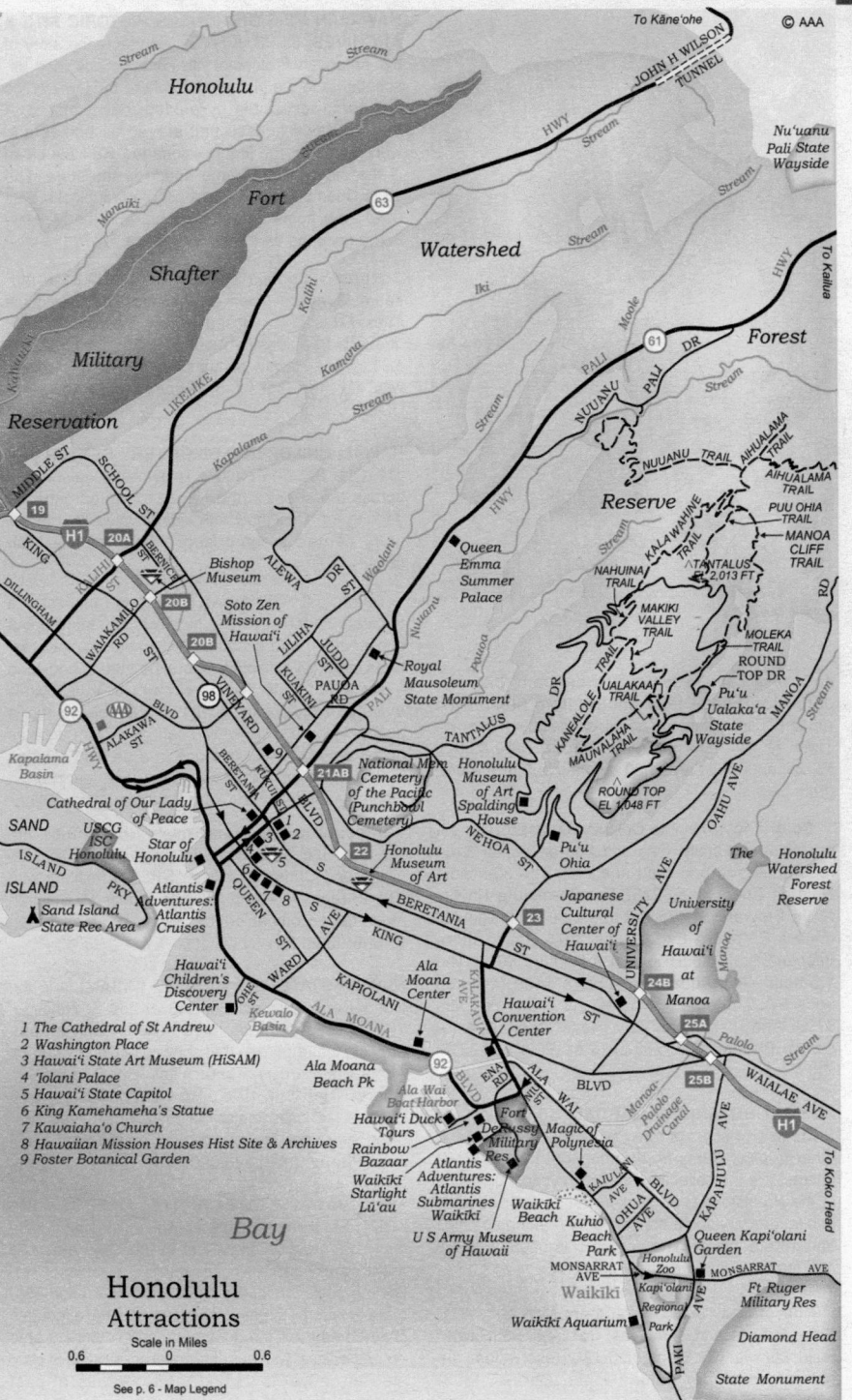

© AAA

Honolulu

Fort

Shafter

Military

Reservation

SAND

ISLAND

Bay

Honolulu
Attractions

1 The Cathedral of St Andrew
2 Washington Place
3 Hawai'i State Art Museum (HiSAM)
4 'Iolani Palace
5 Hawai'i State Capitol
6 King Kamehameha's Statue
7 Kawaiaha'o Church
8 Hawaiian Mission Houses Hist Site & Archives
9 Foster Botanical Garden

Scale in Miles

0.6   0   0.6

See p. 6 - Map Legend

Dolphin Quest Oʻahu

not use a camera during the program, but non-participants may take photos from behind the roped-off area. Inquire about cancellation policies. **Time:** Allow 1 hour minimum. **Hours:** Daily 8:30-5. Participants must arrive 30 minutes before the program begins.

Cost: The 15-minute Dolphin Dip $125. The 15-minute Wee Family, Fins and Fun encounter $149 (one adult and one child age 0-4). The 30-minute Dolphin Encounter $225. The 30-minute Family Swim Program $1,475 (up to six people). The 45-minute Premiere Experience $975 (up to three people). The 1-hour Dolphin Adventure $310. The 1.5-hour Kids' Aquatic Adventure $199 (children ages 5+). The 5.5-hour Trainer for a Day program $700. Age restrictions vary. Reservations are required. **Phone:** (808) 739-8918 or (800) 248-3316. ⑪

FOSTER BOTANICAL GARDEN, 50 N. Vineyard Blvd., has 14 acres of rare trees, palms, orchids and other tropical plants from throughout the world. Of interest are the collection of exotic cycads and ferns in the Prehistoric Glen section, an outdoor butterfly habitat garden, and a conservatory featuring orchids and tropical plants. The garden was begun in 1853 and many original trees still flourish.

Hours: Daily 9-4. Guided tours Mon.-Sat. at 1. Closed Jan. 1 and Christmas. **Cost:** $5; $3 (Hawaiʻi residents with ID); $1 (ages 6-12). Reservations are recommended for guided tours. **Phone:** (808) 522-7066. ⒼⓉ

HAWAIIAN MISSION HOUSES HISTORIC SITE & ARCHIVES, 553 S. King St., connects the story of the American Protestant missionaries and their descendants to the history and culture of Hawaiʻi. The museum, accessible by guided tour, consists of three mission houses that served as homes and workplaces for the first missionaries. Ka Hale Lāʻau is the oldest wood-frame house in the state. The 1831 Chamberlain House, built of coral blocks, was used as a home and storehouse, and the Ka Hale Paʻi functioned as the printing office.

Hours: Grounds Tues.-Sat. 10-4. Guided museum tours are given on the hour 11-3. Archives Tues.-Fri. 10-4. Closed major holidays. **Cost:** Grounds free. Museum tour $10; $8 (ages 55+ and military and Hawaiʻi residents with ID); $6 (students with ID); free (ages 0-5). **Phone:** (808) 447-3910. ⑪

HAWAIʻI CHILDREN'S DISCOVERY CENTER is at 111 ʻOhe St.; free parking is available on-site and across the street in the Kakaʻako Waterfront Park parking lot. Designed with kids in mind, this three-story center is comprised of five main exhibit galleries.

Rainforest Adventures immerses families in a tropical rain forest setting in which they learn about conservation and sustainability. Fantastic You! features interactive displays about the human body and a play area for the 5-and-under crowd. Your Town is a pint-size city complete with an auto repair shop, a post office and a bank. You can blow giant bubbles at a mock coral reef and ride in a pretend airplane in the Hawaiian Rainbows gallery and learn about different cultures in the Your Rainbow World gallery.

Time: Allow 2 hours minimum. **Hours:** Tues.-Fri. 9-1, Sat.-Sun. 10-3. Closed Jan. 1, Easter, Thanksgiving and Christmas. **Cost:** $10; $8 (military with ID); $6 (ages 62+ with ID); free (under 1). Children must be accompanied by an adult at all times. **Phone:** (808) 524-5437. ⑪

HAWAIʻI STATE ART MUSEUM (HISAM) is in the No. 1 Capitol District Building at 250 S. Hotel St. The museum features three galleries and an outdoor sculpture garden that showcase works of art by Aloha State artists. **Time:** Allow 1 hour minimum. **Hours:** Tues.-Sat. 10-4 (also first Fri. of the month 6-9 p.m.). Closed major holidays. **Cost:** Free. Metered street parking and parking garages are available. **Phone:** (808) 586-0900. ⑪

HAWAIʻI STATE CAPITOL, 415 S. Beretania St., reflects many Hawaiian elements. The sunken legislative chambers in the 1969 structure rise to an open crown, resembling a volcano. Reflecting pools symbolize the ocean, and fluted concrete columns suggest palm trees. The executive chambers house the governor's and lieutenant governor's offices. Much of the governor's office is paneled in native *koa* wood, and portraits of past governors adorn the walls.

Brochures for a self-guiding tour may be obtained outside Room 415. **Hours:** Self-guiding tours Mon.-Fri. 9-3:30. Closed major holidays. **Cost:** Free. **Phone:** (808) 586-0222.

HONOLULU MUSEUM OF ART, 900 S. Beretania St. between Victoria St. and Ward Ave., was originally built around the 4,500-piece art collection of founder Anna Rice Cooke. Opening onto a series of lovely garden courts, the museum's galleries now house more than 50,000 works spanning 5,000 years.

Approximately 18,000 paintings, sculpture, decorative art objects and works on paper comprise the European and American collection. Highlights include Hawaiian quilts and feather capes, Italian Renaissance paintings, and works by such renowned artists as Gauguin, Monet, Picasso, van Gogh and Warhol.

The outstanding Asian collection includes examples of Japanese woodblock prints, Buddhist sculpture, Korean ceramics and Chinese paintings from the Qing and Ming dynasties.

Classes, events, special exhibitions and a theater that presents films and concerts round out the offerings. **Hours:** Tues.-Sat. 10-4:30, Sun. 1-5. Phone for tour schedule. Closed Jan. 1, July 4, Thanksgiving and Christmas. **Cost:** (Includes same-day admission to the Honolulu Museum of Art Spalding House) $10; free (ages 0-17 and first Wed. and third Sun. of the month). **Parking:** $5. **Phone:** (808) 532-8700. GT T

Shangri La is accessed via shuttle from the Honolulu Museum of Art at 900 S. Beretania St. Doris Duke was heir to the American Tobacco and Duke Energy fortunes and creator of the Doris Duke Charitable Foundation. Her Middle East-inspired home, set on 5 acres with a stunning ocean view, was completed in 1938. Now a center for Islamic art, the home is filled with works from throughout the Islamic world. Tickets are issued for a given date and time and are not refundable. The tour requires climbing several flights of stairs.

Time: Allow 3 hours minimum. **Hours:** Guided 2.5-hour tours are given Wed.-Sat. at 9, 10:30 and 1, Oct.-Aug. Closed Jan. 1, July 4, Thanksgiving and Dec. 8. **Cost:** (Includes admission to the Honolulu Museum of Art and van transportation to Shangri La) $25. Under age 12 are not permitted. Reservations are required. **Phone:** (808) 532-3853, or (866) 385-3849 for reservations.

HONOLULU MUSEUM OF ART SPALDING HOUSE, 2411 Makiki Heights Dr., features temporary exhibitions that draw from the entire Honolulu Museum of Art collection. The 3.5-acre estate includes lush gardens, sculptures and a permanent David Hockney installation. **Time:** Allow 1 hour minimum. **Hours:** Tues.-Sat. 10-4, Sun. noon-4. Guided tours are given at 1:30. Closed Jan. 1, July 4, Thanksgiving and Christmas. **Cost:** (Includes same-day admission to the Honolulu Museum of Art) $10; free (ages 0-17 and first Wed. and third Sun. of the month). **Phone:** (808) 526-0232. GT T

'IOLANI PALACE, S. King and Richards sts., is the only official royal residence in the United States. The structure was completed in 1882 by King Kalākaua to be a showplace in the Pacific and to demonstrate Hawai'i's status as a modern kingdom among the nations of the world. A 1-hour guided tour as well as a self-guiding audio tour are offered; the audio tour is available in English, French, German, Hawaiian, Japanese, Korean, Mandarin and Spanish.

Note: During audio tours, children ages 0-4 must be secured in either a front carrier worn by an adult or in a stroller provided by 'Iolani Palace. **Hours:** Gallery Mon.-Sat. 9:30-5. Self-guiding audio tours every 10 minutes Mon.-Sat. noon-4. Guided tours every 15 minutes Tues.-Thurs. 9-10, Fri.-Sat. 9-11:15. Closed Jan. 1, July 4, Thanksgiving and Christmas.

Cost: Gallery only $7; $3 (ages 5-12). Self-guiding audio tour $14.75; $6 (ages 5-12). Guided tour $21.75; $6 (ages 5-12). Reservations are required for guided tours; ages 0-4 are not permitted on these tours. **Phone:** (808) 522-0832, or (808) 538-1471 for recorded tour information. GT

JAPANESE CULTURAL CENTER OF HAWAI'I is at 2454 S. Beretania St. The center's first-floor historical exhibit, Okage Sama De—I Am What I Am Because of You, depicts the history of the Japanese in Hawai'i from 1868 to today. The exhibit focuses on such topics as the lives of immigrant plantation workers, the major plantation strike of 1909 and the Japanese involvement in Hawai'i politics. Also featured are mock plantation-era buildings and a 15-minute film about the Japanese experience during World War II.

A resource library houses books, oral history transcripts, photos, diaries and other materials. Special services such as Japanese tea ceremony lessons in an authentic teahouse are offered at certain times of the year.

Smoking, food and beverages are prohibited in the museum. Pets are permitted in the courtyard only. **Time:** Allow 30 minutes minimum. **Hours:** Museum Mon.-Fri. 10-4, Sat. 9-2. Resource library Tues.-Sat. 10-4, Sat. 10-1. Closed Jan. 1, Martin Luther King Jr. Day, Presidents Day, Memorial Day, July 4, Labor Day, Veterans Day, Thanksgiving, day after Thanksgiving, Christmas Eve, Christmas and Dec. 31. **Cost:** $7; $5 (ages 6-17, ages 65+ and students with ID); $3 (military with ID). **Parking:** A fee is charged for on-site parking. **Phone:** (808) 945-7633.

KAWAIAHA'O CHURCH, at King and Punchbowl sts., was built 1837-42 and is Honolulu's oldest church. Noted for its choir, this coral-block building served as the royal chapel of the Hawaiian rulers for nearly 20 years. Within the courtyard is the mausoleum of King Lunalilo. Of interest in the cemetery is the 1912 Stephan Sinding statue of a grieving woman. **Hours:** Office Mon.-Fri. 8-4:30. **Cost:** Free. **Phone:** (808) 469-3000.

KEWALO BASIN, on Ala Moana Blvd. at the foot of Ward Ave., is the home port of charter fishing boats, sightseeing boats and the sampan fishing fleet. **Phone:** (808) 594-0849.

KING KAMEHAMEHA STATUE, outside the Judiciary Building at 417 S. King St., is a replica of the original bronze statue that stands in the Kohala district of Hawai'i Island *(see Kapa'au p. 48)*. On the Friday prior to King Kamehameha I Day, the statue is draped with 13-foot fresh flower *lei* in memory of the monarch. Four tableaux at its base depict great moments in the ruler's life. **Hours:** Daily 24 hours. **Cost:** Free.

KOKO HEAD, on the southeastern tip of O'ahu on SR 72 (Kalaniana'ole Hwy.), embraces about 1,200 acres of rugged lava coastline, scenic Hānauma Bay, and two prominent volcanic landmarks: 642-foot Koko Head and 1,207-foot Koko Crater. A roadside pullout on SR 72 overlooks Hālona Blowhole, where incoming breakers sometimes create a spouting geyser. **Hours:** Daily 4 a.m.-11 p.m. **Cost:** Free. **Phone:** (808) 395-3096.

Hānauma Bay Nature Preserve is just off SR 72 (Kalaniana'ole Hwy.) at 100 Hānauma Bay Rd., following signs. The preserve is in a remnant of a volcanic crater notched into the shore below Koko Head. The bay is a popular scuba diving, snorkeling, swimming and picnicking spot.

The Marine Education Center houses displays and interactive exhibits relating to the bay's inhabitants and geology. Implements used by the settlers also can be seen. A brief film about preserving the bay and other similar environments is required viewing.

Note: The collecting of souvenir coral or any other item is strictly forbidden. The parking lot often fills up early; visitors will not be admitted when the lot is full. Snorkeling equipment and locker rentals are available. Weekends tend to be less crowded than weekdays.

Hours: Wed.-Mon. 6 a.m.-7 p.m., Memorial Day weekend-Labor Day; Wed.-Mon. 6-6, rest of year. Phone ahead for Jan. 1 and Christmas schedules. **Cost:** $7.50; free (ages 0-12, active military and their families, and Hawai'i residents with ID). **Parking:** $1. **Phone:** (808) 396-4229 for recorded information. 🍴 🏕

Koko Crater Botanical Garden is off Kealahou St. at the west end of Kokonani St. The xeriscape garden occupies a basin within its namesake crater and contains a 2-mile trail through its collection of cacti, succulents, plumeria, bougainvillea, palms and other plants from around the world. **Note:** Bikes, motor vehicles and pets are not permitted in the garden. Walking shoes are recommended. **Time:** Allow 1 hour, 30 minutes minimum. **Hours:** Daily dawn-dusk. Closed Jan. 1 and Christmas. **Cost:** Free. **Phone:** (808) 522-7066 or (808) 522-7060.

LYON ARBORETUM is at 3860 Mānoa Rd., about 2.5 mi. n.w. of the University of Hawai'i at Mānoa's main campus. Though not located on campus, it is affiliated with the university and contains native Hawaiian, Polynesian and economically important tropical plants. The 194-acre rain forest can be damp and muddy; rain gear and walking shoes are recommended.

Hours: Mon.-Fri. 8-4, Sat. 9-3. Guided 60- to 90-minute tours Mon.-Sat. at 10. Closed major holidays. **Cost:** Donations. Guided tours $10 per person. Reservations are recommended for guided tours; walk-ins are permitted when space is available. **Phone:** (808) 988-0461. GT

NATIONAL MEMORIAL CEMETERY OF THE PACIFIC (PUNCHBOWL CEMETERY) is at 2177 Pūowaina Dr.; from the H-1 take exit 21A or 21B and follow signs. The approach road offers an excellent view of the city and harbor. Opened in 1949, the military cemetery contains nearly 40,000 graves arranged in concentric circles on the floor of the crater of an extinct volcano. Aptly, the Punchbowl was once called *Pūowaina*—Hill of Sacrifice.

Time: Allow 1 hour minimum. **Hours:** Daily 8-6:30 (Memorial Day 7-7), early Mar.-late Sept.; 8-5:30, rest of year. Persons in private vehicles are permitted to park. **Cost:** Free. **Phone:** (808) 532-3720.

Honolulu Memorial, 2177 Pūowaina Dr. at National Memorial Cemetery of the Pacific (Punchbowl Cemetery), encompasses Courts of the Missing that lists the names of 28,778 service personnel missing in action from World War II, Korea and Vietnam. The landscaped memorial also includes a Court of Honor and two galleries with 10-foot war maps. **Hours:** Daily 8-6:30 (Memorial Day 7-7), early Mar.-late Sept.; 8-5:30, rest of year. Persons in private vehicles are permitted to park. **Cost:** Free. **Phone:** (808) 532-3720.

NU'UANU PALI STATE WAYSIDE, 7 mi. n.e. via Pali Hwy. (Hwy. 61), offers a dramatic panorama of windward O'ahu's valleys and coastline. This windy 1,200-foot-high gap, flanked by cliffs that rise 2,000 to 3,000 feet, was the scene of Kamehameha the Great's decisive victory in the conquest of O'ahu. Winds are usually so intense that visitors can lean against a "wall" created by the current. **Hours:** Daily dawn-dusk. **Cost:** $3 (per vehicle); free (Hawai'i residents). **Phone:** (808) 587-0300.

 PACIFIC AVIATION MUSEUM—see Pearl Harbor p. 169.

PU'U OHIA, popularly known as Round Top-Tantalus Drive, begins at the end of Makiki St., circles Round Top Mountain and provides views of Mānoa Valley and the thickly forested slopes of Mount Tantalus. Vistas of Honolulu and the sea are framed by ferns and philodendrons. The drive, which takes about 1 hour, returns via Tantalus and Pūowaina drives in the Punchbowl area. Many hiking trails begin along the drive. **Note:** Nighttime driving to Tantalus is not recommended. **Phone:** (808) 973-9782 for trail information.

Pu'u Ualaka'a State Wayside, off Pu'u Ohia (also known as Round Top-Tantalus Drive), is a vantage point from which nearly one-third of O'ahu can be seen. Restrooms and drinking water are available. **Note:** Nighttime driving to Tantalus is not recommended. **Hours:** Daily 7 a.m.-7:45 p.m., Apr. 1-Labor Day; 7-6:45, rest of year. **Cost:** Free. **Phone:** (808) 587-0300. 🏕

Koko Head

QUEEN EMMA SUMMER PALACE, 2913 Pali Hwy. (SR 61), was built in 1848 as the summer retreat for Queen Emma, her husband King Kamehameha IV and their son Prince Albert. It is one of three remaining royal residences in the United States. Today the home is a historic site, museum and center for cultural education programs.

Hours: Daily 9-4. Last tour departs at 3. Closed major holidays. **Cost:** Guided tours $10; $8 (ages 65+); $1 (ages 0-17). Self-guiding tours $8; $6 (ages 65+); $1 (ages 0-17). Prices may vary; phone ahead. **Phone:** (808) 595-3167. [GT]

ROYAL MAUSOLEUM STATE MONUMENT, 2261 Nu'uanu Ave., is the sacred burial site of Hawaiian royalty, including members of the Kamehameha and Kalākaua dynasties. Guided tours are available by advance reservation. Picnicking is not permitted. Restrooms are available; drinking water is not. **Hours:** Mon.-Fri. 8-4. **Cost:** Free. **Phone:** (808) 587-2590.

SOTO ZEN MISSION OF HAWAI'I, 1708 Nu'uanu Ave., is a temple of East Indian design noted for its ornate altar. **Hours:** Entry is permitted only between services; phone for schedule. **Cost:** Free. **Phone:** (808) 537-9409 for information.

THE UNIVERSITY OF HAWAI'I AT MĀNOA, off H-1 at University Ave., has 20,000 students enrolled in bachelor's and master's degree programs in more than 85 fields of study, and doctoral degree programs in 51 areas. The 320 acres of landscaped grounds are planted with more than 560 varieties of tropical trees and plants, including the rare sausage tree. Maps and information about plants and art are available at the campus center. **Hours:** Guided tours are given Mon., Wed. and Fri. at 2, except on holidays. Self-guiding tours also are available. **Phone:** (808) 956-7236.

 USS *ARIZONA* MEMORIAL—see Pearl Harbor p. 169.

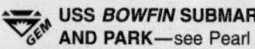 **USS *BOWFIN* SUBMARINE MUSEUM AND PARK**—see Pearl Harbor p. 169.

WASHINGTON PLACE is at 320 S. Beretania St. across from the state capitol. For 55 years this elegant two-and-a-half-story 1847 Greek Revival mansion was home to Queen Lili'uokalani. The queen was arrested here in 1895 on the charge of misprision of treason and subsequently was jailed in 'Iolani Palace *(see attraction listing p. 136)* for almost a year.

Twelve of Hawai'i's governors and their families resided within the coral rock- and wood-framed walls of Washington Place from 1922 to 2002.

Time: Allow 1 hour minimum. **Hours:** Tours, which last approximately 45 minutes, generally depart Thurs. at 10. Closed major holidays. Phone ahead to confirm schedule. **Cost:** Donations. Reservations are required 48 hours in advance. **Phone:** (808) 586-0248.

Honolulu's Waikīkī Area

DIAMOND HEAD STATE MONUMENT, off Diamond Head Rd. between Makapu'u and 18th aves., encompasses a 760-foot-high volcanic crater. The name derives from the volcanic crystals that 19th-century sailors mistook for diamonds. The Hawaiian name is Lē'ahi. A steep .8-mile trail from the crater interior to the summit rim affords a panoramic view of Waikīkī. The 1.3-mile Fort Ruger Pathway runs along the exterior slope of the monument and offers rest stops and picnic areas.

The walk to the site includes a 99-step stairway and may be difficult for the physically impaired. Dark tunnels and staircases are lit. Restrooms are available. Allow 2 hours minimum for the hike. The park is busiest between 9 and noon. When the parking lot fills up, vehicle traffic may be turned away. Wear comfortable walking shoes and a hat. Drinking water is available, but bringing an additional supply is recommended.

Hours: Daily 6-6. Last admission for summit rim hikers 90 minutes before closing. **Cost:** $5 (private vehicle); $1 (person by other means). **Phone:** (808) 587-0300. [🏞]

KAPI'OLANI REGIONAL PARK is at the e. end of Waikīkī, bordered by Kalākaua, Monsarrat and Paki aves. Among the 300-acre park's offerings are recreational facilities, an outdoor bandstand and picnic sites. The Royal Hawaiian Band gives concerts at the bandstand Sun. at 2. **Hours:** Daily 5 a.m.-midnight. **Cost:** Free. **Phone:** (808) 768-4626.

Honolulu Zoo is at 151 Kapahulu Ave. at the corner of Kalākaua Ave. in Kapi'olani Regional Park. This 42-acre zoo is home to 1,000 mammals, birds and reptiles. At the African Savanna exhibits, visitors peer at its jungle inhabitants through foliage, as if in the wild. Other zoo features include children's environmental education programs and a petting zoo.

Hours: Daily 9-4:30 (petting zoo closes at 4). Closed Christmas. **Cost:** $14; $8 (military and Hawai'i residents with ID); $6 (ages 3-12). **Phone:** (808) 971-7171 or (808) 971-7174. [💶] [🏞]

Queen Kapi'olani Garden is behind the Honolulu Zoo at Paki and Monsarrat aves. in Kapi'olani Regional Park. Pathways wind among varieties of hibiscus and other tropical flowering plants. *Kahuna* stones guard the blossoms against pickers. In the 14th century Tahitian *kahuna* arrived and offered spiritual healing to Hawaiians. When they returned to Hawai'i they left their powers in stones for healing and health purposes. **Hours:** Daily 5 a.m.-midnight. **Cost:** Free. **Phone:** (808) 971-2510.

Waikīkī Aquarium, 2777 Kalākaua Ave. in Kapi'olani Regional Park, was founded in 1904 and showcases more than 2,500 species of Pacific marine life, including chambered nautiluses, giant clams, endangered Hawaiian monk seals, sharks and reef fish.

The Northwestern Hawaiian Islands exhibit features a 4,000-gallon aquarium that's home to Hawaiian morwong, masked and bandit angelfish, yellow barbel goatfish and other species indigenous to the string of islands. Visitors can touch sea creatures at an outdoor living coral ecosystem display; observe jellyfish in the Ocean Drifters Gallery; marvel at a self-contained miniature coral reef; and view a sea horse, pipefish and sea dragon exhibit.

Queen Kapi'olani Garden

Note: On-site parking is limited; 4-hour metered parking is available nearby. **Time:** Allow 1 hour, 30 minutes minimum. **Hours:** Daily 9-5. Last admission 30 minutes before closing. Closed Sun. of Honolulu Marathon and Christmas. **Cost:** $12; $8 (active military with ID); $5 (ages 4-12, ages 65+ and the physically impaired). **Phone:** (808) 923-9741.

MAGIC OF POLYNESIA, 2300 Kalākaua Ave. in the Holiday Inn Waikīkī Beachcomber, is a magic show that combines illusions and special effects with Polynesian dancing. Dinner is available with the show. Inquire about cancellation policies. **Time:** Allow 1 hour, 30 minutes minimum. **Hours:** Show daily at 8 p.m. Dinner guests are seated at 6:30; guests attending only the show are seated at 7:30. **Cost:** Dinner shows $104-$149; $69-$79 (ages 4-11). Show only $59; $39 (ages 4-11). Reservations are recommended. **Parking:** $6 (valet only). **Phone:** (808) 971-4321 or (877) 971-4321.

U.S. ARMY MUSEUM OF HAWAI'I, 2131 Kalia Rd. in Battery Randolph at Fort DeRussy, relates the story of early Hawaiian warfare and covers every major military event in the Pacific theater of operations up through the Vietnam War. **Hours:** Tues.-Sat. 9-5. **Cost:** Donations. Audio tour rental (available in English or Japanese) $5. **Phone:** (808) 955-9552 or (808) 941-3900.

WAIKĪKĪ STARLIGHT LŪ'AU, 2005 Kalia Rd., is held on the rooftop of the Mid-Pacific Conference Center at the Hilton Hawaiian Village Waikīkī Beach Resort. Guests can choose from two price points, based on seating and *lei* preference, but both include the buffet, entertainment and two mai tais or tropical juices. Guests who have chosen the general seating option should arrive early to snag a table closer to the stage.

Because this *lū'au* is in a more urban setting, there is no traditional unveiling of the roasted pig in an *imu* (underground oven). The feast does include *kalua* pig, fish, salads and other Pacific Rim and Polynesian dishes.

For the adventurous types, there are conch-shell blowing contests and *hula* lessons before dinner. The after-dinner show features dancers from Hawai'i, Tahiti, Tonga and Samoa and concludes with a fire dance.

Time: Allow 3 hours minimum. **Hours:** Sun.-Thurs. 5-8 p.m. (weather permitting). **Cost:** General seating $99; $79.20 (active military with ID); $49.50 (ages 4-11). Preferred seating $125; $100 (active military with ID); $62.50 (ages 4-11). Reservations are required. **Phone:** (808) 941-5828. *(See ad on insert.)*

Sightseeing
Boat Tours

Cruises and boat tours are available aboard anything from a junk to a catamaran. Some explore the reefs off Waikīkī or visit Pearl Harbor; others offer recreation—chiefly swimming and skin diving—or dinner and dancing.

ATLANTIS ADVENTURES: *ATLANTIS* CRUISES, departing Pier 6 at Aloha Tower Marketplace, offers sightseeing cruises with dinner and entertainment. Seasonal whale-watch cruises also are offered. **Hours:** Dinner cruises depart daily at 5:30 year-round. Whale-watch cruises depart daily at 9 and noon, Dec.-Apr. Phone ahead to confirm schedule.

Cost: Dinner cruise $124-$159; $76-$96 (ages 7-12). Whale-watch cruise $57-$84; $30-$42 (ages 7-12). **Phone:** (800) 381-0237.

SAVE **ATLANTIS ADVENTURES:** *ATLANTIS* **SUBMARINES WAIKĪKĪ** departs from Hilton Hawaiian Village Waikīkī Beach Resort. The company offers narrated underwater voyages during which passengers can see exotic fish, sunken vessels, coral formations and marine animals through large viewing portholes.

Time: Allow 2 hours minimum. **Hours:** Trips depart daily at 9 and on the hour 11-3. Phone ahead to confirm schedule. **Cost:** Trips start at $115; $48 (ages 4-12). Under 36 inches tall are not permitted. Reservations are required. **Phone:** (800) 381-0237.

STAR OF HONOLULU, departing Pier 8 at the Aloha Tower Marketplace, is a 1,500-passenger ship offering a variety of cruises, including a seasonal whale-watch tour with guaranteed sightings. Sunset dinner and holiday cruises also are offered.

Hours: Whale-watch tour departs daily at 8:45 and noon, mid-Dec. to mid-Apr. Phone for other cruise schedules. **Cost:** Whale-watch tours start at $33; $19 (ages 3-11). **Phone:** (808) 983-7827 or (800) 334-6191.

Bus, Limousine, Trolley and Van Tours

One of the best ways to get an overview of Honolulu and the rest of O'ahu is on a guided tour. Costs vary with the mode of conveyance and itinerary. For example, a van tour will run about $60 per adult for a half-day trip and $75 for a full day; a bus tour will cost a little less, a sedan a little more.

One advantage of a smaller vehicle, such as a van or limousine, is that it allows more opportunity for rapport with the driver/guide.

Waikīkī Trolley offers a coastline (Blue Line) tour, a Diamond Head area (Green Line) tour, a historic (Red Line) tour and the Ala Moana Shopping Shuttle (Pink Line). Depending upon the trolley tour chosen, riders may get off and board a later trolley all day. The first trolleys depart between 8:30 and 9 a.m. and the last trolley pickup is between 8 and 10 p.m., depending upon the tour and the day of the week. Trolleys leave every 10 to 40 minutes and run daily. Phone (808) 593-2822 for schedule and fare information.

Gray Line offers a variety of sightseeing tours departing from Waikīkī; phone (808) 833-3000 or (888) 206-4531.

HAWAI'I DUCK TOURS picks up passengers from most Waikīkī hotels. The company offers tours aboard renovated World War II amphibious trucks called "DUCKs." The Maunalua Bay tour features a scenic Maunalua Bay cruise, a drive through the opulent Kahala neighborhood, and more.

Pearl Harbor tour participants enjoy views of downtown Honolulu, Waikīkī and Diamond Head from both land and sea; afterward, they can visit one of three Pearl Harbor attractions. Highlights of the Honolulu City tour include Kalākaua Avenue, Aloha Tower Marketplace and Chinatown.

Hours: Maunalua Bay tour pickups Mon.-Sat. 10:50-11:35 and 1:25-2; closed federal holidays. Pearl Harbor tour pickups Sun. and holidays 11-11:35; closed Jan. 1, Thanksgiving and Christmas. Honolulu City tour pickups Sun. and holidays 7:30-8:45. Phone ahead to confirm schedule.

Cost: Maunalua Bay tour $59; $39 (ages 2-11). Pearl Harbor tour $89-$109; $39-$49 (ages 2-11). Honolulu City tour $49; $29 (ages 2-11). Reservations are required. **Phone:** (808) 988-3825.

Air Tours

BLUE HAWAIIAN HELICOPTERS is off H-1 at 99 Kaulele Pl., just s. of Honolulu International Airport. The Blue Skies of O'ahu Tour lasts 45 to 50 minutes and provides views of Pearl Harbor, Waikīkī, Diamond Head, Nu'uanu Valley, Chinaman's Hat, the North Shore and more. Passengers hear music, two-way communication with the pilot, and the pilot's narration via noise-canceling headsets.

Note: Due to decompression-related sickness, it is recommended that passengers wait 12-24 hours after scuba diving before flying; the amount of time is dependent on particular dive factors. Ask about possible policies regarding minimum wait time between scuba diving and flying; weight restrictions; weather, cancellation and refund policies; and the minimum and maximum number of passengers for flights. All small aircraft may encounter turbulence.

Time: Allow 1 hour minimum. **Hours:** Daily 8-5. **Cost:** $225, plus applicable fuel surcharge . **Phone:** (808) 831-8800 or (800) 745-2583. *(See ad on inside front cover.)*

ISLAND SEAPLANE SERVICE departs from 85 Lagoon Dr., behind the Honolulu International Airport; take the Lagoon exit off Nimitz Hwy. and go s. 1 mi. Complimentary pickup service is available at Waikīkī accommodations and at the Aloha Tower Marketplace. These pilot-narrated flights aboard either a four- or six-passenger seaplane offer spectacular views of O'ahu.

Note: Due to decompression-related sickness, it is recommended that passengers wait 12-24 hours after scuba diving before flying; the amount of time is dependent on particular dive factors. Ask about possible policies regarding minimum wait time between scuba diving and flying; weight restrictions; weather, cancellation and refund policies; and the minimum and maximum number of passengers for flights. All small aircraft may encounter turbulence.

Hours: Flights depart daily at 9:15, 10:45, 12:15, 1:45, 3:15 and 4:45. **Cost:** One-hour flight $299. Half-hour flight $179. Prices may vary; phone ahead. Reservations are recommended. **Phone:** (808) 836-6273.

Lū'au

A *lū'au* is a Hawaiian picnic featuring traditional food and dance. The *lū'au* food is cooked in an *imu*, an underground oven, which is formed by *pōhaku* (heating rocks) in a pit in the ground. The pit is lined with fresh leaves, filled with native vegetables and a prepared pig, then surrounded by heated rocks that also are placed inside the pig. The whole feast is then covered with leaves or canvas and allowed to cook for about 6 hours.

The pork tends to be salty—a nice contrast with the traditional *poi*, the pounded taro-root dish of which there are many variations. Polynesian entertainment adds flavor to the colorful proceedings.

Found at various locations, *lū'au* last about 3-4 hours and are only by reservation. Adult prices generally range from $74 to $153, with discounted prices for students and children. One of the more established Honolulu-area *lū'au* is Germaine's Lū'au, (808) 949-6626 or (800) 367-5655 *(see attraction listing in Kapolei p. 165)*. Another solid choice is Paradise Cove Lū'au, (808) 842-5911 or (800) 775-2683 *(see attraction listing in Kapolei p. 165)*.

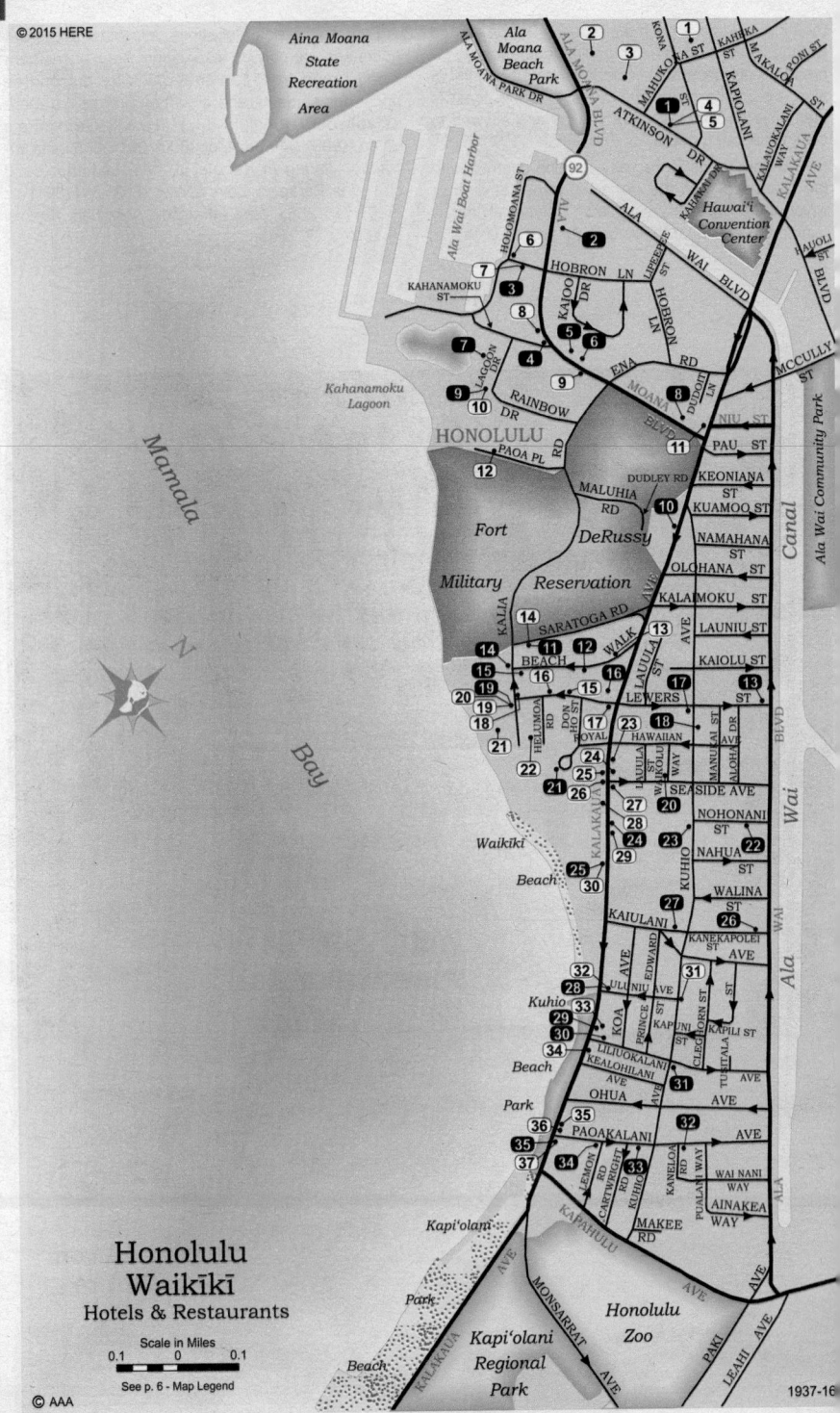

Honolulu
Waikīkī
Hotels & Restaurants

Scale in Miles

0.1   0   0.1

See p. 6 - Map Legend

© AAA

© 2015 HERE

1937-16

Honolulu Waikiki

This index helps you "spot" where approved hotels and restaurants are located on the corresponding detailed maps. Hotel daily rate range is for comparison only. Restaurant price range is a combination of lunch and/or dinner. Turn to the listing page for more detailed rate and price information and consult display ads for special promotions.

HONOLULU (WAIKĪKĪ)

Map Page		Hotels	Diamond Rated	Rate Range	Page
1	p. 142	Ala Moana Hotel	◆◆◆	$129-$499	147
2	p. 142	The Equus Hotel, an Ascend Hotel Collection Member	◆◆	$139-$239	151
3	p. 142	**The Modern Honolulu**	◆◆◆◆	$309-$999 SAVE	153
4	p. 142	Grand Waikikian Suites by Hilton Grand Vacations	◆◆◆	$369-$1900	151
5	p. 142	**Ramada Plaza Waikiki**	◆◆	$140-$200 SAVE	155
6	p. 142	Aqua Palms at Waikiki (See ad p. 150.)	◆◆	$169-$300	147
7	p. 142	Hilton Grand Vacations Club at Hilton Hawaiian Village	◆◆◆	$239-$2100	151
8	p. 142	**DoubleTree by Hilton Alana Waikiki Hotel**	◆◆◆	$189-$279 SAVE	151
9	p. 142	**Hilton Hawaiian Village Waikiki Beach Resort** (See ad on insert.)	◆◆◆	$179-$399 SAVE	152
10	p. 142	**Luana Waikiki**	◆◆◆	$179-$499 SAVE	153
11	p. 142	Trump International Hotel Waikiki Beach Walk	◆◆◆◆	$489-$775	156
12	p. 142	Regency on Beachwalk Waikiki by Outrigger	◆◆◆	$169-$339	155
13	p. 142	**Coconut Waikiki Hotel, a Joie de Vivre hotel**	◆◆	$169-$329 SAVE	147
14	p. 142	**Outrigger Reef Waikiki Beach Resort**	◆◆◆	$209-$989 SAVE	155
15	p. 142	**Embassy Suites by Hilton Waikiki Beach Walk**	◆◆◆	$269-$539 SAVE	151
16	p. 142	Hokulani Waikiki by Hilton Grand Vacations Club	◆◆◆	$349-$649	152
17	p. 142	**OHANA Waikiki Malia**	◆◆	$279-$329 SAVE	155
18	p. 142	**Courtyard by Marriott Waikiki Beach**	◆◆◆	$116-$399 SAVE	151
19	p. 142	**Halekulani**	◆◆◆◆	$482-$1238 SAVE	151
20	p. 142	**Shoreline Hotel Waikiki, a Joie de Vivre Hotel**	◆◆◆	$189-$359 SAVE	156
21	p. 142	**Sheraton Waikiki Resort**	◆◆◆	$199-$540 SAVE	156
22	p. 142	Ilima Hotel	◆◆	$134-$262	152
23	p. 142	**Aqua Waikiki Wave Hotel** (See ad p. 150.)	◆◆	$99-$299 SAVE	147
24	p. 142	Holiday Inn Resort Waikiki Beachcomber	◆◆◆	Rates not provided	152
25	p. 142	**Outrigger Waikiki Beach Resort**	◆◆◆	$249-$959 SAVE	155
26	p. 142	Aqua Aloha Surf Waikiki (See ad p. 150.)	◆◆	$149-$209	147
27	p. 142	**OHANA Waikiki East**	◆◆	$309-$719 SAVE	155
28	p. 142	**Hyatt Regency Waikiki Beach Resort & Spa**	◆◆◆	$180-$510 SAVE	152
29	p. 142	Aston Waikiki Circle Hotel (See ad starting on p. 148.)	◆	$179-$359	147
30	p. 142	**Aston Waikiki Beach Tower** (See ad starting on p. 148.)	◆◆◆	$554-$1214 SAVE	147
31	p. 142	**Hilton Waikiki Beach** (See ad p. 153.)	◆◆◆	$189-$519 SAVE	152
32	p. 142	Aston Waikiki Sunset (See ad starting on p. 148.)	◆◆	$224-$949	147
33	p. 142	**Hyatt Place Waikiki Beach** (See ad p. 154.)	◆◆◆	$139-$449 SAVE	152
34	p. 142	**Hotel Renew** (See ad starting on p. 148.)	◆◆◆	$229-$359 SAVE	152
35	p. 142	**Aston Waikiki Beach Hotel** (See ad starting on p. 148.)	◆◆◆	$219-$709 SAVE	147

Map Page		Restaurants	Diamond Rated	Cuisine	Price Range	Page
1	p. 142	Shokudo Japanese Restaurant & Bar	◆◆	Japanese Fusion	$9-$25	159
2	p. 142	Tanaka of Tokyo West	◆◆	Japanese Steak Seafood	$20-$46	159
3	p. 142	Pineapple Room by Alan Wong	◆◆◆	Pacific Rim	$15-$45	158
4	p. 142	The Signature Prime Steak & Seafood	◆◆◆	Steak Seafood	$30-$65	159
5	p. 142	Royal Garden Chinese Restaurant	◆◆	Chinese Dim Sum	$9-$25	158
6	p. 142	**Chart House Waikiki**	◆◆	American	$24-$52	157
7	p. 142	Morimoto Waikiki	◆◆◆	New Japanese Sushi	$17-$80	158
8	p. 142	Sarento's at the Top of The Ilikai	◆◆◆	Italian	$20-$42	159
9	p. 142	Kobe Japanese Steak House & Sushi Bar	◆◆	Japanese Steak	$15-$50	158
10	p. 142	**Bali Steak & Seafood**	◆◆◆◆	Steak Seafood	$29-$58	156
11	p. 142	Cheeseburger Waikiki	◆◆	American	$10-$15	157
12	p. 142	Waikiki Starlight Luau	◆	Hawaiian	$99-$125	159
13	p. 142	Hard Rock Cafe	◆◆	American	$12-$24 SAVE	157
14	p. 142	BLT Steak	◆◆◆	Steak	$16-$56	156
15	p. 142	Kaiwa Waikiki	◆◆	Japanese	$26-$60	158
16	p. 142	Ruth's Chris Steak House	◆◆◆	Steak	$27-$60	158
17	p. 142	P.F. Chang's China Bistro	◆◆◆	Chinese	$11-$32	158
18	p. 142	Roy's	◆◆◆	Pacific Rim Fusion	$15-$48	158
19	p. 142	**La Mer**	◆◆◆◆◆	French	$110-$195	158
20	p. 142	Orchids	◆◆◆◆	Pacific Rim	$29-$54	158
21	p. 142	House Without A Key	◆◆◆	International	$16-$46	157
22	p. 142	Nobu	◆◆◆	Pacific Rim	$10-$40	158
23	p. 142	Buho	◆◆	New Mexican	$10-$30	156
24	p. 142	Tanaka of Tokyo Central	◆◆	Japanese Steak	$20-$50	159
25	p. 142	Restaurant Suntory	◆◆◆	Japanese Sushi Specialty	$14-$72	158
26	p. 142	Azure Restaurant	◆◆◆	Seafood	$30-$60	156
27	p. 142	Top of Waikiki	◆◆◆	Pacific Rim	$25-$44	159
28	p. 142	Wolfgang's Steakhouse	◆◆◆	Steak	$14-$56	159
29	p. 142	Jimmy Buffett's Restaurant & Bar at the Beachcomber	◆◆	American	$13-$30	157
30	p. 142	Hula Grill Waikiki	◆◆	Regional American	$21-$34	157
31	p. 142	Hy's Steakhouse	◆◆◆	Steak	$28-$80	157
32	p. 142	JAPENGO	◆◆◆	Pacific Rim Sushi	$18-$49	157
33	p. 142	Eggs 'n Things	◆	Breakfast	$9-$17	157
34	p. 142	Oceanarium Restaurant	◆◆	Seafood	$21-$48	158
35	p. 142	Sansei Seafood Restaurant & Sushi Bar	◆◆◆	New Japanese Sushi Fusion	$17-$31	159
36	p. 142	d.k Steak House	◆◆	Steak Seafood	$24-$85	157
37	p. 142	Tiki's Grill & Bar	◆◆	American	$12-$29	159

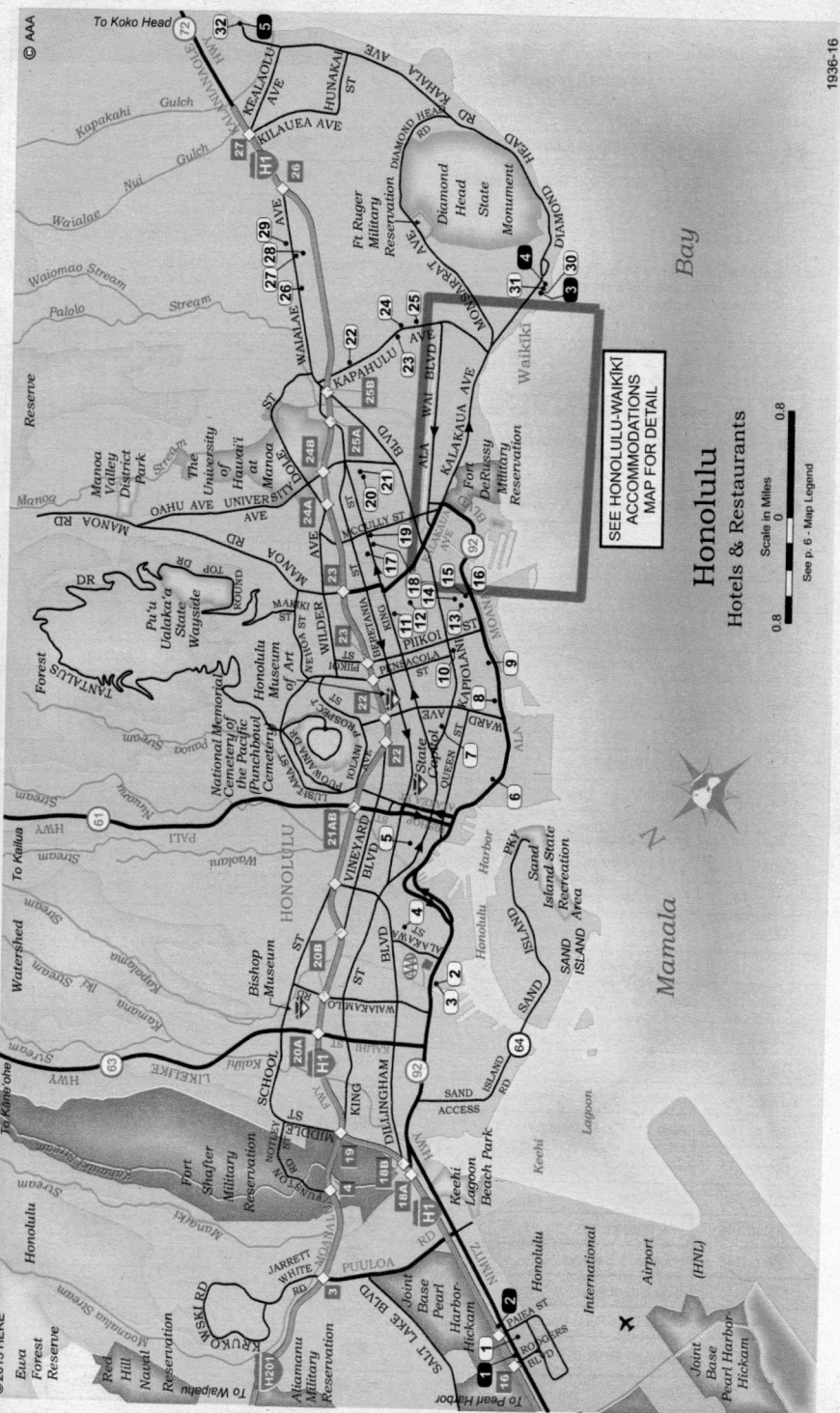

Honolulu
Hotels & Restaurants

SEE HONOLULU-WAIKĪKĪ
ACCOMMODATIONS
MAP FOR DETAIL

Scale in Miles

See p. 6 - Map Legend

✈ Airport Hotels

Map Page	HONOLULU INTERNATIONAL (Maximum driving distance from airport: 0.9 mi)	Diamond Rated	Rate Range	Page
❶ p. 145	Airport Honolulu Hotel, 0.9 mi	🔷🔷	$109-$189 SAVE	160
❷ p. 145	BEST WESTERN The Plaza Hotel, 0.6 mi	🔷🔷	$169-$209 SAVE	160

Honolulu

This index helps you "spot" where approved hotels and restaurants are located on the corresponding detailed maps. Hotel daily rate range is for comparison only. Restaurant price range is a combination of lunch and/or dinner. Turn to the listing page for more detailed rate and price information and consult display ads for special promotions.

HONOLULU

Map Page	Hotels	Diamond Rated	Rate Range	Page
❶ p. 145	Airport Honolulu Hotel	🔷🔷	$109-$189 SAVE	160
❷ p. 145	BEST WESTERN The Plaza Hotel	🔷🔷	$169-$209 SAVE	160
❸ p. 145	The New Otani Kaimana Beach Hotel	🔷🔷	$250-$1800	160
❹ p. 145	Lotus Honolulu	🔷🔷🔷	$319-$409	160
❺ p. 145	The Kahala Hotel & Resort	🔷🔷🔷🔷	$395-$595 SAVE	160

Map Page	Restaurants	Diamond Rated	Cuisine	Price Range	Page
① p. 145	Big Kahuna's Pizza 'n Stuff	🔷	Pizza	$6-$22	160
② p. 145	Nico's Pier 38	🔷	Seafood	$10-$25	162
③ p. 145	Uncle's Fish Market & Grill	🔷🔷	Pacific Rim Seafood	$9-$24	162
④ p. 145	Max's of Manila	🔷🔷	Philippine	$8-$19	161
⑤ p. 145	Little Village Noodle House	🔷🔷	Chinese Noodles	$9-$25	161
⑥ p. 145	Ruth's Chris Steak House	🔷🔷	Steak	$32-$62	162
⑦ p. 145	Yanagi Sushi	🔷🔷	Japanese Sushi	$15-$45	163
⑧ p. 145	Kincaid's Fish, Chop & Steak House	🔷🔷🔷	Steak Seafood	$15-$41	161
⑨ p. 145	Kaka'ako Kitchen	🔷	American	$10-$15	161
⑩ p. 145	Shabu Shabu House	🔷🔷	Japanese Specialty	$10-$60	162
⑪ p. 145	Sushi Sasabune	🔷🔷🔷	Sushi	$20-$60	162
⑫ p. 145	Pagoda Floating Restaurant	🔷🔷	Regional American	$10-$36	162
⑬ p. 145	Saint-Germain Bakery	🔷	Breads/Pastries	$5-$7	162
⑭ p. 145	Longhi's	🔷🔷	Regional American	$14-$45	161
⑮ p. 145	The Mermaid Bar	🔷🔷	American	$10-$16	161
⑯ p. 145	Mariposa	🔷🔷🔷	Pacific Rim	$16-$36	161
⑰ p. 145	Gyotaku Japanese Restaurant	🔷🔷	Japanese	$10-$37	161
⑱ p. 145	Alan Wong's Restaurant	🔷🔷🔷	Pacific Rim	$31-$48	160
⑲ p. 145	Chef Mavro	🔷🔷🔷🔷🔷	Regional Hawaiian	$85-$175	160
⑳ p. 145	Karai Crab	🔷🔷	Seafood	$25-$42	161
㉑ p. 145	The Willows	🔷🔷	Continental	$24-$40	163
㉒ p. 145	Leonard's Bakery	🔷	Breads/Pastries	$3-$6	161
㉓ p. 145	Side Street Inn	🔷🔷	Pacific Rim	$12-$29	162
㉔ p. 145	Uncle Bo's Pupu Bar & Grill	🔷🔷	Fusion	$13-$30	162
㉕ p. 145	Rainbow Drive-In	🔷	Regional American	$3-$9	162
㉖ p. 145	Town	🔷🔷	Mediterranean	$11-$28	162

Map Page	Restaurants (cont'd)	Diamond Rated	Cuisine	Price Range	Page
㉗ p. 145	SALT bar & kitchen	▽▽	New American	$11-$25	162
㉘ p. 145	12th Avenue Grill	▽▽▽	Regional American	$23-$36	160
㉙ p. 145	3660 On the Rise	▽▽	Pacific Rim	$22-$49	160
㉚ p. 145	Hau Tree Lanai	▽▽	Pacific Rim Seafood	$15-$69	161
㉛ p. 145	Michel's at the Colony Surf	▽▽	French Seafood	$42-$85	162
㉜ p. 145	Hoku's	▽▽▽	Pacific Rim	$29-$65	161

HONOLULU (WAIKĪKĪ)

- **Restaurants p. 156**
- **Hotels & Restaurants map & index p. 142**

ALA MOANA HOTEL
(808)955-4811 **1**

▽▽▽ **Hotel** $129-$499 **Address:** 410 Atkinson Dr 96814 **Location:** Adjacent to Ala Moana Shopping Center. **Facility:** 1154 units, some efficiencies. 13-36 stories, interior corridors. **Parking:** on-site (fee) and valet. **Terms:** 3 day cancellation notice-fee imposed. **Amenities:** safes. **Dining:** 4 restaurants, also, Royal Garden Chinese Restaurant, The Signature Prime Steak & Seafood, see separate listings, nightclub. **Pool(s):** outdoor. **Activities:** sauna, steamroom, exercise room, massage. **Guest Services:** valet and coin laundry.

AQUA ALOHA SURF WAIKIKI
(808)923-0222 **26**

▽▽ **Hotel** $149-$209 **Address:** 444 Kanekapolei St 96815 **Location:** Between Kuhio Ave and Ala Wai Blvd. **Facility:** 204 units. 16 stories, interior corridors. **Parking:** on-site (fee). **Terms:** 3 day cancellation notice-fee imposed. **Amenities:** video games, safes. **Pool(s):** outdoor. **Activities:** exercise room, massage. **Guest Services:** valet and coin laundry, area transportation. *(See ad p. 150.)*

AQUA PALMS AT WAIKIKI
(808)947-7256 **6**

▽▽ **Hotel** $169-$300 **Address:** 1850 Ala Moana Blvd 96815 **Location:** Between Hobron Ln and Ena Rd. **Facility:** 215 units, some kitchens. 12 stories, interior corridors. **Parking:** on-site (fee). **Terms:** 3 day cancellation notice-fee imposed. **Amenities:** safes. **Pool(s):** outdoor. **Activities:** limited exercise equipment. **Guest Services:** valet and coin laundry, area transportation. *(See ad p. 150.)*

AQUA WAIKIKI WAVE HOTEL
(808)922-1262 **23**

▽▽ **Hotel** $99-$299

Address: 2299 Kuhio Ave 96815 **Location:** Just s of Seaside Ave. **Facility:** 247 units, some two bedrooms. 15 stories, interior corridors. **Parking:** on-site (fee). **Terms:** 3 day cancellation notice-fee imposed. **Amenities:** safes. **Activities:** exercise room, massage. **Guest Services:** valet laundry, area transportation. *(See ad p. 150.)*

ASTON WAIKIKI BEACH HOTEL
(808)922-2511 **35**

▽▽▽ **Hotel** $219-$709

Address: 2570 Kalakaua Ave 96815 **Location:** Oceanfront. Between Paoakalani and Kapahulu aves. Across from Waikiki Beach. **Facility:** 645 units. 5-25 stories, interior corridors. **Parking:** valet only. **Terms:** 3 day cancellation notice, resort fee. **Amenities:** video games, safes. **Dining:** 2 restaurants, also, Tiki's Grill & Bar, see separate listing, entertainment. **Pool(s):** heated outdoor. **Activities:** exercise room. **Guest Services:** valet laundry. *(See ad starting on p. 148.)*

ASTON WAIKIKI BEACH TOWER
(808)926-6400 **30**

▽▽▽ **Condominium** $554-$1214

Address: 2470 Kalakaua Ave 96815 **Location:** Oceanfront. Corner of Liliuokalani Ave. Across from Waikiki Beach. **Facility:** Each of these incredibly spacious two-bedroom condos feature a fully equipped kitchen, two bathrooms, a washer/dryer and a large balcony facing Waikiki Beach (most with spectacular views). 106 condominiums, some two bedrooms. 5-40 stories, interior corridors. **Parking:** on-site and valet. **Terms:** 7 day cancellation notice, resort fee. **Amenities:** video games, safes. **Activities:** sauna, hot tub. **Guest Services:** complimentary and valet laundry. *(See ad starting on p. 148.)*

ASTON WAIKIKI CIRCLE HOTEL
(808)923-1571 **29**

▽ **Classic Hotel** $179-$359 **Address:** 2464 Kalakaua Ave 96815 **Location:** Oceanfront. Between Uluniu St and Liliuokalani Ave. Across from Waikiki Beach. **Facility:** Built in 1962, this unique, circular high-rise hotel is located directly across the street from Waikiki Beach. Most guest rooms have a balcony. 104 units. 2-14 stories, interior corridors. **Bath:** shower only. **Parking:** on-site (fee). **Terms:** 3 day cancellation notice-fee imposed, resort fee. **Amenities:** video games, safes. **Dining:** Eggs 'n Things, see separate listing. **Guest Services:** valet laundry. *(See ad starting on p. 148.)*

ASTON WAIKIKI SUNSET
(808)922-0511 **32**

▽▽ **Vacation Rental Condominium** $224-$949 **Address:** 229 Paoakalani Ave 96815 **Location:** Between Kuhio Ave and Ala Wai Blvd. **Facility:** Located just two blocks from famous Waikiki Beach, this high-rise condo complex features units with a living room, full kitchen, floor-to-ceiling windows and a large lanai. 338 condominiums. 38 stories, interior corridors. **Parking:** on-site (fee). **Terms:** 3 day cancellation notice-fee imposed, resort fee. **Amenities:** video games, safes. **Pool(s):** heated outdoor. **Activities:** sauna, tennis. **Guest Services:** valet and coin laundry. *(See ad starting on p. 148.)*

COCONUT WAIKIKI HOTEL, A JOIE DE VIVRE HOTEL
(808)923-8828 **13**

▽▽ **Hotel** $169-$329

Address: 450 Lewers St 96815 **Location:** Corner of Lewers St and Ala Wai Blvd. **Facility:** 81 units, some two bedrooms and kitchens. 11 stories, interior corridors. **Parking:** valet only. **Terms:** 3 day cancellation notice-fee imposed. **Amenities:** safes. **Pool(s):** heated outdoor. **Activities:** exercise room. **Guest Services:** valet and coin laundry. **Featured Amenity:** continental breakfast.

Capture Life

AAA Members save
up to 20% Off
our best daily rate

Collect stories, not selfies.

You won't remember the time you spent staring at
your screen, but you'll never forget your time with us.

866·774·2924 | astonhotels.com/AAA

*Not all properties are AAA inspected.

Aston
HOTELS & RESORTS
welcome home

(See map & index p. 142.)

(See map & index p. 142.)

COURTYARD BY MARRIOTT WAIKIKI BEACH
(808)954-4000 **18**

Hotel
$116-$399

COURTYARD Marriott

AAA Benefit: Members save 5% or more!

Address: 400 Royal Hawaiian Ave 96815 **Location:** Jct Kuhio Ave. **Facility:** 403 units. 2-17 stories, interior/exterior corridors. **Parking:** valet only. **Terms:** 3 day cancellation notice. **Amenities:** video games, safes. **Pool(s):** outdoor, heated outdoor. **Activities:** hot tub, exercise room, spa. **Guest Services:** valet and coin laundry.

DOUBLETREE BY HILTON ALANA WAIKIKI HOTEL
(808)941-7275 **8**

Hotel
$189-$279

DOUBLETREE BY HILTON

AAA Benefit: Members save 5% or more!

Address: 1956 Ala Moana Blvd 96815 **Location:** Between Ena Rd and Kalakaua Ave. **Facility:** 317 units. 19 stories, interior corridors. **Parking:** valet only. **Terms:** 1-7 night minimum stay, cancellation fee imposed. **Amenities:** video games, safes. **Pool(s):** heated outdoor. **Activities:** exercise room. **Guest Services:** valet laundry.

EMBASSY SUITES BY HILTON WAIKIKI BEACH WALK
(808)921-2345 **15**

Hotel
$269-$539

EMBASSY SUITES by HILTON

AAA Benefit: Members save 5% or more!

Address: 201 Beachwalk St 96815 **Location:** Between Lewers St and Saratoga Rd; 2 blks from Waikiki Beach. **Facility:** 369 units, some two bedrooms. 21 stories, interior corridors. **Parking:** valet only. **Terms:** 1-7 night minimum stay, cancellation fee imposed. **Amenities:** video games, safes. **Dining:** 3 restaurants, also, Roy's, see separate listing, entertainment. **Pool(s):** heated outdoor. **Activities:** hot tub, exercise room, massage. **Guest Services:** valet and coin laundry. **Featured Amenity:** full hot breakfast.

THE EQUUS HOTEL, AN ASCEND HOTEL COLLECTION MEMBER
(808)949-0061 **2**

Boutique Hotel $139-$239 **Address:** 1696 Ala Moana Blvd 96815 **Location:** Just e of Hobron Ln. **Facility:** This hotel features photos of paniolo (Hawaiian) cowboys and shows some polo influences. Some of the attractive guest rooms offer a balcony and some feature antique furnishings. 67 units. 2-10 stories, exterior corridors. *Bath:* shower only. **Parking:** valet only. **Amenities:** safes. **Pool(s):** outdoor. **Guest Services:** valet laundry.

GRAND WAIKIKIAN SUITES BY HILTON GRAND VACATIONS
(808)953-2700 **4**

Condominium $369-$1900
Address: 1811 Ala Moana Blvd 96815
Location: Enter off Ala Moana Blvd near Ilikai Hotel; jct Kahanamoku St. **Facility:**

AAA Benefit: Members save 5% or more!

Located on the spacious grounds of the Hilton Hawaiian Village, most of the property's one- and two-bedroom units have a private lanai, some with a spectacular ocean view. 331 condominiums. 5-39 stories, interior corridors. **Parking:** on-site (fee) and valet. **Terms:** check-in 4 pm, 1-7 night minimum stay, cancellation fee imposed. **Amenities:** video games, safes. **Dining:** 11 restaurants, entertainment. **Pool(s):** outdoor. **Activities:** hot tub, steamroom, beach access, scuba diving, snorkeling, recreation programs, exercise room, spa. **Guest Services:** complimentary and valet laundry.

HALEKULANI
(808)923-2311 **19**

Hotel
$482-$1238

Address: 2199 Kalia Rd 96815 **Location:** Oceanfront. Just sw of Kalakaua Ave via Lewers St. **Facility:** This service-oriented, Waikiki beachside resort with a luxurious spa provides a central location near all conveniences. 453 units. 17 stories, interior corridors. **Parking:** on-site (fee) and valet. **Terms:** 3 day cancellation notice-fee imposed. **Amenities:** video games, safes. **Dining:** House Without A Key, La Mer, Orchids, see separate listings, entertainment. **Pool(s):** heated outdoor. **Activities:** self-propelled boats, recreation programs, exercise room, spa. **Guest Services:** valet laundry.

HILTON GRAND VACATIONS CLUB AT HILTON HAWAIIAN VILLAGE
(808)953-2700 **7**

Condominium $239-$2100
Address: 2003 Kalia Rd 96815 **Location:** Jct Kahanamoku St; enter off Ala Moana Blvd. **Facility:** Located on the tropical grounds of the Hilton Hawaiian

AAA Benefit: Members save 5% or more!

Village, the property offers studios with wet bars and spacious one and two-bedroom units, some with ocean and lagoon views; most with a lanai. 276 condominiums. 3-24 stories, interior corridors. **Parking:** on-site (fee) and valet. **Terms:** check-in 4 pm, 1-7 night minimum stay, cancellation fee imposed. **Amenities:** video games, safes. **Dining:** 11 restaurants, entertainment. **Pool(s):** outdoor. **Activities:** hot tub, steamroom, scuba diving, snorkeling, recreation programs, kids club, exercise room, spa. **Guest Services:** complimentary and valet laundry.

(See map & index p. 142.)

HILTON HAWAIIAN VILLAGE WAIKIKI BEACH RESORT
(808)949-4321 **9**

Resort Hotel
$179-$399

AAA Benefit: Members save 5% or more!

Address: 2005 Kalia Rd 96815 **Location:** Oceanfront. Jct Ala Moana Blvd. **Facility:** On 22 acres, this exotic, tropical beachfront complex has wildlife on the property. Shopping areas add to the appeal of this expansive resort with five different towers. 2860 units. 2-35 stories, interior corridors. **Parking:** on-site (fee) and valet. **Terms:** 1-7 night minimum stay, cancellation fee imposed. **Amenities:** video games, safes. **Dining:** 11 restaurants, also, Bali Steak & Seafood, Waikiki Starlight Luau, see separate listings, entertainment. **Pool(s):** outdoor, heated outdoor. **Activities:** sauna, hot tub, steamroom, cabanas, self-propelled boats, scuba diving, snorkeling, recreation programs, kids club, exercise room, spa. **Guest Services:** valet laundry, boarding pass kiosk, rental car service. (See ad on insert.)

HILTON WAIKIKI BEACH
(808)922-0811 **31**

Hotel
$189-$519

AAA Benefit: Members save 5% or more!

Address: 2500 Kuhio Ave 96815 **Location:** Between Liliuokalani and Ohua aves. **Facility:** 601 units. 37 stories, interior corridors. **Parking:** valet only. **Terms:** 1-7 night minimum stay, cancellation fee imposed. **Amenities:** video games, safes. **Pool(s):** heated outdoor. **Activities:** hot tub, beach access, exercise room. **Guest Services:** valet laundry. (See ad p. 153.)

HOKULANI WAIKIKI BY HILTON GRAND VACATIONS CLUB
(808)462-4000 **16**

Condominium $349-$649
Address: 2181 Kalakaua Ave 96815 **Location:** Jct Kalakaua Ave and Lewers St. **Facility:** In the heart of Waikiki, this brand-new property is surrounded by many restaurants and shops. The one-bedroom suites feature modern décor and deep soaking tubs. It's just 1 block to the beach. 143 condominiums. 3-15 stories, interior corridors. **Parking:** valet only. **Terms:** check-in 4 pm, 1-7 night minimum stay, cancellation fee imposed. **Amenities:** video games, safes. **Pool(s):** heated outdoor. **Activities:** hot tub, beach access, cabanas, exercise room. **Guest Services:** complimentary and valet laundry.

AAA Benefit: Members save 5% or more!

HOLIDAY INN RESORT WAIKIKI BEACHCOMBER
808/922-4646 **24**

Hotel. Rates not provided. **Address:** 2330 Kalakaua Ave 96815 **Location:** Jct Duke's Ln. **Facility:** 496 units. 2-25 stories, interior corridors. **Parking:** valet only. **Amenities:** safes. **Dining:** Jimmy Buffett's Restaurant & Bar at the Beachcomber, see separate listing, entertainment. **Pool(s):** outdoor. **Activities:** hot tub, beach access, exercise room, spa. **Guest Services:** valet and coin laundry.

HOTEL RENEW
(808)687-7700 **34**

Boutique Hotel
$229-$359

Address: 129 Paokalani Ave 96815 **Location:** Between Kalakaua Ave and Lemon Rd. **Facility:** This Asian-inspired boutique hotel features guest rooms geared more for the business traveler or couples. You'll be pleasantly surprised by the distinctive décor. Try the aroma concierge. 72 units. 9 stories, interior corridors. **Parking:** valet only. **Terms:** 3 day cancellation notice, resort fee. **Amenities:** video games, safes. **Activities:** beach access. **Guest Services:** valet laundry. (See ad starting on p. 148.)

HYATT PLACE WAIKIKI BEACH
(808)922-3861 **33**

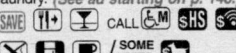

Hotel
$139-$449

HYATT PLACE

AAA Benefit: Members save 10%!

Address: 175 Paokalani Ave 96815 **Location:** Jct Kuhio Ave. **Facility:** 426 units. 2-19 stories, interior corridors. **Parking:** on-site (fee) and valet. **Terms:** cancellation fee imposed. **Amenities:** safes. **Pool(s):** heated outdoor. **Activities:** beach access, exercise room. **Guest Services:** valet and coin laundry. **Featured Amenity:** breakfast buffet. (See ad p. 154.)

HYATT REGENCY WAIKIKI BEACH RESORT & SPA
(808)923-1234 **28**

Hotel
$180-$510

HYATT REGENCY

AAA Benefit: Members save 10%!

Address: 2424 Kalakaua Ave 96815 **Location:** Oceanfront. Between Kaiulani Ave and Uluniu St; entrance on Uluniu St. Across from Waikiki Beach. **Facility:** 1230 units, some two bedrooms. 40 stories, interior corridors. **Parking:** on-site (fee) and valet. **Terms:** 3 day cancellation notice-fee imposed, resort fee. **Amenities:** safes. **Dining:** 2 restaurants, also, JAPENGO, see separate listing, entertainment. **Pool(s):** heated outdoor. **Activities:** hot tub, cabanas, recreation programs, exercise room, spa. **Guest Services:** valet and coin laundry, boarding pass kiosk, rental car service.

ILIMA HOTEL
(808)923-1877 **22**

Hotel $134-$262 **Address:** 445 Nohonani St 96815 **Location:** Between Ala Wai Blvd and Kuhio Ave. **Facility:** 98 kitchen units, some two and three bedrooms. 4-17 stories, interior corridors. **Terms:** 3 day cancellation notice-fee imposed. **Amenities:** safes. **Pool(s):** heated outdoor. **Activities:** sauna, recreation programs, limited exercise equipment. **Guest Services:** coin laundry.

(See map & index p. 142.)

LUANA WAIKIKI

(808)955-6000 **10**

Hotel
$179-$499

Address: 2045 Kalakaua Ave 96815 **Location:** Just w of Namahana St where Kuhio Ave and Kalakaua Ave split. **Facility:** 207 units, some efficiencies and kitchens. 16 stories, interior corridors. **Parking:** valet only. **Terms:** 3 day cancellation notice-fee imposed. **Amenities:** video games, safes. **Pool(s):** heated outdoor. **Activities:** bicycles, exercise room. **Guest Services:** valet and coin laundry, area transportation.

THE MODERN HONOLULU

(808)943-5800 **3**

Contemporary
Resort Hotel
$309-$999

Address: 1775 Ala Moana Blvd 96815 **Location:** Jct Hobron Ln. **Facility:** This beautiful, upscale property boasts amenities and service that will leave a lasting impression. Everything in the hotel is custom designed. Most guest rooms have a private terrace. 353 units, some two bedrooms. 18 stories, interior corridors. **Parking:** on-site (fee) and valet. **Terms:** 3 day cancellation notice-fee imposed. **Amenities:** video games, safes. **Dining:** Morimoto Waikiki, see separate listing, nightclub, entertainment. **Pool(s):** heated outdoor. **Activities:** beach access, spa. **Guest Services:** valet laundry.

▼ See AAA listing p. 152 ▼

HAWOWAII

WE ARE READY TO *WOW* YOU.

With 10% off Best Available Rate, we are bursting with Aloha Spirit. The Hyatt Place Waikiki Beach is mere steps to the beach and just moments from Waikiki's best known attractions.

- Guest rooms feature contemporary decor, divided living and sleeping areas
- Private lanai views of the city, ocean and Diamond Head
- Complimentary Wi-Fi and business center
- Complimentary a.m. Kitchen Skillet
- 24/7 Gallery Menu & Market featuring tropical cocktails and wine tastings
- Complimentary 24-hour StayFit Gym with Life Fitness® cardio equipment

Ready to be WOWED? Visit hyattplacewaikikibeach.com or call 888.421.1442.

Hyatt Place Waikiki Beach • 175 Paoakalani Avenue • Honolulu • Hawaii

HYATT
PLACE™

Waikiki Beach

(See map & index p. 142.)

OHANA WAIKIKI EAST
(808)922-5353

Hotel
$309-$719

Address: 150 Kaiulani Ave 96815 **Location:** Corner of Kaiulani and Kuhio aves. **Facility:** 441 units, some two bedrooms and efficiencies. 19 stories, interior corridors. **Parking:** on-site (fee). **Terms:** 3 day cancellation notice-fee imposed, resort fee. **Amenities:** video games, safes. **Dining:** 3 restaurants. **Pool(s):** outdoor. **Activities:** hot tub, exercise room, massage. **Guest Services:** valet and coin laundry, area transportation.

OHANA WAIKIKI MALIA
(808)923-7621

Hotel
$279-$329

Address: 2211 Kuhio Ave 96815 **Location:** Between Lewers St and Royal Hawaiian Ave. **Facility:** 327 units, some two bedrooms and efficiencies. 2-18 stories, interior/exterior corridors. **Parking:** on-site (fee). **Terms:** 3 day cancellation notice-fee imposed, resort fee. **Amenities:** safes. **Dining:** 2 restaurants. **Pool(s):** heated outdoor. **Activities:** hot tub, exercise room. **Guest Services:** valet and coin laundry, area transportation.

OUTRIGGER REEF WAIKIKI BEACH RESORT
(808)923-3111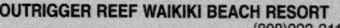

Hotel
$209-$989

Address: 2169 Kalia Rd 96815 **Location:** Oceanfront. Just sw of Kalakaua Ave via Beachwalk. **Facility:** 635 units, some two and three bedrooms. 2-18 stories, interior corridors. *Bath:* shower only. **Parking:** valet only. **Terms:** 3 day cancellation notice-fee imposed. **Amenities:** safes. **Dining:** 3 restaurants, entertainment. **Pool(s):** outdoor. **Activities:** hot tub, recreation programs, exercise room, spa. **Guest Services:** valet and coin laundry, rental car service.

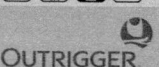 **OUTRIGGER** REEF WAIKIKI BEACH RESORT — Enjoy Hawaiian culture, music & hospitality on Waikiki Beach.

OUTRIGGER WAIKIKI BEACH RESORT
(808)923-0711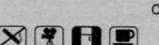

Hotel
$249-$959

Address: 2335 Kalakaua Ave 96815 **Location:** Oceanfront. Between Seaside and Kaiulani aves. **Facility:** 524 units. 16 stories, interior corridors. **Parking:** valet only. **Terms:** 3 day cancellation notice-fee imposed. **Amenities:** safes. **Dining:** Chuck's Steak House, Duke's, Hula Grill Waikiki, see separate listings, entertainment. **Pool(s):** outdoor. **Activities:** hot tub, recreation programs, exercise room, spa. **Guest Services:** valet and coin laundry.

 OUTRIGGER WAIKIKI BEACH RESORT — Located on world famous Waikiki Beach in the heart of Waikiki.

RAMADA PLAZA WAIKIKI
(808)955-1111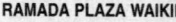

Hotel
$140-$200

Address: 1830 Ala Moana Blvd 96815 **Location:** Between Hobron Ln and Ena Rd. **Facility:** 198 units, some efficiencies. 16 stories, interior corridors. **Parking:** on-site (fee). **Terms:** 3 day cancellation notice-fee imposed. **Amenities:** safes. **Pool(s):** outdoor. **Activities:** exercise room. **Guest Services:** valet and coin laundry.

REGENCY ON BEACHWALK WAIKIKI BY OUTRIGGER
(808)922-3871

Vacation Rental Condominium $169-$339 **Address:** 255 Beachwalk 96815 **Location:** Between Kalakaua Ave and Kalia Rd. **Facility:** These boutique condos have the atmosphere of a private residence yet the sophistication of an upscale hotel with spacious lanais. Pool and business center privileges are offered at the Outrigger Reef. 42 condominiums. 2-9 stories, exterior corridors. *Bath:* shower only. **Parking:** on-site (fee). **Terms:** 2 night minimum stay, 7 day cancellation notice-fee imposed, resort fee. **Amenities:** safes. **Guest Services:** coin laundry.

THE RITZ-CARLTON RESIDENCES, WAIKIKI BEACH
808/445-9083

[fyi] Under construction, scheduled to open May 2016. **Address:** 2112 Kalakaua Ave 96815 **Location:** Jct Kalaimoku St. **Planned Amenities:** 309 units, pets, restaurant, coffeemakers, microwaves, refrigerators, pool, exercise facility.

AAA Benefit: Unequaled service at special member savings!

Discover a wealth of savings and offers

on the AAA/CAA travel websites

(See map & index p. 142.)

SHERATON WAIKIKI RESORT (808)922-4422 **21**

Contemporary
Resort Hotel
$199-$540

Sheraton
HOTELS & RESORTS

AAA Benefit: Members save up to 15%, plus Starwood Preferred Guest® benefits!

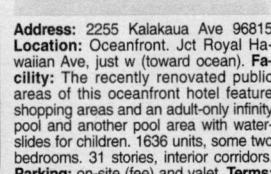

Address: 2255 Kalakaua Ave 96815 **Location:** Oceanfront. Jct Royal Hawaiian Ave, just w (toward ocean). **Facility:** The recently renovated public areas of this oceanfront hotel feature shopping areas and an adult-only infinity pool and another pool area with waterslides for children. 1636 units, some two bedrooms. 31 stories, interior corridors. **Parking:** on-site (fee) and valet. **Terms:** 3 day cancellation notice, resort fee. **Dining:** 5 restaurants, entertainment. **Pool(s):** heated outdoor. **Activities:** hot tub, cabanas, self-propelled boats, snorkeling, recreation programs, kids club, exercise room, spa. **Guest Services:** valet and coin laundry, rental car service.

SHORELINE HOTEL WAIKIKI, A JOIE DE VIVRE HOTEL (808)931-2444 **20**

Boutique
Contemporary
Hotel
$189-$359

Address: 342 Seaside Ave 96815 **Location:** Between Kalakaua and Kuhio aves. **Facility:** This modern boutique hotel is within walking distance of the Royal Hawaiian Shopping Center and just a couple of blocks from famous Waikiki Beach. 135 units. 2-14 stories, interior corridors. **Parking:** valet only. **Terms:** 3 day cancellation notice-fee imposed. **Amenities:** safes. **Pool(s):** outdoor. **Guest Services:** valet laundry.

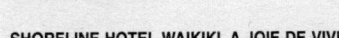

shoreline

TRUMP INTERNATIONAL HOTEL WAIKIKI BEACH WALK (808)683-7777 **11**

 **Contemporary Hotel** $489-$775 **Address:** 223 Saratoga Rd 96815 **Location:** Just sw on Kalakaua Ave via Saratoga Rd. **Facility:** This upscale contemporary hotel with an open-air lobby and wonderful views is across the street from the beach. 305 units, some two bedrooms, three bedrooms, efficiencies and kitchens. 8-38 stories, interior corridors. **Parking:** valet only. **Terms:** check-in 4 pm, 3 day cancellation notice-fee imposed. **Amenities:** safes. **Dining:** 2 restaurants, also, BLT Steak, see separate listing. **Pool(s):** heated outdoor. **Activities:** hot tub, recreation programs, kids club, exercise room, spa. **Guest Services:** valet laundry.

HAWAII PRINCE HOTEL WAIKIKI AND GOLF CLUB 808/956-1111

fyi Not evaluated. **Address:** 100 Holomoana St 96815 **Location:** Oceanfront. Just w of Ala Moana Blvd on Hobron Ln. Facilities, services, and décor characterize a mid-scale property.

MOANA SURFRIDER, A WESTIN RESORT & SPA 808/922-3111

fyi Not evaluated. **Address:** 2365 Kalakaua Ave 96815 **Location:** Oceanfront. Jct Kaiulani Ave. Facilities, services, and décor characterize a mid-scale property.

AAA Benefit: Members save up to 15%, plus Starwood Preferred Guest® benefits!

PACIFIC BEACH HOTEL 808/922-1233

fyi Not evaluated. **Address:** 2490 Kalakaua Ave 96815 **Location:** Oceanfront. Between Liliuokalani and Kealohilani aves. Facilities, services, and décor characterize a mid-scale property.

THE ROYAL HAWAIIAN 808/923-7311

fyi Not evaluated. **Address:** 2259 Kalakaua Ave 96815 **Location:** Oceanfront. Jct Royal Hawaiian Ave. Facilities, services, and décor characterize an upscale property. This lovely historic hotel, built in 1927, offers beautifully renovated public areas and guest rooms in the historic section. The tower offers spectacular ocean views.

AAA Benefit: Members save up to 15%, plus Starwood Preferred Guest® benefits!

VIVE HOTEL WAIKIKI 808/687-2000

fyi Not evaluated. **Address:** 2426 Kuhio Ave 96815 **Location:** Jct Uluniu Ave. Facilities, services, and décor characterize an economy property. Just a couple of blocks from famous Waikiki Beach, this boutique-style hotel offers contemporary and mostly compact guest rooms - great for singles and couples. Complimentary beach gear is offered.

WAIKIKI BEACH MARRIOTT RESORT & SPA 808/922-6611

fyi Not evaluated. **Address:** 2552 Kalakaua Ave 96815 **Location:** Between Kealohilani and Ohua aves. Facilities, services, and décor characterize a mid-scale property.

AAA Benefit: Members save 5% or more!

WHERE TO EAT

AZURE RESTAURANT 808/923-7311 **26**

Seafood. Fine Dining. $30-$60 **AAA Inspector Notes:** Located along the beach at Waikiki, this casual but upscale restaurant with contemporary Moorish architecture features the freshest seafood and small- and large-plate menus that are perfect for sharing. There is also a five course Chef's tasting menu. Reserve a beachside table or cabana on the terrace in advance with a minimum purchase of $175.00 per person. Valet parking for up to four hours is offered. **Features:** full bar, patio dining. **Reservations:** suggested. **Address:** 2259 Kalakaua Ave 96815 **Location:** Jct Royal Hawaiian Ave; in The Royal Hawaiian. **Parking:** valet only.

BALI STEAK & SEAFOOD 808/949-4321 **10**

Steak
Seafood
Fine Dining
$29-$58

AAA Inspector Notes: Skillfully prepared cuisine in an upscale yet relaxing ocean-view dining room makes this place a gem. The fare consists of Black Angus beef, freshly prepared seafood and more, all artfully presented and with an emphasis on locally harvested produce. It's located on the mezzanine level with open windows overlooking the beach and sea. You would be wise to make a reservation at sunset. Validated self and valet parking for up to 4 hours is offered. **Features:** full bar. **Reservations:** suggested. **Address:** 2005 Kalia Rd 96815 **Location:** Jct Ala Moana Blvd; in Hilton Hawaiian Village Waikiki Beach Resort; Rainbow Tower, Mezzanine Level. **Parking:** on-site and valet. **Menu on AAA.com**

BLT STEAK 808/683-7440 **14**

Steak. Fine Dining. $16-$56 **AAA Inspector Notes:** Aged Prime and certified Black Angus beef is prepared by broiling it at 1700 degrees to seal in the flavors. It's served with a selection of delicious sauces. A selection of fresh fish is available, too, at this high-energy restaurant with some creative nightly specials. A pre-fixe three-course meal is offered. Service is professional and attentive. A few outside tables are available. **Features:** full bar, patio dining. **Reservations:** suggested. **Address:** 223 Saratoga Rd 96815 **Location:** Just sw on Kalakaua Ave via Saratoga Rd; in Trump International Hotel Waikiki Beach Walk. **Parking:** valet only.

BUHO 808/922-2846 **23**

New Mexican. Casual Dining. $10-$30 **AAA Inspector Notes:** Take the outside elevator near Victoria's Secret up to the fourth floor to enjoy open-air rooftop dining and drinks among simple contemporary décor with views of Waikiki. The island-influenced modern fare features fresh, locally sourced ingredients. A nice selection of tequila as well as hand-crafted cocktails made with the liquor are offered. Every fifth of the month includes live music, interactive food stations and drink specials. **Features:** full bar, happy hour. **Reservations:** suggested. **Address:** 2250 Kalakaua Ave 96815 **Location:** Jct Royal Hawaiian Ave; in Waikiki Shopping Plaza, Suite 525. **Parking:** street only.

(See map & index p. 142.)

CHART HOUSE WAIKIKI   808/941-6669 6

American
Casual Dining
$24-$52

AAA Inspector Notes: This longtime gathering spot offers sunset views over the Ala Wai Yacht Harbor. Prime steaks and fresh seafood are featured along with signature desserts and drinks. The sunset dinner special is $30.50. Partially validated 4-hour parking is offered at an adjacent garage for $5. **Features:** full bar, patio dining, early bird specials, happy hour. **Reservations:** suggested. **Address:** 1765 Ala Moana Blvd 96815 **Location:** Just ne of jct Hobron Ln; entrance on Holomoana St; at Ala Wai Yacht Harbor. **Parking:** on-site (fee) and street. *Menu on AAA.com* D CALL ♿M

CHEESEBURGER WAIKIKI   808/941-2400 11

American. Casual Dining. $10-$15 **AAA Inspector Notes:** If you're looking for a burger, this open-air dining establishment is the place for you. Choose from several different styles of cheeseburgers, sandwiches, salads, fries and onion rings that are meant for sharing. Service is handled by an enthusiastic young staff. **Features:** full bar, patio dining, happy hour. **Address:** 1945 Kalakaua Ave 96815 **Location:** Corner of Kalakaua Ave and Ala Moana Blvd.

B L D CALL ♿M AC

CHUCK'S STEAK HOUSE   808/923-1228

Steak. Casual Dining. $29-$42 **AAA Inspector Notes:** With its origins in Waikiki since 1959, the concept quickly spread across the country and Pacific Rim. Boasting the first ever self-serve all-you-can-eat salad bar concept and featuring USDA Prime Grade steaks, diners can rest assured that whichever Chuck's they choose they will find consistency in quality and style of operation. The salad bar is included with each entrée. **Features:** full bar, early bird specials, happy hour. **Address:** 2335 Kalakaua Ave 96815 **Location:** Between Seaside and Kaiulani aves; in Outrigger Waikiki Beach Resort. **Parking:** valet only. D CALL ♿M AC

D.K STEAK HOUSE   808/931-6280 36

Steak Seafood. Casual Dining. $24-$85 **AAA Inspector Notes:** Dry-aged or classically aged U.S. high-grade beef is prepared just the way you like it. Locally grown products are used wherever possible. Add some wine from the outstanding wine list—16 wines by the glass are offered. If you'd like something different, try the fresh catch of the day. There's even a keiki (children's) menu with soft drink and choice of ice cream for dessert. There are a few tables on the lanai with ocean views. Enter from Ohua Avenue for self-validated parking. **Features:** full bar, patio dining. **Reservations:** suggested. **Address:** 2552 Kalakaua Ave 96815 **Location:** Between Kealohilani and Ohua aves; in Waikiki Beach Marriott Resort & Spa. **Parking:** on-site (fee) and valet. D CALL ♿M

DUKE'S   808/922-2268

Hawaiian Fusion. Casual Dining. $10-$33 **AAA Inspector Notes:** The sands of Waikiki Beach rise up to the door of this lively establishment. Photographs and memorabilia of Duke Kahanamoku, the famous Olympic swimmer and Hawaiian surfer, adorn the walls. Light choices, including appetizers, burgers and salads, share menu space with a full complement of chicken, fish and seafood entrées. Patrons also can sample the all-you-can-eat salad bar. Live Hawaiian music is featured nightly. Three-hour validated parking is offered at Ohana East for a nominal fee. **Features:** full bar. **Reservations:** suggested. **Address:** 2335 Kalakaua Ave 96815 **Location:** Between Seaside and Kaiulani aves; in Outrigger Waikiki on the Beach. **Parking:** on-site (fee) and valet.

B L D AC

EGGS 'N THINGS   808/926-3447 33

Breakfast. Family Dining. $9-$17 **AAA Inspector Notes:** The expansive breakfast menu at this busy, basic open-air eatery includes a variety of omelets and pancakes. Portions are large, so come hungry. Plan to arrive by 7 am for breakfast to avoid a long wait. Tables are sometimes shared with other patrons and counter seating is available. A few dinner entrée options are available in the evening. **Address:** 2464 Kalakaua Ave 96815 **Location:** Between Uluniu St and Liliuokalani Ave; in Aston Waikiki Circle Hotel. **Parking:** street only. B L D AC

HARD ROCK CAFE   808/955-7383 13

American. Casual Dining. $12-$24 **AAA Inspector Notes:** Rock 'n' roll memorabilia decorates the walls of the popular theme restaurant. Live music on the weekends contributes to the bustling atmosphere. On the menu is a wide variety of American cuisine—from burgers and sandwiches to seafood, steaks and pasta. **Features:** full bar, patio dining, happy hour. **Address:** 280 Beachwalk Blvd 96815 **Location:** Corner of Kalakaua Ave. **Parking:** on-site (fee).

SAVE L D LATE CALL ♿M

HOUSE WITHOUT A KEY   808/923-2311 21

International. Casual Dining. $16-$46 **AAA Inspector Notes:** One of Waikiki's favorite traditions, from the original Halekalani, of cocktails at sunset and Hawaiian music under the 100-year-old kiawe tree is still ongoing at this casual restaurant located near the ocean. The varied menu offers fresh, local ingredients with Hawaiian influences. The staff is well trained. The sunset kiawe grill is offered Tuesday and Thursday 5-8:30 pm. Save room for the signature coconut cake. Arrive early to avoid disappointment as reservations are not accepted. **Features:** full bar, patio dining. **Address:** 2199 Kalia Rd 96815 **Location:** Just sw of Kalakaua Ave via Lewers St; in Halekulani. **Parking:** valet only.

B L D CALL ♿M AC

HULA GRILL WAIKIKI   808/923-4852 30

Regional American. Casual Dining. $21-$34 **AAA Inspector Notes:** This popular spot features an outstanding location with an open-air dining room overlooking Waikiki beach and an island-flavored menu. Diners may enjoy pupu such as imu-style barbecue ribs or Kalua pork pot stickers to start, followed by salads featuring Maui onions. The mains focus on seafood, with choices such as macadamia nut-crusted mahi mahi, fire-grilled ono, or shrimp and lobster selections. Save room for the hula pie. Sunset dinner special from 4:45 to 6 pm. **Features:** full bar, patio dining, early bird specials, Sunday brunch, happy hour. **Reservations:** suggested. **Address:** 2335 Kalakaua Ave 96815 **Location:** Between Seaside and Kaiulani aves; in Outrigger Waikiki on the Beach. **Parking:** on-site (fee) and valet. B D CALL ♿M AC

HY'S STEAKHOUSE   808/922-5555 31

Steak. Fine Dining. $28-$80 **AAA Inspector Notes:** The locals love this place and for good reasons: Flavorful steaks, an attentive waitstaff and cozy surroundings are found in each of the dining rooms. For starters, diners can perk up their appetites with the much-talked-about cheese bread. Then they can select one of several USDA Prime aged beefsteaks broiled over native kiawe wood or fresh Hawaiian fish prepared in a variety of ways. Caesar salads and flaming desserts are prepared tableside. **Features:** full bar. **Reservations:** suggested. **Address:** 2440 Kuhio Ave 96815 **Location:** Jct Uluniu St; in Waikiki Park Heights Hotel. **Parking:** valet only.

D CALL ♿M

JAPENGO   808/237-6180 32

Pacific Rim Sushi. Casual Dining. $18-$49 **AAA Inspector Notes:** This new restaurant offers Pacific Rim and southeast Asian cuisines in a contemporary setting. A few menu selections feature locally grown ingredients from the Hawaiian Islands. Sushi bar and semi-private and private dining areas are available. Validated parking for 4 hours is offered. **Features:** full bar, happy hour. **Reservations:** suggested. **Address:** 2424 Kalakaua Ave 96815 **Location:** Between Kaiulani Ave and Uluniu St; entrance on Uluniu St; in Hyatt Regency Waikiki Beach Resort & Spa. **Parking:** on-site (fee) and valet. D CALL ♿M

JIMMY BUFFETT'S RESTAURANT & BAR AT THE BEACHCOMBER   808/791-1200 29

American. Casual Dining. $13-$30 **AAA Inspector Notes:** Take the elevator up to the second floor. This lively, high-energy restaurant with nightly entertainment offers a buffet at breakfast and sandwiches, burgers and several entrée selections for lunch and dinner. Validated parking when guests use the hotel valet is $3 for 3 hours. **Features:** full bar, patio dining, happy hour. **Address:** 2300 Kalakaua Ave 96815 **Location:** Jct Duke's Ln; in Holiday Inn Resort Waikiki Beachcomber. **Parking:** valet only.

B L D LATE CALL ♿M

(See map & index p. 142.)

KAIWA WAIKIKI
808/924-1555 (15)

▼▼▼ Japanese. Casual Dining. $26-$60 AAA Inspector Notes: Located on the second floor of the new Beach Walk area on Lewers Street, this Tokyo-based teppan fusion and sushi roll restaurant offers an ultra-chic atmosphere inspired by the high energy of Waikiki. Enjoy fresh fish from the Hawaiian waters as well as a large selection of Japanese sake. Outdoor seating overlooks the street scene. Validated parking for a fee is available at the nearby Embassy Suites. Features: full bar, patio dining, happy hour. Reservations: suggested. Address: 226 Lewers St, 2nd Floor 96815 Location: Just s of Kalakaua Ave; in Waikiki Beach Walk. Parking: street only.

[L] [D] CALL [&M]

KOBE JAPANESE STEAK HOUSE & SUSHI BAR
808/941-4444 (9)

▼▼ Japanese Steak. Casual Dining. $15-$50 AAA Inspector Notes: For more than 44 years the skilled antics of the chefs have delighted diners who watch as the steak, chicken or seafood dish of their choice is prepared tableside at shared tables for eight. Although the décor hasn't changed much over the years, this is still a great place to meet and greet your dining partners and enjoy the food and camaraderie. Recommended is the melt-in-your mouth filet mignon. Features: full bar, happy hour. Reservations: suggested. Address: 1841 Ala Moana Blvd 96815 Location: Just w from jct Ena Rd. Parking: valet only. [D]

LA MER
808/923-2311 (19)

▼▼▼ ▼▼

French
Fine Dining
$110-$195

AAA Inspector Notes: The elegant oceanfront setting affords great views of Diamond Head and the surf below. Provence-style French dishes made with fresh island ingredients show meticulous preparation and subtle presentation. Enjoy a European cocktail while perusing the sophisticated menu. Long-sleeve collared shirts or jackets with short sleeve shirts are suggested for gentlemen. Complimentary validated parking for four hours is available. Features: full bar. Reservations: suggested. Semiformal attire. Address: 2199 Kalia Rd 96815 Location: Just sw of Kalakaua Ave via Lewers St; in Halekulani. Parking: on-site and valet.

Menu on AAA.com [D] CALL [&M]

MORIMOTO WAIKIKI
808/943-5900 (7)

▼▼▼ New Japanese Sushi. Fine Dining. $17-$80 AAA Inspector Notes: The open and airy contemporary dining room showcases the distinctive, creative contemporary Japanese cuisine skillfully combining quality Western and local ingredients from the islands wherever possible. The full sushi bar faces the expansive open kitchen. The open-air terrace with fire pits overlooks the yacht harbor. Valet parking is validated for three hours by the restaurant. Features: full bar, patio dining. Reservations: suggested. Address: 1775 Ala Moana Blvd 96815 Location: Jct Hobron Ln; in The Modern Honolulu. Parking: valet and street only. [B] [L] [D] CALL [&M]

NOBU
808/237-6999 (22)

▼▼▼ Pacific Rim. Casual Dining. $10-$40 AAA Inspector Notes: Contemporary Pacific Rim and Peruvian-Japanese cuisine is offered at this restaurant with modern décor and a sushi bar. Servers are attentive. Parking is validated for two hours at the lot adjacent to the Waikiki Parc Hotel. Features: full bar, happy hour. Reservations: suggested. Address: 2233 Helumoa Rd 96815 Location: Just sw of Kalakaua Ave via Lewers St; in Waikiki Parc Hotel. Parking: on-site (fee) and street. [◄] [D] CALL [&M]

OCEANARIUM RESTAURANT
808/921-6111 (34)

▼▼ Seafood. Casual Dining. $21-$48 AAA Inspector Notes: The 280,000-gallon, three-story indoor oceanarium offers tableside views of colorful reef fish. Breakfast, weekend and prime rib and seafood dinner buffets offer an extensive variety with several stations, including seafood pasta and Asian stations. Alaskan king crab legs are featured on Monday and Thursday. Fish feedings by the restaurants' divers and mermaid sightings are featured daily; feeding times can vary. Reserve far in advance to ensure a table near the oceanarium. Features: full bar, Sunday brunch. Reservations: suggested. Address: 2490 Kalakaua Ave 96815 Location: Between Liliuokalani and Kealohilani aves; in Pacific Beach Hotel. Parking: valet and street only. [B] [D] CALL [&M]

ORCHIDS
808/923-2311 (20)

▼▼▼ ▼▼▼ Pacific Rim. Fine Dining. $29-$54 AAA Inspector Notes: Like its namesake flower, this restaurant is elegant, uncomplicated and understated. Patrons can unwind in a comfortable, open-air setting to enjoy creative regional Pacific cuisine that emphasizes contemporary seafood. The best tables are the ones located around the lower patio with views of the ocean. Afternoon tea is offered Monday through Saturday from 3 to 5 pm. Complimentary 4-hour parking is offered with validation. Features: full bar, patio dining, Sunday brunch. Reservations: suggested. Address: 2199 Kalia Rd 96815 Location: Just sw of Kalakaua Ave via Lewers St; in Halekulani. Parking: on-site and valet.

[B] [L] [D] CALL [&M] [✕]

P.F. CHANG'S CHINA BISTRO
808/628-6760 (17)

▼▼▼ Chinese. Fine Dining. $11-$32 AAA Inspector Notes: Trendy, upscale decor provides a pleasant backdrop for New Age Chinese dining. Appetizers, soups and salads are a meal by themselves. Vegetarian plates and sides, noodles, chow meins, chicken and meat dishes are created from exotic, fresh ingredients. Features: full bar, happy hour. Reservations: suggested. Address: 2201 Kalakaua Ave 96815 Location: Jct Lewers St; in Royal Hawaiian Shopping Center. Parking: valet only. [L] [D] CALL [&M]

PINEAPPLE ROOM BY ALAN WONG
808/945-6573 (3)

▼▼▼ Pacific Rim. Casual Dining. $15-$45 AAA Inspector Notes: At this restaurant on the third floor of Macy's in the Ala Moana Center the chef and his staff offer a unique taste of Hawaiian regional cuisine with the freshest locally grown produce and the bounties of the Pacific Ocean. The Hawaiian plantation style décor is welcoming. Features: full bar. Reservations: suggested. Address: 1450 Ala Moana Blvd 96814 Location: Jct Atkinson Dr; in Ala Moana Shopping Center, Macy's Department Store, 3rd Floor. [L] [D]

RESTAURANT SUNTORY
808/922-5511 (25)

▼▼▼ Japanese Sushi Specialty. Fine Dining. $14-$72 AAA Inspector Notes: Skillfully prepared, authentic teppanyaki dishes, shabu shabu, sushi and Washoku dinners with the traditional course menu offerings are featured at this restaurant . The lunch option is a good value. Reservations are suggested for the popular sushi bar. Validated parking, with a nominal fee after the first hour, is offered. Features: full bar. Reservations: suggested. Address: 2233 Kalakaua Ave 96815 Location: Jct Lewers St; in Royal Hawaiian Shopping Center. Parking: on-site and street. [L] [D] CALL [&M]

ROYAL GARDEN CHINESE RESTAURANT
808/942-7788 (5)

▼▼ Chinese Dim Sum. Casual Dining. $9-$25 AAA Inspector Notes: Close to Waikiki, this nicely decorated restaurant offers authentic Hong Kong-style dim sum at lunchtime. The dim sum carts are stacked with bamboo steamer baskets filled with shrimp and pork dumplings, steamed buns and other tasty items. The carts come around frequently and you also can order off the menu at lunch. Dinner features Hong Kong-style dishes. Arrive early without a reservation to avoid a long wait at lunchtime. Features: full bar. Reservations: suggested. Address: 410 Atkinson Dr 96814 Location: Adjacent to Ala Moana Shopping Center; in Ala Moana Hotel. Parking: valet and street only. [◄] [L] [D] CALL [&M]

ROY'S
808/923-7697 (18)

▼▼▼ Pacific Rim Fusion. Fine Dining. $15-$48 AAA Inspector Notes: Enjoy fusion of fresh Pacific seafood, French sauces and Asian seasonings. The ever-changing menu has many entrées such as grilled salmon and barbecue lamb rack, and the signature dessert, chocolate soufflé. Features: full bar, patio dining. Reservations: suggested. Address: 226 Lewers St 96815 Location: Between Lewers St and Saratoga Rd; 2 blks from Waikiki Beach; in Embassy Suites by Hilton Waikiki Beach Walk. Parking: on-site (fee) and valet. [D] CALL [&M]

RUTH'S CHRIS STEAK HOUSE
808/440-7910 (16)

▼▼ Steak. Fine Dining. $27-$60 AAA Inspector Notes: The main fare is steak, which is prepared from several cuts of Prime beef and cooked to perfection, but the menu also lists lamb, chicken and seafood dishes. Guests should come hungry because the side dishes, which are among the a la carte offerings, could make a meal in themselves. Features: full bar, patio dining, happy hour. Reservations: suggested. Address: 226 Lewers St 96815 Location: Just w of Kalakaua Ave; in Waikiki Beach Walk. Parking: valet only.

[D]

(See map & index p. 142.)

SANSEI SEAFOOD RESTAURANT & SUSHI BAR
808/931-6286 (35)

New Japanese Sushi Fusion. Casual Dining. $17-$31 **AAA Inspector Notes:** This upbeat restaurant is a popular addition to Waikiki's dining scene. The menu centers on Japanese and Asian cuisine, including specialty sushi rolls. You also can dine at the sushi bar or on the balcony with views of the ocean. The beverage list is extensive and there are sake flights, too. Open late on Friday and Saturday nights. Parking is validated for 3 hours. **Features:** full bar, patio dining, early bird specials, happy hour. **Reservations:** suggested. **Address:** 2552 Kalakaua Ave 96815 **Location:** Between Kealohilani and Ohua aves; in Waikiki Beach Marriott Resort & Spa. **Parking:** on-site and valet. [D] CALL [&M]

SARENTO'S AT THE TOP OF THE ILIKAI
808/955-5559 (8)

Italian. Fine Dining. $20-$42 **AAA Inspector Notes:** Take the special glass-enclosed elevator up to the 30th floor where you will find an attentive young staff serving this restaurant's hallmark regional Italian fare in any one of four ocean/city-view dining rooms. Seafood fra diavolo served over linguine, chicken rigatoni alla vodka and osso buco are just a few of the delicious menu items offered. Best time to make your reservation is just at sunset to truly appreciate the memorable view. Validated valet parking is $5. **Features:** full bar, happy hour. **Reservations:** suggested. **Address:** 1777 Ala Moana Blvd 96815 **Location:** Between Hobron Ln and Harbor Rd; in Ilikai Hotel. **Parking:** valet only. [D] CALL [&M]

SHOKUDO JAPANESE RESTAURANT & BAR
808/941-3701 (1)

Japanese Fusion. Casual Dining. $9-$25 **AAA Inspector Notes:** Creative, fun modern fusion cuisine is offered at this restaurant with a large patio and comfortable seating out front and a contemporary dining room. Some of the menu items include sushi pizza, chicken teriyaki quesadillas and ishiyaki (food served sizzling in a hot stone bowl), all perfect for sharing. Be sure to make a reservation to avoid a long wait. Validated parking is behind the restaurant; enter on Kona Street. **Reservations:** suggested. **Address:** 1585 Kapiolani Blvd 96814 **Location:** Jct Mahukona St; in Ala Moana Pacific Center, Ground Floor. **Parking:** on-site (fee) and street.
[L] [D] [LATE] CALL [&M]

THE SIGNATURE PRIME STEAK & SEAFOOD
808/949-3636 (4)

Steak Seafood. Fine Dining. $30-$65 **AAA Inspector Notes:** Plan to arrive early enough to catch the sunset and wonderful views of the Waikiki skyline. Bone-in rib-eye, miso butterfish and rack of lamb are just a few of the savory menu items at this sophisticated upscale restaurant. Take the exclusive elevator from the hotel lobby to the 36th floor. Live piano music is offered, and you can even sit at the piano and dine. **Features:** full bar, happy hour. **Reservations:** suggested. **Address:** 410 Atkinson Dr 96814 **Location:** Adjacent to Ala Moana Shopping Center; located in Ala Moana Hotel. **Parking:** valet only. [⊟] [D] CALL [&M]

TANAKA OF TOKYO CENTRAL
808/922-4702 (24)

Japanese Steak. Casual Dining. $20-$50 **AAA Inspector Notes:** Patrons watch master teppanyaki chefs prepare certified Black Angus sirloin and quality seafood in front of them on tabletop grills. Service is attentive. Two-hour validated parking is available. **Features:** full bar. **Reservations:** suggested. **Address:** 2250 Kalakaua Ave 96815 **Location:** Jct Royal Hawaiian Ave; in Waikiki Shopping Plaza, 3rd Floor. **Parking:** on-site (fee). [D]

TANAKA OF TOKYO WEST
808/945-3443 (2)

Japanese Steak Seafood. Casual Dining. $20-$46 **AAA Inspector Notes:** Steak and seafood are prepared by teppanyaki chefs with flair at your tabletop grill. Experience first hand the onion volcano, the egg roll and all the fork-and-knife twirling you can handle! **Features:** full bar. **Reservations:** suggested. **Address:** 1450 Ala Moana Blvd 96814 **Location:** Jct Atkinson Dr; in Ala Moana Shopping Center, Hookipa Terrace, 4th Floor.
[L] [D] CALL [&M]

TIKI'S GRILL & BAR
808/923-8454 (37)

American. Casual Dining. $12-$29 **AAA Inspector Notes:** Overlooking Waikiki Beach, this restaurant's second-floor location is perfect for evening sunsets or simply people watching. The menu features a mix of local seafood entrées as well as burgers and sandwiches. The large outdoor patio bar is usually hopping each evening and has live music nightly. Three-hour validated parking is offered. **Features:** full bar, patio dining, happy hour. **Reservations:** suggested. **Address:** 2570 Kalakaua Ave 96815 **Location:** Between Paoakalani and Kapahulu aves; in Aston Waikiki Beach Hotel. **Parking:** valet only. [L] [D] [LATE] CALL [&M]

TOP OF WAIKIKI
808/923-3877 (27)

Pacific Rim. Fine Dining. $25-$44 **AAA Inspector Notes:** Dine on nicely prepared entrées from a varied menu that offers some island inspirations at Hawaii's only revolving restaurant on three levels. The real draws are the dramatic skyline views; it takes about an hour for one revolution. Take the elevator up to the 18th floor and then the escalators to reach the restaurant. Be sure to make a reservation to enjoy the sunset views. Prix fixe dinners are available. **Features:** full bar, happy hour. **Reservations:** suggested. **Address:** 2270 Kalakaua Ave, 21st Floor 96815 **Location:** Jct Seaside Ave; in Waikiki Business Plaza. **Parking:** on-site (fee). [D]

WAIKIKI STARLIGHT LUAU
808/941-5828 (12)

Hawaiian. Casual Dining. $99-$125 **AAA Inspector Notes:** This lū'au offers a large buffet of Polynesian-style foods and a nicely narrated Polynesian show in an idyllic urban setting on the rooftop at the Mid-Pacific Conference Center. Plan to arrive when the doors open at 5 pm for better seating. Complimentary validated self or valet parking is offered. **Features:** full bar. **Reservations:** required. **Address:** 2005 Kalia Rd 96815 **Location:** Jct Ala Moana Blvd; in Hilton Hawaiian Village Waikiki Beach Resort. **Parking:** on-site and valet.
[D] CALL [&M] [🎵]

WOLFGANG'S STEAKHOUSE
808/922-3600 (28)

Steak. Fine Dining. $14-$56 **AAA Inspector Notes:** Take the escalator up to the third floor to find this restaurant with a few tables overlooking the street scene of Kalakaua Avenue. USDA Prime dry-aged Black Angus beef is served, along with a few seafood selections. The side dishes are meant to be shared. The menu can be pricey, but the servers are always courteous. Brunch is served Saturday and Sunday. Parking is validated for one hour when you park in the Royal Hawaiian Center lot on Royal Hawaiian Ave. **Features:** full bar, Sunday brunch, happy hour. **Reservations:** suggested. **Address:** 2301 Kalakaua Ave 96815 **Location:** Jct Seaside Ave; in Royal Hawaiian Shopping Center, 3rd Level. **Parking:** on-site (fee) and street. [L] [D] CALL [&M]

YARD HOUSE
808/923-9273

American. Casual Dining. $10-$28 **AAA Inspector Notes:** Loud and bustling and blaring classic rock music, the bar area takes center stage at this popular ale house and dinner spot that boasts more than 100 beers from around the world on tap with the kegs viewable in the transparent keg room. The menu offers favorites ranging from steaks and burgers to chicken, fish and pastas. Come thirsty. **Features:** full bar, happy hour. **Address:** 226 Lewers St 96815 **Location:** Just s of Kalakaua Ave. **Parking:** street only.
[L] [D] [LATE] CALL [&M]

BEACHHOUSE AT THE MOANA
808/931-8383

[fyi] Not evaluated. This delightful dining room is filled with Hawaiian tradition and, while expensive, is worth a visit for breakfast, traditional afternoon tea or a sunset dinner. Dining also is offered on a covered outdoor veranda. The setting is magical, facing a huge 100-year-old banyan tree in the outdoor patio area and featuring Hawaiian entertainment each evening. The menu offers a nice selection of steak, lobster and other seafood. **Address:** 2365 Kalakaua Ave 96815 **Location:** Jct Kaiulani Ave; in Moana Surfrider, A Westin Resort & Spa.

WAILANA COFFEE HOUSE
808/955-1764

[fyi] Not evaluated. Reasonably priced good food is offered in a casual setting. Across from the Hilton Hawaiian Village, this is the place to go when feeding a family on a budget. The waitresses serve up breakfast, burgers, sandwiches, dinner entrées and daily specials. A salad bar is available. Breakfast is available 24 hours. Large windows overlook busy Ala Moana Boulevard. This restaurant has been around for more than 40 years and is part of the history of Waikiki. **Address:** 1860 Ala Moana Blvd 96815 **Location:** Corner of Ena Rd and Ala Moana Blvd.

HONOLULU (I-5)

- Attractions map p. 118
- Hotels & Restaurants map & index p. 145

AIRPORT HONOLULU HOTEL   (808)836-0661 **1**

Hotel
$109-$189

Address: 3401 N Nimitz Hwy 96819 **Location:** Jct Rodgers Blvd. Next to busy interstate. **Facility:** 307 units. 4 stories, interior corridors. **Parking:** on-site (fee). **Terms:** 3 day cancellation notice-fee imposed. **Pool(s):** outdoor. **Activities:** exercise room. **Guest Services:** valet and coin laundry.

BEST WESTERN THE PLAZA HOTEL   (808)836-3636 **2**

Hotel
$169-$209

AAA Benefit: Save 10% or more every day and earn 10% bonus points!

Address: 3253 N Nimitz Hwy 96819 **Location:** Just e of jct Paiea St. Next to busy interstate. **Facility:** 274 units. 6-12 stories, interior/exterior corridors. **Parking:** on-site (fee). **Terms:** cancellation fee imposed. **Pool(s):** outdoor. **Activities:** exercise room. **Guest Services:** valet and coin laundry.

THE KAHALA HOTEL & RESORT   (808)739-8888 **5**

Hotel
$395-$595

Address: 5000 Kahala Ave 96816 **Location:** Oceanfront. E of Diamond Head at end of Kahala Ave. Located in a quiet residential area. **Facility:** Just minutes from Waikiki Beach, this luxury resort in Oahu's most exclusive residential area has hosted honeymooners and multigenerational families. Romantic beach dining is offered. 338 units. 2-10 stories, interior corridors. **Parking:** on-site (fee) and valet. **Terms:** 3 day cancellation notice-fee imposed. **Amenities:** video games, safes. **Dining:** 5 restaurants, also, Arancino at the Kahala, Hoku's, see separate listings, entertainment.

Pool(s): heated outdoor. **Activities:** sauna, hot tub, steamroom, cabanas, self-propelled boats, fishing, scuba diving, snorkeling, recreation programs, kids club, bicycles, spa. **Guest Services:** valet laundry, rental car service, area transportation. **Featured Amenity:** breakfast buffet.

LOTUS HONOLULU   (808)922-1700 **4**

Boutique Contemporary Hotel $319-$409 **Address:** 2885 Kalakaua Ave 96815 **Location:** East end of Kapiolani Park. Located at Diamond Head end of Waikiki. **Facility:** Rooms at this small boutique hotel have been recently renovated and have some upscale enhancements to include private, spacious lanais with Diamond Head and partial ocean views. 51 units, some two bedrooms and kitchens. 12 stories, exterior corridors. **Parking:** valet only. **Terms:** 3 day cancellation notice-fee imposed. **Amenities:** video games, safes. **Activities:** beach access, bicycles. **Guest Services:** valet and coin laundry, area transportation.

THE NEW OTANI KAIMANA BEACH HOTEL
(808)923-1555 **3**

Hotel $250-$1800 **Address:** 2863 Kalakaua Ave 96815 **Location:** Oceanfront. Southeast end of Kapiolani Park. **Facility:** 125 units. 9 stories, interior corridors. **Parking:** valet only. **Terms:** 3 day cancellation notice-fee imposed. **Amenities:** safes. **Dining:** 2 restaurants, also, Hau Tree Lanai, see separate listing. **Activities:** self-propelled boats, exercise room, spa. **Guest Services:** valet and coin laundry.

MARINA TOWER   808/949-0061

fyi Not evaluated. **Address:** 1700 Ala Moana Blvd 96815 **Location:** Just e of Hobron Ln. Facilities, services, and décor characterize an economy property.

WHERE TO EAT

12TH AVENUE GRILL   808/732-9469 **28**

Regional American. Casual Dining. $23-$36 **AAA Inspector Notes:** Located outside of Waikiki, this wonderful neighborhood bistro serves contemporary cooking such as braised short ribs, pork chops, Big Island rib-eye steak and organic chicken breast. Fresh ingredients from island farms are utilized. There are daily specials and a fresh fish of the day prepared according to the chef's desire. Be sure to save room for their mouthwatering desserts. **Features:** full bar, happy hour. **Reservations:** suggested. **Address:** 1120 12th Ave 96816 **Location:** Between Waialae and Harding aves. **Parking:** street only. **D**

3660 ON THE RISE   808/737-1177 **29**

Pacific Rim. Fine Dining. $22-$49 **AAA Inspector Notes:** Just outside of the Waikiki area in the Kaimuki neighborhood, this popular restaurant is ideal for a pleasant evening out. Unwind with a drink from their extensive martini list. Known for its signature ahi katsu and New York steak alaea dishes, the menu mixes the flavors of Hawaii, Europe and Asia. The restaurant shares space with a bank. Complimentary validated parking is located under the building. Another pay lot is behind the building. **Features:** full bar. **Reservations:** suggested. **Address:** 3660 Waialae Ave 96816 **Location:** Between Wilhelmina Rise and 13th Ave. **Parking:** on-site and street. **D** CALL

ALAN WONG'S RESTAURANT   808/949-2526 **18**

Pacific Rim. Fine Dining. $31-$48 **AAA Inspector Notes:** Just outside Waikiki, this is among Oahu's longtime favorite restaurants. Service is handled by attentive and eager young staff members whose knowledge of the menu is impressive. Menu listings marked with a pineapple designation are signature dishes. Best of all is the coconut dessert, a chocolate shell that looks like a coconut but is filled with soft ice cream. Prix-fixe menus are available. A few tables have mountain views. Valet parking is $5. **Features:** full bar. **Reservations:** suggested. **Address:** 1857 S King St, 3rd Floor 96826 **Location:** Between Pumehana and Artesian sts. **Parking:** valet and street only. **D** CALL

BIG KAHUNA'S PIZZA 'N STUFF   808/833-5588 **1**

Pizza. Quick Serve. $6-$22 **AAA Inspector Notes:** Not far from the airport, this cash-only eatery offers traditional and several specialty pizzas with a local twist. You might try the Kalua pork pizza, chicken teriyaki pizza or the Portuguese sausage pizza. Sandwiches and garlic cheese balls also are offered. Call ahead to reserve a table and place your order; your pizza will be ready when you arrive. **Address:** 550 Paiea St 96819 **Location:** Off Nimitz Hwy, just e on Paiea St, jct Koapaka St; in Airport Trade Center. **L** **D** CALL

CHEF MAVRO   808/944-4714 **19**

Regional Hawaiian Fine Dining
$85-$175

AAA Inspector Notes: Elegant island décor created by local designer Mary Philpotts immerses diners in a soft, mellow glow. Chef Mavrothalassitis is the founding member of Hawaiian Regional Cuisine and, with his dynamic team of chefs, is on the cutting edge of trendsetters focused on only the freshest seafood and produce from trusted local purveyors. **Features:** full bar. **Reservations:** suggested. **Address:** 1969 S King St 96826 **Location:** Corner of S King and McCully sts; enter on S King St. **D** CALL

(See map & index p. 145.)

GORDON BIERSCH BREWERY RESTAURANT 808/599-4877
♦♦ American. Casual Dining. $10-$28 **AAA Inspector Notes:** As the name implies, this restaurant features fresh, handcrafted beers, brewed on-site, which are crafted in a German tradition. What may not be evident is the wide variety of foods like meal-sized salads, burgers and sandwiches, made-from-scratch pizzas and flatbread, pastas, steaks and seafood offered for a casual dining experience. A lighter menu is available, too. The lanai looks out onto the harbor. Live music most nights. **Features:** full bar, patio dining, happy hour. **Reservations:** suggested. **Address:** 1 Aloha Tower Dr, Suite 1123 96813 **Location:** In Aloha Tower Marketplace. **Parking:** on-site (fee) and valet. [L] [D] [LATE] CALL 🅐Ⓜ 🅐Ⓒ

GYOTAKU JAPANESE RESTAURANT 808/949-4584 (17)
♦♦ Japanese. Casual Dining. $10-$37 **AAA Inspector Notes:** Dine downstairs or upstairs at this restaurant with simple décor. It's known for its popular "ten-pura"—not tempura—a crispy, light batter that coats a serving of deep-fried vegetables. The menu is visually appealing with pictures of all the items, making it easy to decide on what to order. Order individual sushi or complete meals at reasonable prices. Lunch and early specials are available on certain days. A variety of sakes is offered. **Features:** beer & wine, early bird specials, senior menu. **Address:** 1824 S King St 96826 **Location:** Just w of McCully St. [L] [D]

HAU TREE LANAI 808/921-7066 (30)
♦♦♦ Pacific Rim Seafood. Fine Dining. $15-$69 **AAA Inspector Notes:** *Classic.* Watching the sunset is an event at this longtime restaurant. Dine on fresh seafood from the Hawaiian waters or the prix fixe four-course menu for $69. The restaurant overlooks the beach beneath ancient hau trees where author Robert Louis Stevenson once relaxed and wrote. Validated 3-hour parking is offered for $5. **Features:** full bar, patio dining. **Reservations:** suggested. **Address:** 2863 Kalakaua Ave 96815 **Location:** Southeast end of Kapiolani Park; in The New Otani Kaimana Beach Hotel. **Parking:** valet only. [B] [L] [D] 🅐Ⓒ

HOKU'S 808/739-8780 (32)
♦♦♦♦ Pacific Rim. Fine Dining. $29-$65 **AAA Inspector Notes:** The locally popular restaurant offers wonderful daylight views of the Pacific Ocean and Diamond Head from the multilevel dining room. Lining the varied menu are whole fish, lobster and dishes that exemplify a fusion of contemporary island, Asian and European cuisines. The chef's tasting menu is worth the splurge. Three-hour complimentary parking with validation. **Features:** full bar, Sunday brunch. **Reservations:** required. **Address:** 5000 Kahala Ave 96816 **Location:** E of Diamond Head at end of Kahala Ave; in The Kahala Hotel & Resort. **Parking:** on-site and valet. [D] CALL 🅐Ⓜ

KAKA'AKO KITCHEN 808/596-7488 (9)
♦ American. Quick Serve. $10-$15 **AAA Inspector Notes:** Popular with the area business crowd, the simple restaurant is great for fresh sandwiches, local plate lunches and daily meat and veggie specials. Local fresh ingredients are used wherever possible. Diners order from the counter, then grab an outside table on the covered patio to wait for their meals to be delivered. **Features:** patio dining. **Address:** 1200 Ala Moana Blvd 96814 **Location:** Jct Kamakee and Auahi sts; Ward Centre, Ground Floor. **Parking:** on-site and valet. 🔲 [B] [L] [D] CALL 🅐Ⓜ

KARAI CRAB 808/952-6990 (20)
♦♦ Seafood. Casual Dining. $25-$42 **AAA Inspector Notes:** This fun, casual eatery offers several seafood selections (not just crab) and seasoning sauces to go with your spice level. Karai means 'spicy crab' in Hawaiian. Arrive early or make a reservation to avoid a long wait. The outdoor garden setting with a small pond and fountain are enjoyable. Valet parking is $3 with validation. **Features:** full bar, happy hour. **Reservations:** suggested. **Address:** 901 Hausten St 96826 **Location:** From Date St, just n. **Parking:** valet and street only. [D] CALL 🅐Ⓜ

KINCAID'S FISH, CHOP & STEAK HOUSE 808/591-2005 (8)
♦♦♦ Steak Seafood. Fine Dining. $15-$41 **AAA Inspector Notes:** This popular restaurant has a bustling, warm ambience. The varied menu includes seafood, steak and excellent prime rib. Ample wine and dessert choices round out the meal. **Features:** full bar, happy hour. **Reservations:** suggested, for dinner. **Address:** 1050 Ala Moana Blvd 96814 **Location:** Jct Ward Ave and Auahi St; Ward Warehouse, 2nd Floor. 🔲 [L] [D]

KONA BREWING CO. 808/396-5662
♦♦♦ American. Casual Dining. $11-$28 **AAA Inspector Notes:** Handcrafted beers and pub fare along with pupus (appetizers), hand-tossed pizzas, sandwiches and local seafood are served at this casual waterfront restaurant overlooking the marina. Live music on the weekends. **Features:** full bar, patio dining, happy hour. **Address:** 7192 Kalanianaole Hwy 96825 **Location:** Jct Lunalilo Home Rd; in Koko Marina Center. [L] [D] CALL 🅐Ⓜ 🅐Ⓒ

LEONARD'S BAKERY 808/737-5591 (22)
♦ Breads/Pastries. Quick Serve. $3-$6 **AAA Inspector Notes:** *Classic.* Since 1952, this establishment has been famous for its malasadas, a traditional Portuguese pastry of sweet, deep-fried yeast dough coated in sugar and served hot. They're a must-have treat in Hawaii. An assortment of bakery goods, including pao doce, also are offered. A line forms, especially on the weekends, so it is best to arrive early in the morning as parking can be difficult. **Address:** 933 Kapahulu Ave 96815 **Location:** Jct Charles St. [B] [L]

LITTLE VILLAGE NOODLE HOUSE 808/545-3008 (5)
♦♦ Chinese Noodles. Casual Dining. $9-$25 **AAA Inspector Notes:** When visiting Chinatown, be sure to try this restaurant with varied and tasty menu offerings, some of which are uncommon on the mainland. No MSG is used in the preparations. Service is friendly and courteous. It's popular with the downtown business crowd, so plan to arrive early or later for lunch during the week. Parking is available at nearby lots. **Features:** wine only. **Address:** 1113 Smith St 96817 **Location:** From Nimitz Hwy, just e; jct Hotel St; downtown. **Parking:** on-site and street. [L] [D] [LATE] CALL 🅐Ⓜ

LONGHI'S 808/947-9899 (14)
♦♦♦ Regional American. Casual Dining. $14-$45 **AAA Inspector Notes:** Take Longhi's private elevator to the fourth floor to enjoy the distant views of the ocean and Ala Moana park framed by the large, graceful archways. The light and airy open-air setting at this casual dining spot features fresh local fish, steak, chicken and pasta dishes. Extensive wine list. **Features:** full bar, happy hour. **Reservations:** suggested. **Address:** 1450 Ala Moana Blvd, Suite 3001 96814 **Location:** In Ala Moana Shopping Center, oceanside, mall level. [B] [L] [D] CALL 🅐Ⓜ 🅐Ⓒ

MARIPOSA 808/951-3420 (16)
♦♦♦ Pacific Rim. Casual Dining. $16-$36 **AAA Inspector Notes:** On the third floor of Neiman Marcus, this popular and slightly upscale restaurant with distant ocean views offers amazing lunch and dinner selections with locally sourced ingredients when available. Recommended choices include the lobster club sandwich, ahi melt and rib-eye roast beef sandwich. Dinner features Dungeness crab tagliatelle, braised lamb shank and seared Diver scallops. High tea is served Sunday 3-5 pm and reservations are highly recommended. Terrace seating is available, too. **Features:** full bar, Sunday brunch. **Reservations:** suggested. **Address:** 1450 Ala Moana Blvd 96814 **Location:** Jct Atkinson Dr; in Ala Moana Shopping Center. [L] [D] CALL 🅐Ⓜ

MAX'S OF MANILA 808/599-5033 (4)
♦♦ Philippine. Family Dining. $8-$19 **AAA Inspector Notes:** Just 15 minutes from Waikiki and set back from Dillingham Boulevard is where you'll find this popular chain restaurant that offers dishes along the lines of chicken and pork adobo, kare-kare, pancit, bangus (milkfish), pinakbet and more. There's a small patio out back. **Features:** beer & wine, patio dining. **Address:** 801 Dillingham Blvd 96817 **Location:** Off Nimitz Hwy, just e on Alakawa St, just s; near Dole Cannery Shops and Costco. [L] [D] CALL 🅐Ⓜ

THE MERMAID BAR 808/951-3428 (15)
♦♦ American. Casual Dining. $10-$16 **AAA Inspector Notes:** The small cafe puts together fresh salads and sandwiches. Featured desserts are worth a look, as are the ice creams and sorbets. Everything can be ordered for carry-out. **Features:** beer & wine. **Address:** 1450 Ala Moana Blvd 96814 **Location:** Jct Atkinson Dr; in Ala Moana Shopping Center, in Neiman Marcus, 2nd Floor. [L] CALL 🅐Ⓜ

(See map & index p. 145.)

MICHEL'S AT THE COLONY SURF   808/923-6552 31
▼▼▼▼ French Seafood. Fine Dining. $42-$85 **AAA Inspector Notes:** *Classic.* With stunning views of the beach and sea, this romantic oceanfront restaurant serves up tastefully prepared seafood and beef entrées with a French classical influence in an upscale environment. Tableside preparations of select menu items and a chef's tasting menu for $95 are offered. Brunch is served the first Sunday of each month. Dine early to take in the sunset. Valet parking is complimentary. **Features:** full bar. **Reservations:** suggested. **Address:** 2895 Kalakaua Ave 96815 **Location:** Southeast end of Kapiolani Park. **Parking:** valet only. [D] [JC]

NICO'S PIER 38   808/540-1377 2
▼ Seafood. Casual Dining. $10-$25 **AAA Inspector Notes:** Located on the docks in Iwilei, this basic eatery commands excellent views from the large windows of fishing vessels unloading their daily catches. Fresh fish direct from the auction block is served here. While there's often a line out the door at lunch, it moves quickly. Salads, sandwiches, burgers and other meat entrées are available; the daily special of incredibly fresh fish can sell out. The fresh poke appetizer is recommended. **Features:** full bar, patio dining, happy hour. **Address:** 1129 N Nimitz Hwy 96817 **Location:** At Pier 38. **Parking:** on-site and street. [B] [L] [D] [JC]

PAGODA FLOATING RESTAURANT   808/948-8356 12
▼▼ Regional American. Family Dining. $10-$36 **AAA Inspector Notes:** Dinner and weekend buffets are featured in a relaxed setting that includes a koi pond, waterfall and Japanese garden. Breakfast and lunch are a la carte. Parking in the adjacent lot is $1 per hour. **Features:** full bar, early bird specials, Sunday brunch. **Address:** 1525 Rycroft St 96814 **Location:** Jct Keeaumoku St, just ne of Ala Moana Shopping Center; in Pagoda Hotel. **Parking:** on-site (fee). [B] [L] [D] CALL [&M]

RAINBOW DRIVE-IN   808/737-0177 25
▼ Regional American. Quick Serve. $3-$9 **AAA Inspector Notes:** *Classic.* Since 1961, this drive-in has been a local favorite for inexpensive plate lunches, burgers, teriyaki beef, boneless chicken and sandwiches. **Features:** patio dining. **Address:** 3308 Kanaina Ave 96815 **Location:** Corner of Kapahulu Ave and Castle St. [B] [L] [D] CALL [&M] [JC]

ROY'S   808/396-7697
▼▼▼ Pacific Rim Fusion. Fine Dining. $15-$56 **AAA Inspector Notes:** Enjoy fusion of fresh Pacific seafood, French sauces and Asian seasonings. The ever-changing menu has many entrées such as grilled salmon and barbecue lamb rack, and the signature dessert, chocolate soufflé. **Reservations:** suggested. **Address:** 6600 Kalanianaole Hwy 96825 **Location:** Corner of Kalanianaole Hwy and Keahole St; in Hawaii Kai Towne Center. [D] CALL [&M]

RUTH'S CHRIS STEAK HOUSE   808/599-3860 6
▼▼▼ Steak. Fine Dining. $32-$62 **AAA Inspector Notes:** The main fare is steak, which is prepared from several cuts of Prime beef and cooked to perfection, but the menu also lists lamb, chicken and seafood dishes. Guests should come hungry because the side dishes, which are among the a la carte offerings, could make a meal in themselves. **Features:** full bar, early bird specials, happy hour. **Reservations:** suggested. **Address:** 500 Ala Moana Blvd, Suite 6C 96813 **Location:** jct South St; at Restaurant Row; in Waterfront Plaza. **Parking:** on-site (fee). [⊞] [D] CALL [&M]

SAINT-GERMAIN BAKERY   808/955-1711 13
▼ Breads/Pastries. Quick Serve. $5-$7 **AAA Inspector Notes:** This moderately priced bakery offers a limited variety of tasty sandwiches, a varied assortment of French-style pastries and several flavors of French macarons, along with cakes and artisan breads made with all-natural fresh ingredients utilizing authentic European recipes. **Address:** 1450 Ala Moana Blvd 96814 **Location:** In Ala Moana Shopping Center, Level One, near post office. [L] [D] CALL [&M]

SALT BAR & KITCHEN   808/744-7567 27
▼▼▼ New American. Casual Dining. $11-$25 **AAA Inspector Notes:** This high-energy eatery with limited, compact seating upstairs and deafening noise, offers fresh, high-quality, creative contemporary cuisine with local and Mexican inspirations. Small and large plates are available. Counter seating is offered downstairs. Reserve in advance. **Features:** full bar, happy hour. **Reservations:** suggested. **Address:** 3605 Waialae Ave 96816 **Location:** Between 11th Ave and Center St; in Kaimuki neighborhood. **Parking:** street only. [D] [LATE]

SHABU SHABU HOUSE   808/597-1655 10
▼▼ Japanese Specialty. Casual Dining. $10-$60 **AAA Inspector Notes:** Shabu shabu, which translates to "swish swish," is what you do with thinly sliced beef, pork or seafood to cook it in your own hot pot. Each set comes with a variety of vegetables and is a healthy option. The paitan broth is recommended for cooking. Dipping sauces are tasty. Hot pots are even at the counter seating area. The staff is helpful and friendly. Partial validated parking is available just a few doors down from the restaurant. **Features:** full bar. **Reservations:** suggested. **Address:** 1221 Kapiolani Blvd 96814 **Location:** Jct Pensacola St. **Parking:** on-site (fee) and street. [L] [D] CALL [&M]

SIDE STREET INN   808/739-3939 23
▼▼ Pacific Rim. Casual Dining. $12-$29 **AAA Inspector Notes:** Local comfort food is served in large portions at this restaurant not far from Waikiki and located on 'da strip,' as the locals say. Salads, Hawaiian-style Pulehu short ribs, Korean-style short ribs with kimchi and ahi fillet prepared with furikake are a sampling of the menu items. Valet parking for $5 or self-paid parking in a nearby lot is available. **Features:** full bar, happy hour. **Reservations:** suggested. **Address:** 614 Kapahulu Ave 96815 **Location:** Just s of Mooheau Ave; in Prudential Building. **Parking:** valet and street only. [B] [L] [D] CALL [&M]

SUSHI SASABUNE   808/947-3800 11
▼▼▼▼ Sushi. Casual Dining. $20-$60 **AAA Inspector Notes:** This small restaurant with a nondescript exterior prepares exquisite sushi (and the prices reflect this). Sushi is the only option, and a minimum of four orders per person is required. The watchful chef instructs patrons on how to best eat each preparation. The baby squid appetizer is recommended. A variety of hot and cold sakes is available. **Features:** beer & wine. **Reservations:** suggested. **Address:** 1417 S King St 96814 **Location:** Jct Keeaumoku St, just e. **Parking:** street only. [L] [D]

TOWN   808/735-5900 26
▼▼ Mediterranean. Casual Dining. $11-$28 **AAA Inspector Notes:** Located in the trendy neighborhood of Kaimuki, this slightly eclectic and thoroughly casual American bistro aims to serve "local first, organic whenever possible, with aloha always." With that spirit in mind, the kitchen sources out the freshest ingredients available and creates unpretentious but clean-flavored dishes such as black mussels served with cavatelli pasta, tomato and fennel in a Cinzano broth and succulent grilled chicken with smoked pancetta, bread and roasted grapes. **Features:** full bar, patio dining. **Reservations:** suggested. **Address:** 3435 Waialae Ave 96816 **Location:** Jct 9th Ave. **Parking:** street only. [B] [L] [D]

UNCLE BO'S PUPU BAR & GRILL   808/735-8310 24
▼▼ Fusion. Casual Dining. $13-$30 **AAA Inspector Notes:** A variety of tasty pupus (appetizers), perfect for sharing, and steaks, seafood, pasta and pizzas, often with Asian inspirations, are offered at this lively bistro-style restaurant that offers new menu items frequently and is just a 15-minute walk from the Honolulu Zoo. The décor is eclectic. Street parking can be difficult to find. Large portions are offered, so come hungry. **Features:** full bar, happy hour. **Reservations:** suggested. **Address:** 559 Kapahulu Ave 96815 **Location:** Jct Campbell Ave. **Parking:** street only. [D] [LATE] CALL [&M]

UNCLE'S FISH MARKET & GRILL   808/275-0063 3
▼▼ Pacific Rim Seafood. Casual Dining. $9-$24 **AAA Inspector Notes:** A nautical theme prevails at this casual eatery featuring fresh fish right off the boats. Sandwiches and entrées are prepared several different ways. A few sidewalk tables are offered. **Features:** full bar, patio dining, happy hour. **Reservations:** suggested. **Address:** 1135 N Nimitz Hwy 96817 **Location:** At Pier 38; in Fisherman's Village. [L] [D] CALL [&M]

(See map & index p. 145.)

THE WILLOWS   808/952-9200 [21]

▼▼ Continental. Casual Dining. $24-$40 **AAA Inspector Notes:** One of Hawaii's original garden restaurants is serving locals and tourists with a magnificent buffet lunch and dinner. What makes this restaurant special is the wonderful setting with its many waterfalls and lush tropical touches. The residential neighborhood location offers plenty of parking. Diners who take the time to try this well-kept secret won't be disappointed. **Features:** full bar, Sunday brunch. **Reservations:** suggested. **Address:** 901 Hausten St 96826 **Location:** Between Date St and University Ave. **Parking:** valet and street only. [L] [D] [AC]

YANAGI SUSHI   808/597-1525 [7]

▼▼ Japanese Sushi. Casual Dining. $15-$45 **AAA Inspector Notes:** Since 1978 this restaurant has offered an extensive variety of fresh sushi, sashimi, noodles and pupus (appetizers) along with combination dinners. A nice sake selection also is offered. Observe the chefs preparing selections at one of the two sushi bars. Late-night specials are available. **Features:** full bar. **Reservations:** suggested. **Address:** 762 Kapiolani Blvd 96813 **Location:** Just nw from jct Ward Ave. **Parking:** valet and street only. [L] [D] [LATE] CALL [M]

ARANCINO AT THE KAHALA   808/739-8888

[fyi] Not evaluated. This new fine-dining restaurant offers Napoli-style cuisine with Japanese inspirations. Many of the ingredients are imported from Italy. Pizza, baked in a wood-burning pizza oven, and pasta are offered. Prix fixe menus are offered only at dinnertime, with three- or four-course dinners from $56 or $79. **Address:** 5000 Kahala Ave 96816 **Location:** E of Diamond Head at end of Kahala Ave; in The Kahala Hotel & Resort.

HAKONE   808/956-1111

[fyi] Not evaluated. This buffet with harbor views offers made-to-order sushi along with other featured items depending on the availability. The price for the buffet is $54. **Address:** 100 Holomoana St 96815 **Location:** Just w of Ala Moana Blvd on Hobron Ln; in Hawaii Prince Hotel Waikiki and Golf Club.

HELENA'S HAWAIIAN FOOD   808/845-8044

[fyi] Not evaluated. Since 1946, this is where you've been able to find your Hawaiian favorites such as squid lū'au, pipikaula and kalua pig. Parking can be difficult. Cash only. **Address:** 1240 N School St 96817 **Location:** H-1 exit Houghtailing St, just ne, then just s.

KA'A'AWA (F-4) pop. 1,379, elev. 6'
- **Attractions map p. 118**
- **Part of Honolulu area — see p. 122**

The town of Ka'a'awa extends along O'ahu's windward coast at the base of steep, fluted mountains. Crouching Lion, a rock formation beside SR 83 north of town, is a local landmark. Legend holds that it is the figure of a Tahitian demigod turned to stone as he fled from jealous sisters. The crumbling ruins of a sugar mill that operated from 1863 into the early 1870s are along the highway 2.5 miles north.

Kualoa Regional Park, about 3.5 miles south on SR 83, is a large grassy expanse facing the sea. Ancient fishponds adjoin the park's western margin. Offshore rises the conical islet of Mokoli'i, popularly known as Chinaman's Hat due to its distinctive shape.

KUALOA RANCH & ACTIVITY CLUB, 49-560 Kamehameha Hwy. across from Kualoa Park, has been a working ranch since 1850. A number of motion pictures have been filmed here, including "Jurassic Park," "Pearl Harbor" and "50 First Dates." The television series "Lost" also has been filmed on the premises. A tour of the movie sets, a jungle expedition, and an Ancient Fishing Grounds & Tropical

Gardens Tour are among the tours offered. Other activities include 1- or 2-hour horseback and ATV trips and children's horseback rides.

Ask about minimum age and size requirements. **Time:** Allow 1 hour minimum. **Hours:** Daily 8-5. Movie set tours, jungle expeditions, and Ancient Fishing Grounds & Tropical Gardens Tours depart several times daily. Closed Jan. 1 and Christmas. Phone ahead to confirm schedule. **Cost:** Movie set tours, jungle expeditions, and Ancient Fishing Grounds & Tropical Gardens Tours each $35; $25 (ages 3-12). Other fees vary depending on activity. **Phone:** (808) 237-8515, or (808) 237-7321 for reservations. [🍴]

KAHALU'U (G-5) pop. 4,738, elev. 3'
- **Part of Honolulu area — see p. 122**

SENATOR FONG'S PLANTATION AND GARDENS is at 47-285 Pulama Rd. Established in the windward O'ahu rain forest, this 700-acre garden estate encompasses lush valleys and plateaus. A guided 1-mile walking tour explores landscaped gardens, fruit orchards and tropical foliage. Sen. Hiram Fong, who purchased the land in 1950 and is the gardens' namesake, was the first Asian American elected to serve in the United States Senate. Guests are invited to sample fruits off the trees and, for an additional charge, make lei at the visitor center.

Time: Allow 1 hour, 15 minutes minimum. **Hours:** Visitor center Sun.-Fri. 10-2. Tours depart at 10:30 and 1. Closed Jan. 1 and Christmas. **Cost:** Tour $14.50; $13 (ages 65+); $9 (ages 5-12). Lei-making $6.50 per lei. Cash only. **Phone:** (808) 239-6775.

KAHUKU (E-4) pop. 2,614, elev. 20'
- **Hotels p. 164** • **Restaurants p. 164**
- **Attractions map p. 118**
- **Part of Honolulu area — see p. 122**

At the northern end of O'ahu's windward coast, Kahuku grew around a large sugar mill that operated from 1890 to 1971. The town was at the end of the O'ahu Railway line from Honolulu; train service ended in 1947. The former cane fields north and west of town now produce vegetables and fruit, and aquaculture ponds nurture fish and shrimp. The old Kahuku Sugar Mill is now home to a variety of shops.

HELE HULI ADVENTURE CENTER, 57-091 Kamehameha Hwy. on the grounds of Turtle Bay Resort, conducts guided off-road Segway tours. Each 90-minute tour begins with a 20-minute training session that allows participants to get acquainted with the two-wheeled transportation devices. While following a path that winds along the ocean and through a forest and golf course, riders are treated to gorgeous scenery and interesting narration. Hawaiian monk seals are known to frequent the beach area along the route.

The center offers a variety of other outdoor activities—from hiking, horseback riding and kayaking tours to bicycle and moped rentals.

Note: Closed-toe shoes are recommended; high-heeled and platform shoes are not permitted. Portions of the path are bumpy and/or sandy. Participants must be able to stand on a Segway for up to 40 minutes without a break. Snacks are available. **Time:** Allow 2 hours minimum. **Hours:** Tours depart daily at 9 and 11. **Cost:** $99. Ages 0-13 are not permitted. Reservations are recommended. **Phone:** (808) 293-6024.

TURTLE BAY RESORT — 808/293-6000

▼▼▼ **Resort Hotel.** Rates not provided. **Address:** 57-091 Kamehameha Hwy 96731 **Location:** Oceanfront. 3 mi nw off SR 83. **Facility:** This resort has a magnificent oceanfront location on the famous North Shore on attractive, expansive grounds with a swimming beach, snorkel area and activity center. A shopping service is available. 478 units, some two bedrooms, three bedrooms, kitchens and cottages. 6 stories, interior/exterior corridors. **Parking:** on-site (fee) and valet. **Amenities:** safes. **Dining:** 6 restaurants, also, North Shore Kula Grille, Ola, Pa'akai, see separate listings, entertainment. **Pool(s):** outdoor. **Activities:** hot tub, self-propelled boats, fishing, snorkeling, regulation golf, tennis, recreation programs, bicycles, trails, spa. **Guest Services:** valet and coin laundry, rental car service.

[icons]

WHERE TO EAT

GIOVANNI'S SHRIMP TRUCK — 808/293-1839

▼ Specialty. Quick Serve. $4-$13 **AAA Inspector Notes:** When visiting the North Shore be sure to join the throngs of shrimp-loving tourists. This famous graffiti covered shrimp truck offers made-to-order shrimp prepared three different ways with the shells on. For the garlic lover, I recommend the shrimp scampi - it is loaded with garlic and olive oil. It's best to arrive early at mealtimes to avoid standing in a long line. There is a wash station just behind the covered patio after you are through licking your fingers. **Features:** patio dining. **Address:** 56-505 Kamehameha Hwy 96731 **Location:** Center.

L D CALL 🖳M 🎒

NORTH SHORE KULA GRILLE — 808/293-6000

▼▼ Regional American. Casual Dining. $14-$39 **AAA Inspector Notes:** This casual ocean-view spot offers breakfast and farm-to-table dining in the evening. A variety of tasty menu items are featured. **Features:** full bar, patio dining. **Reservations:** suggested. **Address:** 57-091 Kamehameha Hwy 96731 **Location:** 3 mi nw off SR 83; in Turtle Bay Resort. **Parking:** on-site and valet.

B D CALL 🖳M

OLA — 808/293-0801

▼▼ Regional American. Casual Dining. $10-$62 **AAA Inspector Notes:** Ola in the Hawaiian language means "life, healthy and well-being." This boisterous bistro overlooks Kuilima Bay and sits right on the beach with a few tables set in the sand. Contemporary Hawaiian-style cuisine is served in a casual atmosphere. Be sure to make a reservation before sunset. **Features:** full bar, patio dining. **Reservations:** suggested. **Address:** 57-091 Kamehameha Hwy 96731 **Location:** 3 mi nw off SR 83; in Turtle Bay Resort. **Parking:** on-site and valet. L D CALL 🖳M 🎒

PA'AKAI — 808/293-6000

▼▼▼ Regional American. Fine Dining. $32-$52 **AAA Inspector Notes:** Pa'akai translates to "sea salt" in the Hawaiian language. Locally sourced menu items along with fresh local fish prepared several different ways and sea salt produced in Hawaii are offered at this casually upscale restaurant with views of the ocean. Recommended is the Hawaiian monchong fish with Kona crab risotto. There is a five-course tasting menu for $75. **Features:** full bar, happy hour. **Reservations:** suggested. **Address:** 57-091 Kamehameha Hwy 96731 **Location:** 3 mi nw off SR 83; in Turtle Bay Resort. **Parking:** on-site and valet. D CALL 🖳M

KAILUA (H-5) pop. 38,635, elev. 10'
• Attractions map p. 118
• Part of Honolulu area — see p. 122

An easy drive over the mountains through the Nu'uanu rain forest via Pali Highway (SR 61), Kailua and nearby Lanikai are among Honolulu's best-known beach communities. Offshore are the Mokulua Islands, known locally as the "twin islands."

Kailua Chamber of Commerce: 600 Kailua Rd., Suite 107; P.O. Box 1496, Kailua, HI 96734. **Phone:** (808) 261-7997, (808) 261-2727 or (888) 261-7997.

KAILUA BEACH PARK is entered via Kailua Rd.; Pali Hwy. (SR 61) becomes Kailua Rd. just after Castle Hospital in town. Kayaking, windsurfing and other small-craft sailing are popular, as is swimming, at this wide, fine sandy beach with shaded picnic areas. Windsurfing equipment rentals and lessons are available. **Note:** Because of prevailing strong onshore winds, the stinging blue jellyfish known as Portuguese man-of-war can be a hazard. Lifeguards are on duty. **Hours:** Daily 5 a.m.-10 p.m. **Cost:** Free. **Phone:** (808) 233-7300.

RECREATIONAL ACTIVITIES
Kayaking
• **Kailua Sailboards & Kayaks** is at 130 Kailua Rd. Other activities are offered. **Hours:** Mon.-Sat. 8-5. **Phone:** (808) 262-2555 or (888) 457-5737.

BACI BISTRO — 808/262-7555

▼▼▼ Italian. Casual Dining. $15-$25 **AAA Inspector Notes:** This intimate, romantic bistro serves a variety of tempting pastas as well as risottos, veal, chicken and fish entrées. The ravioli is made fresh daily. Recommended is the lobster ravioli. **Features:** full bar, patio dining. **Reservations:** suggested. **Address:** 30 Aulike St 96734 **Location:** Just n of jct Kuulei Rd. **Parking:** on-site and street.

L D CALL 🖳M

FORMAGGIO GRILL — 808/263-2635

▼▼ Mediterranean. Casual Dining. $16-$45 **AAA Inspector Notes:** Steaks and seafood, pastas, thin-crust pizzas and panini with a Mediterranean flair are served at this casually upscale restaurant with high energy (it can be noisy). Reserve in advance for the "Dining in the Dark" event where you dine on a four-course meal blindfolded. **Features:** full bar, happy hour. **Reservations:** suggested. **Address:** 305 Hahani St 96734 **Location:** SR 61 (Pali Hwy which becomes Kailua Rd), just n on Kailua Rd, then just e; across from Kailua District Park. **Parking:** on-site and street. L D CALL 🖳M

BUZZ'S ORIGINAL STEAK HOUSE — 808/261-4661

[fyi] Not evaluated. This casual restaurant serves a limited variety of steaks. **Address:** 413 Kawailoa Rd 96734 **Location:** Across from Kailua Beach Park.

KĀNE'OHE (H-5) pop. 34,597, elev. 80'
• Attractions map p. 118
• Part of Honolulu area — see p. 122

Connected to Honolulu by Likelike Highway (SR 63), Kāne'ohe is a growing residential city on the shore of Kāne'ohe Bay. The southern end of the bay, protected from the strongest winds by the Mōkapu Peninsula, offers sailing and fishing. Beneath the bay off the He'eia area lie coral gardens that can be explored by snorkelers.

Haiku Gardens, 46-336 Haiku Rd., is accessed via a paved walking path that begins at the Haleiwa

Joe's restaurant. Exotic plants and flowers, two ponds, an open-air chapel, a gazebo and a mountain backdrop all contribute to the beauty of this tranquil spot; phone (808) 247-0605.

Shopping: The more than 110 stores and eateries of Windward Mall, 1 mile north at 46-056 Kamehameha Hwy., include Macy's and Sears.

BYODO-IN TEMPLE is at 47-200 Kahekili Hwy. (SR 83), 2.5 mi. n. of SR 63 in Valley of the Temples Memorial Park. Within this private cemetery is a replica of a 10th-century Buddhist temple in Uji, Japan. On the grounds are a 3-ton brass peace bell (said to clear the mind of impurity or bring good luck), a statue of a 9-foot tall Buddha perched atop a lotus flower and hundreds of koi in a reflection pond. Mosquito repellent is recommended. **Hours:** Mon.-Sat. 9-5, Sun. 10-4. Closed Jan. 1, Thanksgiving and Christmas. **Cost:** $3; $2 (ages 65+); $1 (ages 1-11). Cash only. **Phone:** (808) 239-9844.

HO'OMALUHIA BOTANICAL GARDEN, 1.7 mi. s. to 45-680 Luluku Rd., is a 400-acre recreational facility with programs and activities that promote environmental awareness. Paved walking trails feature signs identifying foliage native to Hawai'i and other tropical regions. **Time:** Allow 45 minutes minimum. **Hours:** Daily 9-4. Reservations are required for camping. Closed Jan. 1 and Christmas. **Cost:** Free. **Phone:** (808) 233-7323. 🔺 🏕

HALEIWA JOE'S - HAIKU GARDENS RESTAURANT
808/247-6671
▼▼▼ American. Casual Dining. $10-$34 **AAA Inspector Notes:** Overlooking the lush and tropical Haiku Gardens and with a beautiful view of the Koolau mountain range, this open-air restaurant serves seafood and steaks with an island flair and small- and big-plate options. Be sure to arrive at around 5 pm, as the restaurant fills quickly with diners vying for tables with a view of the gardens and reservations are not accepted. **Features:** full bar, patio dining, Sunday brunch, happy hour. **Address:** 46-336 Haiku Rd 96744 **Location:** SR 83, just w. [D] CALL 🄫🅼 🕱

KAPOLEI (H-2) pop. 15,186, elev. 20'
- **Restaurants p. 166**
- **Attractions map p. 118**
- **Part of Honolulu area — see p. 122**

GERMAINE'S LŪ'AU is at 91-119 Olai St.; complimentary transportation to and from Waikīkī hotels is available. Hawaiian *hula* dancers as well as Tahitian, Samoan and Maori dancers provide entertainment at this 3-hour oceanside *lū'au.* Try to arrive when the gates open so you can snag a picnic table close to the stage.

At 6 p.m. you'll watch the ceremonial uncovering of the *kalua* pig that will be served. Shortly thereafter, you'll head to the buffet line for all-you-can-eat foods like mahi-mahi, teriyaki beef and *haupia* (a firm, coconut-flavored pudding). Unlimited soft drinks, coffee and tea are provided; three alcoholic beverages are included in the ticket price for those 21 and older.

Casual clothing, flat shoes and a light jacket are recommended. Allow 1 hour for the drive from

Waikīkī. **Time:** Allow 5 hours minimum. **Hours:** Daily at 6 p.m., May-Aug.; Tues.-Sun. at 6 p.m., rest of year. Gates open at 5:15. Closed Jan. 1. **Cost:** $88; $78 (ages 14-20); $68 (ages 6-13). Reservations are required. **Phone:** (808) 949-6626 or (800) 367-5655. 🍴

PARADISE COVE LŪ'AU is at 92-1089 Ali'i Nui Dr.; transportation to and from Waikīkī hotels is available for a fee. Guests can choose one of four different *lū'au* experiences: the Hawaiian Lū'au Buffet, the Orchid Lū'au Buffet, the Deluxe Lū'au Package or the Dolphin Snorkel Tour & Lū'au Combo.

Upon arrival you'll be welcomed with a mai tai and a *lei.* During the 4-hour oceanside event you can participate in Hawaiian activities like spear throwing, *lei*-making, outrigger canoe rides and a *hukilau* (a fishing method involving a big group of people and a big net) ceremony. Highlights include the ceremonial unveiling of the roasted pig and the Shower of Flowers (in which tree-climbing experts toss flowers from palm trees). Conch shells are blown to call guests to dinner, where entertainment includes *hula* and fire-knife dancing.

Note: Casual clothing, flat shoes and a light jacket are recommended. Allow 1 hour for the drive from Waikīkī. Inquire about cancellation policies. **Time:** Allow 6 hours minimum. **Hours:** *Lū'au* daily at 5 (weather permitting). **Cost:** Hawaiian Lū'au Buffet $94; $84 (ages 13-20); $74 (ages 4-12). Orchid Lū'au Buffet $125; $111 (ages 13-20); $97 (ages 4-12). Deluxe Lū'au Package $161; $144 (ages 13-20); $131 (ages 4-12). Dolphin Snorkel Tour & Lū'au Combo $209.70; $200.70 (ages 13-20); $169.20 (ages 4-12). Reservations are required. **Phone:** (808) 842-5911 or (800) 775-2683. 🍴

[SAVE] **WET 'N' WILD HAWAI'I,** 400 Farrington Hwy., is a water park featuring more than 25 rides and attractions. **Time:** Allow 2 hours minimum. **Hours:** Park opens daily at 10:30, Memorial Day-Labor Day; Thurs.-Mon. at 10:30, rest of year. Closing times vary. Phone ahead to confirm schedule. **Cost:** $47.99; $37.99 (ages 65+ and under 42 inches tall); free (ages 0-2). Prices may vary; phone ahead. **Parking:** $8. **Phone:** (808) 674-9283. 🍴

AULANI - A DISNEY RESORT & SPA IN KO OLINA, HAWAII
(808)674-6200
▼▼▼ ▼▼▼ **Resort Hotel** $449-$634 **Address:** 92-1185 Ali'inui Dr 96707 **Location:** Oceanfront. 20 mi w of Honolulu International Airport via I-H1 W exit Ko Olina, just s. Located in Ko Olina resort area. **Facility:** This new beachfront resort on 21 acres offers the rich traditions and culture of Hawaii with just a touch of Disney magic. There's something for everyone, from kids to teens to adults. 1051 units, some two bedrooms, three bedrooms and kitchens. 16 stories, interior corridors. **Parking:** on-site (fee) and valet. **Terms:** 6 day cancellation notice-fee imposed. **Amenities:** safes. **Dining:** 4 restaurants, entertainment. **Pool(s):** heated outdoor. **Activities:** sauna, hot tub, cabanas, self-propelled boats, snorkeling, recreation programs, kids club, playground, game room, picnic facilities, spa. **Guest Services:** valet and coin laundry, boarding pass kiosk, rental car service, area transportation.
🍴 🧑 🍸 🆔 CALL 🄫🅼 ➳ ➕ [BIZ] [HS] 🛜
🆇 📱 💻 / [SOME UNITS]

MARRIOTT'S KO OLINA BEACH CLUB   808/679-4700

[fyi] Not evaluated. **Address:** 92-161 Waipahe Pl 96707 **Location:** Oceanfront. 20 mi w of Honolulu International Airport via I-H1 W exit Ko Olina, just s. Facilities, services, and décor characterize a mid-scale property. Located on a private lagoon with three pools and attractive tropical landscaping. Attractive units, most with kitchens and modern amenities.

AAA Benefit:
Members save 5% or more!

WHERE TO EAT

CHUCK'S STEAK & SEAFOOD   808/678-8822

Steak Seafood. Casual Dining. $24-$45 **AAA Inspector Notes:** With its origins in Waikiki over 50 years ago, the concept quickly spread across the country and Pacific Rim. Boasting the first ever self serve salad bar concept and relying on a single purveyor of Western choice beef, diners can rest assured that whichever Chuck's they choose they will find consistency in quality and style of preparation. The menu features a complete line-up of steaks and seafood. **Features:** full bar, patio dining, happy hour. **Reservations:** suggested. **Address:** 92-161 Waipahe Pl 96707 **Location:** 20 mi w of Honolulu International Airport via I-H1 W exit Ko Olina, just s; in Marriott's Ko Olina Beach Club. **Parking:** on-site (fee) and valet.

[D] CALL [S/M] [X]

GERMAINE'S LUAU   808/949-6626

Hawaiian. Casual Dining. $80 **AAA Inspector Notes:** Experience a casual, fun luau in a private setting along the ocean. Picnic tables are set in the sand. Be sure to watch the uncovering of the whole roasted pig from the imu pit on the luau grounds, then feast on Hawaiian favorites buffet-style. Three complimentary alcoholic beverages for adults and free hotel pickup. The Polynesian show includes a spectacular fire knife dance. **Features:** full bar. **Reservations:** required. **Address:** 91-119 Olai St 96707 **Location:** 17 mi w of Honolulu International Airport via I-H1 W exit 1, Campbell Industrial Park/Kalaeloa Blvd/Barbers Point, 2.2 mi s, then just w.

[D] CALL [S/M] [X]

MONKEYPOD KITCHEN BY MERRIMAN   808/380-4086

American. Casual Dining. $13-$35 **AAA Inspector Notes:** Wood-fired pizzas are served at this casual bi-level eatery. Some tables have views of the adjoining golf course. More than 45 craft brews are on tap. Live music and valet parking are offered in the evening. **Features:** full bar, patio dining, happy hour. **Reservations:** suggested. **Address:** 92-1048 Olani St 96707 **Location:** 20 mi w of Honolulu International Airport via I-H1 W exit Ko Olina Resort, just sw on Ali'inui Dr, then just w; in Ko Olina resort area. **Parking:** on-site and valet. [L] [D] CALL [S/M]

PARADISE COVE LUAU   808/842-5911

Hawaiian. Casual Dining. $88-$153 **AAA Inspector Notes:** On the ocean on a private lagoon, this lū'au begins with Hawaiian games and crafts, with several venues of live entertainment. After the unveiling of the roasted pig at the imu pit, the feast begins with a buffet of various island-style foods. There is a Polynesian show with Hawaiian hula dancers, of course, and a fire knife dancer. Several lū'au packages are available. **Features:** full bar. **Reservations:** required. **Address:** 92-1089 Ali'inui Dr 96707 **Location:** 20 mi w of Honolulu International Airport via I-H1 W exit Ko Olina Resort, just w to Ali'inui Dr, past the guard shack. [D] CALL [S/M] [X]

ROY'S   808/676-7697

Pacific Rim Fusion. Fine Dining. $16-$32 **AAA Inspector Notes:** Enjoy fusion of fresh Pacific seafood, French sauces and Asian seasonings. The ever-changing menu has many entrées such as grilled salmon and barbecue lamb rack, and the signature dessert, chocolate soufflé. **Features:** full bar, patio dining, happy hour. **Reservations:** suggested. **Address:** 92-1220 Ali'inui Dr 96707 **Location:** 20 mi w of Honolulu International Airport via I-H1 W exit Ko Olina Resort, just s to Ko Olina Golf Course. [L] [D] CALL [S/M]

LĀ'IE (F-4) pop. 6,138, elev. 10'
- Attractions map p. 118
- Part of Honolulu area — see p. 122

In addition to being a locale for summer homes, this windward coast town is the Hawaiian center of the Church of Jesus Christ of Latter-day Saints. The development of about 6,000 acres has been a major church project since 1864.

LĀ'IE HAWAI'I TEMPLE, 55-600 Naniloa Loop, is approached through formal terraced gardens with reflecting pools. Visitors may not enter the temple, but the grounds and visitor center contain exhibits and audiovisual presentations. **Hours:** Visitor center daily 9-8. Guided tours depart from the Polynesian Cultural Center *(see attraction listing)* daily every 20 minutes 3-7. **Cost:** Free. **Phone:** (808) 293-9297.

POLYNESIAN CULTURAL CENTER is on SR 83 next to Brigham Young University. The 42-acre center preserves and shares the heritage of the South Pacific region: Hawai'i, Samoa, Tahiti, Tonga, Fiji and Aotearoa (New Zealand).

While visiting each village, you'll interact with native people of these island cultures and enjoy presentations, exhibits and hands-on Go Native! activities. More than 100 natives perform in the evening "Ha: Breath of Life" show. "Hawaiian Journey" is a 15-minute cinematic experience featuring 4-D special effects. An exhibition area devoted to Rapa Nui (Easter Island) is another highlight.

General admission includes walking and canoe tours of the facility; the Lā'ie tram tour and Mission Settlement; Go Native! activities; the Rainbows of Paradise canoe pageant; and "Hawaiian Journey." Other packages include enhanced tours, special *lei* greetings, a variety of dining options and the "Ha: Breath of Life" show.

Hours: Center Mon.-Sat. 11:45-9; box office closes at 8. Island villages close between 5 and 5:30. Canoe pageant at 2:30. *Lū'au* at 5. Evening show at 7:30. Closed Thanksgiving and Christmas. **Cost:** General admission $49.95; $39.96 (ages 5-11). Show package $74.95; $59.96 (ages 5-11). Ali'i Lū'au package $99.95; $79.96 (ages 5-11). Ambassador Lū'au or Ambassador Prime Rib package $139.95; $111.96 (ages 5-11). Super Ambassador package $199.95; $159.96 (ages 5-11). Prices may vary; phone ahead. **Phone:** (808) 293-3333 or (800) 367-7060.

COURTYARD BY MARRIOTT OAHU NORTH SHORE
(808)293-4900

[fyi] Hotel $237-$378 Too new to rate, opening scheduled for May 2015. **Address:** 55-400 Kamehameha Hwy 96762 **Location:** 1.2 mi s. **Amenities:** 150 units, restaurant, coffeemakers, refrigerators, pool, exercise facility. **Terms:** 3 day cancellation notice.

AAA Benefit:
Members save 5% or more!

MOKULĒ'IA (F-2) pop. 1,811, elev. 5'

- **Attractions map p. 118**
- **Part of Honolulu area — see p. 122**

Mokulē'ia is a North Shore community fronting a 6-mile stretch of beach. Dillingham Airfield, a former Air Force base on SR 930 west of town, is a popular jumping-off point for gliding and skydiving flights.

From the end of the paved Farrington Highway (SR 930) 5 miles west of Mokulē'ia, a trail continues 2.5 miles to Ka'ena Point, O'ahu's westernmost point. Here the Wai'anae Range tapers to a land's end finger of black lava rock, thrashed by crashing waves. The point has the island's largest remaining tract of dunes, and its shrubby patches host nesting Laysan albatross. Endangered monk seals occasionally haul out on the rocks. Ka'ena Point is a state park and wildlife refuge. Visitors should stay on the trails and not disturb the landscape or animals.

The point also is accessible from the Wai'anae side, via a 2.5-mile hike from the end of SR 93, which is 7 miles north of Mākaha. Although this access route is more scenic, a short stretch of the trail is washed out and hikers have to clamber along the cliff side. **Note:** Hikers should carry water and not leave valuables in their vehicles. *See Recreation Areas Chart.*

MR. BILL'S ORIGINAL GLIDER RIDES departs from Dillingham Airfield on SR 930. Tours for one or two passengers lasting 15 to 60 minutes offer spectacular views of O'ahu's North Shore via sailplanes. Whale sightings are common December through April. Additional flight options are available to single passengers for a fee.

Note: Due to decompression-related sickness, it is recommended that passengers wait 12-24 hours after scuba diving before flying; the amount of time is dependent on particular dive factors. Ask about possible policies regarding minimum wait time between scuba diving and flying; weight restrictions; weather, cancellation and refund policies; and the minimum and maximum number of passengers for flights. All small aircraft may encounter turbulence. **Hours:** Daily 10-5:30. **Cost:** Fare for solo passenger $79-$215. Combined fare for two passengers $128-$390. Reservations are recommended. **Phone:** (808) 637-0207.

Let Your Voice Be Heard

If your visit to a TourBook-listed property doesn't meet your expectations, tell us about it.

AAA.com/TourBookComments

RECREATIONAL ACTIVITIES

Hang Gliding

- **Paradise Air Hawai'i** departs from Dillingham Airfield on SR 930. **Hours:** Trips depart daily in the morning; phone for schedule. **Phone:** (808) 497-6033.

Skydiving

- **Pacific Skydiving** departs from Dillingham Airfield, 68-760 Farrington Hwy.; look for the big white tent at the third building on the left. **Hours:** Trips depart daily. Closed Christmas. Phone ahead to confirm schedule. **Phone:** (808) 637-7472.

PEARL CITY (H-3) pop. 47,698, elev. 89'

- **Attractions map p. 118**
- **Part of Honolulu area — see p. 122**

UNIVERSITY OF HAWAI'I URBAN GARDEN CENTER is at 955 Kamehameha Hwy., via the Home Depot parking lot. Hibiscus, subtropical vines, herbs, plumeria, a subtropical fruit orchard, a children's garden and a hedge maze are some of the 30-acre garden's highlights. **Note:** Water, sunscreen and mosquito repellent are recommended. **Time:** Allow 1 hour minimum. **Hours:** Mon.-Fri. 9-2 (also second Sat. of the month 9-noon). Closed major holidays. **Cost:** Free. **Phone:** (808) 453-6050.

PEARL HARBOR (H-3)

- **Attractions map p. 118**
- **Part of Honolulu area — see p. 122**

The Japanese attack on Pearl Harbor on the morning of Dec. 7, 1941, "a date which will live in infamy," precipitated the entry of the United States into World War II. The attack lasted almost 2 hours and left 2,403 Americans dead and another 1,178 wounded.

Although specialists in Washington had decoded a Japanese message indicating that an attack in the Pacific was imminent, atmospheric difficulties and human error kept the message from being delivered in time. As it became apparent that O'ahu would be caught off guard, the commander of the Japanese squadron signaled the attack to begin. Despite their short-run victory, Japan went on to lose the war.

The loss of life in the attack was substantial, but not all of Japan's objectives had been met. All but three of the 18 warships damaged during the raid—the *Arizona, Utah* and *Oklahoma*—were repaired and returned to duty. The fleet's three aircraft carriers, away from Pearl Harbor during the attack, were undamaged. The oil-storage tanks, a prime Japanese target, were not destroyed. Pearl Harbor survived and continued to function as a Pacific base of naval operations throughout the war.

The value of the harbor, which is the double estuary of the Pearl River, was recognized in 1840 by U.S. Navy Lt. Charles Wilkes. He discovered that dredging an outlying reef would make Pearl Harbor readily accessible. About 30 years later U.S. Army Col. John M. Schofield recommended that the United States secure harbor rights. This was done in 1873; work began in 1898.

Pearl Harbor has grown dramatically in value and covers more than 10,000 acres of land. Most of the United States Navy commands in the Pacific have headquarters at Pearl Harbor. A naval shipyard, supply center and submarine base are among the harbor's various facilities.

The World War II Valor in the Pacific National Monument, established by presidential proclamation in 2008, consists of nine historic sites in Pearl Harbor, Alaska's Aleutian Islands and California. Among the five Pearl Harbor sites are the USS *Arizona* Memorial *(see attraction listing)*, the USS *Utah* Memorial and the USS *Oklahoma* Memorial; the *Arizona* and *Utah* vessels are under the jurisdiction of the U.S. Navy and are not considered parts of the monument.

The USS *Utah* Memorial is on Ford Island, about three-quarters of a mile east of the USS *Arizona* Memorial, and is accessible to civilians with a military sponsor. The USS *Oklahoma* Memorial, also on Ford Island, stands near the entrance to the Battleship *Missouri* Memorial *(see attraction listing)* and may be visited after a tour of the *Missouri*.

BATTLESHIP *MISSOURI* MEMORIAL, next to the Pearl Harbor Memorial Museum & Visitor Center off SR 99, is moored at Pier Foxtrot-5 on Ford Island. The shuttle bus ride from the USS *Bowfin* Submarine Museum and Park to the pier features stories of the history of the area and the *Missouri*, from the 1940s to the present.

The ship, also known as "Mighty Mo," is a veteran of World War II as well as the Korean and Gulf wars. Visitors can explore the decks of this ship launched in 1944 and decommissioned in 1998 and observe its 16-inch guns. Particularly stirring is a walk on the Surrender Deck, where, on Sept. 2, 1945, Japan signed the "Instrument of Surrender" ending World War II.

The guided 90-minute Battle Stations Tour focuses on the people and places involved in the ship's various battles.

Note: No bags of any type may be carried on board; bags may be stored for a fee. Tickets are sold at the Pearl Harbor Memorial Museum & Visitor Center. **Time:** Allow 1 hour minimum. **Hours:** Daily 8-5, June-Aug.; 8-4, rest of year. Last admission 1 hour before closing. Closed Jan. 1, Thanksgiving and Christmas. **Cost:** Mighty Mo Pass with choice of 35-minute guided, audio or iPod tour $25; $13 (ages 4-12). Heart of the *Missouri* Tour (in addition to Mighty Mo Pass) $25; $12 (ages 10-12). Reservations are recommended for the Heart of the *Missouri* Tour. Under age 10 are not permitted on the Heart of the *Missouri* Tour. Combination tickets with other Pearl Harbor sites may be purchased online in advance at www.pearlharborhistoricsites.org/deals. **Phone:** (877) 644-4896. GT

PACIFIC AVIATION MUSEUM is at 319 Lexington Blvd. in Hangar 37 on Ford Island; shuttle buses provide transportation from the Pearl Harbor Memorial Museum & Visitor Center. World War II aircraft and artifacts from the Pacific are showcased in a 42,000-square-foot former seaplane hangar that weathered the attack on Pearl Harbor.

Upon arrival visitors step back in time to December 7, 1941, the date of the Pearl Harbor bombing. Film footage shown in a 200-seat theater; a P-40 fighter; a diorama of a Japanese Zero aboard a carrier; an exhibit about a Japanese Zero that crash landed on Ni'ihau; and a damaged civilian plane create an impressive portrait of the momentous event.

Several aircraft displays help re-create other significant World War II happenings. Highlights include a B-25B characteristic of those used during the Doolittle Raid; a Guadalcanal diorama featuring a Grumman Wildcat; an SBD Dauntless dive bomber representing the Battle of Midway; and a Stearman N2S-3 training plane flown by President George H.W. Bush.

Celebrating the iconic Pan American World Airways and its role in aviation history, the Come Fly With Me exhibit features a collection of Pan Am memorabilia housed in a mock airliner cabin.

The Aviator's Tour explores hangars 37 and 79, in addition to a rebuilt aircraft service unit where planes are restored. Flight simulators let visitors test their own piloting skills.

Note: Bags are not permitted on the trolleys. Tickets are sold at the Pearl Harbor Memorial Museum & Visitor Center. **Time:** Allow 1 hour, 30 minutes minimum. **Hours:** Daily 8-5. Aviator's Tour departs daily at 9, 11, 1 and 3. Closed Jan. 1, Thanksgiving and Christmas. **Cost:** $25; $15 (military and Hawai'i residents with ID); $12 (ages 4-12); $10 (ages 4-12 with military or Hawai'i-resident parent). Aviator's Tour $35; $25 (military and Hawai'i residents with ID); $22 (ages 4-12); $20 (ages 4-12 with military or Hawai'i-resident parent). Flight simulator $10. Combination tickets with other Pearl Harbor sites may be purchased online in advance at www.pearlharborhistoricsites.org/deals. **Phone:** (808) 441-1000.

PEARL HARBOR MEMORIAL MUSEUM & VISITOR CENTER, reached via H-1 w. to Arizona Memorial/Stadium exit 15A, then SR 99 to 1 Arizona Memorial Pl., recounts the Dec. 7, 1941, attack and its causes and aftereffects from both an American and a Japanese perspective. The LEED-certified, indoor-outdoor complex serves as the gateway to and ticketing location for the USS Arizona Memorial, the USS Bowfin Submarine Museum and Park, the Battleship Missouri Memorial and the Pacific Aviation Museum (see attraction listings).

Museum galleries feature interactive exhibits, audiovisual displays, artifacts and photos. Highlights include a collection of medals, a salvaged fragment of the USS Arizona and a model of the Japanese aircraft carrier Akagi. Visitors with USS Arizona Memorial tickets can watch a 23-minute documentary in a theater. Outside the buildings are interpretive wayside exhibits; designated areas for oral history presentations and special activities; and Remembrance Circle, which pays homage to those killed during the attack on Pearl Harbor.

The National Park Service conducts a public commemorative ceremony on December 7.

Note: Articles that offer concealment, such as fanny packs, purses and camera bags, are prohibited. Lockers are available for a fee (suitcases are not permitted). Pets are not permitted. Arrive early to ensure a parking spot. **Time:** Allow 1 hour minimum. **Hours:** Daily 7-5. Closed Jan. 1, Thanksgiving and Christmas. **Cost:** Free. Self-guiding audio tour $7.50. **Phone:** (808) 422-3300.

USS ARIZONA MEMORIAL is reached via H-1 w. to Arizona Memorial/Stadium exit 15A, then SR 99 to the Pearl Harbor Memorial Museum & Visitor Center, 1 Arizona Memorial Pl. Part of the World War II Valor in the Pacific National Monument, the offshore memorial is a white concrete and steel structure that spans the 106 by 608 foot hull of the sunken USS Arizona. Most of the 1,177 killed on the Arizona during the attack on Dec. 7, 1941, are entombed in the sunken hull.

The USS Arizona Memorial is divided into three sections: the entry room; the assembly area, which is used for ceremonies and as a viewing platform; and the shrine room, wherein are engraved the names of those killed aboard the USS Arizona during the attack. The ship is visible fore and aft. The 75-minute self-guiding tour includes a short orientation and boat transportation to and from the memorial; a 2.5-hour audio tour also is offered.

Note: Shoes and shirt are required. Articles that offer concealment, such as fanny packs, purses and camera bags, are prohibited. Lockers are available for a fee (suitcases are not permitted). Timed-entry tickets are distributed at the Pearl Harbor Memorial Museum & Visitor Center on a first-come, first-served basis starting at 7; tickets often are gone by early afternoon in summer. In the busy seasons, wait times may reach 3 hours. Reservations are accepted online.

Time: Allow 3 hours minimum. **Hours:** Visitor center daily 7-5. Memorial tours 7:30-3. Closed Jan. 1, Thanksgiving and Christmas. **Cost:** Visitor center and self-guiding tour free. Audio tour $7.50. Under 12 should be accompanied by an adult. Combination tickets with other Pearl Harbor sites may be purchased online in advance at www.pearlharborhistoricsites.org/deals. **Phone:** (808) 422-3300.

USS BOWFIN SUBMARINE MUSEUM AND PARK, next to the Pearl Harbor Memorial Museum & Visitor Center off SR 99, commemorates those who served in the "silent service." The park centerpiece is the 1,500-ton USS Bowfin, also known as the "Pearl Harbor Avenger." Launched in 1942, this Balao-class submarine could remain submerged for 24 hours. A museum traces the history of submarine design.

A theater in the park shows film footage from World War II and submarine-related videos. Other highlights include a periscope and conning tower viewing facility, a Japanese one-man "suicide submarine" from World War II and a memorial to the 52 U.S. submarines and more than 3,500 crewmen lost during this world war.

Tickets are sold at the Pearl Harbor Memorial Museum & Visitor Center. **Time:** Allow 1 hour minimum. **Hours:** Daily 7-5. Last tour of the submarine begins 30 minutes before closing. Closed Jan. 1, Thanksgiving and Christmas. **Cost:** Museum only $5; $4 (ages 4-12). Museum and submarine $12; $8 (ages 60+ and military with ID); $5 (ages 4-12). Under age 4 are not permitted on the *Bowfin* but are allowed in the museum and theater. Combination tickets with other Pearl Harbor sites may be purchased online in advance at www.pearlharborhistoricsites.org/deals. **Phone:** (808) 423-1341.

SCHOFIELD BARRACKS (G-3) pop. 16,370
• **Attractions map p. 118**
• **Part of Honolulu area — see p. 122**

TROPIC LIGHTNING MUSEUM is accessed through Lyman Gate. The museum is in Carter Hall (Building 361) at jct. Waianae Ave. and Flagler Rd. The 25th Infantry Division, nicknamed "Tropic Lightning" in the mid-1940s while fighting in the Philippines, has fought in World War II, Korea, Vietnam and both Gulf wars. The unit also has participated in various international peacekeeping missions. The museum showcases the history of the 25th Infantry Division and Schofield Barracks through archives, artifacts, photos and interactive exhibits.

Note: For security purposes all vehicles will be inspected prior to entrance. A photo ID is required for adult visitors. Photography is permitted in the museum but not on the grounds. **Time:** Allow 1 hour minimum. **Hours:** Tues.-Sat. 10-4. Closed major holidays. **Cost:** Donations. **Phone:** (808) 655-0438.

WAHIAWĀ (G-3) pop. 17,821, elev. 920'
• **Attractions map p. 118**
• **Part of Honolulu area — see p. 122**

Inland on the 1,000-foot Leilehua Plain, Wahiawā is the shopping center for the surrounding villages and for military station personnel. Schofield Barracks and Wheeler Army Airfield are in the area.

DOLE PLANTATION is 2.5 mi. n. at 64-1550 Kamehameha Hwy. (SR 99). The plantation features exhibits about the history of pineapple farming techniques and the industry's impact on Hawai'i's economy. The Plantation Garden Tour offers a close-up look at tropical crops such as coffee and cacao. The Pineapple Express is a narrated 20-minute, 2.2-mile-long trip on a narrow gauge railroad

through fields of growing pineapples, bananas and coffee. The Pineapple Garden Maze is situated on more than 3 acres with nearly 2.5 miles of pathways flanked by more than 14,000 tropical plants.

Time: Allow 1 hour minimum. **Hours:** Grounds and visitor center daily 9:30-5:30. Plantation Garden Tour, Pineapple Express and maze daily 9:30-5. Closed Christmas. **Cost:** Grounds and visitor center free. Plantation Garden Tour $5; $4.50 (military with ID); $4.25 (ages 4-12). Pineapple Express $8.50; $7.75 (military with ID); $6.50 (ages 4-12). Maze $6; $5 (military with ID); $4 (ages 4-12). **Phone:** (808) 621-8408.

WAHIAWĀ BOTANICAL GARDENS, 1396 California Ave., consists of 27 acres of tropical conifers, sub-tropical palms, tree ferns, epiphytes, aroids, gingers, heliconias, palms and many varieties of native plants. A visitor center distributes self-guiding tour brochures. **Hours:** Daily 9-4. Closed Jan. 1 and Christmas. **Cost:** Free. **Phone:** (808) 621-5463.

WAI'ANAE (G-1) pop. 13,177, elev. 8'
• **Attractions map p. 118**
• **Part of Honolulu area — see p. 122**

Wai'anae is the most central of several settlements along Farrington Highway (SR 93) on the little-traveled west coast. It lies on the semiarid outwash plain below Kolekole Pass. The only highway across the Wai'anae Range cuts through the pass but is a military road and is closed to the public.

The west coast is noted for surf that sometimes reaches 40 feet in height. Championship surfing competitions are held at Mākaha Beach, north of Wai'anae, in winter.

DOLPHIN STAR (HOKU NAI'A) departs from Wai'anae Boat Harbor, 85-371 Farrington Hwy.; pickup and drop-off service is available from Waikīkī hotels for a fee. This 149-passenger catamaran offers eco-friendly, narrated dolphin-watching cruises with guaranteed sightings. Whale sightings are possible December through April.

The 2-hour Wild Dolphin Watch & BBQ tour, with a crew of certified naturalists, includes a children's program, a video presentation, fruit punch, drinking water and lunch. The 3-hour Wild Dolphin Watch, BBQ and Snorkel tour is led by trained divers. Snorkel equipment is provided, and participants can expect to see coral formations and such marine creatures as the Hawaiian green sea turtle.

Smoking is not permitted. Comfortable clothing and shoes are recommended for the dolphin-watching tour. A towel and sunscreen are recommended for the snorkeling trip. Inquire about cancellation policies.

Time: Allow 3 hours minimum. **Hours:** Departures daily; phone for schedule. Closed Jan. 1, Thanksgiving, day of Honolulu Marathon and Christmas. Passengers should arrive 30 minutes prior to departure. **Cost:** Wild Dolphin Watch & BBQ tour $66; $40 (ages 3-11). Optional lunch additional $17; $10 (ages 3-11). Wild Dolphin Watch, BBQ and Snorkel tour (includes lunch) $111; $67 (ages 3-11). Reservations are required. **Phone:** (808) 983-7827 or (800) 334-6191. [¶]

WAIMĀNALO (H-6) pop. 5,451, elev. 23'
• Attractions map p. 118
• Part of Honolulu area — see p. 122

SEA LIFE PARK, 41-202 SR 72 (Kalaniana'ole Hwy.) at Makapu'u Point, offers marine mammal shows and exhibits ranging from sea lion or dolphin shows to an aquatic theater to a seabird sanctuary. The Pirates' Lagoon area has children's attractions. Interactive programs let visitors swim with dolphins or sharks, befriend sea lions, snorkel with stingrays and dive in a reef tank.

Time: Allow 3 hours minimum. **Hours:** Daily 10:30-5. **Cost:** (Including shows, exhibits and Pirates' Lagoon) $29.99; $19.99 (ages 3-12). Hawaiian Ray Encounter $19.99. Sea Lion Swim or Swim With Sharks $99.99. Dolphin Encounter $119.99. Dolphin Swim Adventure $184.99. Dolphin Royal Swim $249.99. Photo and video of the experience are available for purchase. Reservations are required for interactive programs. **Parking:** $5. **Phone:** (808) 259-2500. [¶]

WAIMEA (F-3) elev. 30'
• Attractions map p. 32
• Part of Honolulu area — see p. 122

After Capt. James Cook was slain on Hawai'i Island in 1779, his crew stopped here to replenish their water supply. They were the first Europeans to visit O'ahu and described the Waimea Valley as lush, picturesque and densely settled. Floods that devastated the valley and silted up the mouth of the bay in 1894 forced most of the population to relocate. Perched on a bluff above Waimea Bay, the town is accessible via Pūpūkea Road.

The nearby North Shore beaches are world-renowned surfing venues. Waimea Bay, just south of town, offers a steep crescent of sand. Giant waves that form here in the winter attract surfers from around the world. In summer the sea can be as flat as a lake. **Note:** Swimmers should always check with lifeguards about conditions.

Pūpūkea Beach Park, just north of Waimea in the Pūpūkea Marine Life Conservation District, features tide pools to explore at Old Quarry—the lava and coral rock are very sharp, so water shoes are a good idea.

South of Pūpūkea Beach Park on Pūpūkea Road is Pu'u O Mahuka Heiau, which is believed to have been built in the 1600s. This temple site covers more than 5 acres. Signs have been placed on the grounds describing its significance to ancient Hawaiian culture. Some believe human sacrifice occurred here. The site offers a good view of the Pacific Ocean. **Note:** *Heiau* are culturally significant and should be treated with respect.

Ehukai Beach Park, 2.5 miles north on SR 83, has the famous Banzai Pipeline, a curling wave that forms off the left end of the beach.

With waves that can reach 25 feet in height, Sunset Beach, 3 miles north on SR 83, is among the island's top winter surfing spots. Even in the calmer summer months, swimmers should beware of the long shore current. Windsurfers flock to Backyards, a surf break off the north end of Sunset Beach.

WAIPAHU (H-3) pop. 38,216, elev. 40'
• Attractions map p. 118
• Part of Honolulu area — see p. 122

Located northwest of Pearl Harbor, Waipahu was the site of the giant O'ahu Sugar Company Mill, the largest sugar processor on the island. Built in 1898, the mill operated until 1995. All that remains is the 170-foot high smokestack, a laboratory and the generator building. The sugar industry, once king in Hawai'i, has all but disappeared.

Shopping: Waikele Premium Outlets, off H-1 exit 7, offers discount shopping in 50 outlets such as Barneys New York and Coach.

HAWAI'I'S PLANTATION VILLAGE is at 94-695 Waipahu St.; from H-1 eastbound or westbound take exit 7, go s. on Paiwa St., then w. on Waipahu St. On a 50-acre site below the former O'ahu Sugar Mill, this outdoor museum features 25 restored and replica early 20th-century buildings. Furnishings, artifacts, clothing and artwork reflect the multiethnic plantation workers—Chinese, Filipino, Japanese, Korean, Native Hawaiian, Okinawan, Portuguese and Puerto Rican. A library and photographs document Hawaiian plantation history from 1830s to 1950s.

Hours: Guided 90-minute walking tours depart Mon.-Sat. on the hour 10-2. Closed major holidays. **Cost:** $13; $10 (ages 62+); $7 (military with ID); $5 (ages 4-11). **Phone:** (808) 677-0110.

The Hawaiian Language

While English is the universal language of the islands, visitors will find it liberally sprinkled with words and phrases Hawaiian, a dialect of the Polynesian language that contains only 12 letters.

The vowels are as follows: *a* as in among, *e* as in let, *i* as in ring, *o* as in no, *u* as in too. Vowels are pronounced separately, except when they appear as diphthongs, and when marked with a *kahakō* (a line above a vowel) they are longer and always stressed. Diphthongs emphasize the first letter: *ai, ae, ao, au, ei, eu, oi, ou,* and *iu.* When vowels are separated by an *'okina* ('), indicating a glottal stop, there is a distinct separation of sound, as in *oh-oh.* For example, *pa'u* is PA-oo.

The consonants *h, k, l, m, n, p* and *w* have sounds similar to those in English. However, *w* is pronounced like *v* after *i* and *e,* like *w* after *o* and *u,* and like *w* or *v* after *a* or initially—Pu'uwai is POO-oo-VAI.

Another form of speech used in the islands is pidgin—a mixture of English, Hawaiian and other Pacific languages that penetrates, to varying degrees, daily life and interactions. Because it is so much a part of the Hawaiian whole, a few of its words and phrases are included among the Words in Common Use list.

Place Names

Place	Pronunciation	Meaning
'Ewa	*EH-vah*	angular, crooked
Hā'ena	*HA-eh-na*	red-hot
Haleakalā	*HA-leh-ah-ka-LA*	house of the sun
Hāmoa	*Ha-MO-ah*	possibly interchangeable with "Samoa"
Hāna	*HA-na*	alert
Hānalei	*HA-na-lay*	lei valley
Hānapēpē	*HA-na-PAY-PAY*	crushed bay
Hilo	*HEE-lo*	twisted
Honoka'a	*HO-no-KA-ah*	rolling bay
Honolulu	*HO-no-LOO-loo*	protected bay
'Īao	*EE-ow*	toward the dawn
Iwilei	*EE-weh-LAY*	collarbone
Kahala	*Ka-HA-la*	a screw pine
Kailua	*Kai-LOO-ah*	two ocean currents
Kāne'ohe	*KA-neh-OH-heh*	slim man
Kealakekua	*KEH-ala-KEH-kua*	pathway of the gods
Kīlauea	*KEE-low-eh-ah*	spewing volcano eruption
Kōke'e	*Ko-KEH-eh*	to bend
Koko Head	*KO-ko*	blood
Kona	*KO-na*	leeward
Lahaina	*La-HAI-na*	cruel sun
Lā'ie	*LA-ee-eh*	'ie leaf
Moloka'i	*Mo-lo-KA-ee*	child of the goddess Hina
Nu'uanu	*NOO-oo-AH-noo*	cool height
O'ahu	*OH-ah-hoo*	gathering place
Puna	*POO-na*	spring
Punahou	*POO-na-hoe*	new spring
Wahiawā	*WA-he-ah-WA*	place of noise
Wai'anae	*WAI-ah-NAI*	mullet water
Waikīkī	*wai-KEE-KEE*	spouting water
Wailua	*Wai-LOO-ah*	two waters
Wailuku	*Wai-LOO-koo*	water of destruction
Waimānalo	*Wai-MA-na-lo*	potable water
Waimea	*Wai-MEH-(y)ah*	reddish water
Wai'oli	*WAI-oh-lee*	joyful water

Words in Common Use

Word	Pronunciation	Meaning
'a'ā	*AH-ah*	rough lava
aikāne	*aye-KA-neh*	friend

akamai	a-ka-MYE	clever, smart
ala	AH-la	road
aloha	ah-LOW-ha	greeting, love, welcome, farewell
brah	BRAH	brother, friend, pal (pidgin)
bumby	bum-BYE	after a while, by and by (pidgin)
da kine	da KINE	whatchamacallit (pidgin)
'Ewa	EH-vah	toward the west, generally
hale	HA-leh	house
haole	HOW-lee	Caucasian, mainlander
hāpai	ha-PAI	lift, carry; pregnant
hau'oli	HOW-o-lee	happy, rejoice
heiau	hey-ee-AU	temple
holokū	HO-lo-KOO	a loose, seamed dress
holomū	HO-lo-MOO	a long fitted dress
honi	HO-nee	to kiss
ho'omalimali	HO-oh-MA-lee-MA-lee	to flatter
huhū	hoo-HOO	angry
hukilau	hoo-KEE-lau	group fishing
hula	HOO-la	Polynesian dance
humuhumunukunukuāpua'a	HOO-moo-HOO-moo-NOO-koo-NOO-koo-AH-poo-AH-ah	a triggerfish
imu	EE-moo	underground oven
ipo	EE-po	sweetheart
kai	KYE	ocean
kālā	KA-LA	money
kama'āina	KA-ma-AH-ee-na	Hawai'i resident
kāne	KA-neh	man
kapu	KA-poo	taboo, forbidden, keep out
keiki	KAY-key	child
kōkua	KO-KOO-ah	help
kuleana	koo-leh-AH-nah	property
lāna'i	LAH-nigh	porch
lei	lay	garland or wreath
lōlō	LOH-loh	stupid
lū'au	LOO-aow	taro leaf, feast
mahalo	ma-HA-loh	thanks
maika'i	MY-kah-ee	good, fine
ma kai	mah-KYE	toward the ocean
malihini	mah-lee-HEE-nee	newcomer
ma uka	MAOW-ka	toward the mountains, upland or inland
Menehune	MEN-eh-HOO-ney	3-foot-tall people of Hawaiian legend
moana	moh-AH-nah	ocean
mu'umu'u	MOO-oo-MOO-oo	Mother Hubbard dress
nui	NOO	big, huge, much
ōkolehau	OH-koh-LEH-how	ti root liquor
'ono	OH-no	tastes good
'ōpū	OH-poo	stomach, abdomen
pāhoehoe	PAH-ho-eh-ho-eh	smooth, unbroken lava
pākē	PAH-KE	Chinese
pali	PA-lee	cliff
paniolo	pa-nee-OH-lo	cowboy
pau	pow	finished
pā'ū	PAH-oo	wraparound skirt for riding
pilikia	pee-lee-KEE-ah	trouble
puka	POO-kah	door, hole of any kind
pūpū	POO-poo	appetizer, hors d'oeuvre
pupule	poo-POO-ley	crazy

shaka .... *SHAH-kah* .... well done, great, terrific (pidgin)
wahine .... *wa-HEE-neh* .... female, girl, woman
wikiwiki .... *WEE-kee-WEE-kee* .... fast, quickly

Phrases and Greetings

Good morning. .... *Ah-LOW-ha Ka-ka-he-AH-ka.* .... Aloha kakahiaka.
Good evening. .... *Ah-LOW-ha AH-hee-AH-hee.* .... Aloha ahiahi.
How are you? .... *Pe-HEH-ah OH-eh?* .... Pehea ʻoe?
I am fine. .... *MY-kye.* .... Maikai.
Many thanks. .... *Ma-HA-low AH-noo-ee.* .... Mahalo ā nui.
What is the trouble? .... *He-AH-ha Kah Pe-lee-KEY-ah?* ...... Heaha ka pilikia?
No trouble. .... *Ah-OH-le Pee-lee-KEE-ah.* .... ʻAʻole pilikia.
Come here. .... *HEH-leh MYE.* .... Hele mai.
Come on in. The house is yours. .... *KO-mo MYE. NO-oo Kah HAH-leh.* .. Komo mai. Nou ka hale.
I love you. .... *Ah-LOW-ha Ah-oo EE-ah OH-ee.* .... Aloha au ia oe.
Much love .... *Ah-LOW-ha NOO-ee LOW-ah.* .... Aloha nui loa.
Happy Birthday. .... *HOW-O-lee La HA-now.* .... Hauʻoli lāhānau.
Merry Christmas. .... *MAY-leh Kah-LEE-kee-MA-ka.* .... Mele Kalikimaka.
Happy New Year. .... *HOW-OH-lee MA-ka-HEE-kee HO.* .. Hauʻoli Makahiki Hou.
Bottoms up. .... *Oh-KO-leh Mah-LU-nah.* .... Okole Maluna.

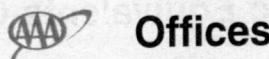 Offices

Main office listings are shown in **BOLD TYPE** and toll-free member service numbers appear in *ITALIC TYPE*.
All are closed Saturdays, Sundays and holidays unless otherwise indicated.
The addresses, phone numbers and hours for any AAA/CAA office are subject to change.
The type of service provided is designated below the name of the city where the office is located:

✚ Auto travel services, including books and maps, and on-demand TripTik® routings.
● Auto travel services, including selected books and maps, and on-demand TripTik® routings.
▦ Books/maps only, no marked maps or on-demand TripTik® routings.
▲ Travel Agency Services, cruise, tour, air, car and rail reservations; domestic and international hotel reservations; passport photo services; international and domestic travel guides and maps; travel money products; and International Driving Permits. In addition, assistance with travel related insurance products including trip cancellation, travel accident, lost luggage, trip delay and assistance products.
✪ Insurance services provided. If only this icon appears, only insurance services are provided at that office.
C Car Care Plus Facility provides car care services.
▣ Electric vehicle charging station on premises.

AAA NATIONAL OFFICE: 1000 AAA DRIVE, HEATHROW, FLORIDA 32746-5063, (407) 444-7000

HAWAII

HONOLULU—**AAA HAWAII**, 1130 N NIMITZ STE A170, 96817. WEEKDAYS (M-F) 9:00-5:00, SAT 9:00-2:00. (808) 593-2221, *(800) 736-2886*. ✚▲✪

Metric Equivalents Chart

TEMPERATURE

To convert Fahrenheit to Celsius, subtract 32 from the Fahrenheit temperature, multiply by 5 and divide by 9. To convert Celsius to Fahrenheit, multiply by 9, divide by 5 and add 32.

ACRES

1 acre = 0.4 hectare (ha)   1 hectare = 2.47 acres

MILES AND KILOMETERS

Note: A kilometer is approximately 5/8 or 0.6 of a mile. To convert kilometers to miles multiply by 0.6.

Miles/Kilometers		Kilometers/Miles	
15	24.1	30	18.6
20	32.2	35	21.7
25	40.2	40	24.8
30	48.3	45	27.9
35	56.3	50	31.0
40	64.4	55	34.1
45	72.4	60	37.2
50	80.5	65	40.3
55	88.5	70	43.4
60	96.6	75	46.6
65	104.6	80	49.7
70	112.7	85	52.8
75	120.7	90	55.9
80	128.7	95	59.0
85	136.8	100	62.1
90	144.8	105	65.2
95	152.9	110	68.3
100	160.9	115	71.4

Celsius ° / **Fahrenheit °**

Celsius		Fahrenheit
100	BOILING	212
37		100
35		95
32		90
29		85
27		80
24		75
21		70
18		65
16		60
13		55
10		50
7		45
4		40
2		35
0	FREEZING	32
-4		25
-7		20
-9		15
-12		10
-15		5
-18		0
-21		-5
-24		-10
-27		-15

LINEAR MEASURE

Customary	Metric
1 inch = 2.54 centimeters	1 centimeter = 0.4 inches
1 foot = 30 centimeters	1 meter = 3.3 feet
1 yard = 0.91 meters	1 meter = 1.09 yards
1 mile = 1.6 kilometers	1 kilometer = .62 miles

WEIGHT

If You Know:	Multiply By:	To Find:
Ounces	28	Grams
Pounds	0.45	Kilograms
Grams	0.035	Ounces
Kilograms	2.2	Pounds

LIQUID MEASURE

Customary	Metric
1 fluid ounce = 30 milliliters	1 milliliter = .03 fluid ounces
1 cup = .24 liters	1 liter = 2.1 pints
1 pint = .47 liters	1 liter = 1.06 quarts
1 quart = .95 liters	1 liter = .26 gallons
1 gallon = 3.8 liters	

PRESSURE

Air pressure in automobile tires is expressed in kilopascals. Multiply pound-force per square inch (psi) by 6.89 to find kilopascals (kPa).

24 psi = 165 kPa	28 psi = 193 kPa
26 psi = 179 kPa	30 psi = 207 kPa

GALLONS AND LITERS

Gallons/Liters			
5	19.0	12	45.6
6	22.8	14	53.2
7	26.6	16	60.8
8	30.4	18	68.4
9	34.2	20	76.0
10	38.0	25	95.0

Liters/Gallons			
10	2.6	40	10.4
15	3.9	50	13.0
20	5.2	60	15.6
25	6.5	70	18.2
30	7.8	80	20.8
35	9.1	90	23.4

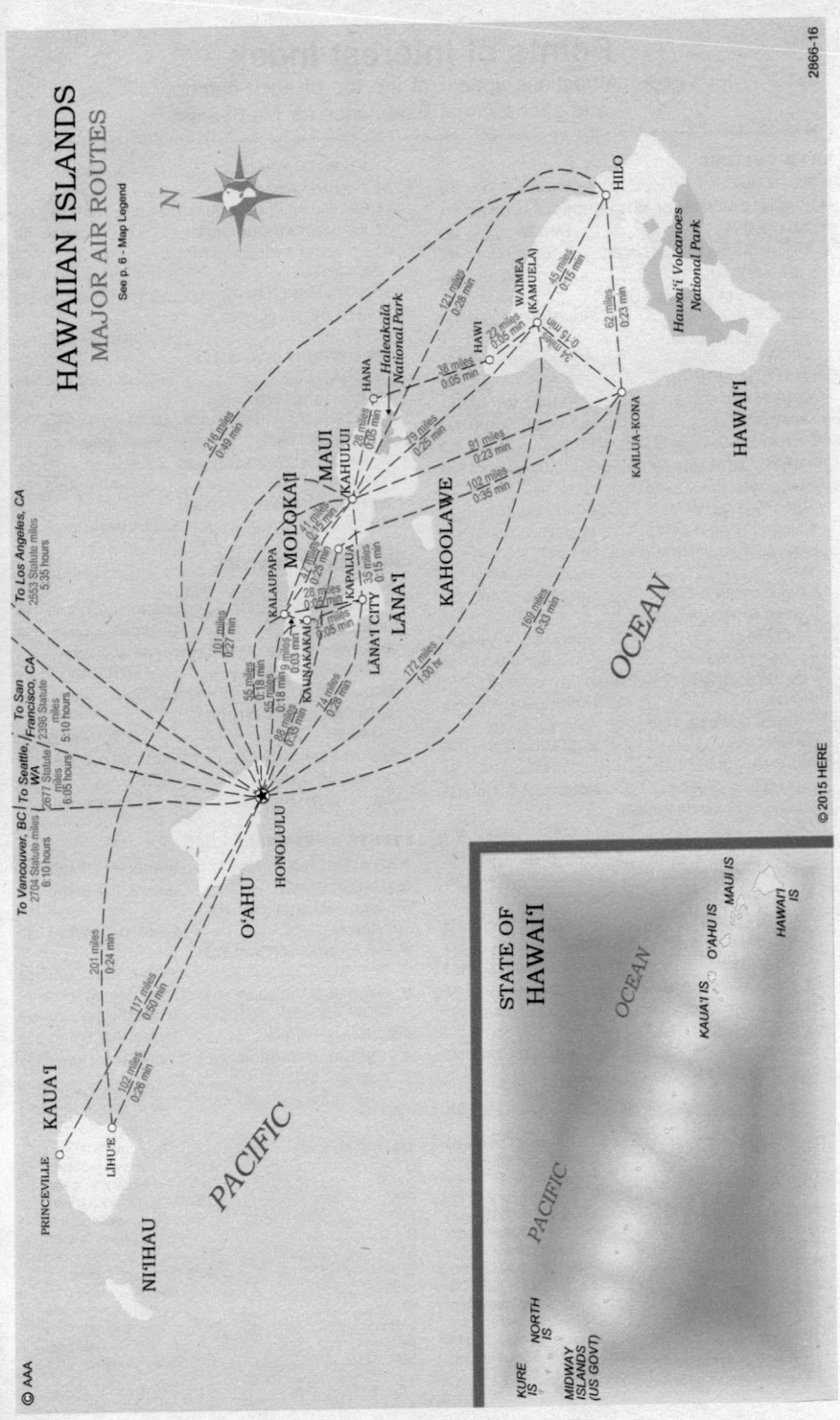

Points of Interest Index

Attractions appear at the top of each category
and offer a Great Experience for Members®.

Index Legend

NB...................................... national battlefield	NR..national river
NBP.........................national battlefield park	NS....................................national seashore
NC...............................national cemetery	NWR.........................national wildlife refuge
NF..................................national forest	PHP......................provincial historic(al) park
NHM.............. national historic(al) monument	PHS.........................provincial historic(al) site
NHP..................... national historic(al) park	PP...provincial park
NHS....................... national historic(al) site	SF..state forest
NL............................. national lakeshore	SHM................. state historic(al) monument
NME............................. national memorial	SHP....................... state historic(al) park
NMO.............................national monument	SHS........................ state historic(al) site
NMP.....................national military park	SME....................................state memorial
NP.....................................national park	SP.. state park
NRA........... national recreation area	SRA.............................state recreation area

HISTORIC SITES & EXHIBITS

OUTDOORS & SCIENCE

SHOPPING & NIGHTLIFE

SPORTS & RECREATION

TOURS & SIGHTSEEING

Ask about AAA/CAA Associate membership
to share the benefits you value

Photo Credits

Page numbers are in bold type. Picture credit abbreviations are as follows:
■ (i) numeric sequence from top to bottom, left to right ■ (AAA) AAA Travel library.

■ (Cover) Nāpali Coast, Kauaʻi / © Masa Ushioda / age fotostock

■ **2** (i) © Boykov / Shutterstock.com

■ **2** (ii) © Eddy Galeotti / Shutterstock.com

■ **2** (iii) © Francesco Carucci / Shutterstock.com

■ **12** (i) Courtesy of Berry Manor Inn

■ **12** (ii) © Chris Dew / Killarney Lodge

■ **12** (iii) Courtesy of Hyatt Hotels

■ **12** (iv) Courtesy of Montpelier Plantation and Beach

■ **12** (v) © Elisa Rolle / Wikimedia Commons

■ **12** (vi) Courtesy of The Shores Resort & Spa

■ **12** (vii) Courtesy of All Star Vacation Homes

■ **12** (viii) Courtesy of Bryce View Lodge

■ **12** (ix) Courtesy of Vista Verde Guest Ranch

■ **13** Courtesy of Divi Resorts

■ **18** (i) © mdlart / Shutterstock.com

■ **18** (ii) © Eddy Galeotti / Shutterstock.com

■ **19** © Francesco Carucci / Shutterstock.com

■ **20** (i) © Susanne Sims / PhotoResourceHawaii.com

■ **20** (ii) Office of the President

■ **23** (i) Published with permission from AAA associate Diana Beyer

■ **23** (ii) © Jennifer Crites / PhotoResourceHawaii.com

■ **23** (iii) © Hayball / Shutterstock.com

■ **23** (iv) © Shane Myers Photography / Shutterstock.com

■ **23** (v) © col / Shutterstock.com

■ **24** (i) © Boykov / Shutterstock.com

■ **24** (ii) © iStockphoto.com / Janugio

■ **24** (iii) © iStockphoto.com / jewhyte

■ **24** (iv) © iStockphoto.com / gregobagel

■ **29** © Lessadar / Shutterstock.com

■ **31** © Jennifer Crites / PhotoResourceHawaii.com

■ **62** © Sahani Photography / Shutterstock.com

■ **81** © Marc Schechter / PhotoResourceHawaii.com

■ **85** © Henner Damke / Shutterstock.com

■ **112** © Jon Ogata / PhotoResourceHawaii.com

■ **117** © Tibor Bognar / Alamy

■ **122** © Shaiith / Shutterstock.com

■ **124** © Peter French / age fotostock

■ **125** © Ellen Isaacs / Alamy

■ **126** © Masa Ushioda / Alamy

■ **127** Courtesy of Ala Moana Center

■ **128** Published with permission from AAA associate Diana Beyer

■ **129** © EpicStockMedia / Shutterstock.com

■ **130** © Brandon Tabiolo / age fotostock

■ **134** © Havoc / Shutterstock.com

■ **137** © iStockphoto.com / muchemistry

■ **139** © Istvan Molnar / Shutterstock.com

Remember, car seats, booster seats and seat belts save lives